PENGUIN

LEON BATTIST.

'The career of this true "Renaissance man", and the world he not only inhabited but came to influence profoundly, are brought vividly to life in a magnificent *tour de force* of intellectual biography by one of the world's leading experts on the period . . . Grafton's portrait does full justice to a remarkable man' Andrew Crumey, *Scotland on Sunday*

'A convincing and engaging account of Alberti's intellectual milieu in what is arguably the most important general contribution to Albertian studies of recent decades' Bruce Boucher, *The New York Times Book Review*

'This is a wonderful book . . . Anthony Grafton makes a complex subject accessible to the general reader' Shane de Blacam, *Irish Times*

'Densely informative and very well-written . . . Grafton explores the sources and contexts of [Alberti's] unusually revealing self-portrait. He distinguishes what is borrowed or traditional in it from what is new and original, and thus shows Alberti at work creating a very finely tuned and comprehensive persona, which was indeed a kind of blueprint for the new *uomo universale*, or, as we would say, "Renaissance man"' Charles Nicholl, *Literary Review*

'Admirable . . . the most convincing portrait to date of Alberti as a man in a social environment' Jack M. Greenstein, *Wall Street Journal*

'Excellent . . . Grafton's portrait of Alberti is a joy to read. His approach is rigorous and scholarly, yet he writes with a detailed concern for social context and interaction that brings the distant past alive' Robert Tavernor, *Architects' Journal*

'[Grafton] has made himself the master interpreter of European thought between the fifteenth and eighteenth centuries . . . an unusual and stimulating book' Michael Dirda, *Washington Post Book World*

ABOUT THE AUTHOR

Anthony Grafton teaches European intellectual history at Princeton University. He is the author of *Joseph Scaliger: A Study in the History of Classical Scholarship*, *Defenders of the Text* and *The Footnote: A Curious History*.

LEON BATTISTA ALBERTI

MASTER BUILDER OF THE ITALIAN RENAISSANCE

ANTHONY GRAFTON

PENGUIN BOOKS

PENGUIN BOOKS

Published by the Penguin Group
Penguin Books Ltd, 80 Strand, London, WC2R 0RL, England
Penguin Putnam Inc., 375 Hudson Street, New York, New York 10014, USA
Penguin Books Australia Ltd, 250 Camberwell Road, Camberwell, Victoria 3124, Australia
Penguin Books Canada Ltd, 10 Alcorn Avenue, Toronto, Ontario, Canada M4V 3B2
Penguin Books India (P) Ltd, 11, Community Centre, Panchsheel Park, New Delhi - 110 017, India
Penguin Books (NZ) Ltd, Cnr Rosedale and Airborne Roads, Albany, Auckland, New Zealand
Penguin Books (South Africa) (Pty) Ltd, 24 Sturdee Avenue, Rosebank 2196, South Africa

Penguin Books Ltd, Registered Offices: 80 Strand, London, WC2R 0RL, England

www.penguin.com

First published in the USA by Hill and Wang, a division of Farrar, Straus & Giroux 2000
First published in Great Britain by Allen Lane The Penguin Press 2001
Published in Penguin Books 2002
1

Printed in England by Clays Ltd, St Ives plc

FOR ANNA

CONTENTS

ACKNOWLEDGMENTS

The research for this book was carried out in the Firestone and Marquand Libraries of Princeton University, the Avery and Butler Libraries of Columbia University, the Biblioteca Apostolica Vaticana, the Bibliothèque Nationale de France, the British Library, the Warburg Institute of the University of London, the libraries of the Free University of Berlin and the University of Hamburg, the Kunstbibliothek Berlin, the Biblioteca Riccardiana, and the library of the University of California, Berkeley. The Wissenschaftskolleg zu Berlin, the Warburg-Haus Hamburg, the Ecole Normale Supérieure de Paris, and Princeton University gave me time to work. But my greatest single debt is owed to the Department of Art History and Archaeology at Columbia University, which invited me to serve as Meyer Schapiro Visiting Professor during 1996–97, and more particularly to Joseph Connors, who urged me to devote a series of public lectures to Alberti. My friends at Columbia gave me the ideal occasion to turn what had seemed to be disparate research projects into a story about Alberti and his world. Their questions—as well as others asked by the graduate students who took my Columbia seminar—have helped me to correct errors and clarify my thoughts on dozens of points. Thanks, too, to Pierre Petitmengin, who invited me to present some of my findings on Alberti in a series of lectures at the Ecole Normale Supérieure, and to my listeners there—especially Jean-Louis Ferrary, François Hartog, Françoise Waquet, and Henri Zerner—for their questions and responses.

No historian knows all of Alberti's fields of interest—or even a majority of them—at first hand. After many years of concentrating on Renaissance humanism and natural philosophy, I came as an outsider to many of the problems and subjects discussed here. I feel a special gratitude, accordingly, to the scholars in a number of fields, without whose meticulous investigations of Alberti's work and its context it would have been impossible to attempt this interpretation of his life. Many distinguished philologists have traced the textual histories of Alberti's works, edited them and translated them into modern languages. Since World War II alone, the late Cecil

Grayson, Eugenio Garin, Giovanni Orlandi, Paulo Portoghesi, Laura Goggi Carotti, Lucia Cesarini Martinelli, Joseph Rykwert, Riccardo Fubini, Anna Menci Gallorini, Renée Neu Watkins, David Marsh, Lucia Bertolini, Massimo Danzi, Roberto Cardini, and many others have not only given us usable texts and translations of many works, but also revolutionized our understanding of how Alberti plied the writer's trade in Latin and Italian.

At the same time, historians of art and architecture have analyzed Alberti's buildings, self-portrait, and works on the theory of painting and building, setting them into context and exploring their qualities and their impact. The works of Erwin Panofsky, Rudolf Wittkower, Richard Krautheimer, Trude Krautheimer-Hess, Charles Mitchell, John Spencer, E. H. Gombrich, Michael Baxandall, Charles Dempsey, Charles Hope, Joseph Rykwert, Robert Tavernor, and Charles Burroughs, among others, have shaped my thinking in diverse ways. A number of art historians have generously given me the benefit not only of their written work, but also of their criticism: warm thanks to Katherine Weil-Garris Brandt, Caroline Elam, Elizabeth Cropper, Keith Christiansen, and Marvin Trachtenberg, for comments which were sometimes sharp in tone but always constructive in content.

Sections of this book set Alberti's life and thought into a series of different urban environments. My own teacher, Eric Cochrane, first showed me that a letter by Machiavelli could reveal a past street-corner society in living color. The great tradition of Florentine historiography created and founded by such scholars as Hans Baron, Felix Gilbert, Nicolai Rubinstein, and Gene Brucker, and the highly original work on the history of Rome produced in the last generation by Massimo Miglio, Silvia Maddalo, Anna Modigliani, and other scholars associated with that wonderful enterprise, *Roma nel Rinascimento*, were endlessly instructive. The experience of teaching about the cultural history of cities in Princeton's undergraduate Program in European Cultural Studies gave much food for thought, as did the examples of urban history offered by Carl Schorske and Jerrold Seigel.

Patricia Brown and John Pinto generously took the time to read substantial sections of this book in manuscript and to make many suggestions, of which I have taken full advantage. Leonard Barkan, Fabio Barry, Christopher Celenza, Brian Curran, Martin Davies, Arthur Field, Francesco Furlan, Thomas DaCosta Kaufmann, Jill Kraye, David Marsh, Elizabeth McCahill, Ingrid Rowland, and Giovanni Zanovello let me benefit from their deep knowledge of fifteenth-century humanism and the arts. The sections of this book that connect Alberti's career with the history of Renaissance science and engineering draw on the teaching of Noel Swerdlow and discussions with Mike Mahoney, Tom Kuhn, and Nicholas Adams. Debora Krohn, Peter Miller, and Nancy Siraisi provided a support that was moral—but also much more. Discussions with David Quint about Alberti and much else began in Zion, Illinois, almost thirty years ago, and have gone on ever since, to my continuing profit. Lauren Osborne and her colleagues treated each draft of the book with imperturbable courtesy and impeccable care. Their editorial work—like the support and criticism offered by so many colleagues—provided a superb example of the sort of intellectual and literary collaboration that Alberti demanded, and did not always receive, from his interlocutors.

Princeton, NJ
21 March 2000

LEON BATTISTA ALBERTI

I

WHO WAS LEON BATTISTA ALBERTI?

MAKING AN IDENTITY IN THE 1430S

A stage, in a fifteenth-century Italian city square. Behind the proscenium, drops and wings depict the stone facades and tile roofs of houses, severe and classical. Some of the roofs extend over covered terraces, and some of the ground floors have loggias opening to the street. Other houses are completely enclosed by rusticated stone. Before one of them, a stone gatepost, worn down by centuries of rain, supports a statue of Pluto, the Roman god of the underworld. On one side, a path leads to an inn. On the other, steps run down to a small square, where a sign bearing a Latin motto in golden capital letters appears before an impressive villa. Ancient Rome has temporarily come back to life.[1]

Male actors make their entrances, some dressed as men, others as young women. Some wear the fine fabrics that proclaim high social standing, others are clearly slaves or servants. Standing and conversing in a formal, self-consciously dignified way, they speak neither the Italian they would use in daily life nor the modern, functional Latin of the medieval church and university, but rather the ancient Latin of Roman comedy, a language the playwright has had to reconstruct for them. They act out a complex, somewhat cumbersome story—the tale of how young Philodoxus ("the lover of glory") seeks to win the hand of a young woman, Doxia ("glory"), with the help of his slave Phroneus ("the intellect"). Another young man, Fortunius ("fortune"), the adoptive son of Tychia, also seeks to win Doxia, by force. Not finding her, he takes her sister Phimia ("fame"). Still other characters appear, and the action takes a number of twists. Finally Chronos ("time"), the father of Alithia ("truth"), arranges for Philodoxus and Doxia to marry.[2]

The play's plot, as this summary suggests, is an allegory, a creaky clockwork device designed to produce the right moral at the right time. The characters, as their names proclaim, do not embody individual personalities but personify abstract qualities. They spend more time declaiming than conversing. Leon Battista Alberti, who wrote the first version of this script at the age of twenty, confessed as much in a commentary: "This play has to do with conduct: for it teaches that a man dedicated to study and hard work can attain glory, just as well as a rich and fortunate man."

For all its moralism, Alberti's play had some strikingly fresh qualities: above all, its rich and consistently classical style. Though other Renaissance scholars had previously tried to compose plays in the manner and idiom of the Roman comic poets Plautus and Terence, none had anticipated Alberti's effort to place the action of a play before a unified classical setting. Some of the scenes that Alberti's abstract characters played out, moreover, attacked vital literary and moral problems. Doxia, the love interest, naturally is beautiful; early in the play, the slave Potentio describes her to Philodoxus's rival, Fortunius, in a set piece, a fragile, elegant construction of contrasting clauses that deftly balances panegyrical terms and their moral implications, setting beauty against character, and the open display of beauty against the carefully preserved modesty that paradoxically revealed a woman's good character:

FORT: Is she beautiful?
POT: She is so beautiful, and so good, that nothing could be added to her, and nothing more could be wished—so much so, indeed, that I think her either more beautiful than Venus, or very like her. Her head is fine, her face lovely, her appearance gay, her walk modest: she holds herself and moves exactly as an honorable matron and a Roman citizen should.

Beauty and decorum—a young woman's physical grace and charm and the stern discipline that could prevent these qualities from causing bad behavior in men—preoccupied the young author as well as his characters.

In the first version of Alberti's play, when Philodoxus describes the effect that Doxia has on him, his eloquence carries him to the point of clever eroticism. Imagining himself as a statue holding a light for her at night, admiring her "as you stand there, without law or fantasy, in your robe and your hair," he bursts out, "O gods, I wish I could be your lyre, and while you played me, I would produce pleasant, harmonious, sweet notes. . . . O gods, how happy this would make me." This fantasy disappeared from Alberti's second draft: in the course of revision, as in the speech itself, self-discipline celebrated a hard triumph over desire.

Alberti's experiments in dialogue embraced not only the emotions of the inexperienced, handsome young but also the hard-nosed, wised-up talk of older men and women. When Phrontisis ("thought") confronts the maid Mnimia ("memory"), for example, she tells the whole sad story of her unhappy marriage, admitting her own guilt for its failure:

MNI: Ah, me. So the fates have decided, so must it be for us. The gods command, so we must wish to have it so.

PHRON: Why are you standing there? Why don't we go home?

MNI: Alas! I am remembering a great many things, some of which I wish were different, others I prefer and wish to be as they are.

PHRON: That's the human condition: to wish and not to wish. Wise men know how to wish and not to wish for something at the right time. Not to want the things you must want, or to want the things you can't have, is for those who only believe in and desire things for themselves. Criminals always give off a certain smell, that of their crime. It accompanies them everywhere, revealing itself, and bringing the proper penalty in its wake. This will not go unavenged.

MNI: I expect it will be as you think. But I also rebuke myself for my own madness, for disagreeing with my husband, with whom I quarreled three years ago at Athens. I refused to give him the gold signet rings that he had deposited with me for safekeeping. I did what we foolish women usually do, especially if we are also pretty: I wanted him to beg for them. The next day he left. Now your name has brought him back to mind. If I had not done this, I would be living a pleasant and rather lavish life, and would not have gone wrong, as I continue to do.[3]

In one speech, Mnimia has managed to range across several urgent contemporary topics: marriage, property relations, the physical beauty of women, and their inborn moral defects. In one burst, from the sharp tongue of a single female character, a fascinating mixture of acute social observation and conventional misogyny emerges. Her biting wit etches sharp sketches of the grasping bourgeoisie of the Italian cities: "Greedy men are especially bold when they deal with spinsters and widows."

Like the turn-of-the-twentieth-century playwright Alfred Jarry, whose schoolboy farce about his lycée science teacher became a lifelong obsession and turned into *Ubu Roi*, Alberti laid out in this youthful comedy themes and issues that would occupy him for the rest of his life: beauty and property, ancient settings and modern families, the visual world and how to represent it with lines and colors, the social world and how to analyze it in words. Like Jarry, Alberti found inspiration for a lifetime of artistic and literary experiments in his early experiences—which included breathtaking encounters with radical new forms of art as well as chastening confrontations with philistines. Like Jarry, finally, Alberti amazed and enthralled his contemporaries by bringing together images and ideas, levels of expression and artistic motifs, that had previously existed separately. The inexperienced playwright would soon become a creator of the fifteenth-century avant-garde. Who was he?

In a literal sense, the question seems surprisingly easy to answer. A fair number of historical documents attest to Alberti's central accomplishments as a scholar, writer, and architect, while others identify the brilliant company that he kept. Alberti, they tell us, was born in Genoa in 1404, one of two illegitimate sons of a Florentine merchant, Lorenzo Alberti. The Alberti—like many other great clans that fared badly in the dangerous, loser-take-nothing game of Italian city politics—had been exiled from their native city by the rulers of its republican government, the Albizzi family and their allies.

Still prosperous, the Alberti possessed a large-scale business, which they ran as a family partnership. Branch offices served as the nodes of a trading network that stretched as far west as France and England and as far east as the Greek islands and the remains of the Byzantine empire. Though Leon Battista and his brother Carlo were bastards, their father treated them as his own and educated them very well. Leon Battista studied the Latin classics, and possibly some Greek ones, at the famous school of Gasparino Barzizza in Padua, which he attended from around 1416 to 1418. Like a great many other ambitious young men, he then studied law at the ancient University of Bologna. He seemed on the way to a successful career, perhaps as a judge or a professor of law. But his father's death, which took place after his first year as a student, deprived him of protection and financial support. Soon afterward his health gave way under the pressure of academic work. He diverted himself by turning to the study of nature and the visual arts—fields that would fascinate and preoccupy him throughout his life. He also began, slowly, to write—mostly, at first, formal pieces of literature in the most classical Latin he could compose.

Early in the 1430s, Leon Battista joined the first of many courts. He took a job at the papal curia (the administrative offices of the papacy), where he served as an abbreviator and put his stylistic skills at the service of influential members of the higher clergy. He began to write in Italian as well as Latin, and his dialogues in both languages began to find readers. Church benefices—ecclesiastical offices with income from an estate—gave him some financial independence. (The first and crucial one was the priory of San Martino in Gangalandi, a Gothic church on a small hill overlooking a town outside Florence.) At some point after 1428, when the Florentine government lifted the ban on the Alberti family, Leon Battista entered the city of his ancestors for the first time. In the mid-1430s, he moved to Florence with Pope Eugenius IV, who had been driven out of Rome by popular demonstrations. Soon he became a canon of the Florentine Cathedral; his career would remain entwined with the history of the city from then on.

Between 1435 and 1452, Alberti's creative energies exploded in an astonishing number of directions. He wrote and rewrote brilliant, original treatises on the practices of Florentine painters and the lives of the great Florentine clans. He organized a public poetry contest (which flopped prominently), experimented with the possibilities of Italian prose and verse, and performed a brilliant analysis of the history and structure of the Tuscan dialect. In Rome and elsewhere, he made himself one of Italy's three leading experts on the remains of ancient art and architecture, collecting every passage from a classical text that bore on ancient buildings and statues and turning over the rubble of every site he could reach. By the middle of the fifteenth century, he had set out to write the most ambitious of all his books: the first modern manual of classical architecture, a work designed to rival, and if possible displace, the standard ancient work by Vitruvius on building and city planning. To be sure, the greed of his fellow Florentines soon alienated him, and this feeling was confirmed and deepened by the harsh criticism with which they greeted many of his attempts at innovation. Still, his ambitious writings on these vital, very current topics won him attention from fellow scholars, patrons of the arts, and some artists in central and northern Italy.

Alberti's career coincided with a transformation of the Italian urban world. The mercenary captains and adroit diplomats who ruled small independent cities like Ferrara, Mantua, and Urbino came to see cultural patronage as essential, not only to express their own interests and tastes but also to assert their status and legitimacy, which they had not inherited. So, eventually, did a series of popes who thought spectacular buildings and fine art could preserve the faith of the ordinary Christian in the Catholic Church. And so, on the grandest scale of all, did the Medici—the family that came to dominate Florence after Cosimo de' Medici returned from a brief political exile, early in the 1430s. At midcentury, several Italian courts supported new forms of art and architecture. The learning, fearlessness, and social adroitness that enabled Leon Battista to offer advice on many subjects without seeming arrogant or servile made him a valued adviser at these courts, an erudite consultant on aesthetic questions, with impeccable taste.

Soon he also established himself as a designer of major projects in his own right, one who directed architects and builders. His services were valued highly by brilliant, brutal soldier-princes like the Este of Ferrara, Sigismondo Malatesta of Rimini, and Federigo da Montefeltro of Urbino. He probably advised Pope Eugenius IV and his successor, Nicholas V, on the restoration of the city of Rome. Later he certainly did the same for the most learned of all fifteenth-century popes, Pius II. Mantuan legend identifies Alberti with an older man who whispers in the ear of the city's ruler, Ludovico Gonzaga, in one of Mantegna's great frescoes in the Camera degli Sposi. Whether or not the story is true, he certainly became a habitué of splendid courts in Mantua and elsewhere, where leggy and disdainful young men attended the greats of state and church at the banquet table and the battlefield.

Florentine cultural patronage had traditionally been ambitious and lavish and public. But under the Medici family, who ruled the city from 1434 onward, values and patterns of cultural consumption shifted. Both the city's rulers and those who supported their regime came to value splendid displays, great buildings, and breathtaking parties—the common change of court life in the period—more than the older Florentine practice of concealing wealth to avoid public suspicion and higher taxes. By contrast, the Medici and their friends prized, and enjoyed exercising, the Aristotelian virtue of "magnificence." Classical architecture was soon identified as a primary way to practice this virtue. Eventually Alberti found a friend as well as a patron in the person of the great builder Giovanni Rucellai. In Florence as in Rimini and Ferrara, Alberti's tastes and his vision of the ancient world found widespread favor.

Between the middle of the century and his death in 1472, Alberti lived in a fairly regular orbit that took him from Florence to his favorite courts—like that of Urbino, where he often spent part of the hot-weather season with his friend, the learned soldier-prince Federigo da Montefeltro. He designed, or helped to design, some of the most original and influential buildings of the fifteenth century: the Malatesta Temple in Rimini, Santa Maria Novella and the Rucellai Palace in Florence, Sant'Andrea in Mantua, and others. At the same time, he composed a full-scale treatise on architecture, On the Art of Building, and continued to write shorter works in many fields, from sculpture through moral philosophy to cryptography. He died a celebrity, renowned for his originality and versatility, which had won him many powerful friends and patrons. His books survived him, doing much to spread the taste for a classical style to Northern Europe and to form a language in which Italians and northerners alike could discuss works of art critically. No wonder that highly influential Florentine writers like Cristoforo Landino and Angelo Poliziano heaped up phosphorescent metaphors when they praised his intellect and his erudition.[4]

Yet if Alberti's vital statistics are easily gathered and presented, his achievements—and many vitally important minor details of his work—remain controversial. What accounted for his ability to achieve so much in so many fields? Did any common themes and methods connect his work as a writer to his practical efforts as artist and builder? More than a century ago, the Basel historian Jacob Burckhardt proposed what remains the most influential single answer to this question. Burckhardt's dazzling study, The Civilization of the Renaissance in Italy: An Essay, called the modern study of the Renaissance into existence, and his deeply sympathetic portrait of Alberti has shaped much subsequent research, even though scholars' knowledge of Alberti's life, work, and context has since changed beyond recognition. Until recently, most of the new materials about Alberti that scholars have discovered in the last century have been forced into the mold that Burckhardt crafted.

With unforgettable brilliance and pathos, Burckhardt depicted Alberti as the ideal combination of intellectual and athlete, the perfect example of the "universal man." He could ride the wildest horses and jump from a standing start over the head of a man standing next to him. When Alberti's memory failed him after an illness, he turned to the study of nature and natural philosophy. He invented practical devices, like the cipher used at the papal curia; he devised a magnificent "show box," in which he created spectacularly effective renderings of sky and landscape; he wrote in every literary genre and in both Italian and Latin; and he practiced all the fine arts. He had a gift for cultivating friendships with men of radically different kinds, from pious monks to humanist pornographers.

Alberti, in short, mastered all the traditional arts of the medieval courtier and all the new ones of the Renaissance intellectual. At the same time, he made the presentation of self in everyday life into a new art of its own. Alberti, as Burckhardt emphasized, trained himself systematically to walk, ride, and converse in attractive ways—and never to reveal the effort that had gone into doing so. He thus adumbrated the courtier's steely, subtle discipline of self-cultivation, the elegant, sometimes deadly performance art that Baldassare Castiglione would describe definitively in his *Book of the Courtier*, long after Alberti's death. Yet all this severe self-discipline did not dull the keen edge of Alberti's sensibility. On the contrary, he responded emotionally to every setting. He loved the countryside, even though spring flowers and fall fruits filled him with melancholy, making him feel unproductive, and he delighted in the sight of virtuous old men. In short, he expressed a new creative ideal in his everyday life as well as in his treatises— the first modern ones—on painting, architecture, and society. His easy "inner contact" with the world even enabled him, Burckhardt claimed, to predict the future. He foresaw a terrible crisis that faced the Este in Ferrara, foretold the troubled future of Florence and Rome for years to come, and read the characters of his acquaintances from their physiognomies. A unique force of will united all of these qualities. Alberti believed that men could do anything, "if they only have the will to do so."[5]

For Burckhardt, moreover, Alberti's overriding desire for fame—and the discipline and passion with which he developed every talent he had to win it—stemmed directly from the environment he inhabited, and to which he had to adapt himself. In Renaissance Italy, as tyrants without inherited claims to their thrones took power in state after state, achieving and maintaining political and social standing became infinitely difficult. Only talent, not high birth, could enable an artist to win the ear and favor of one of the soldier-kings, whose trademark was the brutal rapidity with which they could shed blood in a crisis. Danger promoted deftness: walking a tightrope over the shark-pool of such courts forced men to develop every sense and every strength they had. Alberti, who cultivated arms and letters together, was the quintessential product of his age. Even his iron will depended for its existence on conditions that affected all his fellow citizens—conditions that produced, after Alberti's death, a second "universal man," who was to Alberti as the virtuoso to the dilettante: Leonardo da Vinci.

Burckhardt's beautiful profile of Alberti stamps itself on the memory of every reader and has continued to inspire studies of Alberti. Girolamo Mancini, the erudite Italian scholar whose expert research in archival documents and literary texts turned up most of what is known today about the details of Alberti's life, wanted to show how Alberti's achievements in many fields precisely fitted the needs of his time. In the 1960s, a pioneering social and cultural historian, Joan Gadol, took Burckhardt as the inspiration for her effort to draw connections among all areas of Alberti's work and thought. Tireless in her pursuit of substantive links between Alberti's scholarship and his scientific work, Gadol shirked no difficulty, textual or intellectual, and broke much new ground, especially in her exploration of Alberti's work on perspective and practical arithmetic. Like Mancini's detailed, informative biography, Gadol's rich study, *Leon Battista Alberti: Universal Man of the Early Renaissance*, remains a standard work, one inspired by the belief that Alberti's diverse achievements formed a coherent response to the world he knew. So does the erudite book in which the French scholar Paul-Henri Michel tried to find the unity in Alberti's varied pursuits— though he noted the persistence of medieval elements in many areas of Alberti's thought, an idea that would be pursued by many later scholars as well.[6]

Gadol's work, however, was unusual for its time. In the late nineteenth and twentieth centuries, historical scholarship became increasingly specialized, even fragmented. Art history, Renaissance intellectual history, and the history of Italian literature (among other fields) established themselves as independent disciplines, each with its own methods, standards, and burgeoning scholarly literature. German scholars, attracted by unexplored archives as well as the lively streetcorner society outdoors, flooded into Italy. Italians responded to national unification and the challenge of the German empire by declaring the production of solid, document-based history to be a fundamental patriotic duty. By the turn of the century, adventurous Americans and Britons were also taking an active part in research. After World War II, Australians, New Zealanders, and Canadians joined them.

The various facets of Alberti's life and work attracted the attention of specialists in each field. But few scholars could muster all the skills needed to address the full dazzling range of his pursuits. Monographs multiplied—but as they did, the possibility of achieving a synthesis became more and more elusive. The new specialized scholarship gave Alberti an enhanced—even a dramatic—role in central areas of Renaissance culture. From the 1920s onward, the great German art historian Erwin Panofsky studied perspective, a complex tradition belonging to both art and science and based on geometry and optics, one form of which enabled painters and sculptors in the early fifteenth century, for the first time, to create a convincing illusion of three-dimensional space in a two-dimensional painting or a low relief. Alberti's achievement—which was not to invent this crucial form of applied geometry, but to give its principles coherent written form for the first time—loomed large, even central, in the story of the Renaissance. The humanistic scholars of the fourteenth and fifteenth centuries, Panofsky argued, showed their contemporaries how to see the ancient world from a fixed point in time—their own. They grasped, for the first time, the full chronological distance that stretched, the great social and political changes that had taken place, between the time of Cicero and Virgil and their own day. Alberti showed them how to see the visual world in a similar way: from a fixed viewpoint, and in logically coherent terms. The *space* of Renaissance painting—and indeed of Renaissance science—reflected the same cultural origins as the *time* of humanistic scholarship. It was Albertian space, subject to a rigorous geometry, as historical time was subject to a rigorous philology. Alberti stood revealed as one of the creators of the modern world.[7]

Rudolf Wittkower, another of the eminent German art historians whose emigration to England and the United States transformed the humanities in so many vital ways, advanced a similar thesis about Alberti and architecture. Alberti, he argued, devised a visual language for modern architecture in the classical style—a lexicon of ancient forms, like the triumphal arch and the dome, whose proportions and shapes were determined by rigorous mathematical ratios like those that underlay musical harmony. This system, as developed in Alberti's own practice and perfected by later architects like Andrea Palladio and Sebastiano Serlio, yielded churches and palaces of a new kind—an architecture as radically new as Albertian perspective.[8] A third great German scholar, Richard Krautheimer, ranged across Alberti's world and the disciplines he practiced, shedding light on everything he touched, from Alberti's texts to the Florentine and Roman contexts in which he composed them.

These detailed studies and the dozens of others they inspired did more, over time, than make individual aspects of Alberti's life and work appear with greater clarity. They also gave rise to disagreements, some of them radical. In the first place, they made it harder and harder to see all of Alberti's activities as fitting together in a coherent way. Julius von Schlosser, a prolific and influential Viennese art historian of the first part of the twentieth century, took a deep and passionate interest in the formal treatises and commentaries devoted to the visual arts by scholars and philosophers in antiquity and afterward. He collected the texts and wrote what remains, in updated form, the standard survey of them—the magnificent, indispensable *The Literature of Art.*

Alberti, the pioneering author of *On Painting, On Sculpture,* and *On the Art of Building,* naturally received a prominent place in Schlosser's cast of characters. The historian and critic emphatically praised Alberti, not only for his ambition and learning but also for his practical mastery of the arts, which enabled him to formulate central problems of creativity in ways that remained provocative for centuries. Yet as Schlosser continued to work on Alberti and the arts, as he tried to embrace not only Alberti's writings but his buildings as well, in a synthetic treatment, he found himself unable any longer to discern the unity that had so impressed Burckhardt. For Schlosser, finally, Alberti was not a "universal man" but an intellectual dilettante. In trying not only to write but to cultivate all the arts and sciences, he revealed—as most, if not all, critics would have—his own catastrophic lack of artistic talent. The temple he built for the Malatesta in Rimini was "a masquerade"; his Church of Sant'Andrea in Mantua amounted to "a purely decorative form, almost like a stage setting."[9]

Schlosser conceded that Alberti's treatises were informative and historically important. But he dismissed his architectural work as pedantic and incoherent, and he insisted that Alberti himself played no active role in the history of the arts. Alberti had been an overambitious scholar, whose work rewarded the art historian not with a hidden unity but with problems of comprehension.

In recent years, monographic work on all these aspects of Alberti's work—and others—has multiplied. Scholars have studied and edited many of Alberti's texts, though to this day, few of them are available in critical editions, and two ongoing projects to produce editions of his complete works will not reach completion for some time to come. But this painstaking, indispensable work has yielded neither clarity nor consensus. Some estimable scholars firmly believe that Alberti knew and worked with practicing artists;

others argue that he remained essentially a theorist, aloof from the world of practice (which, in turn, remained largely aloof from him). Some hold that Alberti's treatises had a powerful impact on painters and sculptors, while others argue that it had little or none. Some ascribe a great many buildings to Alberti or to architects working in consultation with him; others maintain that no surviving building reflects his concrete activity as planner and builder.

One school—nowadays the dominant one—has found a dark, mysterious world of irony and self-torment under the smooth classical surface of Alberti's built and written work, especially in his satire on court life, the *Momus,* and his short dialogues, the *Dinner Pieces.*[10] These scholars' investigations have revealed stress fractures cutting jaggedly across the smooth bright self that Burckhardt ascribed to Alberti. In the past, many historians saw Alberti as an optimistic urbanist and architect who eagerly worked with Pope Nicholas V to redesign Rome as a magnificent ideal city. But, as Eugenio Garin, the leading Italian historian of Renaissance thought, and Manfredo Tafuri, a brilliant, contentious specialist on architectural history, point out, Alberti devoted the *Momus* to a scarifying satire on all such grandiose plans. Alberti, long seen as a deft and willing courtier, turns out to have harbored subversive, radical feelings against the very rulers he supposedly served.

Alberti, the optimist, was at times deeply pessimistic. The engineer who wrote about how to create great bridges and praised man's power to dominate and master nature also evoked, with a modern environmentalist's horror, the destruction wrought by man's demonic, excess energy on an innocent natural world. The warm-hearted idealist who held that any individual could accomplish any feat, however difficult, on his own, longed for the love and support that his own extended family, the Alberti, denied him. He gave expression to his mourning in magnificent prose—when they refused to treat him as a legitimate member of the clan. The glorious summer of Burckhardt's Alberti was haunted by the perpetual winter of this newer Alberti's discontent.

How then to restore the unity—or retrace the partial coherence—of a portrait of this fascinating, labile, passionate man? One way may simply be to return to Burckhardt and his first encounter with the sources—and to ask whether he could have followed—or hacked out—other paths in his treatment of this central figure. Students of Burckhardt, above all the great Basel scholar Werner Kaegi, who wrote his biography in seven fascinating volumes, have reassembled much of the material he used. They have shown that Burckhardt's dazzlingly compressed paragraphs on Alberti actually omitted the bulk of what he knew about Alberti.

By the middle of the 1850s, when Burckhardt began writing what he called his "essay" on *The Civilization of the Renaissance*, he had enjoyed a superb training in ancient, medieval, and modern history and art history at the University of Berlin, a preeminent center of innovation in historical and humanistic research. He had developed a dazzlingly original historical method of his own, one that had already enabled him to produce an innovative study of the late antique world of the Roman emperor Constantine. Doing cultural history of the Italian Renaissance, as Burckhardt understood it, required both long years of travel in Italy, where he mastered the art and architecture of the period, object by object, sketching as he went; and long bouts of systematic digging in the primary sources, which he read not in order to reduce them to a single reliable narrative but to make them exude, like teabags dipped in hot water, the flavor and color of the age that produced them. For his study of Constantine, Burckhardt wanted to know not what Constantine had done, day by day, but how he and his contemporaries had thought and felt. For the Renaissance book, he worked in the same way.

It took Burckhardt five years of intermittent work to prepare *Civilization of the Renaissance*, and he did so by adapting a technique handed down directly from the Renaissance humanists—notably Alberti. He read and took careful notes from the primary sources, which he later reassembled into glittering mosaics of striking detail that supported his assertions about the artistry of public life, the independent role of women, and the proliferation of universal men. A famous letter of 1858 to his friend Paul Heyse vividly conveys the nature of Burckhardt's working method:

> Yesterday, for example, I cut apart 700 little sheets with citations just from Vasari, which I had copied out in a notebook, and sorted them for gluing up in topical order. From other authors I have around a thousand quarto pages of excerpts on art and two thousand on culture. How much of all this will I really be able to process?

Only capitalists, he reflected sadly, had the time for research on this massive scale, but they devoted that time to other activities.[11]

Burckhardt excerpted Alberti's works carefully and fully. In fact, he dedicated one of his three earliest preserved sets of notes on the Renaissance to Alberti. His notes were precise and insightful. With characteristic prescience, he noted Alberti's general appreciation for the new art of the Florentine 1420s and 1430s, his belief that artists should claim a new social and intellectual status, and his interest in the artistic representation of hair and garments set into motion by the wind:

> The Germanic period is over. He discovers the Renaissance, already underway in five great representatives [the artists praised in Alberti's dedicatory letter to Brunelleschi, which Burckhardt had summarized]. Modern consciousness of fame . . . *Movement of the soul* . . . Movement of hair, limbs, and clothing—Even Giotto had still let them fall as they fell—The motif of movement [in the air] caused by a single wind god.[12]

All of these themes still require careful discussion in any modern analysis of Alberti's thought. Yet Burckhardt took note not only of these colorful details—exactly the ones that another great historian of art and culture, Aby Warburg, would seize on, a generation later, without knowing Burckhardt's excerpts—but of many drier ones as well. He recorded Alberti's argument that architecture derived from painting, and compared it with the very different history of the arts that Alberti offered in his work on architecture. He remarked on the careful investigations of ancient sites that underpinned that work, compared its recommendations with Alberti's buildings, and called attention to its key aesthetic term: *concinnitas* (harmony of the parts with the whole). Burckhardt would use these notes extensively, many years later, in his detailed *History of Architecture in the Renaissance*, in which he showed that he had studied Alberti's treatise *On the Art of Building* as carefully as he had drawn the ancient and modern buildings that Alberti had known.

But in the text of *Civilization of the Renaissance*, Burckhardt omitted details like these—just as he omitted the detailed treatment of the visual arts that he had originally intended as an essential companion to this essay. Burckhardt saw the full aesthetic development of personality as the Renaissance's highest creative work; the search for lives lived as art, rather than a precise analysis of texts, dominated his research. Years later he told another historian that the real inspiration for his work on the Renaissance had come to him in Rome in 1847, when he read the fifteenth-century Florentine bookseller Vespasiano da Bisticci's colorful, anecdote-filled lives of his contemporaries.[13]

The search for the ideal type of the Renaissance man meant the reading, above all, of biographies—like the historian Paolo Giovio's *Eulogies* of famous men and the painter Giorgio Vasari's *Lives of the Artists*, both written in the sixteenth century. Giovio had had nothing to say about Alberti, and Vasari only a little. But Burckhardt had found a biographical witness that was as rich in details as it was puzzling. His description of Alberti's character rested less on Alberti's own writings—to say nothing of his buildings— than on a short Latin biography of Alberti, written in the third person and anonymous, which was also translated into Italian and published in the first edition of Alberti's Italian writings.[14] Anilio Bonucci, who supervised this collection, suspected that Alberti himself had written this biography, and Burckhardt seems to have found this suspicion plausible.

It may seem curious that Burckhardt retailed at length all of the short biography's tall stories about Alberti's physical and intellectual prowess. But he knew exactly what he was doing. He saw in the *Anonymous Life* of Alberti an individual personality experienced in its full development. Evidently, Alberti had sought glory above all and had seen the full development of his every talent as the natural way to go about that great quest. As long as the high aspirations that the text conveyed were genuine period ideals, Burckhardt did not care that some exaggeration might have crept into Alberti's account of how he fulfilled them.

Burckhardt relied on this text as a modern analyst might rely on an unreliable narrative or interview for the understanding of a personality. But he also selected as he read, omitting details that did not support or dramatize his larger arguments. He did not, for example, mention a fact repeatedly referred to in the *Anonymous Life*: that Alberti made strenuous efforts to win support from the other members of his family, and he vividly recorded the pain he felt when these attempts failed. Alberti, student of all the arts and crafts, portrayed himself as a depressive who was repeatedly paralyzed by grief or fear, unable to produce any creative work. A brilliant athlete and public performer, he sometimes withdrew in misery from all contact with others and made vicious fun of others' aspirations. These elements are as prominent in the *Life* as the ones that Burckhardt singled out, yet they found no mention in his brilliantly biased summary of the text.

Alberti, as Burckhardt saw so clearly, desperately needed an identity, both personal and professional, in the 1430s, when he almost certainly wrote the *Anonymous Life* (a precocious autobiography, the text seems to have been written in 1438). Like a young Balzac character, he went to live in big, dangerous cities where he had no support system. Though a scion of a great family, he began his adult life deprived of the rank and money needed to make his life secure, and the connections that would have given him immediate access to desirable positions. For this initial wound, anyone might have felt the need to compensate. Like many others in his time, Alberti tried to avenge in the realm of the intellect his initial defeats in the countinghouse.

So far, Burckhardt's analysis retains all its poignant precision. But a closer look at Alberti's *Life*—both its content and its composition—will show that Alberti did not create himself out of whole cloth. He drew on existing cultural resources of many kinds, and the drama of his life—like that of most lives—played itself out in acts of artful and creative adaptation to his surroundings. These, in the end, enabled him to surmount enormous obstacles and to make good terrible losses—but not to create the seamless, perfect self that Burckhardt ascribed to him.

To begin, where Burckhardt did, in midlife: Alberti's autobiography certainly portrays, as Burckhardt held, a dazzling figure. Alberti, according to the third-person narrative, exhibited in one brilliant self the whole range of human potentiality. He schooled himself to show the self-discipline of a convinced Stoic. To counter the severe physical pains and discomforts that were a normal part of experience in the fifteenth century, he applied moral as well as physical therapies: "He could tolerate pain and cold and heat. Once, when not yet fifteen, he had received a serious wound in his foot. As the doctor, following medical custom, sewed up the separated parts of the foot, he had to tie them together by passing his needle through the skin. Alberti did not let forth a single wail. Rather, he helped the doctor who was healing him with his own hands, despite the intense pain, and treated the wound himself." Alberti hired musicians to help him bear severe cold sweats; refused to wear a hat, however cold and windy the weather; and even trained himself to accept the presence near him of honey and garlic, two substances that had originally filled him with violent disgust. "He conquered himself, by making a practice of looking at and handling the things he loathed, to the point that they ceased to offend him; and he thus offered an example to show that men can make anything of themselves, if they wish."[15] Developing a tolerance for garlic proved the plasticity of the self: Alberti's terrible vulnerability to social and physical injury was accompanied by tenacious efforts to achieve a state of balance. Though threatened by demons, Alberti remained on his high wire and danced.

Balance is a motif that appears and reappears throughout Alberti's *Life*—and his own life. The English art historian Michael Baxandall, who has recreated with great originality and insight the intellectual practices of the world in which Alberti came to maturity, devoted a brilliant essay to this point. He showed that Alberti systematically tried, again and again, to find in his life or to make in his art places where extremes could meet, or at least be balanced against each other.[16]

Despite Alberti's ferocious training and rigorous personality remodeling, despite his efforts to harden himself, to give himself an exterior as rigid and impervious as a suit of armor, his senses and his sensibilities remained undimmed. Everything he saw affected him, and some sights filled him with profound joy, a sense that the world was orderly and beautiful: "He took a special pleasure in seeing things that had a certain beauty. He loved to marvel at old men endowed with dignity and health, and declared that he venerated them as miracles of nature. He said that four-footed beasts, birds and other animals of great beauty deserved the warm affection of humanity, because nature had endowed them with a particular grace. He wrote a funeral oration for his charming dog, after its death." Seeing jewels, flowers, and beautiful landscapes could even restore Alberti to health—a form of therapy by beauty, which the Florentine philosopher and medical man Marsilio Ficino would later codify in a book that became a European best-seller.

A lover of friendship, Alberti freely shared his real and intellectual property with others. He did his best to ally himself with his relatives in Florence as well, but all his efforts, or most of them, were in vain—at least as he later told the story. He found himself rejected by his family and beset by critics who carped at everything he did. Even though he refused to return their insults, he often found himself unable to restore his friendships with them. The open-hearted man lived surrounded by bitter, close-mouthed enemies.

Alberti's intellectual life also spanned extremes. On the one hand, he loved to relax. He invited friends for endless discussions of "literature and learning." He enjoyed rigorous outdoor exercise, especially mountain climbing. And he spent time contemplating the beauty of plants, animals, and handsome old men. Yet he also worked so continually that many thought him antisocial: "He never took time off from meditation and invention: he rarely came home from the city without devising something, and did so even at meals. As a result, he came to seem somewhat taciturn and solitary, and a bit off-putting in appearance." Despite these constant efforts to create, Alberti continually reproached himself for his own infertility. Then, as now, therapy could backfire. Alberti's country walks, for example, did not always have their intended effect. The sight of spring flowers or fall fruits filled him with depression, and he would urge himself on with a desperate football coach's clichés: "Battista, now it's your turn to promise some sort of fruits to the human race." The great dilettante who tried to shape his own character as a seal imprints a form on hot wax oscillated throughout his life between creative hyperactivity and paralyzing depression.

Even Alberti's most striking and remarkable intellectual achievements revealed profound underlying divisions and paradoxes, as he inspected them with the assumed objectivity of his third-person autobiographical narrator. In predicting the future—for which he claimed to have a considerable gift—"he combined learning and intelligence with the arts of divination." In some cases, Alberti evidently used the art of astrology, exchanging letters on the future of the papacy with the renowned astrologer Paolo Toscanelli. But in others, he depended on a personal prophetic gift, a "ray in his heart," that enabled him to make out the characters and intentions of others at a glance.[17] A trained reader of the stars, Alberti was also an inspired reader of the soul. He thus combined the scientific prowess of a medical man, based on close study of texts and the application of precisely formulated rules and protocols, with the charismatic gifts normally found in saints like his older contemporary Bernardino of Siena, who startled hearers of his sermons with his ability to detect their flagging attention and failing determination.

Alberti loved classical literature and plunged into studying it at Padua and Bologna: but while he was a student at Bologna, in the 1420s, he became ill from overwork, forgetting even the names of his best friends. The very words on the pages of his beloved books, which he had always seen as a garden of floral delight, turned threatening. They assumed the shapes of scorpions—a brilliant, terrifying transformation of the image of Dialectic, the art of reasoning, who, as Alberti knew from illuminated books, holds flowers in her right hand and a scorpion in her left.[18] At the same time, his ears rang with frightening noises. Always a lover of the visual arts, Alberti turned to "the arts of nature and medicine," since he thought he could practice them without taxing his memory further. The master humanist was also a committed, even obsessive lover and student of nature. In some moods, Alberti considered his versatility a virtue. He praised himself, for example, for learning music on his own, without a teacher, so well that learned musicians praised him and took his advice. On the other hand, he also hurried home to practice what he called "his duty"—without explaining what that might be.

At times Alberti presented himself as a master of all the rational arts of living upon which his contemporaries set great store. He tried to teach a lesson in applied aesthetics with every gesture that he made: "Therefore he wished both to be and to seem worthy of the affection of others, in every aspect of his life, with every gesture, and in every utterance. Above all, he said that one must apply the greatest artistry in three things: walking in the city, riding a horse, and speaking, for in each of these one must try to please everyone. But a further art must also be added to the other three: namely, that none of these seem to be done in an artful way."[19] He portrayed himself, in other words, as the courtier of courtiers; the avatar of grace in every word and movement; the possessor of an exterior shell so polished and so beautiful that it repelled all criticism; a performer of consummate agility and elegance who always kept his audience in mind. At the same time, however, he freely admitted his vulnerability: for his fragile mind and body responded immediately both to the sight of natural beings and to the insults of fellow men. For all his efforts at self-protection, he suffered pains and diseases too powerful even for one of his profound self-mastery to overcome. The wound inflicted by his family's rejection was particularly painful.

What did Alberti hope to achieve by portraying himself as both the master and the victim, the sovereign Stoic and the victim of hostile men and friendly nature? By the time he wrote, in the 1430s, other writers had already begun to compose biographies of scholars—elaborate literary works devoted to men whose achievements lay in the realm of the mind and letters rather than on the battlefield or in the parliament. Leonardo Bruni, a brilliant Florentine scholar and government figure whom Alberti knew fairly well, wrote lives of Dante, Petrarch, and Boccaccio in Italian, just before Alberti wrote his own autobiography in Latin. Bruni too set his protagonists into the worlds in which they had lived, portraying in detail the violent political struggles in which Dante had taken an active part and the decline of classical learning that Petrarch had been the first to begin to remedy. Bruni not only narrated his subjects' lives, moreover, he also offered profound and serious judgments of them. He explained at length, for example, that one could become a poet in two quite different ways, "through the incitement and motion of personal genius by some inner and hidden force," as Saint Francis had achieved the state of mystical union with God, or "through knowledge and study, through learning and art and prudence." Bruni did not hesitate to describe the first form of poetic career as "the highest and most perfect"—or to designate Dante as of the "second sort."[20]

Ultimately, Bruni made his comparison of his two heroes, Dante and Petrarch, into a sustained exploration of the relation of cultural to political achievement. Dante he saw as clearly "of greater worth than Petrarca in the active and civic life, for he served laudably both at arms for his land and in the government of the Republic." Petrarch, by contrast, had shown his wisdom by dedicating himself to "the quiet and leisurely life" and using his opportunities to gain a mastery of Latin and literature denied to Dante. Yet each had "his own excellence in part," and Dante's greatest Italian works surpassed Petrarch's even as Petrarch's Latin works surpassed Dante's. Bruni's probing studies of character and context, talent and tradition, may well have stimulated Alberti to attempt his own self-analysis—though his decision to write about himself, rather than another, reveals a dramatic concentration on his own character and fate that Bruni seems not to have shared.[21]

When Alberti decided to produce a self-portrait rather than an image of someone else, he may well have had in mind the examples of Dante and Petrarch, as well as some of the ancient sources that inspired them. Both had written substantial works of autobiography and self-analysis—texts that not only recounted the stories of their lives but also laid bare to contemporary and later readers their spiritual and emotional histories. Petrarch, for example, cast his own efforts to achieve peace and virtue into an allegorical account in a letter on his ascent of Mount Ventoux. He devoted long and elaborate treatises and dialogues to other moments in the same struggle.

Petrarch may have provided Alberti with his model in another sense as well. When he set out to dramatize his own divided self, Petrarch played off ancient literary models. In his letter on Mount Ventoux, he used terms that deliberately echoed Augustine's account (in books eight and nine of *Confessions*) of the drama of his own conversion. Like Augustine, Petrarch confronted his refractory self in desperation, unable to feel the single-hearted devotion that a Christian should. In his hour of crisis, Augustine was in a garden where he heard a child's voice singing, *Tolle, lege* ("Take, read"). The passage from the life of Saint Antony he then picked out and contemplated sent him on his way to Christianity. Book bit man. Petrarch, by contrast, sitting on his mountaintop, opened the pocket-sized copy of Augustine's *Confessions* that he had brought with him and found a passage which condemned the curiosity that made men explore nature rather than their inner selves. This threw him into a spasm of self-examination and self-criticism. He cast his thoughts into literary form at once, so he claimed, in case his mood might change. Yet Petrarch's life made no radical swerve, as Augustine's had, even in a parallel moment of high drama: he had not, and presumably would not, find the total peace and resolution that Augustine had attained when he became a Christian. Petrarch's dramatic account of his inner life, in other words, would have infuriated and disgusted the author of its model.[22]

Alberti made similarly creative use of ancient pigments when he painted his own self-portrait. In the later 1420s and early 1430s, a long and quirky collection of *Lives of the Philosophers*, attributed to one Diogenes Laertius and probably compiled in the third century C.E., attracted much attention in Italian scholarly circles. This substantial work included not only short biographies but a rich range of curious anecdotes and short texts by Greek philosophers from the early sages Thales and Solon onward, down to Epicurus. Though Diogenes summarized the philosophers' positions and told stories about them rather than analyzing their views in depth, he gave an intellectual and historical profile of thinkers who were mentioned or quoted in well-known texts but whose own works had not been transmitted to posterity. His work offered a massive demonstration that Greek sages like Thales and Solon had created philosophy—one that could be cited against the view, also widespread in antiquity, that ancient near eastern writers like Hermes Trismegistus and Zoroaster had been the first wise men. The full text of Diogenes' work had been preserved only in Greek in the Middle Ages, and was accordingly little known in western Europe. In the 1430s, the Camaldolensian monk Ambrogio Traversari translated the whole text into Latin, and Alberti's friend Lapo da Castiglionchio did the same for the life of Thales. Soon Diogenes found attentive readers.

Many parallels show that Alberti used Diogenes' life of Thales as a central model for his *Life*. Like Diogenes' text, Alberti's consisted not in a chronological narrative but in a series of stories and a collection of witty sayings. Alberti presented himself as an autodidact. Similarly, Diogenes remarked that Thales "was taught by no one" except some mysterious priests he had visited in Egypt. Like Alberti, Thales predicted the future—"foreseeing that it would be a good season for olives, [he] rented all the oil-mills and

thus amassed a fortune." Thales led his personal life with evident delibera-
tion, carefully avoiding having children of his own. He too changed interests, "becoming interested in nature after engaging in politics."[23]

Clearest of all is the relation between the provocative, sometimes cryptic
sayings that Diogenes ascribed to Thales and those that Alberti ascribed to
himself. Both texts reported not coherent arguments but short, charged
jokes and exchanges of question and answer, pulled from their original context and presented, presumably, both to amaze and tease potential readers.
Each man appeared as a master of the rapid, devastating retort. "Thales," according to Diogenes, "held that death did not differ from life: 'Why don't
you die, then?' said someone. 'Because,' he said, 'there is no difference.' " Alberti, according to the Life, produced extemporaneously a vast range of both
serious and comic remarks, which others collected. For example, "when a
foreigner asked which way he should go to reach the place where justice was
administered, he said, 'My friend, I don't know.' 'Don't you know the palace
of the Signoria?' said Alberti's fellow citizens, who were present. 'I hadn't remembered, my friends,' he answered, 'that justice had its dwelling there.' "

At one point, Alberti even quoted Thales explicitly, though he characteristically changed what his classical source—in this case, not Diogenes
Laertius but the slightly earlier biographer and essayist Plutarch—had to say
even as he used it. According to Plutarch, the Egyptian king Amasis posed
questions to an Ethiopian, who answered them in an unsatisfactory way:
"What is the oldest thing? Time. The biggest? The universe. The wisest?
The truth. The most beautiful? Light. The most common? Death. The most
helpful? God. The most harmful? The devil. The hardest? Fortune. The eas-
iest? Pleasure." Thales then answered the same questions, more profoundly:
"What is the biggest thing? Space . . . The wisest? Time . . . The most common? Hope."

According to Diogenes, as we have already seen, Thales noted that there
was no difference at all between life and death. Alberti described his own
replies to a similar set of riddles in the Life: "Asked what would be the
biggest of all things among mortals, he answered, 'Hope.' As to the smallest,
he said, 'The difference between a man and a corpse.' And as to the sweetest
of all things: 'Time, which makes free with bitterness'—that is, as he would
explain in a later work, time, which both brings bitter experiences in its
wake and frees us from them."[24]

Alberti, in other words, fitted the trajectory of his own life to that of one
of Greece's ancient sages. In doing so, he made powerful claims for his own

standing. He portrayed himself as a man of strong and independent mind: a thinker able not only to solve problems but also to amaze his contemporaries with enigmatic, witty sayings, produced with contemptuous ease and certainty. He revealed himself as a master of many trades and an autodidact. And at the same time, he cloaked himself in some of the mystery that hung about his ancient spiritual counterpart. Alberti genuinely described himself, as Burckhardt held, as a man of deep and penetrating insight, of wide vision and ambition. But he did so by applying to himself a ready-made template from an ancient text. The originality of his work—and of his life, as he himself understood it—lay in the speed and adroitness of his adaptive responses to challenges, his remarkable ability to seize and apply the right tool for each intellectual job.

As Alberti deftly pieced segments of older texts together, he revealed central truths about himself. In depicting himself as an essentially isolated figure, eager to find contacts and committed to winning respect but lacking a firm social and political base in his own family, he described what was and would remain his situation. Throughout his life, he remained a celibate cleric. Moreover, though he eventually made an impressive career as a writer and builder, he never came to rest in any single institution, but moved restlessly between the Florence of the Medici, the courts of Rimini and Ferrara, Urbino and Mantua, and the curia, welcome everywhere but nowhere firmly at home. A valued, vital member of many groups, he did not occupy a central position in any of them.

Even more revealing is the method Alberti used to create the *Life*. He was—in his own terms—a rhetorician, someone who saw himself as a skilled performer, whose use of language was in fact as calculated as it seemed spontaneous. Alberti, as we will see, had mastered the formal art of oratory, which had played so central a role in the political and legal life of ancient cities like Athens and Rome and which scholars in the fourteenth and fifteenth centuries revived in the hope of reanimating their own politics and culture. The rhetorician—so a vast body of ancient theory and practice showed—disposed of a wide culture, literary, historical, and philosophical. He had to learn all the skills that went into public speaking—five in all, including finding subject matter, arranging it in a suitable order, adorning it with a proper style, memorizing it, and performing it. He also had to know how to use literary references and historical allusions, both of which could serve as warm evocations of the institutions and traditions he shared with his hearers and help him win assent to the program or the verdict he supported. And he had to be able to address, seemingly without preparation, any subject that might come up in public life. Alberti—as he made clear in the *Life*—was deeply concerned with how he appeared in public—with the impression he made when walking in the city, riding, or conversing, all activities normally carried on before an audience. The art of oratory, as conceived of by Cicero, who had devoted a series of massive works to it, and as taught by Quintilian in his detailed handbook *The Education of an Orator*, offered exactly the skills in appropriate speech and movement that he needed.[25]

Alberti enjoyed an excellent rhetorical training. He even drew up a manual for young orators that laid out, in the form of a wheel, what he saw as the crucial points for any text on practical problems. Simply by turning this wheel, itself adapted from medieval precedents, the student would see that he must discuss certain "places" (*loci*): virtue and vice, utility and cost, ease and difficulty. These terms sounded vague, even labile, but they were vital nonetheless. Philosophers might pursue issues wherever they led, going deeply into implications and using words in senses quite different from those they bore in everyday conversation. But the orator needed only to keep in mind the normal meanings of terms, to organize what he read and knew into the categories already given on his wheel—and then to mobilize his materials whenever practical considerations called for him to do so. By doing so, he could always present himself and his policies in the best light.[26]

The orator who, like Alberti, used ancient sources and rhetorical techniques in the modern world had to be aware that he lived in a new time. Circumstances naturally altered cases: a practice that had once been highly moral, like the Old Testament requirement to marry the widow of one's brother, could become undesirable or even immoral over time. But if the orator simply collected good materials and used them with due regard for his own circumstances, his speech would almost write itself, proving as lucid, effective, and original as the governing conventions of its genre would allow. Alberti's encomium for himself, the *Life* that he based on cleverly chosen ancient models, was a splendid case in point.

Alberti knew that rhetoric was traditionally connected with morality, and responded in some of his works to Cicero's classical discussions of their relation. But in his manual he did not attend to the question of whether the orator's ends, or his character, were good. That sobering fact may help to explain some of the paradoxes and mysteries of Alberti's own character, so appealingly laid bare in the *Life*. Alberti portrayed himself as an emotional and moral acrobat, a master at finding a balance between extremes: a man who could encompass all of nature in a single moment of oceanic feeling or retreat into a tiny ball, the size of a point, when psychically wounded. He could do so because as he entered new situations, his character constantly adjusted itself, allowing one side or the other to prevail for a moment or in a text. Proud and humble, autonomous and dependent, Alberti subordinated ends to means. And only capturing the regard of others—winning applause, gaining assent—could show that he had been successful at a given task.

As a rhetorician, Alberti concentrated on the response of his audience: as he put it in the *Life*, he tried to thrill all who watched him with his deft gestures and conversation. Burckhardt emphasized, rightly, that Alberti very much wanted glory. But glory is always the gift of others. To win it, the rhetorician had to know his audience, polish his craft, and constantly accommodate the one to the other. Since he addressed many different groups, Alberti had to draw on cultural resources of many kinds in order to speak their special, technical languages. And since addressing each of these groups presented its own difficulties, he had to try at least to prepare a favorable reception for what he produced. In every discipline or pursuit Alberti attempted, he set out to organize and learn from his audience's first responses to him. He built communities of hearers and readers, critics who could reassure and correct him as proved necessary. But communities had to communicate. Hence he spent much of his life, as we will see, trying to construct languages that did not yet exist: languages whose users could regulate the practice of different arts. In the end, Alberti called into being not only a classical theater but a whole range of imaginary and real institutions: communities of scholars, of literati and painters, of architects and patrons. For only groups, as the orator knew, could usefully approve of or improve on the text, or the image, or the building that an individual had conceived. Alberti set out not only to perform but to create a whole series of arenas in which others could do the same. Surprisingly often, he succeeded at this ambitious, self-imposed task, deploying the resources of his classical culture to become not only a pioneering architect but a master builder in a much wider sense: the creator of new cultural systems and institutions.

An approach complementary to Burckhardt's seems most likely to do justice to the complexity of Alberti's strategies and the range of conditions that shaped them. The lack of personal primary sources—only a handful of Alberti's letters survive, for example—makes it difficult, if not impossible, to write a day-by-day biography that would do justice to Alberti's constant shifts of sensibility and mood. By contrast, a series of studies in the different forms of intellectual work that Alberti undertook, one that also investigates the environments and communities in which he undertook them, will enable us to watch him turning his rhetorical wheel, using different conventions, always creatively, and trying to build social institutions to regulate new cultural practices, like the learned painting and classical architecture that began to flourish in his time.

These tasks were never easy. Alberti insisted, over and over again, on the difficulties he had encountered as a writer. In his *Life*, he evoked the dedication with which he had pursued classical literature and devised modern literary forms, and the disdain with which his work had been received by sour contemporary readers, whom he nonetheless thanked for their useful criticisms. He underlined his powerful drive to change entire fields of study and application. He dwelt on his move from the study of letters to that of nature, from the verbal to the visual arts, and on his passion to master every new field of activity, from music to the crafts. He described at great length his successes as artist and craftsman, the innovative devices he had created and the responses they had evoked from his audience—a set of practical experiments and experiences more reminiscent of Plutarch's life of Archimedes than of Diogenes' life of Thales. And he expressed in vivid language the hurts he had received from his family, who "had scarcely bothered to read the titles" of his dialogues *On the Family*, though foreign readers showed a real passion for them.

Autobiography is never transparent. But it seems reasonable to take these themes as expressing views that Alberti himself passionately held. Lapo da Castiglionchio, trying to sum up his friend's achievement in 1438, emphasized as strongly as the *Vita* Alberti's extraordinary facility at pursuing new interests with skill and originality: "He is the sort of man who easily and quickly becomes better than anyone else at whatever pursuit he undertakes."[27] Lapo felt easy, in other words, using Alberti's own categories to describe his friend. Let us begin, then, by following the shape of Alberti's own life as he himself saw it, looking back in his mid-thirties: as an ambitious effort to win success as a particular kind of writer and scholar and as an even more unusual kind of artist and inventor—while simultaneously trying to win acceptance as a full member of the Alberti family and as an insightful observer of contemporary Florence. In following Alberti into each of these realms, we will examine not only his autobiography but a wide range of other documents and materials fabricated by his friends and enemies, his critics and supporters. These may enable us, if not to reveal the real man behind the brilliantly crafted mask, at least to re-create something of Alberti's own sense of what he had lived and achieved.

By dissolving Alberti's autobiography, the completed self-portrait, into its traditional and its novel ingredients, we have gained some understanding of the multiple ways in which his individual talent reshaped tradition—and in which tradition shaped the possibilities for his individual talent. In doing so, we used Alberti's own cherished method in reverse: we turned the wheel backward, to discover which "places" he had touched on and what their contents were. In each of the studies to come, we will apply a similar method, and we will come to appreciate Alberti's art of apparent spontaneity as the work of craft that it was.

II

HUMANISM:

THE ADVANTAGES AND

DISADVANTAGES OF SCHOLARSHIP

Alberti was still in his twenties when he composed a memorable account of his early career as a student of the classics and a writer of Latin. He did so in a single mordant Latin diatribe on a perpetually attractive subject: the uselessness of the humanities and the ineptness of humanists, at least for ordinary life. The savage little book *On the Advantages and Disadvantages of Letters* (variously dated to 1428 and to the early 1430s), which he dedicated to his brother Carlo, turned out to be an intellectual time bomb. Centuries after Alberti's own time, his book caught the eye of another mordant critic of professional scholarship, Friedrich Nietzsche, who imitated it in his own treatment of the advantages and disadvantages of applying history to one's life.

Like Nietzsche, Alberti left the reader in no doubt that he loved the classics. Like Nietzsche, too, however, he portrayed the prospects of the classical scholar as truly dismal. Badly dressed and ill at ease, confined all day to the company of books written on the skins of dead animals, scholars might master the arts of reading, but they could not learn and apply the arts of living. A simple look at these scholars' physical appearance—in an age when the science of physiognomics offered a key to character analysis—would reveal the miserable condition to which their pursuit of learning reduced them:

> We see them, dedicated from boyhood to letters, chained to the reading of manuscripts, and condemned to solitary confinement: so worn down by the rule and by their teachers, by the effort of learning, their continual reading and rereading and work, that they are absolutely worn out. Indeed, they often seem more cold-blooded than is normal for boys. Then comes youth: their faces will show you how pleasant and joyous they find that. See how pale they are, how flaccid their bodies, and how weighed down they seem, as they emerge from their long confinement in the prison of their schools and libraries.

Such feeble beings could neither amuse young women nor impose their wills on powerful men. Nor could they engage in any of the forms of recreation and exercise proper for young men of rank: "If any of them is inclined to ride horses, train dogs, or exercise in the gymnasium, or carry out any of the other activities worthy of a free man, think how wretched he will be when forced to give up everything that makes youth attractive to hide himself in the wretched obscurity of libraries."[1] More sharply than any later opponent of humanistic studies, Alberti formulated the parodic figure of the bumbling scholar, detached and dessicated.

Unable to dance, ride, or travel, Alberti continued, obsessed with the pursuit of philological trivia, such a pedant could never achieve either wealth or power. Worse still, he would probably never even become one of the shaky, frail pillars of his own academic society. Out of every thousand young scholars, only three hundred would reach the age of thirty—the minimum age for distinction. Only a hundred of these three hundred would retain their humanistic interests, only ten of the hundred would do really interesting work—and only three of those ten would win fame. By comparison, the prospects of a modern graduate student look positively rosy.[2]

In tallying up the odds against academic success, Alberti knew what he was talking about. As the scion of a great Florentine family, he had cherished great expectations in his youth. But his father's death and his relatives' greed and neglect, or so he felt, deprived him of the private means that would have made his way easy. Like many ambitious young men before and since, Alberti knew that he lived in a deeply hierarchical society and that his own position was low. For his social world forced the facts of his case on his attention. The quality, color, and shape of people's clothing and other easily legible, external signs located every individual in a place in the society of premodern Europe. One who changed costume, putting on the purple of a prince or the long gown of a scholar, claimed membership in a different social order and gained the privileges that belonged to it.[3] A fine house, schooled gestures, and the presence of servants and dependents immediately identified the men who held real power. Alberti came from a great family that within his memory had enjoyed all the visible appurtenances of wealth and standing. When his father Lorenzo married in Genoa in 1408, the French ambassador reported, the state ordered the bankers to close their shops for three days so that the wedding festivities could take place with suitable splendor in the Piazza de' Banchi. Sumptuary laws were temporarily repealed, so that women could wear "as many real pearls as they wish" and dress in silk of any color and quality they desired.[4] Leon Battista was four when this splendid wedding took place: a child of privilege. But when his father died while he was studying law at Bologna, he inherited no property. An illegitimate orphan, Leon Battista found he had to make his way on his own.

Later, as a young adult, Leon Battista made clear how fiercely he resented this situation: "When the rich man goes for a stroll," he told his brother Carlo, "a long retinue of friends and servants attends him, and he bears himself and gesticulates with visible pride."[5] Somehow Alberti had to find a way to rise—or else resign himself to the fate that the ambitious young find hardest of all to accept: poverty and obscurity. The quest for rank and dignity presented itself to him with special force after he returned to Florence. His relatives there not only flaunted their own prosperity but apparently pressed Leon Battista to follow Carlo—also a gifted scholar and writer—in taking uncongenial employment in a concern controlled by the Alberti cousins.[6] Alberti apparently rejected offers of such high-paying jobs, which would have forced him to abandon the intellectual life he loved.

If the problem was clear, so was one potential solution: the sort of career for which Alberti was already prepared when his father died. Italian cities had long harbored universities—institutions designed to turn out specialists who could perform certain demanding tasks that a sophisticated mercantile society and independent city governments required.[7] Students began, normally at the public schools that Italian communes also supported, by mastering Latin grammar and learning to read and compose Latin texts.[8] Then they could devote themselves, in a formal way, to three formal disciplines, two of which were taught in the higher faculties of the universities. Theoretically, those who pursued knowledge did so for its own sake. "Knowledge," so ran a proverb, "is the gift of God, and therefore cannot be sold." In fact, however, Alberti remarked, these studies "serve only the goods of the body and of fortune, and these arts are organically connected to the pursuit of gain."[9]

With relatively little expense of time and money, a young man could become a notary: a professional producer of contracts, wills, and other legal documents, as well as official and personal letters. By the early fifteenth century, notaries were deeply entrenched in the Italian cities, producing vital documents in large numbers for public as well as private use. Coluccio Salutati, the celebrated, erudite scholar and patron of scholars who served as chancellor of Florence, and Gian Francesco Poggio Bracciolini, a witty, eloquent papal secretary and writer of Latin treatises and dialogues, both made their way to impressive offices and stately fortunes by learning the notary's art, attaining membership in the notarial guild, and using their formal skills to establish themselves as valued public servants. These men—who also wrote official histories and propaganda for the states that employed them— enjoyed immense prestige as well as large incomes.[10]

A young man willing and able to invest more time and money could embark on the formal study of law or medicine. To do so, he must first master logical argument, learning in a university faculty of arts how to construct elaborate, rigorous chains of formal inferences. He would find both the premises for these inferences and the ways to connect them in the canonical texts of Aristotle, "the philosopher," and his Greek, Arabic, and Latin commentators. Then in one of the higher faculties, he would master a more specialized textual corpus. Lawyers had to assimilate both the Roman *Corpus iuris*, with its glosses by Accursius and other medieval commentators, which served as the basis of civil law, and the twelfth-century canon law compilation of Gratian, which codified the law of the church. (In medieval Europe, the church and its legal code regulated marriages, wills, and much more.) Medical students had to work their way through an equally demanding and difficult corpus—one, moreover, riven by seeming contradictions between its main authorities, Galen and Aristotle. Medical students read not only ancient medical works but also later commentaries and textbooks by such writers as the Arabic philosopher Avicenna and the fourteenth-century scholastic Pietro d'Abano, who tried to resolve apparent contradictions in the canonical texts.[11]

Whichever learned profession the young man chose, he needed one basic skill: a knowledge of how to apply ancient texts to modern problems. He was taught to assume that works written long ago by pagans offered principles directly relevant to his own world. (Laws about the property of temples, for example, could be taken to hold also for Christian churches.) He was also trained as a skilled debater, one who could use logical techniques to justify his readings and applications of the canonical works. Once he obtained his doctorate, he could become a highly respected and well-paid member of the local elite, often as both a practitioner and a professor. The successful doctor Taddeo Alderotti and the great lawyer Bartolus of Sassoferrato used their skills to write detailed *consilia*, formal opinions, about the illnesses that afflicted their acquaintances and the legal and political problems with which popes and emperors presented Italian cities that claimed independence from their supposed lords.[12] More than one young scholar admitted that naked ambition, not intellectual curiosity, drove him to these higher studies. As one of Alberti's friends, the Sicilian poet Antonio Beccadelli, or Panormita, put it,

> Let fame arrive when I am safely dead,
> So that its noise can't penetrate my head.
> A prudent stylist, I don't write for free,
> But sell my gifts at court, for a high fee.[13]

Lawyers, as Beccadelli suggested, had power, knowledge, and noble rank. Medical men, though their professional duty to analyze urine specimens and examine corpses lowered their social standing, reputedly enjoyed great wealth as well. But attaining a doctorate in law or medicine took many years and much expense. Alberti described one Bolognese father's complaint: His son had won the coveted doctoral degree, but he had cost his father far more than the degree was worth. The father had had to buy the boy new suitable clothing; to pay for elaborate feasts; and even to rebuild his house to fit his son's new rank: "if the money that is buried in my son's books and clothing were invested as it could be," he complained, "it would have yielded an enormous profit; I would still have the money I have spent on my son and I would have harvested a yearly profit as well."[14] The path to study—like the other paths of ambition—required financial as well as intellectual resources, and Alberti once again resented the trivial social snobbery that required scholarly progress to be celebrated in such vulgar ways.

Alberti nonetheless obtained a doctorate in canon and civil law at

Bologna in 1428, and his training probably helped to gain him his place as a secretary in the papal curia. Still, legal studies posed at least as many technical demands as they offered financial rewards. The very language used there—as precise, serviceable, and particular as the Yiddish spoken in a yeshiva—seemed impenetrable to nonspecialists. The huge glossed texts that lawyers displayed in their consulting rooms, resting on impressive rotating reading stands, appeared to many contemporaries, including Alberti, as a source of mystification rather than enlightenment: external symbols of professional authority, more like the framed diplomas on the wall of a modern lawyer's or doctor's office than an intellectual's dented, well-used working tools.[15] Only those who continually spoke and wrote the technical language of the law, keeping abreast of its conceptual and linguistic development, could retain command of its vocabulary. Alberti's early book on *The Advantages and Disadvantages of Letters* already expressed some dissatisfaction with lawyers, whom he described as showing little interest in the Roman law they supposedly studied and none in using it to achieve just outcomes in the courts. Writing in 1437, less than a decade after he took his degree, Alberti claimed that he had already lost "this legal faculty, [which] requires of its practitioners that they have the law constantly in mind and study it."[16] And he set out a stringent, closely argued program for the pursuit of justice—one as impressive in its formal coherence as it was irrelevant to the everyday practice of Roman law in Italian cities. The law, in other words, did not offer Alberti a royal road to the social and cultural position that he saw as rightly his.

A fourth technical field was also coming into its own in Italy in the years when Alberti was reaching maturity.[17] In the twelfth and thirteenth centuries, theology—the third of the higher studies, along with law and medicine—had been a specialty of northern European rather than Italian universities. Paris had attracted the most talented young theologians, from Peter Abelard to the Italian Dominican Thomas Aquinas, to teach Christian doctrine in ways that ranged from the sharply provocative to the calmly synthetic. By contrast, the Italian universities had concentrated on law and medicine, the higher studies for which their sophisticated cities had a clear use. In the fourteenth and fifteenth centuries, however, the Dominicans and Franciscans—the mendicant friars who preached in churches, streets, and piazzas against the moral excesses of the new commercial society and the theological heresies of newly literate laymen and dissident clerics—founded study houses in the Italian universities as well.[18] Formal works on theology, cast in the ferociously precise Latin and argued in the intensely formal way characteristic of the medieval north, began to be written and studied in northern and central Italy as well.[19] Contemporaries of Alberti like the dynamic Franciscan preacher Bernardino of Siena showed, in sermons that attracted thousands of listeners, how to apply the precepts of theology to the economic and social divisions of Italy's urban society.[20] Men and women throughout northern and central Italy thereupon devoted themselves to quiet lives of contemplation within religious communities or to noisy careers of public debate about the structure of the Roman Church and the validity of its central beliefs. Alberti took the teachings of Christianity seriously, devoted himself to the service of the church, and subjected many of its customs and institutions to severe criticism. But he seems never to have felt the attraction of theology or to have considered studying it formally.

One other path remained, also a relatively new one, though it grew from medieval roots. In the fourteenth century, Petrarch and a host of other scholars had devoted themselves to the study of the Latin classics. Petrarch, like Alberti, had tried the law, in southern France. But he too found it deeply unsatisfactory. True, he loved the many facts about Roman history and life that he found embedded in the legal texts. But the anachronistic application of these ancient books to modern life filled him with intellectual and emotional discontent. Petrarch could not accept the principle that texts written and legislation passed in ancient Rome could be applied to the modern world in which he despairingly lived. Instead of continuing in the field, he turned to the precise study and systematic imitation of the greatest Roman writers.

Petrarch built up an extraordinary library, the richest of his age. He filled the margins of his books with meticulous annotations, corrected textual errors by comparing manuscripts and sources, solved philological and historical problems, and applied his new understanding of the ancients to moral and practical problems. Soon he achieved fame, both as a scholar and as a writer of Latin letters and poems, dialogues, and treatises, which many readers found as powerful as those of Cicero and Virgil. So profound was his attachment to these Roman writers that he wrote letters to them, in which he analyzed, praised, and criticized their lives and writings. But he also tried to emulate them: to become a classic in his own right, for readers who would live long after him. He directed another letter, modeled on the verse epistles that the Roman poet Ovid had addressed to his imagined future readers, "To Posterity." Here he made clear that he expected later readers to feel the same kinds of interest in his writing and curiosity about his life that he felt for the ancients.[21] He found warm support for his pursuit of a literary career on the ancient model not only from other scholars but also from great ecclesiastical families like the Colonna and from the rulers of Italian states like Robert of Naples, who crowned him with the poet's laurels in Rome, and the Carrara of Padua, who became his patrons. At the same time, he rejected the scholastic method, which was becoming increasingly fashionable in Italy, with vehemence: if anything, he showed more scorn for doctors, who also used the scholastic method of textual interpretation, than for lawyers. Gradually he created a new model for an intellectual career, one based on literary and philological pursuits. Alberti—who also expended great efforts on communicating with his future readers—owed Petrarch an enormous amount, especially this personal example in the tradition of classical studies.[22]

But Petrarch and his followers also offered Alberti a cultural style and a career pattern. For Petrarch was far from the only Italian intellectual in the fourteenth century who seriously pursued an interest in ancient writings. By the time he died, in 1374, he had many allies and followers, some of whom—like Coluccio Salutati—occupied positions of great influence (in Salutati's case, chancellor of Florence). In the course of the next two generations, the new literary culture that Petrarch had cultivated as an individual found permanent institutional form.[23] Popes, princes, and patricians realized that writers of classical Latin could state their political cases to an increasingly discriminating European public. Every Italian government that could manage it soon boasted a humanist chancellor like Salutati, who could not only organize the state papers and compose treaties and ordinances but also write effective propaganda and official history. The papacy, which dealt by necessity with rulers and bishops, monastic houses, and universities across Europe, needed effective writers in even greater numbers than secular governments—especially during the long crisis in which, as we will soon see, it was involved for the first half and more of Alberti's lifetime.

Even before the rise of the new classical culture, Italian universities and towns had employed public teachers of Latin grammar.[24] In the course of the fifteenth century, more and more of these jobs went to humanists—classical scholars after Petrarch's model, men who could impart to the young not only the basics of Latin grammar, which had been taught throughout the Middle Ages without overmuch respect for its particular details, but the newly accessible secrets of ancient Latin rhetoric, history, and moral philosophy. The most effective of these teachers became celebrities. Their textbooks formed the basis of a new, alternative curriculum. They promised that their schools would train young men not to carry out a single defined specialist function but to become effective generalists—activist scholars prepared, like the ancient orators on whom they modeled themselves, to deploy their knowledge of history and morality in every arena of public life. Few humanists earned incomes or enjoyed reputations that could compare with those of successful doctors and lawyers. But they could compensate for material defeats with achievements in the realm of the spirit, arguing that their studies, unlike those of the higher-paid professionals, cultivated the spirit as well as the body. Unlike the dismal disciplines of the lawyers and doctors—so Petrarch and his followers claimed—the historical examples and moral precepts they culled from the ancients not only showed the right course of action but formed readers and hearers to follow it. By the time that Alberti wrote his own work on letters, with its sharp condemnation of both the greed of the professionals and the unworldliness of the humanists, he was contributing to a lively ongoing debate on the status of the professions—a debate that had already engaged Petrarch, Salutati, and many others.[25]

Even before Alberti went to law school, he had studied the classics from around 1416 to 1418 with one of the most effective and widely respected of humanist teachers, Gasparino Barzizza, at Padua.[26] His time with Barzizza seems to have marked him for life, even more deeply than his later period as a law student. Alberti learned the technical lessons that Barzizza had to offer, and very well indeed. But he also developed a close relationship with his teacher, one that became the model for many future friendships with scholars on whose learned advice and moral support Alberti relied. Frantic with worry when his father Lorenzo refused to leave Venice during an outbreak of plague, Alberti went to his teacher "weeping, at around the second hour of the night," and succeeded in persuading him to write to Lorenzo and ask him to seek safety.[27]

Studying with Barzizza meant being inducted into a coterie culture. Barzizza belonged to a tight if informal network of well-established scholars and teachers who informed one another as rapidly as possible of the discovery of new classical texts and put them to use as soon as they could in their own work. Alberti's friend Beccadelli, for example, also seems to have studied with Barzizza.[28] He harvested acclaim for deftly applying the erotic and scatological vocabulary of Roman poets like Martial and Catullus in his own

Hermaphrodite—a collection of wittily scabrous verse in Latin, roughly modeled on the priapic poems ascribed to Virgil but even lewder. Beccadelli chose the title for his book because, he said, the hermaphrodite had both a penis and a vagina.[29] The city poets of early imperial Rome had celebrated their rough, erotic life, their long nights of drinking, gluttony, and sex with men and women. Their vocabulary—rich in terms for the genitals and their uses—was ready-made for the sophisticated modern, like Beccadelli, who wanted to celebrate his own rough nights in Florentine streets and bawdy houses. "Go," he instructed his own poems in the envoi to the *Hermaphrodite*,

> To Florence. Once inside her mighty walls,
>   There is a fine and pleasant place,
> Easy to find, right at the crossing of her malls,
>   I'll tell you just which steps to trace.
> Seek Santa Reparata, or St. John,
>   the Baptist with the lamb. Then go
> Hard right, and walk as briskly as you can;
>   Then say you seek the good old Mercato.
> There's the jolly brothel, they will love my song.
>   Don't worry, you will know it by its pong.

Beccadelli went on to describe the welcome that the book would receive, whore by whore ("blond Elena and sweet Matilda, skilled at the wiggling of their bottoms," "Giannetta, with her puppy at her heels," "Clodia, with her bare, painted nipples.")[30] No wonder that *Hermaphrodite* horrified rigorist clerics who distrusted the study of the classics—or that it ravished the humanists, who made copies of the book for their friends. The rediscovered Latin of the classics became the special language of a social and intellectual avant-garde—experimental, cheerfully misogynistic, and openly sexual.

Thanks to Barzizza's lessons, Alberti spoke this language well. Beccadelli even addressed one of the poems in the *Hermaphrodite* to Alberti, praising Leon Battista's high birth, pure character, and learning before asking him for advice on how to deal with his mistress:

> If my accounts were on ten trading floors,
>   Ursa could quickly piss them all away.
> If I had books by dozens and by scores,

> *Ursa would pawn them in a single day.*
> *However high my seminal output rose,*
> > *Ursa could drain it like a human bucket.*
> *If I became a giant, man-sized nose,*
> > *Her smell alone would be enough to stuff it.*[31]

Beccadelli's poem made a vivid, if not a tasteful, passport for Alberti, a literary identification card that proved his citizenship in the nascent republic of letters. Only young men of talent received such signal recognition from their peers.

Alberti rapidly found a node of his own in the network of the humanists. Not all the textual discoveries that made news in Barzizza's world were sexy in the literal sense. One that generated special excitement was the uncovering, in 1421 in the cathedral archive at Lodi, of a number of texts on rhetoric by Cicero, including the complete text of his dialogues *On the Orator* and *Brutus*. In these works, Cicero offered detailed, fascinating commentary about the history of the humanists' favorite art and complex, thoughtful reflections on its use and abuse. Alberti soon obtained his own copy of the *Brutus* (which still survives). Schooled in the proper way to read and personalize such texts, he made the manuscript not only a favored source but even a confidant. He recorded the births of children in Alberti households and other family achievements in the highly selective diary that he kept on a blank leaf at the end of the book.[32] Alberti also referred to Cicero's work in his own treatise on the study of literature, in a way that would be unmistakable for humanist insiders. His father Lorenzo, Leon Battista remarked, had always told his sons never to be idle—and he himself, as a result, could never bear to spend a day without reading and writing something.[33] This apparently autobiographical description of Alberti's own working habits had at its core a quotation of what Cicero had said about Hortensius, who had never let a day pass without speaking in the forum or working hard on a speech outside it.[34] Reading and writing were inextricably intertwined.

Alberti's interactive way of using classical texts was the natural product of his school's regime. Barzizza, who had a keenly developed sense of practicality, did more than read through classical texts with his students. He also provided them with precise instructions for employing sentiments and anecdotes from the ancients in their own original compositions—as Beccadelli had done with the Roman poets of the street. In a short, punchy treatise *On Imitation*, Barzizza explained in a strikingly frank way how the young Latinist should go about his basic task: "Imitation can be understood and carried out in four ways—by addition, subtraction, transferral, and transformation"—but not, of course, by direct copying. Sometimes relatively simple changes could make a classical sentiment new without debasing it: "If Cicero says 'Brutus said that neatly,' I will add, 'Our friend Brutus said that neatly and elegantly.'" More ambitious tactics included the inversion of the classical source: "If Cicero, whom we wish to imitate, praised someone to the skies, we could blast him to the depths."[35]

Barzizza regularly put these rules into practice. When he wrote, at Leon Battista's request, to ask his student's father Lorenzo not to risk contracting the plague by remaining in Venice; he cast this urgent, personal plea in highly artificial Latin prose. Barzizza heaped up elaborate metaphors drawn from the still richer collection of literary devices that he could have unleashed had he thought it necessary: "Free yourself from so great a danger, and us from so great a fear. You cannot undergo shipwreck alone. Everything that belongs to you is in the same boat: your children, your wife, the members of your household, your friends. Since you are their patron, it is shameful if you, in full sight and knowledge of the situation, should prefer to hold your very dangerous course amid the waves and hail when you could immediately seek a safe port."[36] Eloquent composition in the modern world, Barzizza's students rapidly came to see, required the skilled reuse of classical components—however simple and practical the message they had to send.

To process the information and absorb the style models that the classical texts provided, students learned to make systematic notebooks, organized by *loci* ("places" or "headings") which would give rapid access to these materials whenever they might prove relevant.[37] The great teacher Guarino of Verona, for example, instructed his Ferrarese pupil Leonello d'Este (later one of Alberti's closest friends and patrons), "whenever you read . . . have ready a notebook, in which you can write down whatever you choose and list the materials you have assembled. Then whenever you decide to review the passages that struck you, you will not have to leaf through a large number of pages. For the notebook will be at hand, like a diligent and attentive servant, to provide what you need."

Another letter of Guarino's, to a different pupil, made clear how such notebooks were to be used in practice:

Remember when you praise the countryside or denounce the city to take the reasons for the praise or blame from four "places." That is, show that utility, pleasure, virtue, and excellence belong to the country. Contrariwise, damage, wretchedness, defects, and flaws belong to the city. I recall that I once set these rules out in a distich. You should note this down and memorize it so that you will always have it to hand:

> Four things to praise all topics amply go:
> Virtue and use, pleasure and goodness show.[38]

Like a modern reporter adapting the latest reports from an on-line news service, the young humanist should not create something totally new but piece together, from existing ingredients of high quality, a mosaic with a novel form of its own.[39] Late in life, Alberti was to codify these practices, as we have seen, in a short rhetorical handbook of his own.

He also applied them at every turn. His frank and emotional autobiography adapted classical models and combined classical sources in original ways. His first original composition, his play about Philodoxus, was really a careful pastiche of phrases drawn from the ancient comedies of Plautus and Terence—a mosaic so meticulously assembled that when his friend Beccadelli put an "uncorrected" copy of it into circulation (against the author's will), many readers took it for a genuinely classical text.[40] "It gave off," Alberti later recalled, "a powerful scent of the ancient comic genre and a sort of deep antiquity."[41] Resigning himself to his own success at imitation, Alberti attached to his play a short prose foreword. Here he attributed the work to one Lepidus, though he left enough broad hints that he would later be able to claim the text as his. Then he let the work enter the public domain with his approval, where "everyone read it with the greatest admiration, many committed it to memory, and more than a few spent a good deal of time copying it out." Even those readers who suspected that Alberti had written the comedy evidently played along with the joke in a creative way, inserting new obscene passages. Ultimately, "no one who did not know the play was considered to have a proper appreciation of the comic." It would be hard to imagine a more successful exercise in imitation. No wonder that Alberti, in his middle years, used the art of the mosaic as a metaphor for his own art of writing.[42]

The young Alberti enjoyed his skill at performing these literary equivalents of musical scales and exercises. He self-consciously referred, especially in his early works, to the formal techniques of imitation and argumentation that he had learned at Barzizza's side and that he still used. Even so, he did not simply empty all his notebooks onto the pages of *The Advantages and Disadvantages of Letters*, he insisted, but rather selected only a few of the formally relevant topics to treat: "In discussing these matters, I have made every effort to be brief, passing over many *loci* [topics] without stopping even briefly there, leaving many arguments without examples to bear them out, and many efforts at persuasion without rhetorical developments."

Alberti returned again and again to the topic of literary tools. At one point in *The Advantages and Disadvantages of Letters,* he took up a favorite humanist question: whether the mere fact that notaries, lawyers, and doctors enriched themselves from the suffering and death of others sufficed to condemn them. An artful use of preterition—the literary device by which one addresses a topic in the very act of claiming not to—enabled him to win credit for knowing all the subheadings he could have marshaled and declined to use, as well as those he had used:

> I shall pass over this *locus* briefly, to avoid giving the impression that I am making a pedantic collection of materials that can be used to bring the study of letters into discredit. Therefore, I will say nothing of their deceitfulness, their perfidy, their bearing of false witness, their falsifications of contracts and wills—nothing of their administration of poisons, their instilling of fevers, their use of prescriptions and drugs to cause diseases; and I will silently omit the many vile crimes of greedy notaries and doctors.

A similarly adroit turn of phrase enabled Alberti to give vent to feelings he evidently shared with Beccadelli: "But it is better not to mention the nature and folly of women than to ventilate, so to speak, so large a subject, and one so well-known."[43] Alberti, in other words, seems to have enjoyed giving readers a peep into his own literary workshop, showing off his ability to apply his reading in his writing. His technique seems a little mechanical now—but the depth of his commitment to humanistic culture and to this particular creative adaptation of the past is beyond doubt. For years to come, as we will see, he continued to apply these same methods with self-conscious artistry and pride.

Alberti's decision to concentrate on the classics gave his life an intellectual and creative direction. But it did not provide him, all at once, with the practical results that he clearly hoped for. He composed his first literary works, he claimed, as part of the discipline that he adopted to console himself for the problems he suffered as an orphan and the neglect of his kinsmen: they were a form of scholarly and literary self-help.[44] But most of those who produced substantial, inventive pieces of literary Latin, he knew perfectly well, did so for at least two other reasons as well. They wanted to test or prove their own powers, and they wanted to make connections with their fellow scholars and patrons of learning, to whom they dedicated their efforts.

Alberti pursued both ends himself. But for all his skill and learning, as he confessed to his brother, he had encountered a problem that was as simple as it was drastic: his literary offerings, however original, did not have their intended effect of providing him with a livelihood. In grim detail, he made clear exactly how little a humanist could hope to earn through the sorts of literary services they usually performed. Carried away by the flow of his language, he even argued that law and medicine yielded few profits—a view he denied elsewhere in the same work:

> Tell me, please, o student: do you hope to become rich from the tiny fees you will collect when you teach a boy, when one of your little works appears, when you plead a case, when you cure a fever, or when you speak at some length on a question of law? Hardly. The gains realized in this way are so modest that they hardly suffice to pay your day-to-day expenses, and they come so infrequently that they can hardly mount up to any sort of fortune, at least for a very long time.

Scholar, as Alberti learned from bitter experience, does not rhyme with *dollar*; "to put it in a nutshell: the learned don't become rich, or if they do become rich from literary pursuits, the sources of their wealth are shameful."[45] By the late 1420s, in other words, Alberti had become a highly skilled classicist in the most up-to-date style. But how, or if, his learning would fit him for life remained unclear. *On the Advantages and Disadvantages of Letters*, though idealistic, vibrated with Alberti's fundamental uncertainty about the direction of his life. Every passage in which he proclaimed his unselfish love for the classics, the superiority of the humanist who read his books for love over the lawyers and doctors who read theirs for gain, was flanked by another in which he complained bitterly of the pitiful rewards that true scholars reaped. The unworldly scholar, bleary-eyed and hesitant in the company of men of practical experience, was a self-portrait in the mode of Daumier, drawn with a sharply bent nib—but it seems to have affected Alberti like his image in the mirror on his worst mornings.

At times, moreover, Alberti found that he could not take pleasure even in his prized and hard-won skills as a Latin stylist. His training in formal imitation rested on the assumption that the ancients were excellent in every way—so excellent that a modern writer could express himself only by assembling centos of quotations from them. But this assumption inspired an understandable melancholy in the young writer. At the outset of *On the Advantages and Disadvantages of Letters,* he told his brother how "often I thought about what sort of composition I could devise which would enable me to test the powers of my own intellect and to gratify the members of my family." Finding a way to do this had been difficult, he admitted, since "no subject ever occurred to me which the ancients had not already treated in a splendid way . . . the ancients dealt with every topic, serious and comic alike, so well that they have left us nothing to do but read and admire their skillful work." Previous scholars in modern times, he noted, had managed to win praise for their treatments of subjects that the ancients had not addressed. In resignation, he claimed for himself and other young writers the right, if not to address such serious topics as history, then at least to produce "exercises" that might please their elders and betters. A young man who prized action above all thus found himself confronted with the possibility of stasis—or, perhaps, forced to seek a different field of action, where the neglect of his relatives and the excellence of his models would not strip him of all freedom to move forward.

Two peculiar institutions—the papal curia and the Florentine chancery—offered Alberti the clearest opportunities for advancement. In the early fifteenth century, the papacy found itself confronted on every side with criticism and contumely. For much of the previous century, after a brutal confrontation between the French king, Philip the Fair, and Pope Boniface VIII ended in the latter's humiliation, the popes had resided not in their historic seat in Rome but in Avignon, in territory that is now French (but then belonged to the Angevin princes of Naples). Though the popes used the period of the so-called Babylonian Captivity in Avignon, 1308–77, to reorganize the institutions of the curia, they also received bitter criticism from those who felt that the church had become rich, corrupt, and dependent on the French monarchy. Even after the papacy returned to Rome in the 1370s, its troubles persisted. The popes had to wage bitter warfare to regain the sizeable portions of their secular holdings, the Papal States, that other Italian powers had nibbled away during the Babylonian Captivity. Worse still, more than one rival claimant to the papacy found support from substantial parts of the church, since many of the cardinals, being French, resisted the papacy's return to Rome, and on 20 September 1378 they elected a French pope of their own, Clement VII, in opposition to the Neapolitan Urban VI who held office in Rome. The Great Schism that began in this way lasted until 1417. For a brief period, after 1409, three popes simultaneously claimed Peter's throne. Most influential theologians held that church supremacy should rest not with any individual, even the pope, but with the church as a whole, as represented by a universal council. Still, as many conciliarists also recognized, only the pope could call an orthodox council, a principle that posed especially serious problems in a time of schism. The councils of the early fifteenth century—that of Pisa (1409), called by dissident cardinals, and that of Constance (1414–18), called by the Holy Roman Emperor Sigismund—attracted great theologians, radical clerics with strong views about the need to control and discipline the papacy, and representatives of secular states who hoped to preserve the freedom of their national churches.

The Council of Constance achieved a great deal. It deposed three supposed popes and chose a member of a great Roman noble family, the Colonna, to succeed them as Martin V. The large-scale heresies of the followers of John Wyclif in England and Jan Hus in Bohemia had challenged the doctrinal authority and liturgical practices of the church in vital areas, from the uses of the Bible to the form of communion for the laity. The council attacked these problems by burning Hus himself and asserting orthodox doctrines. And it enacted a system by which regular future councils would administer the church.

But the papacy was confronted by other forms of opposition as well, many of them hard to accommodate and impossible to stamp out. Major controversies regularly erupted over such questions as the nature of true Christian poverty—controversies that split the great religious orders into warring groups. Formal and informal groups of laymen and women claimed to offer a purer, more internal form of religious life than the older, established orders. The Orthodox Church, headed by the patriarch of Byzantium, refused to recognize Roman supremacy and differed from the Catholics on vital questions of Christology and much else. Though the Borgo, the papal district of Rome, began to recover its fourteenth-century prosperity, and though papal power began to reassert itself from the time of Martin V onward, councils continued to meet, at Basel in 1431 and Ferrara/Florence in 1438–39. The head that wore the tiara barely had time to rest.[46]

The more severe and visible the problems that faced the popes and prelates, the richer the opportunities that offered themselves to young humanists. Every debate within the church required the pope and other authoritative figures to take formal positions, which had to be explained in crisp, effective Latin. Often the debates stimulated the production of innovative literary works, like the dialogue that the humanist Poggio Bracciolini dedicated to the controversial theme of avarice. The church councils—magnificently staged meetings of prelates from all over Europe—not only challenged papal authority but provided an intoxicating atmosphere of ecclesiastical wealth and power. Here scholars could meet colleagues from radically different worlds, exchanging everything from manuscripts of long-forgotten texts to ideas about Christian devotion. Skilled writers and articulate speakers of Latin could make friends, exchange texts, and pick up valuable information. At the same time, they could find preferment in the papal curia itself or in the households of the cardinals, who surrounded the pope like so many satellites and whose courts sometimes rivaled his in wealth if not in size.

The administrative branch of the curia, known as the chancery, employed "writers" (*scriptores*) who drew up papal bulls and the less formal documents known as briefs, and "abbreviators" (*abbreviatores*) who produced official summaries of papal bulls. Both the chancery and the apostolic chamber, which oversaw papal finances, employed "secretaries"—one of whom might be the pope's "secret" or "domestic secretary," his personal assistant. Cardinals had secretaries, too, and could ease the way to papal employment for those who enjoyed their favor. Not all these jobs went to humanists, of course; kinship ties—older, stronger, and more pervasive than intellectual networks—ensured that members of great families obtained more posts than their scholarship warranted.[47] Still, the possibilities were exciting. Alberti's friend Lapo da Castiglionchio, Jr., who detested the luxuriousness and sexual license of the curia, celebrated the many opportunities it offered for working and learning: "Every day some news is conveyed by letters, messengers, and rumors, and no day or even hour in the whole year goes by in which something new is not put forward. Nothing that is done in the whole world is not known directly in the curia. . . . Wherever you are in the curia, then, you hear some bit of news."[48]

As exciting as the papal curia was the Florentine intellectual world that centered on the city's chancery, which produced official correspondence, propaganda, and even histories of the city. In the fourteenth century, Florence had been crippled economically by royal bankruptcies and plague, and it had been severely challenged by Milan and Naples in the years around and after 1400. But thereafter it began to prosper again and became the center of a territorial empire, ruling previously independent states like Pisa and Lucca. The Florentines staged their city as a citadel of splendid production, expensive consumption, and political power, all symbolically basking in divine favor.[49] They celebrated the city's power on 24 June, the Feast of Saint John, a great ritual occasion when every subject state had to provide floats and tribute for a magnificent celebration. The Florentine merchants and their expensively dressed wives and daughters solemnly watched the procession, sitting, with their most expensive wares, before their closed stores. But Florence needed humanists, too, to write its propaganda and celebrate its traditions. And the chancery, from Salutati's time on (he was chancellor from 1375 to 1406), became a center not only of official document writing but also of scholarly and literary discussion. Under the eye of the erudite, benevolent chancellor, manuscripts of every kind were studied and copied. Scholars and scribes collaborated in developing a new, classical-looking script, which they used for ancient texts, and the history of the city itself was interpreted and reinterpreted.[50]

Connections between the curia and chancery were close—and not only because Florence, which boasted an ancient Guelf, or pro-papal, tradition, proclaimed its ancient loyalty to the Holy See and exercised much practical influence on the papacy (though they had waged war with each other in the 1370s). Young scholars moved easily between the two official communities.[51] Both Bruni and Poggio spent large parts of their professional lives in Rome, but they kept property in Florence and eventually returned there, serving as chancellors of the republic in their turn. While Poggio wearily traveled the northern roads of Europe in ecclesiastical service, moreover, he also followed the scholarly directions of the great Florentine book collector Niccolò Niccoli. Poggio ransacked monastic libraries where his friend had heard that a rare text or a better manuscript of a well-known one might be lurking. The intellectual avant-garde of Italy had branches in many locales, including the courts of Naples and Milan, Ferrara and Urbino. Alberti's friend Beccadelli overcame the scandal of *Hermaphrodite*—which was burned by public executioners in some cities though it was also read with relish by scholars throughout Italy—to make a brilliant career as a valued royal secretary and diplomat in the Aragonese court at Naples. There he helped to create a vibrant, sometimes violent world of literary cliques.[52] But in the 1420s, the intellectual pipeline that connected Florence with Rome offered possibilities of swift career progress that were not easily to be found elsewhere.

Not everyone traveled these roads as easily as Bruni and Poggio did. Skilled humanists wound up in places far less attractive than Rome and Florence. Stefano Fieschi of Soncino, who studied with Barzizza ten years after Alberti, wrote brilliantly successful textbooks on the vital field of Latin usage. He served as chancellor and headmaster of the humanist school in Ragusa—not exactly a hardship post, and not so marginal to the humanist networks as it may seem in retrospect, but not a spectacularly prestigious position either.[53] The Benedictine Girolamo Aliotti, a friend and admirer of Alberti's, cultivated his connections with the influential scholar Poggio and others. But he found himself sitting, again and again, before closed doors at the curia, railing at the indifference he encountered everywhere.[54] Lapo complained bitterly of the "ill will of certain criminals and wicked men, who not only try to prevent me from attaining glory, but also want to humiliate and destroy me utterly."[55] He died of the plague before he managed to obtain a post—or even, as he put it less demandingly in another letter, "to be among famous and learned men, and to enjoy a certain esteem and rank there."[56] Organizations that depended, as most did, on family ties and the personal patronage of great men proved accessible to those who approached them already equipped with the keys to the kingdom—birth and money—or armed with a sharply realistic sense of how to seek them. They certainly did not offer "careers open to talent." The humanist seeking work there knew, as well as the great men he wooed, that "fortune governs and rules all human affairs."[57]

Worse, the institutions that offered humanists their richest opportunities also offered the greatest dangers. Every time a pope died, the Roman people had the right to sack and pillage his apartments, even as his followers mourned him in accordance with an elaborate ancient ritual. But during the interregna known as "vacant sees," chaos reigned in other realms as well. The humanists who held places in the previous pope's retinue had to scramble to win his successor's favor or give up their jobs: "Some," wrote one humanist dryly, "mourn the dead pope, as is the way of the human intellect, because they are cast down by the loss of so great a father and lord; others, because they have lost any hope of private advantage."[58]

The atmosphere in which humanists had to earn support, moreover, did not always prove collegial and supportive. For much of the 1420s and 1430s, the curia and the circles connected with it in Florence formed a white-hot crucible where intellectual and cultural fashions took shape under high intellectual and social pressure.[59] Years later, when Poggio Bracciolini published his famous Latin collection of jokes, he looked back with a Proustian nostalgia to the years when he, Antonio Loschi, and other curial intellectuals had created what they called the Lie Shop (*bugiale*). There they discussed all the gossip, sexual and literary, sparing no one:

> In the day of Martin V, we used to choose a certain place in the more private part of the court. There the news was reported, and we used to converse about all sorts of things, both for relaxation, which was usually our purpose, and sometimes in a serious way. There we spared no one when we set out to debunk all the things of which we did not approve, and our criticism very often started with the pope himself. Therefore many would come, fearing that we would start with them. The chief roles were played by Razello of Bologna, that brilliant conversationalist, some of whose anecdotes I have included here; Antonio Loschi, a very witty man, who appears here often as well; and Cencio the Roman, a man whose vocation lay in joking. I have also added a good many stories of my own, which I thought not without flavor. Today they are all dead, the Lie Shop has ceased to be. It is the fault both of the times and of men that this whole practice of witty conversation has disappeared.[60]

These papal officials collected manuscripts and antiquities, argued over the moral and political issues of the day, and when the discussion became especially intense, rolled on the floor, clutching each other's testicles and poking at each other's eyes.[61] A slew of obscene poems, sharp satires, and jokes about ignorant and lustful friars—the Vatican is to this day one of the world's richest sources of anticlerical humor—preserves their portraits—or at least lively caricatures of them—for posterity. Winning prominence in this highly competitive world came easily for no one—especially for a young man who had few high connections.

Distinction was earned by writing: writing texts in convincing classical Latin. But the producer of artistic Latin prose or verse confronted special difficulties of a kind known nowadays only, in a lesser form, to those who write for publication in a highly formal second language, like French or German. From Petrarch onward, humanists wanted to write a Latin comparable to that of the ancient authors they esteemed most. But to do so, they had not only to learn but actually to reconstruct a lost literary language, no native speakers of which survived.[62]

Some of the necessary tools were easy to find. Ancient lexica and glossaries offered essential help, by no means all of it elementary. The grammarians of late antiquity, like Servius and Priscian, had already addressed students who used in daily life a Latin very different from that of Cicero and Virgil. Their textbooks and commentaries offered help in recovering classical patterns of usage and syntax.[63] Unfortunately, these useful works also contained many errors: the more closely the humanists studied the classical texts, the less they felt they could trust postclassical textbooks—to say nothing of the medieval ones, which they simultaneously disdained and plagiarized. Every humanist knew that the Latin spoken and written in most schools and universities—a highly sophisticated but entirely modern academic jargon—had permanently marked his choice of words and framing of sentences. When Alberti made one of his characters declare, in his dialogue On the Family, that a father should see to it that his children learned Latin "from Priscian and Servius, and became most familiar not with *cartule* and *gregismi* but with Cicero, Livy, and Sallust," he referred to medieval texts that were still widely used—and propagating errors—in his own time. Alberti and his colleagues knew how hard it was to rid themselves of the diphthongless spelling, bad grammar, and wrong usage that most of them had learned from such works as boys.[64]

Every humanist soon learned that making a public mistake in Latin could drop him into deep hot water. Poggio Bracciolini encountered this hard literary fact in the course of a bitter controversy with another humanist, Lorenzo Valla. Valla wrote a sharp dialogue in which the cook and stableboy of Guarino of Verona, as well as the great teacher they served, read aloud and dissected passages from Poggio's Latin. Though they were Germans and therefore barbarians, the servants exposed dozens of the Italian humanist's errors—for example, his use of the impersonal verb *taedet* ("it is wearisome") with a nominative subject and accusative object, instead of the proper genitive and accusative. Playing with the term *accusative*, the cook says, "Let us then both accuse him." No, replies Dromo the stableboy: "Instead, let us beat him," invoking the standard penalty paid by schoolboys who made grammatical mistakes.[65]

Mistakes about content—placing mythological figures in the wrong places or historical figures in the wrong times, or interpreting ancient histories in problematic ways—could sometimes prove just as devastating. A dialogue by the Milanese scholar Angelo Decembrio records the terrible fate meted out to Ugolino Pisani. Pisani wrote a Latin dialogue, the characters in which were pots and pans, and tried to present a copy to the cultivated prince Leonello d'Este. According to Decembrio, Pisani's reward was a public humiliation at the hands of a brash young Ferrarese Latin poet, Tito Vespasiano Strozzi, who took pleasure in skewering every one of Pisani's many errors in taste and violations of decorum.[66] Critical discussions like these—which also went on at the Neapolitan court of Alfonso of Aragon, where the learned king Alfonso called the scholars at his court together for official "hours of the book" and listened with pleasure as they tore and rent one another's Latin prose—could be purely destructive in their aims and effects: participants read to kill.[67]

From Petrarch onward, accordingly, the humanist who wished to 'scape whipping had to make his writing, as well as his reading, into a systematic, long-term scholarly enterprise. Petrarch himself, for example, rewrote his works as he became aware of new rules and distinctions. As he revised, poetic substantives replaced prosaic ones, subjunctives replaced indicatives, hypotaxis replaced parataxis.[68] He had read in the Roman rhetorical handbook of Quintilian that the orator, since he must "emend" his draft writings, should leave enough space for additions and corrections in the wax tablets in which he wrote them. Leaving too little space, Quintilian warned, could lead to laziness in rewriting. "I know from experience how profoundly true this is," wrote Petrarch—in the margin of his own copy of Quintilian.[69] He proudly presented a heavily revised copy of his work *On His Own Ignorance and That of Many Others* to his friend Donato degli Albanzani and recorded the fact that he had done so in his dedicatory letter. Like the emperor Nero, he boasted, he had left many things "crossed out, inserted, and written above the lines," so to prove his authorship not only of the text but of the manuscript—and to highlight the work he had put in on revision.[70]

Before 1400, some humanists began to see "emendation" not only as a normal stage in the composition of their own works, but also as a specialized service they could offer to others. Salutati—who was at least as dedicated to training others in the proper spelling and punctuation of Latin as to the cause of the Florentine republic—revised Latin works on Florentine history by Filippo Villani, including the first version of his life of Salutati himself.[71]

A generation later, the learned antiquarian Flavio Biondo sent one of his works to three erudite friends in three different cities and refused to make it publicly accessible until all of them had read and evaluated it.[72] His precautions failed; after his death, the humanist pope Pius II, himself a far more skillful Latinist, regretted with silky lack of compassion that the learned Biondo "did not examine what he wrote carefully enough" and expressed the hope that a more skillful writer might someday "emend and embellish" Biondo's works.[73]

Emendation mattered, dramatically. It became a coded move in the games of formal male friendship that each humanist had to play. When Biondo sent Lapo da Castiglionchio his history of Italy to "read and reread critically," Lapo thought, he was doing a remarkable honor to a scholar whom he had not met: "for we normally do not share such our most cherished and personal efforts except with our intimates, with whom we enjoy a long established friendship and on whom we know we can rely." As Lapo read Biondo's work, accordingly, he felt himself to be in possession "of a pledge and testimony of your sentiments toward me, so that I may hope that the friendship between us, which has begun in this way, will last forever, or at least for a long time."[74] Both men were Alberti's friends: he would have recognized both Biondo's gesture and Lapo's interpretation of it.

In the first decades of the fifteenth century, moreover, the details and uses of learned editing became both a topic of debate and a theme of literary works in its own right. The influential Salutati and the young men in his circle, like Bruni and Poggio, devoted themselves to working out whether a writer should refer to himself as *I* or *we*. They worried endlessly about the spelling of commonly used Latin words. Nowadays, it might seem that arguing over whether one should write *nihil* or *nichil* is much ado about nothing. But these apparently trivial arguments reflected a larger debate about a whole style of life and art. Its protagonists formed something like the first modern aesthetic movement, the results of which included the transformation of so basic an art as writing itself.[75] Creative correction of texts—systematic improvement of modern writings in Latin—seemed so exciting to the humanists that they incorporated glamorous or scandalous scenes of textual editing into literary works. Valla, as we have seen, showed servants "emending" Poggio. He also represented Beccadelli, his bitter personal and scholarly enemy, offering to "emend" an anecdote told by Plato.[76]

Classical Latin writers had occasionally described the emendation of literary works. Tacitus, for example, depicted a former orator turned poet reading his work aloud to a select audience in the hope of receiving helpful criticism.[77] This work, discovered in a monastery at Hersfeld, in Germany, in the 1420s, excited Florentine readers like Angelo Poliziano, and it certainly showed that helpful ancient precedents existed for the humanists' text processing.[78] But the humanists of the 1420s and 1430s did not know Tacitus' *Dialogue on Oratory*. Scenes of detailed, word-by-word editing, with all the sadistic and masochistic pleasures it could inspire, became a more prominent part of Renaissance literature than they had ever been in the classical texts that the humanists most admired. Emendation, evidently, glowed with the allure of novelty and fashion with which practices like net surfing and Web site design are charged nowadays.

One of the central figures of Florentine cultural life, Niccolò Niccoli, first became famous when he insisted that editing was useless, since no modern writer could actually produce a decent piece of Latin. Niccoli could speak with some authority, for he had rich resources, both spiritual and material, to draw on. He expended a fortune working with Poggio and other book hunters to assemble a collection of some eight hundred classical manuscripts, which eventually became the first public library of the Renaissance, that of San Marco.[79] He also collected coins and statues, making his house into one of the first museums of antiquities, where he assessed—and dealt in—gems and cameos.[80] Vespasiano da Bisticci, the well-informed *cartolaio* or book dealer who wrote Niccoli's biography, found it "a civilized pleasure" to watch the old man eat like an ancient Roman from his splendid crystal vessels.[81]

As a recognized connoisseur of the classical, Niccoli repeatedly claimed that he could see through the pretenses to scholarship and eloquence of any modern. Like a Renaissance equivalent to F. R. Leavis, he hoped to save the literary tradition by destroying all efforts to add to it. More than one diatribe against Niccoli—and he attracted many—offers a vivid portrait of this sovereign critic at work, demolishing the reputation of yet another reputed masterpiece.[82] Leonardo Bruni brought him onstage in book one of a famous pair of dialogues. Instead of praising the Florentine classics—Dante, Petrarch, and Boccaccio—Bruni's Niccoli denounced them for their incorrigible violations of grammatical propriety and rhetorical decorum. Dante, for example, not only misinterpreted Virgil's text, he also made gross historical and literary errors: "He describes Marcus Cato, who perished in the civil wars, as a very old man with a long white beard—an obvious display of ignorance, since he died at Utica in the forty-eighth year of his life and in his prime."

Worse still, Dante condemned the heroic Brutus to the underworld for killing Caesar in defense of Roman liberty—even though he placed the earlier Brutus who put an end to the Roman monarchy in the Elysian Fields. Niccoli's criticism annihilated the "three crowns of Florence" for that worst of all literary sins in the age of humanism, lacking "Latinity." These offenses against Niccoli's sense of historical and literary decorum condemned their writings out of hand.[83]

In book two of Bruni's work, however, Niccoli—the literary character, not the historical individual—retracted his attacks, offering half-hearted support for the thesis that the moderns could write something of value.[84] And in fact, in the 1420s and 1430s, life imitated art. F. R. Leavis turned into Maxwell Perkins. Niccoli began to collaborate with Poggio and other writers, trying to make their works acceptable even by his own sere rhetorical and philological standards. Vespasiano, a connoisseur of writers and scribes, recalled that Niccoli had become something like a professional editor—one whom many writers sought out, though he chose to work with few of them:

> It chanced one day that a scholar brought some of his writings to show to him, but neither the subject nor the style of them was to Niccolò's liking. After he had read separate portions of the work, the writer begged for his opinion, but Niccolò demurred, being unwilling to vex him, and answered, "I have already to deal with several hundred volumes of authors of repute before I shall be able to consider yours" (for every writer of that time would ask him to read his work and give an opinion), and handed the manuscript back to the writer, who was much astonished, and failed to understand what his verdict was.[85]

Poggio portrayed Niccoli in a less conciliatory mode:

> Many bother me, seeking to have me praise their stupidity. They bring something that they have produced—something tasteless, chaotic, inelegant, worthy only to be taken out to the latrine—and they want my opinion. I make a habit of speaking freely—for I cannot praise a poet, if he is bad—and I tell the truth. I warn them not to publish, I forbid it, I reveal the work's faults, I insist that their writings are not eloquent, weighty, stylish, prudent, written in good

Latin, or correct. But some, shameless in their self-inflation, go away angry, complaining under their breath that I am moved by envy.[86]

Evidently even Niccoli's sincere admirers did not find him a diplomatic editor.

Poggio knew Niccoli's methods at first hand. When he finished his dialogues on the urgent contemporary problem of avarice, he sent them to Niccoli for criticism.[87] For some time Poggio heard nothing back, which naturally made his nerves quiver. When Niccoli's judgment arrived, anxiety turned into depression. Poggio's friend made a sweeping call for changes in everything from the names he had assigned to his characters to the Latin style he had adopted. Like a modern author replying to a stern letter from an editor, Poggio plaintively answered that other erudite humanists had read his work "with approval." But eventually he admitted that Niccoli was right: "Everything shall be polished up to suit you."[88] Evidently it did not take the invention of printing for the calling of the editor to come into being—or for those who labored in that trade to begin complaining that "an editor's life is not all beer and skittles."

The humanist writer knew, accordingly, that sharp criticism awaited him as soon as he dared to publish some of his work. At least in Florence, to be sure, such discussion purportedly had a powerful constructive end in view. But even there, correction—like the witty conversation celebrated by Poggio—posed inherent social risks. The scholar who entrusted his work to another humanist's criticism, as Alberti's friend Lapo remarked, "offered a remarkable, open show of love" by doing so. Sharing one's "intimate and domestic studies" made one vulnerable—and doing so was a declaration of confidence in the other. Yet even expert critics—like another friend of Alberti's, Leonardo Dati—found themselves having to apologize to those who had asked for their help for the surgical sharpness of the commentaries they provided.[89] Ages of criticism—from Quattrocento Florence to Fifties America—are not hospitable to faint-hearted writers.

Alberti knew as well as anyone that he was treading dangerous ground in becoming a humanist writer. He began, accordingly, in the normal, cautious way: by writing relatively short, experimental pieces, in both prose and verse, that demonstrated his strengths as both reader and writer. He soon found a particularly fertile field to explore in the works of the Greek writer

Lucian,[90] whose satirical texts were immensely popular in the fifteenth century. Lucian's shortest dialogues made ideal reading for students beginning the study of the Greek language. They offered both examples of finely written classical Greek and treasuries of useful historical and mythological information. His more elaborate satires, which included mordant, outspoken portraits of human folly and sustained descriptions of gods and goddesses, beliefs and practices, were rich quarries, materials from which could be stored in notebooks and adapted to new purposes.

Over and over again, when a new work of Lucian reached Alberti in one of the fresh Latin translations that Guarino, Lapo, and others regularly carried out, he set himself to produce an emulative response to it. When he read Lucian's oration in praise of the fly, which Guarino had just translated, he proclaimed himself cured of a fever by his amusement, then wrote his own work on the same topic—a dazzlingly clever mock-heroic speech in which the fly's piety and heroism come in for effusive praise.[91]

Alberti's early experiments in this Lucianic line generally took the form of short dialogues and stories. These works, to which he eventually gave the collective title *Intercenales (Dinner Pieces)*, were clearly designed to entertain. He had collected them in "short books so that they may be more easily read over dinners and drinks," he explained. Here as in his earlier Latin writings, Alberti made clear that he valued the formal tricks of the humanist's trade. In one early *Dinner Piece*, "The Deceased," in which he described the experiences of a discontented intellectual who returned as a ghost to watch his own funeral, Alberti made his protagonist criticize the funeral oration itself. By doing so, he demonstrated his mastery of such exercises:

> He said not a word about my learning, knowledge, talent, liberal studies, fortitude, constancy, moderation, restraint, chastity, wisdom, judgment, historical erudition, and prudence. He passed over in silence every aspect of my integrity and dignity.

Adding insult to injury, the bishop in question delivered the oration as badly as he composed it, shouting "in a loud voice, like someone calling the night watch," and waving his arms.[92] Here and elsewhere Alberti's early works retain something of the character of set pieces: skillful, but the work of one who had only recently left his formal training behind him.

In time, the form of the short dialogue proved highly flexible in Alberti's hands. He used it to treat a wide variety of issues, some of them highly controversial in his immediate social and cultural environment. The humanists of the fifteenth century were gradually reviving the ancient notion of a virtuous secular life: the life of the solid citizen, one who lived in the world and made constructive use of his fortune. Leonardo Bruni and others translated and commented on the ancient works of Aristotle and Xenophon that had discussed household management and defended the productive use of wealth.[93] In the 1420s, more than one humanist devoted an original work to this controversial set of themes. Some denounced the pursuit of money as antisocial or sinful; others defended it as vital to the preservation of society; and still others—like Poggio, who devoted an extended dialogue to avarice—canvassed both views and others.[94]

Alberti addressed these questions in one of his *Dinner Pieces* with all the bitterness of the wounded orphan he still was—or at least he put the bitterness he felt into the mouth of his grandfather, Benedetto, who served as his spokesman. Driven into exile, lying on his deathbed, Benedetto is urged by friends to draw up his will. He asks them what he should include in it, and they reply that Benedetto, as the richest man in Tuscany, should dispose of his estates and his property.

He said: "I assure you that there is nothing of which I am more ignorant and unaware. As for those things which I suppose you mean, I scarcely know now what is mine. But in my youth, I labored many years under such an error, and imprudently deemed mine those things which are popularly thought to belong to a person. I followed the common usage of my fellow-citizens, and called them *my* estates, *my* property, and *my* wealth, as people do."

"But weren't they yours?" his friends asked.

"No," my grandfather replied. "Even more surprisingly, I have long realized that even this body which confines me was never really mine. For I recall how against my will these members were always subject to cold, to heat, or to various pains, and how they hindered and opposed my nobler intentions and desires. I recall how this body continually suffered hunger, thirst, and other such harsh and savage masters. And I perceive how in a single day fortune, mistress of our affairs, has snatched from me all my wealth and goods and even my homeland, and has driven me into exile. What, then, dare I call mine, either past or present?

"Now, wealth in human life is like a game with a ball. For it is not holding the ball in your hands a long time, but throwing it with skill and returning it accurately, that helps you win the victory. Just so, I judge that it is not the possession but the use of wealth that contributes to happiness."

The issues that Alberti broached here—the uses of wealth in family and civic life, the power of fortune over human affairs, the ease with which the bases of existence can be lost—would all recur in his later writings. So would his literary method, in which vivid metaphors, rather than elaborate arguments, conveyed the essence of human situations in all their fragility and darkness. Some of the dinner pieces are less vivid—for example, those in which Alberti developed at length his belief that most women have a propensity to vicious conduct in general and sexual unfaithfulness in particular. In others, he coined powerful new images—as in the short text in which the stones in the foundation of a Tuscan temple rebel against the slavery imposed on them by "the insolent and idle stones that weigh upon our shoulders." They succeed in breaking out, and enjoy the light and the sun—only to bring the whole temple down with a crash. The masons who clear away the damage grind up some of the former foundation stones to make mortar and use the others to line the bed of a sewer. The stones that had fomented the revolution repent, warning all the other stones, "It is better to tolerate ancient custom, even if it is harmful and unjust, than it is to seek changes that may plunge you and others into loss and utter ruin"—a provocative way, at least when read in retrospect, for a future architect to denounce the Florentine propensity to engage in the kind of self-consuming civil strife that had destroyed his own family's wealth and position.[95] The value of letters and the need for rigorous household economy, the vital importance of industry and the folly of astrologers—these and many other political and social issues received cogent discussions in Alberti's short works, some of which he published separately even before he made them into a collection, probably in the early 1440s.

One of the most striking characteristics of Dinner Pieces as a whole, however, is the amount of space that their author devoted to expressing his own feelings of failure and insecurity as a writer, and to analyzing the larger conditions to which he ascribed the problems. Sometimes Alberti portrayed himself as Lepidus, a neurotic, harried individual whose every effort to make his way led only to disaster:

For by some fate, ever since my birth, not the least affair has turned out as I wished. It is strange how everything happens contrary to my hopes and expectations. If I seek to win friends through courtesies and favors, I make enemies. If I seek to win favor by liberal studies, I am repaid by envy. If I attend to my affairs in tranquillity and modesty, offending no one, I meet with detractors, denouncers, secret foes, and villainous betrayers who confound my plans and projects. In short, no matter what I undertake or pursue, nothing turns out as I wish it.

In the dinner piece "Rings," Alberti represented himself as Philoponius, an artist who had tried to make his way by producing new works of art from old materials: a practitioner of a form of visual art that nicely paralleled Alberti's style as a writer. "They promised me that I would win your favor, Minerva," Philoponius complains,

by drawing select pebbles from the sacred fount, by cleaning and polishing them, and by consecrating them on the altar to adorn the candelabra of Posterity. Was I at all negligent in doing this? Did you find my efforts lacking in any way? Can you deny that before the thirtieth day I had extracted more than thirty rare and remarkable pebbles? But recall how I was rewarded. I drew forth several pebbles which were cleaned, polished, and cut in various facets. No one contemned or openly scoffed at these, which were rather modest. Yet they muttered that "these are nothing compared to the pearls of old, and many are missing," and they walked away. Need I mention the others? How often hard times and evil men [let me offend no god] caused me to regret this labor! Everyone deplored these wrongs, and I should justly hate you for causing me to meet with so many setbacks. Then, with a new plan to torment me, you urged me to gather golden sands from the sacred fount. I obeyed. You urged me to cast rings. I obeyed. You urged me to inscribe and engrave them. I obeyed. You urged me to display them, so that their price would free me from Poverty's harsh yoke. And although I knew how ridiculous and futile my task was, still I obeyed to avoid your accusing me of being stubborn. But what happened as I wandered through the market, the theater, the meeting-house, the crossroads, and even the inns? As evening fell, no one had bought my wares, few had even looked at them, and everyone denied that such gold could be sold. And who did not scorn my gems? "They are vulgar," they said, not caring for them at all.

In this text, Alberti treats his counterpart's cultural pessimism as ill-founded. Another character, Counsel, urges Philoponius on into the literary marketplace:

I cannot remain silent, but must tell you, Philoponius, that you are completely mistaken. I have often told you what all your friends have impressed on you. I tell you again and again that you possess many rare and worthy things. If only you show that you have them, they will be valued more than you think by men who desire them. How many varied and elegant pebbles do you have from the fountain? May I perish if you even know their number! Yet, whatever their quality, you must display them publicly. Ignorant folk won't praise them? Misers won't buy them? Still, no one will disparage them. If you are wise, you will do your best in all you do. Don't fail yourself. Bring them out and display them.

Eventually Genius, Counsel, Confidence, and Minerva, pushing and pulling Philoponius, manage to persuade or force him to enter "the basilica," where "learned men" and "experts" await. "The learned will save the learned, if they are truly learned," says Confidence—quoting a line from the Greek writer Plutarch's Life of Antony, which Leonardo Bruni had translated into Latin, and evidently expressing Alberti's hope that his works would find a welcome from the expert readers in Rome and Florence.[96]

For the most part, however, notes of vulnerability and despair, rather than measured confidence or justified pride, pervade Alberti's early work. He made clear, more than once, why he felt so certain that literary prowess would not bring him social and cultural success. The environment in which he worked, he argued, was marked by such sharp rivalry among writers and so much severity on the part of critics, by such deliberate efforts to over-shadow all rivals and such excessive insistence on applying a single, overly high standard to all modern writers and their works, that no contemporary Latinist could hope to succeed. Alberti regularly submitted his own writing to the judgment of critics he respected. He asked his brother Carlo to emend On the Advantages and Disadvantages of Letters. He urged Leonardo Bruni to read over and emend the second book of his Dinner Pieces. He even requested an opinion on his Aesopian fables, a few years later, from Aesop himself, who answered favorably—at least to judge from the reply that Alberti composed in his name.[97]

But the critics read each new text so critically, and with so little interest in the author's own intentions, that their judgments did only harm: "There isn't a single scholar whose judgment is definitive or even compatible with the opinions of others. Some are delighted only by elevated bombast, while others regard all meticulous compositions as harsh and severe. Still others cull and savor flowery ornaments, elegant turns of phrase, and rounded periods as they read. Yet few pay attention to the power of a writer's genius or the method in his art." In these conditions, Alberti complained, even Cicero "would undoubtedly forget how to speak." Criticism, far from honing Alberti's eloquence, threatened to silence him. The protocols of collective authorship, as the Florentine learned world had developed them, looked more like a conspiracy of furious imbeciles than a way of averting error and raising standards.

Alberti not only blamed the critics in general for the death of intelligent writing: he also made clear which critic he had in mind. In more than one work, he described Tuscany as a particularly critical, unwelcoming environment. And within Tuscany he identified Niccoli, the critic of critics, as especially dangerous. Early in the 1430s, Alberti was already making fun of Niccoli in his *Dinner Piece* "The Deceased." The dead protagonist complains, bitterly, of the way his heirs had sold his precious library and collection of antiques, his "many splendid and sumptuous Greek and Latin volumes decorated with silver," and "my statues, my paintings and the other objects which had given me pleasure." But he speaks with even greater dismay of the fate of the text on which he had been working—a "history" that he had left "rough and unpolished," and the pages of which his kinsmen tore out, to use them to wrap a particularly precious salve which he had also bequeathed. Alberti could hardly have found a clearer way to identify Niccoli—the great bibliophile and collector, the pathologically self-critical scholar who could never bring himself to publish anything he himself wrote.

Or at least Alberti could not do so until a couple of years later, when he had spent some time in Florence. Like many others, Alberti found Niccoli more infuriating as he came to know him better. Accordingly, he devoted a whole series of texts to dismantling his reputation. In these dialogues between Lepidus (Alberti) and Libripeta (the Bookhound), Niccoli emerges as irreligious and cynical, devoted only to buying rather than reading books. In one horrifying text, Libripeta (Niccoli) emerges from a sewer. Lepidus suggests that the collector must have heard that it contained valuable books. In fact, however, Libripeta explains that he has just returned from the land of the dreamers: he had to cross a grotesquely solid river, made up of human faces, that bit all those who tried to cross, rolling themselves into balls and spinning across: "If I hadn't been long accustomed to wounding men with my own teeth," says Libripeta, "and tough-skinned from the many bites I've received in continual insults and quarrels, you'd see me torn to shreds. But I thank the heavens, since I crossed the river with my nose intact."[98] The critic has, at least, the virtue of a thick skin. Otherwise, however, Niccoli emerges as a savage, misanthropic pedant: one whose continual criticisms of others' works were aimed not to improve them but to destroy their authors' confidence. For all their artistry, their confident manipulation of the literary weapons and armor needed to fight through the crowd of young humanists, Alberti's dialogues also convey a powerful impression of intellectual losses suffered—of vulnerability and melancholy, inflicted not only by the great inimitable presence of the classics but also by the constant back-biting of the critics. When he asked his brother Carlo to edit and emend *The Advantages and Disadvantages of Letters* and begged Florentine luminaries like Poggio, Bruni, and the mathematician Paolo Toscanelli to correct his *Dinner Pieces*, he was seeking protection against what he experienced as real harms.

Despite all his difficulties, Alberti managed to go on writing—and, very much like the fictional protagonist of "Rings," to combine and refine ancient materials in sophisticated new ways. He received important material support, moreover. Pope Eugenius IV awarded him a priory outside Florence and issued a bull that enabled him to take ecclesiastical orders despite his illegitimate birth. (This handicap would otherwise have kept Alberti from becoming a priest.) Soon he also became a canon of Florence's cathedral. Alberti's receipt of these signs of respect and sources of income signaled that important figures in the curia had discovered his abilities. He soon felt himself in a solid position—solid enough to point out, to a friend who picked a fight with him, that he enjoyed financial security and could play the useful role of an "interpreter" with the head of the papal chancery—the patriarch of Grado, Biagio Molin.[99]

At some point between late 1432 and March 1434, Molin asked Alberti to write a series of lives of the early Christian martyrs, beginning with that of Potitus, whom the Roman emperor Julian had put to death. Molin presumably had the authority to command literary performances from the young men who were beginning careers as abbreviators. In this case, obeying Molin required Alberti to join in what was becoming a fashionable new kind of research. During the 1420s, under Martin V, a Roman pope from a Roman family, Poggio and his friends had made it fashionable in the curia to explore the city's past. They scrutinized ancient arches, temples, and public buildings, and searched the great waste spaces, which included the ancient Forum, for interesting Roman inscriptions.[100] Rome became a center of creative historical research. Much of it, naturally enough, was devoted not only to the Roman republic and empire but also to the early development of Christianity. Some of these scholars, like Alberti himself, applied new tools of historical criticism to the sources for the early history of the city and the church, asking to whom a given event had actually happened, and when, and where, and how—and finding that such aggressive interrogation revealed long-accepted sources and stories to be fabulous.[101]

In response to Molin, Alberti professed his modesty, remarking that many would have refused such a commission "because they would have tried above all not to seem foolish or arrogant, like those who had set out to deface the writings of the ancients with their own new efforts to show off." But he also admitted that "I think that I can deny you nothing even so, when you order me to carry out an exercise of this kind." Accordingly, he asked Molin both to choose a martyr for him to work on and to correct the results.[102] Here, as in *The Advantages and Disadvantages of Letters*, Alberti tried to make productive use of the system of literary criticism that he found so wounding. Like Poggio, he hoped that the criticism supplied by his first readers would enable him to produce a text impervious, or at least resistant, to later, more public attacks.

Alberti not only asked his superior for editorial help but found a contemporary to advise him as well—one whose literary advice and personal friendship he would rely upon for the remaining forty years of his life. Leonardo Dati, a Florentine a few years younger than Alberti, enjoyed the patronage of the influential Camaldolensian monk, scholar, and translator Ambrogio Traversari, who in turn brought him into contact with Cardinal Giordano Orsini. Dati, becoming a priest, entered Orsini's service in Rome in 1432. For the next few years he stayed there, in the company of Poggio, Loschi, and other humanists, studying the classics, writing erotic verse, and beginning to accumulate benefices.[103] Alberti and Dati apparently became friends when Molin decided that Alberti should attack, as his first martyrological project, the life of Potitus. Dati was one of the constructively nosy humanists who enjoyed reading and criticizing others' writings—and Alberti put Dati's editorial skills to good use.

In a detailed letter to his friend, Alberti confessed that he found his task challenging, even daunting. The surviving sources on Potitus were for the most part simple lives in the vernacular, swarming with pious stories about miracles—a form of edifying tradition, popular and unclassical, that many humanists had long wanted to eliminate from historical writing, except when it described the portents that announced the dramatic deaths of tyrants.[104] Alberti knew how to do historical research, as he made clear by listing, in his characteristic way, the *loci* that a good historical account should touch on: "I bore in mind that scholars have many requirements for history: they want to have full descriptions of the causes of events, the events themselves, the places, the times, and the full dignity of the protagonists." But after assembling and comparing the sources, he was forced to confess that the evidence for Potitus' life was unusually scanty:

> I saw that older writers had provided clear and full accounts of the acts of the Apostles and the lives of the other popes and martyrs. But I also saw that the accounts of the life of this Potitus were so careless that one could easily conclude that incompetents, rather than those great scholars, drew up this life.

Learned readers, he feared, might take the whole story as a fiction rather than a history.

Eventually, Alberti managed to tie his man down to a specific place and time. The early Christian writer Tatian mentioned a Potitus, and the letters of the Christian martyrs of Lyons, quoted by one of the Greek fathers of the church, Eusebius, in his *Ecclesiastical History* (fourth century), recorded that a Ponticus had suffered with them. Presumably the two martyrs were one and the same, separated only by a scribal error. Like a scholarly counterpart to Archimedes, Alberti boasted of his philological triumph: "I have this Ponticus, accordingly; his date and deeds correspond perfectly with the period of Antoninus. And those letters were written in the period of Antoninus." Accordingly, he claimed no longer to fear "the judgment of those who may think this history a fiction"—even though he went on to complain of the corruption of the sources he had to use.

The text Alberti finally wrote shows his literary skills to good effect. The story of a Christian martyr who died in the arena, *The Life of Potitus* gave him opportunities to compose rhetorical set pieces. Alberti characteristically remarked, "The constancy of this youth, who is remarkable for the many miracles he worked, would give the writer who sought to praise him both

plenty of material for amplification and a chance to win wide attention."
Accordingly, Alberti turned out some pretty speeches, like the one in which
Potitus, urged by his father to worship the pagan gods, replies in a sharply
iconoclastic vein: "Who can force me to adore false idols of stone, or to
make sacrifice to images made by human hands?"

Alberti also took a number of opportunities to paint pictures of events in
the martyr's life, and even to interpret them, as if he were already thinking
about the ways painters should choose and execute their subjects—a theme
that would soon become central to his thought. The same moral issues that
Alberti addressed in his Latin dialogues appeared in this text as well, in the
accessible form of easily deciphered moral emblems. When a devil tries to
tempt Potitus, and the young Christian sees through his words, the "fan-
tasm" grows to a height of fifteen cubits and then disappears. Alberti comments:

> O, what a fine image of the evanescence of things! For when you
> want the goods that are subject to fortune, you find it hard to realize
> how much damage they can do. But when, with God's help, you man-
> age to escape them and despise them, you understand much more
> clearly that there is nothing greater than that plague, that it far ex-
> ceeds the strength of men. But they say that when the youth had seen
> the terrible character of the monster, he blew, and it vanished. This
> also fits our picture very neatly. For either when we die, we lose in
> one breath everything that we have accumulated throughout our life;
> or even before that, during our lifetimes, they can suffer shipwreck
> because of one blast from fortune.[105]

Alberti's short Life of Potitus thus served, at least in part, the central task of
written history as Cicero had defined it in antiquity, and as most humanists
of the Renaissance still understood it: to provide examples of good and evil
conduct that readers could learn to imitate or avoid, offering the factual un-
derpinnings for effective oratory and moral philosophy.[106]

Alberti also told miracle stories: how the animals that were set on Potitus in the arena did not devour him but adored him instead; how the boy,
though tortured, beaten, and deprived of eyes and tongue, continued with
God's help to confess his true faith. Passages like these were designed not to
stimulate emulation but to promote contemplation: the deep, warm, inward
feeling of piety that the mystics and devout laymen of fifteenth-century Eu-

rope systematically strove to attain.[107] Some of Alberti's most vivid word-pictures embodied religious rather than merely moral sentiments. When Potitus was brought, beaten and bruised, into pagan temples, all the idols rotted and fell apart like so many transfixed vampires.

At times, however, Alberti treated Potitus' story less as a coherent, edifying narrative than as a framework on which he could hang episodes, some of which expressed his personal views so strongly that they challenged the validity of his hagiographical enterprise as a whole. As a boy and young man, as we have seen, Alberti resented the pomp and pride of the great men he observed in the streets of Padua and Bologna. The contemporary church had more than its share of pomp and pride as well, and the contemplation of early Christianity—even in the dim and problematic form it took in his sources for the life of Potitus—made the defects of the modern church seem all the more striking. "Some work for profit," Alberti complained, "some strive to render military service, others starve themselves and study letters deep into the night. But all of them do this so they may become famous in the eyes of man, not so that they may win glory before the face of God."[108]

Digressions that applied ancient examples to modern times were nothing new in history, even if Alberti's brand of plain speech was unusually sharp and frank. Elsewhere, however, Alberti's sharp pen proved capable of doing some real damage. The value of money had become an urgent moral question, as we have already seen, in fifteenth-century Italy. This mercantile society, like others before and after it, often felt ashamed, for both social and theological reasons, of the pursuits that had made it rich.[109] Monks and mendicant friars—especially the stricter Franciscans, whose founder had insisted that they literally "take no thought for the morrow"—offered in theory a shaming example of life lived for God, without private property, to the rich men and women who supported them. But in practice the convents often seemed as collectively prosperous as their inhabitants were individually poor. Alberti, as we have already seen, detested idleness, insisting that he himself never passed a day without writing. No wonder, then, that he put into the mouth of no less a character than the Roman emperor Antoninus a swinging denunciation of the idleness of Christian monks: "I say . . . that no breed of men is lower than these. They have decided to spend their whole lives in idleness, without industry or work: they avoid, demean, and hate all the worthwhile arts—military pursuits, letters, everything that serves to adorn human life." Such excursuses can hardly have pleased all of Alberti's readers. Alberti himself expressed some nervousness when sending his work on to another authoritative figure, Marino Guadagni.[110] At least in Florence, however, Alberti apparently gained the reputation of an able biographer of saints.[111]

In other, more classical areas, Alberti's continual experiments also paid off. He composed texts that showed, in form as well as content, considerable originality and prescience. More than one of his dinner pieces contained literary innovations even more extended and systematic than those in *The Life of Potitus*, such as long set pieces describing works of visual art. Such descriptions, which had formed part of artistic prose in the Hellenistic and imperial worlds, came to new life in Renaissance Italy, as Michael Baxandall has shown in work of great originality and insight.[112] Humanists set themselves to describe both real and imagined paintings, buildings, and cities. They did so in various styles, which they could—at their most skillful—even adapt to fit the styles of particular artists and patrons.

In a dinner piece entitled "Paintings," Alberti described a temple of good and ill fortune, supposedly situated "in the land of the gymnosophists"—the land of the naked Indian ascetics whom Greek and Roman writers generally identified with the Brahmins, and whom many of them took as one of the elder races of thinkers from whom the Greeks had derived their own philosophy. Alberti skipped quickly past the splendid decorations of the building itself—a range of capitals and architraves carved from Parian marble, with vases and caldrons, gold and gems that seem oddly incongruous with the austerity of the temple's supposed creators. But he described in great detail the twenty symmetrically arranged paintings of personified goods and evils that appeared on opposite walls—for example, Humanity herself:

> In the first place, there is painted an extraordinary image of a woman, around whose neck are gathered various faces, young, old, happy, sad, joyful, serious, and so forth. Numerous hands extend from her shoulders, some holding pens, others lyres, some a polished gem, others a painted or carved emblem, some various mathematical instruments, and others books. Above her is written: Humanity, mother.

Similar images, equally crowded with striking features, expressed the nature of Misery and Calamity, Peace and Happiness.

Alberti made clear to readers at the outset of his text that he saw these works as exemplary both in the luxurious plenitude of visual detail they afforded and in the moral lessons they embodied: "The reader will not only delight in the paintings' variety and the artist's invention, but will be grateful, I believe, when he finds in our work pleasing and enjoyable counsels for living wisely." At the end, he repeated that he had meant to offer serious counsels for good living in this accessibly vivid form: "By these paintings, unless we err, we have offered our readers some pleasure and some counsel for living well and happily. Having achieved this, we have reaped the greatest and most desired reward for our studies. Scholars, applaud!"[113] Evidently Alberti already saw the visual arts—like history—as a particularly effective medium for conveying basic truths about the good and the good life.

Alberti's bold, sometimes radical Latin writings aroused the attention of many readers. Individual dinner pieces and short collections of them circulated widely. *The Life of Potitus* evidently thrilled one pious humanist, the Benedictine humanist Girolamo Aliotti, who campaigned to win Alberti a second assignment in hagiography as well. Thanks to his priory, moreover, he enjoyed the basic income necessary to pursue scholarship and style with security. Nonetheless, Alberti found neither his situation nor his rate of progress satisfying. If—as one scholar has recently suggested—he actually composed his treatise *On the Advantages and Disadvantages of Letters* in the early 1430s (or revised it then), rather than in the late 1420s, its evidence would strengthen the theory that he felt himself hemmed in and pursued by difficulties. Ever a believer in man's capacity to alter his own fortunes, ever energetic, he found another way forward. Alberti the scholar turned himself into Alberti the engineer. His most original early writings would arise from an ambitious effort to fuse two originally distinct occupations and cultures.

III

FROM NEW TECHNOLOGIES

TO FINE ARTS:

ALBERTI AMONG THE ENGINEERS

Sometime before July 1436, Alberti dedicated the Italian text of his book *On Painting* to Filippo Brunelleschi.[1] Alberti's book—his earliest finished work to become a classic—is famous for many reasons. He composed *On Painting* in two languages, Latin and Italian, but neither his own references to the work nor the evidence of the two versions definitively identifies either of them as the original.[2] Its first section offers the earliest precise description of how to create a systematic, coherent perspective space in two dimensions. The rest of the book provides a still more elaborate description of how a new sort of learned artist should be trained and, once equipped with expertise and erudition, how he should apply his skills to painting and other tasks. This lastingly influential work and its context in Alberti's life and world require examination from several points of view. The best way to confront the work for the first time, however, is probably to begin as Alberti wanted readers of his Italian text to: with his eloquent and evocative dedicatory letter. After using the dedication to explain how Alberti came to write a work on painting, we will examine the text itself in the next chapter.

On a first reading, the dedication resembles a travelogue. Alberti offers an account of the wonders of recent Florentine art and architecture, as a traveler coming from Rome might encounter them as he rode through the district of Oltr'Arno, crossed the river on the Ponte Vecchio, and passed Or San Michele on his way to the Cathedral:

I used both to marvel and to regret that so many excellent and divine arts and sciences, which as we know from their works and from historical accounts were possessed in great abundance by the talented men of antiquity, have now disappeared and are almost entirely lost. Painters, sculptors, architects, musicians, geometers, rhetoricians, augurs, and distinguished and remarkable intellects of that sort are very rarely to be found these days, and are of little merit. Consequently I believed what I heard many say, that Nature, mistress of all things, had grown old and weary, and was no longer producing intellects any more than giants on a vast and wonderful scale such as she did in what one might call her youthful and more glorious days. But after I came back here to this most beautiful of cities from the long exile in which we Alberti have grown old, I recognized in many, but above all in you, Filippo, and in our great friend the sculptor Donatello and in the others, Nencio [Ghiberti], Luca [Della Robbia], and Masaccio, a genius for every laudable enterprise in no way inferior to any of the ancients who gained fame in these arts. I then realized that the ability to gain the highest distinction in any meritorious activity lies in our own industry and diligence no less than in the favors of Nature and of the times. I admit that for the ancients, who had many precedents to learn from and imitate, it was less difficult to master those noble arts which for us today prove arduous; but it follows that our fame should be all the greater if without preceptors and without any model to imitate we discover arts and sciences hitherto unheard of and unseen. What man, however hard of heart or jealous, would not praise Filippo the architect when he sees here such an enormous construction towering above the skies, vast enough to cover the entire Tuscan population with its shadow, and done without the aid of beams or elaborate wooden supports? Unless I am wrong, this was a feat of engineering that people did not believe feasible these days, and it was probably equally unknown and unimaginable among the ancients. . . . If you should have some leisure, I shall be glad if you will look over this little work of mine on painting, which I did into

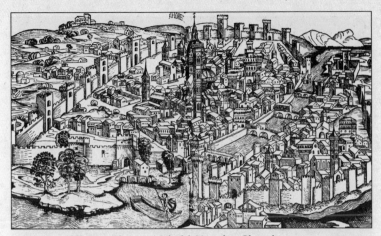

1. Panorama of Florence. Hartmann Schedel, *Nuremberg Chronicle*. Department of Rare Books and Special Collections, Princeton University.

2. Florence, Cathedral. Alinari/Art Resource, NY.

3. Lorenzo Ghiberti. North Doors. Baptistery, Florence. Alinari/Art Resource, NY.

Tuscan for you. . . . Please, therefore, read my work carefully, and if anything seems to you to need amendment, correct it. No writer was ever so well informed that learned friends were not very useful to him; and I want above all to be corrected by you, so as not to be bitten by detractors.[3]

Alberti's letter is a fine example of literary practices he had mastered long before: the stitching together of classical sources to produce a patchwork, one that imposed a new meaning on antique materials. Here as elsewhere, Alberti juxtaposed two recently discovered classical sources in an artful way. The younger Pliny, whose uncle wrote the *Natural History*, the richest of all literary sources for the history of art in antiquity, had described in one of his letters a public reading held by a comic poet, Vergilius Romanus. Pliny thought Vergilius' work so good an imitation of the ancient (Greek) comedians that it could serve as a literary model in its own right.[4] The Epicurean philosopher Lucretius had expressed a more pessimistic view in his great poem *On the Nature of Things*, a work passionately praised by Virgil but little read in the Middle Ages and rediscovered by the humanists as recently as the 1410s. Lucretius held that nature, grown weak with time, no longer brought forth giants: the earth, which had once produced giant animals, now had difficulty bearing even tiny creatures.[5]

Like Pliny, Alberti took human creativity as proving that the world had not grown old. Like Lucretius, he took the great physical dimensions of the creation, rather than its high artistic quality, as proof of the creative force that man shared with nature herself.[6] By putting the two passages together, he neatly managed to twist one of them (that of Lucretius) into a radically different shape, and to make the other (that of Pliny) far more pointed than its author had intended. Pliny had insisted only that the men of his own day and the future could still carry on the tradition of writing based on ancient models. Alberti, by contrast, suggested that Brunelleschi had surpassed the ancients. He had done so, moreover, without the aid of a model or a teacher to follow.[7] As in his earlier text on the pursuit of letters, moreover, Alberti adapted not only well-known ancient books but the freshest finds of the erudite humanist book hunters in his circle.[8] Barzizza himself could not have provided a neater example of creative anachronism in the service of high style. Alberti's citation-riddled text would have identified him at once as a humanist of a particular kind—but only to readers who, unlike Brunelleschi, had a sound enough classical education to recognize the changes he had rung on his sources.

The form of the letter also amounted to a code, the symbolic subtext of which any humanist would have found easy to detect. At the end of the text, Alberti asked Brunelleschi to serve as his editor: not just to read and approve his work but to emend it and by doing so to protect its author from detractors. In making this request, as we now know, Alberti was following his own custom and the larger norms of Florentine literary life—except in one crucial respect. Normally humanists addressed such letters to their colleagues, believing, as Alberti liked to say, that "the learned will be saved by the learned."[9] When he identified Brunelleschi as a man of learning and asked for his technical advice, Alberti suggested that their relationship was one of scholar and scholar. More still, he declared his friendship for the artist, as well as his willing vulnerability to Brunelleschi's sharp tongue. He thus made clear, in terms no contemporary humanist could miss, that he saw the architect as his colleague in a particular form of intellectual work. Alberti could not have meant that Brunelleschi, whose knowledge of Latin was modest, was a humanist in the same sense that he was. Rather, he forcefully acknowledged that Brunelleschi too practiced a liberal art or arts, arts that required the use of the intellect (a point that Brunelleschi himself had made, two years before, when he refused to pay guild dues).[10] At the same time, Alberti claimed for himself, alongside his first identity as a scholar, a second identity as a master of technology—one who recognized Brunelleschi's superiority but still asserted collegiality with him. Though middle-aged, Alberti boldly used the prefatory letter to assert that he was entering a new territory.

Neither the letter's hidden allusions nor its conventional form necessarily mattered much to Brunelleschi. An architect, sculptor, and engineer, he was a practical man, literate in Italian and, as the son of a notary, presumably able to read Latin but hardly in a position to match citations with a highly skilled humanist like Alberti.[11] To that extent, the art historian E. H. Gombrich, a pioneer in the study of Alberti's work and that of his contemporaries, pointed out long ago, discovering the sources on which Alberti drew serves only a limited purpose. It enables us to gain a clearer sense of how he composed texts, how he reshaped the fragments into splendid new shapes—mosaics in composition but not in form, their pieces so seamlessly fitted together that only an expert could even detect them. It also shows how deftly Alberti could draw on his classical reading to create a technical language appropriate to new intellectual tasks. But identifying Alberti's sources does not offer help with a central problem: understanding what the letter might have meant to Brunelleschi and his colleagues. Rules of composition cannot necessarily be employed as rules of interpretation—especially in the case of a text written to cross social and intellectual boundaries. When read against a different background, however—that of Brunelleschi's own social and professional world—the letter takes on a different color, one that Brunelleschi and others like him could certainly have detected.

At the outset, Alberti remarked that nature no longer seemed to produce "painters, sculptors, architects, musicians, geometers, rhetoricians, and augurs." This list of job titles sounds arbitrary, but it has a double logic. The disciplines Alberti listed were, in the first place, the very ones in which he claimed competence, from painting to predicting. Readers who knew him could not miss that he was, at the start as at the end of the letter, asserting that he himself played a vital role in the Renaissance of the arts that he evoked so eloquently. In the second place, and more important, Alberti was not the first to bring these disciplines together. When he connected the crafts of painting and sculpture with the liberal arts of geometry and astrology, and both of these sets of pursuits with architecture, he associated himself with a technological and social revolution—one that radically changed both the social structures that created buildings and works of art and the products that resulted. The protagonists of this revolution, as Jacob Burckhardt suggested long ago, were engineers like Brunelleschi, whose characteristic pursuit of many different interests and skills he found strikingly reminiscent of Alberti.[12]

The new technology began to develop long before Alberti's time. From the twelfth century onward, western Europeans watched with astonishment as a new set of experts raised huge church towers to challenge the skies, hurled stone bridges across once impassable rivers, and used wind and water mills to exploit the powers of nature. One pioneer, Villard d'Honnecourt, left a fascinating notebook behind that records in detailed, often curious diagrams the results of his study of buildings, technical devices, human anatomy, and animals, among many other subjects. Villard insisted, more than once, that he had made his sketches of lions and churches from the originals, emphasizing the skill of his hand and the range of his personal experience.[13] But he also proclaimed that architecture, as he practiced it, was an intellectual pursuit. He and other masters, he said, had settled points *inter se disputando* ("in disputation with one another")—using the technical term for formal debate that had long been standard in the schools, to underline the fact that his art too rested on firm intellectual principles that could be applied in systematic argumentation.[14] And he boasted that his readers would learn how useful the art of geometrical drawing, as well as the machines that it described, could be.[15] Dozens of others whose names are lost also took part in this larger movement, which reshaped cityscapes and settlement patterns across Europe, and more than one agreed with Villard's challenge to the belief that the work of the mind was both completely separate from, and higher than, the work of the hand.[16]

By the fourteenth and early fifteenth centuries, this technological movement was entering a new phase.[17] The Italian and German engineers who worked in Italy in the decades around 1400 devised startling innovations in every area. For the pageants lavishly staged by Renaissance cities and courts, they created spectacular floats that moved without visible draft animals to pull them—a startlingly vivid demonstration of the power of a state, or an individual ruler, to harness hidden powers. During the wars so bitterly waged across the Italian landscape in the same period, as Milan, Florence, Naples, and other centers used force to build territorial states, the engineers built fortifications, diverted rivers, and cast enormous, powerful-looking cannon—the newest and most terrifying of weapons, if not at this point the most effective ones, at the disposal of European states.[18]

Engineers whose skills lay in these attention-getting areas enjoyed the patronage of the powerful and were entrusted with the solution of vital military problems. Buonaccorso Pitti, a wealthy Florentine merchant who held office as one of the standard-bearers of the militia companies in 1403, recalled how the Ten of War, the committee in charge of Florence's military affairs, learned from a priest that an old gate in the walls of Pisa, though bricked up so that it was flush with the rest of the surface, was hollow and unguarded: "The Ten took counsel on this matter with a clever engineer who, having heard them out, went secretly to examine the bricked-in stretch of wall for himself and, seeing the holes left in the exterior by the scaffolding, concluded that it must indeed be hollow." The engineer promised to fill the holes with gunpowder and knock the wall down, enabling the Florentines to enter Pisa. This bold plan ultimately did not work, any more than Brunelleschi's more famous effort to defeat the Pisans by changing the course of the river they depended on. The Pisans dug trenches in front of the old gate and set guards, preventing the Florentines from setting their charges.[19] But though the engineer failed on this occasion, the public esteem that his skills enjoyed from the hard-nosed managers of the city is clear. The very title that the engineers used highlighted their brilliance. An *ingeniator* or *engignour* derived the name of his occupation not, like a baker or a ropemaker, from the material on which he worked, but from the brilliance of his intellect, his *ingenium*, and the cleverness of the weapons or devices (also called *ingenia*) that it enabled him to create.[20]

The power of the new technology impressed even observers familiar with the once-magnificent marble cities of the eastern Mediterranean. Bessarion, the learned Greek from Trebizond who became a cardinal of the Roman Church in 1439, was an erudite philosopher who yielded to none of his contemporaries in his passion for the truths found in ancient books. His magnificent collection of Greek manuscripts, which he bequeathed to the city of Venice, became the nucleus of the Biblioteca Marciana. But the new tools and devices he saw in his adopted home in Italy impressed him as deeply as the richest classical texts—and seemed at least as relevant to the defense of his native land. Writing to Constantine Palaeologus, who ruled the independent Greek state of Morea, he urged that four or eight young men be sent from Greece to Italy to learn the vital new crafts the Italians practiced: "boards are sawn automatically, mills turn as rapidly and exactly as possible; in metallurgy bellows are inflated and deflated without the touch of human hands, separating the metal from the baser material in the flux." Iron founding, weapon making, shipbuilding—all the skills vital for protecting the remnants of the Greek Christian world against the Turks could be mastered in Italy and then brought back and taught to the Greeks.[21] For hundreds of years, western travelers to Constantinople had gawked in wonder at the carefully preserved late antique technology of the court, from the imperial throne that rose and sank at the touch of a lever and the emperor's artificial tree crowded with automata that sang like birds, to the Greek fire that burned across the water to destroy enemy ships. Now western Europe harbored powerful technologies that the ancients had never known. Even non-Christian observers agreed, to judge from the eagerness with which the Ottoman sultan hired Christian, or formerly Christian, gun founders to make enormous siege cannon.[22]

Engineers and architects of this new kind combined practical studies like building and gun casting with theoretical studies like music and geometry, making every effort to use the latter to support their practical proposals. When construction at Milan Cathedral came to a halt around 1400, for example, the architects associated with the project engaged in sharp public debates about what form of arch was the strongest. Both factions made clear that they considered it impossible to make such arguments rigorously without invoking mathematics and Aristotelian natural philosophy in their support. These men probably worked, for the most part, by traditional rules learned at the building site. But they set their innovative efforts to exploit natural forces and use natural materials into a wide theoretical and cosmological context. Astrology, the most rigorous and comprehensive explanatory system that existed in the fourteenth century, provided them with vital tools. Both Georg Kyeser, a doctor from the Holy Roman Empire who worked in Italy, and Mariano di Jacopo, known as Taccola, a Sienese engineer who described his military devices to no less prominent a customer than the Holy Roman Emperor Sigismund, argued that military specialists must know their astrology. Only by making use of this predictive science could a ruler gauge the strengths and weaknesses of his opponents and determine a favorable time for going to war against them.[23] The engineers, in short, were augurs as well as mathematicians and artists—a fact that helps to explain Alberti's choice of disciplines to mourn, and later to celebrate. And they made no fine distinction between what we would now call the fine arts, like painting and sculpture, and the applied ones, like bridge building. On the contrary, the same masters often carried on projects in all of these areas. Alberti's letter, in other words, not only claimed collegiality with Brunelleschi but specified the fields of interest and competence that they shared. Most viewers of Alberti's performance would have recognized at once the role that he was trying to play.[24]

Alberti implicitly argued for a joint revival of the arts of writing on the one hand, the crafts on the other. His position sounds radical: he placed the abstract, classically grounded pursuits of the well-born and the sweaty, paint-smeared crafts of men who worked with their hands on the same level. But even here he remained within the engineering tradition. Fifty years ago, Erwin Panofsky argued in a brilliant essay that the Renaissance saw barriers fall—barriers that for centuries had blocked traffic between the city of books and contemplation where scholars cogitated and the city of labor and energy where the craftsmen cut stone and wood. Artists as well as medical men, for example, now began to dissect human bodies. Some of the artists—above all Leonardo—went so far as to claim that their mastery of perspective, foreshortening, and other artistic techniques, which enabled them to record the results of their investigations far more vividly and usefully than writers could, actually made them more effective and profound students of nature than traditional scholars and medical men. Panofsky used Leonardo's famous manuscripts, with their profuse, endlessly creative interplay of illustrations and text, to document the artists' claim to occupy a new social and intellectual position.[25]

Leonardo, however, was an engineer as well as a painter and draftsman. In fact, when he offered his services to Ludovico Sforza, he began by describing the wonderful tanks and other military devices he could produce, waiting until the very end to refer to his artistic abilities. His combination of pursuits, moreover, was not unusual. True, generalizations are dangerous. Italian courts varied radically in size and style: in some of them, like that of Ferrara, the prince was the main source of patronage, while in others court officers and local nobles also took part in choosing the engineers and artists who would build palaces, churches, forts, and bridges. Some innovative providers of technical services described themselves, or were described, as specialists: painters or architects. Others, like Leonardo, offered to put their hand to any imaginable task—and to some unimaginable ones. What seems clear, however, is that fifteenth-century courts offered those with technological skills extensive opportunities to explore new areas.[26] Artists who worked there routinely carried out practical tasks as well. Jean Fouquet, now best known for his brilliant, bizarre portrait of the jester Gonella, also produced gunpowder and armaments for the Estensi of Modena.[27] Leonardo's claims to high standing are particularly well known, of course, because he took the vital step of making them in writing. His magnificent, highly personal form of writing fused words with images, in order to record his continuous, intense exploration of the relation between human joints and artificial machines, the movement of air and that of water. Leonardo did not expend this enormous effort, practical and intellectual, only to gratify his curiosity. By producing books, the artist made clear his claim to be a man of learning. When Leonardo devoted long sections of his manuscripts to arguing with Alberti and other learned men who had treated similar subjects, he evidently saw what he was doing from exactly this point of view.

In this respect too, moreover, Leonardo followed a path that others had already cleared. Since the fourteenth century, engineers had been producing texts that strikingly resembled his: manuscript descriptions of mechanical devices, with captions or longer texts. Some of these included schematic diagrams of the machinery designed to pull ferries, lift weights, and tell time. Other engineering books enticed the reader with more imaginative drawings of military and transport devices, as they would look when in use in real time. Taccola, for example, provided his readers with diagrams of siphons and other devices practical enough that later engineers would copy and apply them for the next century, but he also drew vivid sketches of devices that surely never found employment on the field of battle. One of his most curious inventions involved a dog, tied by a long line to a bell at the top of a tower. The dog's desperate efforts to reach food and water left just beyond his range would make the bell ring, creating the illusion that a deserted fort was still occupied.[28]

Alberti knew this world of applied science from the inside; he wrote a treatise on practical geometry, which survives, and a work on weights and measures, which does not.[29] He used the language, and even repeated the clichés, of the engineering tradition, as it had been framed in the past two centuries, not only by northern Italian laymen, but also by the northern European monks and friars who carried out similar projects, designing astronomical clocks and other mechanical devices of their own. In his *Life*, Alberti emphasized the close contacts he had enjoyed with craftsmen: "From craftsmen, architects, shipbuilders, and even from cobblers and tailors, he tried to learn, wishing to acquire any rare and secret knowledge contained in their particular arts." He repeatedly expressed his admiration for their energy and assiduity, which he tried to emulate: "He would leave his house for the relief of his spirit and go out into the city to watch all the artisans working diligently in their shops, then hurry back as if admonished by some grave teacher, saying, 'We, too, must exercise the office we have undertaken to fill.' "[30]

Here, as Alberti's contemporaries knew, he used a language long familiar in the tradition of engineering and technology. The rediscovery of Aristotle had brought with it, along with much else, a realization that man and nature worked in the same way: that human crafts and natural processes followed the same laws, and that human energy and intelligence, if rightly applied, could actually perfect nature.[31] Roger Bacon emphasized the utility of craft knowledge two centuries before Alberti did: "For my part, I often learn far more useful things from people of very modest condition, whose very names are unknown in the universities, than from the most famous doctors." And he made clear that he had classical precedent for stating this thesis, by calling Aristotle to witness to the truth of his declaration.[32] Bacon's famous evocations of nature as a world of powerful forces open to manipulation by man, ones that technology could imitate and tame, connected the Aristotelian assertion of the value of working experience to Alberti's insistence on the need to connect brain and hand. As we have seen, much evidence suggests that Alberti, for all his skill in using classical tags and texts, remained liable to massive attacks of the anxiety of influence. Confronting the perfection of the ancients on paper was always daunting. All the better, then, if he could muster classical arguments in favor of his position.

Engineers also insisted on the value of tradition. They collected and plagiarized ancient and medieval texts on machines as eagerly as they accumulated personal experience. But the language of the technological tradition, which emphasized human energy and forward motion, had a predominantly positive and cheerful flavor. Though Alberti drew some of the wording of his dedication from Pliny and Lucretius, the line of argument he followed came not from ancient texts but from a modern, vernacular tradition that took shape in the course of discussions among articulate artisans.[33]

Alberti did more than use the language of the engineers, moreover; he set out to become one in his own right. In the next twenty years or so, he would write a whole series of texts that directly emerged from the vernacular world of the engineers and other practical urban types. His *Mathematical Games*, a text on problems of measurement, surveying, and ballistics that he wrote in the 1440s, resembles not only the demanding treatises of engineers like Taccola but also the humbler textbooks on practical mathematics, the so-called abacus books, that Italian boys studied in urban schools.[34] Many of the problems Alberti solved in this work were conventional. When he used similar triangles to measure the height of a distant tower, for example, he solved problems that had cropped up in dozens of mathematics texts before Alberti grappled with them. The more complex techniques that he applied to problems of land measurement came directly from the tradition of practical mathematics created by the thirteenth-century mathematician Leonardo Fibonacci and many others.[35] But the *Games* also show ample signs of connection to the engineering tradition. Though Alberti's own manuscript of the work does not survive, those that do show that he peppered the text with technical diagrams and referred to them in his exposition, just as Taccola and other engineers had done.[36] Alberti's treatise on the mapping of the city of Rome, on which he began work before he finished *Games*, used some of the same surveying techniques, as we will see. And many chapters of his book on architecture rested on firsthand technical work—surveying and measurement, for example, of exactly the same sort that the professional engineers carried out. When Alberti devoted elaborate discussion to the building of piers for bridges, he attacked a problem that Taccola had also worked on, as a consulting engineer in Rome.

Alberti's interest in mathematical approaches to problems of many kinds seems to have taken root early. In his little book on the study of literature, for example, he explained that a formal computation would make the life chances of humanists clearer—as if he and his audience were used not only to reading literary texts but also to decoding calculations and diagrams.[37] It is certainly possible that Alberti encountered the practical engineering tradition in his early years in northern Italy. Padua, for example, had been the site of notable engineering work by Giovanni Dondi dell'Orologio in the fourteenth century. In the 1420s, Giovanni Fontana, whose bafflingly encrypted manuscripts record hallucinogenically strange and wonderful experiments in the design of automobiles and cannon, was also active there.[38]

At some point, Alberti mastered many standard instruments and their applications. Sadly, only fragmentary testimonies describe how he learned to do so. He carried out observations of the sun's path with the Florentine medical man and astronomer Paolo Toscanelli. The experience proved formative. A standard instrument for such observations, the quadrant, became one of the bases of Alberti's practice as a surveyor and an engineer: he adapted it, for example, to draw up his plan of Rome.[39] Alberti became proficient with such devices.[40] But this particular application of astronomical instrumentation to surveying problems was no departure from tradition. Taccola, for example, offered both careful instructions and vivid illustrations of the uses of a similar surveying instrument, in his treatises of the 1420s.[41] Alberti, in other words, was not innovative in every aspect of his engineering practice. But he did amass a wide range of skills, which he regarded with the fierce pride of possession natural in a literary man set loose in a world of instrument makers and surveyors. As late as the 1460s, in On Sculpture, Alberti vividly described, in a passing remark, the difficulty of recording with precision astronomical observations made at night with hand-held instruments.[42]

The style, as well as the substance, of Alberti's engineering work links it closely to that of Brunelleschi and other contemporaries. In On Painting, Alberti referred briefly to what he called "the demonstrations of painting, which our friends marveled at when we did them, and called them 'miracles of painting.' "[43] In his autobiography, Alberti described these miracles in detail, in the third person:

He wrote little books on painting, and in that art did unheard-of things, incredible to those who saw them, which he showed in a little box with a small opening. There you might have seen huge mountains, vast provinces, the immense round of the sea surrounding them, and regions so distant from the eye that sight was dimmed. He called these things "demonstrations," and they were such that expert and layman alike would insist that they saw, not painted things, but real ones in nature. There were two kinds of demonstrations, those he called diurnal and those he called nocturnal. In the nocturnal ones you would see the North Star, the Pleiades, Orion, and that kind of bright signs, and the dawning moon rising from the lofty summit of cliffs and heights, while the stars that appear before daybreak were shining brightly. In the diurnal demonstrations, the brilliance that appears after Homer's early-born dawn would brighten every part and illuminate the immense world far and wide.[44]

Alberti framed his discoveries not only in words, but also in a device that he made the centerpiece of a public show. By doing so, he subjected himself to what had become the standard test for innovative technologists and artists: a collective judgment based on a contest, usually held in the glare of open discussion before a panel of experts and patrons.[45]

From the early fifteenth century at the latest, contests decided the assignment of major Florentine projects like the doors of the Baptistery—the symmetrical twelfth-century church that stood in the center of Florence, across from the main entrance of the Cathedral, which was considered in the fifteenth century to be a converted Roman temple of Mars. The sources for the competition—fragmentary, biased, and in part contradictory—do not make the full course of events clear. But it seems that a number of goldsmiths offered proposals for the bronze relief doors that the church needed. Brunelleschi and Ghiberti were selected as semifinalists and were given bronze to make sample panels. A jury with thirty-four members, many of them craftsmen, decided the competition. It remains uncertain whether they simply gave the commission to Ghiberti, as he later claimed, or asked Brunelleschi and Ghiberti to share it, only to have the former turn them down. What is clear, however, is that those who hoped to make their mark in the arts—in this case, to make a permanent addition to an ideologically charged, central building, one that proved the noble Roman origins of Florence—had to be willing to give displays of their innovative techniques.[46]

Such exercises in technical showmanship were not the exclusive province of sculptors and painters. The engineers of the fourteenth and fifteenth centuries aimed their work deliberately at making dramatic, publicly accessible effects, which could establish reputations and win patronage. Dondi's astronomical escapement clock, which simulated the movement of the planets with geared mechanical models, was one of the sights of Padua. Brunelleschi became almost as famous for the flying mandorla, or almond-shaped panel, with which he raised a young man, representing Jesus in an Ascension Day play, to the roof of the Church of Santa Maria del Carmine, as for the hoists and other devices with which he reared the cupola of the Cathedral.[47] All of these displays appealed to two audiences at once: the smaller community of the competent, who could appreciate the subtle techniques by which they were executed, and the larger circle of citizens, who could be dazzled by their elegance, wit, and unexpectedness. Dondi, for example, declared that he had designed his clock both to give expert astronomers precise information and to help less expert individuals understand the planets' motion.[48] The theatrical engineering culture of the Quattrocento laid down the precedents that the more celebrated inventors of the next century followed when they created gardens and grottoes in which secret hydraulic devices soaked the unwary, or when they used a hidden bellows to inflate carefully washed bulls' intestines until they became enormous, transparent balloons that forced courtiers into corners.[49]

Public display was vital but dangerous. Only by showing a working model could an inventor assert his intellectual property rights, or an artist prove his ability to capture a biblical scene. But producing the model exposed its creator to the risk of ridicule or plagiarism—or both at the same time. Brunelleschi railed bitterly to his younger colleague Taccola: "Do not share your inventions with many, share them only with the few who understand and love the sciences." Some would criticize the inventor's work—only to steal it themselves some months or a year later. Others, thicker witted, would simply ridicule these new devices, saying to the engineer: "Please, shut up about these things, or everyone will think you are a beast."[50] Taccola, who listened respectfully to and echoed these complaints, apparently disagreed with Brunelleschi, since he did produce manuscript accounts of his inventions. But he too played a deliberate game of concealment with his readers, illustrating devices with deliberately imprecise, if charmingly executed, illustrations, and pacifying the reader with the remark that experts should not need further elucidation in any case.[51] It remains unclear to this day how the expert reader would have convinced a bull to deploy one of

4. Filippo Brunelleschi. The Sacrifice of Isaac. Museo Nazionale del Bargello, Florence. Alinari/Art Resource, NY.

5. Lorenzo Ghiberti. The Sacrifice of Isaac. Museo Nazionale del Bargello, Florence. Alinari/Art Resource, NY.

Taccola's military devices, a burning kettle that the animal was meant to hold in a harness as it charged an enemy army.[52]

Like Brunelleschi and Taccola, Alberti downplayed the element of display in his work as an engineer. In the autobiography, he remarked severely that he had "worked more on investigating these things than on making them known, for he was more attached to the service of mind than of glory."[53] But he nonetheless followed the self-dramatizing traditions of the engineers when he used his device to evoke wonder, as he himself said, from "expert and layman alike." He did the same, a few years later, in his *Games*, in which he described over and over again the "delight" that his surprising devices for making water clocks and drawing up plans of cities elicited from those he displayed them to.[54] Alberti's "miracles of painting" belonged to a highly particular, theatrical culture of technology, one shaped by the highly competitive environment in which engineers won and lost their commissions.

Alberti's visual device is sometimes described as a form of camera obscura, a device for projecting images. The text of the *Life*, however, does not support this analysis. It states that Alberti built "a small box with an opening," into which the onlookers peered. This was presumably a "show box"—a device that forced anyone using it to view an image from a set distance. Alberti's brief description of the device in *On Painting* follows a very precise statement that "no objects in a painting can appear like real objects unless they stand at a determinate distance from the viewer."[55] One should imagine, in other words, a box of modest size, with an eyepiece for viewing on one side and small images—perhaps painted on glass to admit light—on the opposite one: a device designed to ensure that the viewer sees the image from exactly the distance needed to make its illusion of three dimensions effective.[56]

This analysis suggests that Alberti's demonstration pieces would have been small—perhaps no larger than manuscript illuminations. Remarkably, a series of illuminations, carried out in the mid-fifteenth century and closely associated with one of Alberti's most memorable architectural projects, seems to record the demonstrations in visual as well as verbal detail. In 1449 the humanist Basinio of Parma came to Rimini, where he served as court poet. In a long poem, *Hesperis*, he celebrated the exploits of his master, Sigismondo Malatesta, finishing off with the creation of the Malatesta Temple: the radically innovative rebuilding of a medieval church, carried out to Alberti's design, which imposed a facade strongly resembling a Roman triumphal arch on a Christian church. The original manuscript of this commissioned epic stayed in Rimini and seems to have disappeared. But three copies survive, in Oxford, Paris, and the Vatican. All were illuminated by an artist named Giovanni da Fano, and a number of his miniatures—images that stand out strikingly from the norms of Italian manuscript painting—seem to illustrate Alberti's "miracles."[57] Four appear in the endpapers.

Giovanni's most famous miniature shows the Gothic cathedral of Rimini being clothed with Alberti's classical stone shell. The illuminator celebrated the skills and technologies of the building workers in intense Albertian detail. For the temple, if not for the smaller stones being shaped before it; he also used a single, strict perspective system: all lines perpendicular to the temple front converge on a vanishing point at the left side of the picture, just at the height of the central doorframe—a feature still unusual in an illumination in this period. Albertian art celebrated an Albertian structure—a neat trick for any artist.

Other miniatures innovated still more dazzlingly. One series represents ships at sea—a rare subject. The first recreates in minute detail the hull, sails, and rigging of an intact ship. The little roof that forms the center of the picture is a formal exercise in perspectival construction, a dramatic piece of drafting that recalls the trellis in Paolo Uccello's fresco of the drunkenness of Noah in the green cloister of Santa Maria Novella. The second shows a ship foundering, as seen from a dramatically low point of view. The illuminator pays special attention to the movement of the violent waves on the water's surface. Giovanni clearly took an interest in the technical details of shipbuilding and the movement of water—passions he shared with the Tuscan technologists. Brunelleschi tried to divert a river for military purposes and worked extensively both on naval technology and on waterside construction.[58]

Equally revealing is the artist's effort to solve that central problem of the early fifteenth century: the representation of the action of light itself. Alberti stated, in On Painting, that his "demonstrations of painting" could show how "rays of light, reaching the surface of water, are reflected upward and strike the beams of a house."[59] In Giovanni's image of the ship passing an island, the sun sends its rays directly down, producing shadows under the little roof and along the ship's side rail. At the same time, however, light reflected upward from the water brilliantly illuminates the ship's hull and the shore of the tiny island it passes. The water itself changes color dramatically where the hull passes through it.

Most striking of all, however, are two other images which apparently draw on the innovations of two of the most influential Florentine painters of the 1420s—painters whose work Alberti could well have seen in Rome. In one of them, Giovanni attacks an especially difficult technical problem— that of showing galleys, from a high viewpoint, sailing at a range of distances from the viewer. The solution he adopts is essentially the same one devised by Masaccio for representing a circular group of people in his *Tribute Money* fresco—a device that has been memorably christened "horizon-line iso-cephaly."[60] Alberti explained the point with a graphic example in *On Painting*: "in churches we see the heads of men walking about, moving at more or less the same height, while the feet of those further away may correspond to the knee-level of those in front of them."[61] Giovanni deftly applied this counterintuitive but vital illusionistic technique to the masts of the ships— as Fra Angelico, for example, did not do in his exactly contemporary image of *Scenes from the Life of Saint Nicholas*.

In a second image, where Sigismondo's army moves down a shore by night, Giovanni attacked the coloristic problem of representing a night sky. He adopted the conventions for representing both a starry night and the illumination of the scene taking place under it devised by Gentile da Fabriano. Giovanni worked with minute care to show the stars' reflection in the surface of the water and the stark, almost shadowless illumination given by the moon. The miniatures in this sequence, in other words, amount, like *On Painting* itself, to a partial summa of the discoveries of the Florentine 1420s— as they presented themselves to Alberti in Rome and then in Florence itself.

It seems reasonable on the face of it to connect these manuscripts to Alberti. They were produced with the official support of the brilliant despot who employed Alberti in and around Rimini, and their final, most glamorous illumination celebrated his masterpiece, the Malatesta Temple. But the evidence of the *Vita* clinches the case:

He drew great admiration from certain Greek captains, to whom the sea was well known, for when he showed them this artificial immensity of world through, as I have said, a little opening, and asked them what they saw there, this is how they responded: "Ah," said they, "we see a fleet of ships in the midst of the waves. It will be here by noon, unless that cloud to the East and that awful approaching storm stops them. We see, too, that the sea has grown wild, and a sign of danger are the rays of the sun too sharply reflected from the sea."[62]

6. Giovanni da Fano. View of the Malatesta Temple under construction. Oxford University, Bodleian Library.

Like Giovanni da Fano's illuminations in the *Hesperis*, Alberti's demonstrations represented ships approaching at a great distance, in a way that satisfied expert mariners. They offered a convincing portrait of an approaching storm—"the sea," cried the Greek captains, "has grown wild." And they made a serious effort to show how ocean water reflects light. The illuminations offer a series of historically specific perspectival and coloristic effects, which correspond closely to Alberti's description. They give us the best sense we can have of what Alberti showed through the peephole in his box.

More than any of his other practical projects, Alberti's show box offers a close parallel to Brunelleschi's work of the 1410s and 1420s. In those years, Brunelleschi—an architect and hence presumably an expert at such skills as surveying, making ground plans and elevations, and predicting the visual effect that a given structure would have on onlookers—carried out his own experiments on the same problems of representation that fascinated Alberti.

7. Baptistery, Florence.
Alinari/Art Resource, NY.

8. Palazzo Vecchio, Florence.
Alinari/Art Resource, NY.

He fashioned two panels, one representing the Baptistery and the other the Piazza della Signoria, in which a geometric picture space and careful use of converging lines created a spectacularly effective illusion of three dimensions in two. And he showed other artists what he had achieved by clever tricks—like making them look, through a hole at the vanishing point in his panel of the Baptistery, at the painting's image reflected in a mirror held before it at a predetermined distance—and then perhaps whipping the mirror away to reveal the real building behind it. Like Alberti's "miracles," Brunelleschi's demonstrations were dramatically staged on the steps of the Florentine Cathedral, facing the Baptistery, and in the Piazza della Signoria, two of the most historically and ideologically loaded spaces in Florence. Like Alberti's "miracles," Brunelleschi's demonstrations evidently caused some amazement, stimulating other artists to try to obtain the same effects. "Paolo Uccello and other painters came along later," Antonio Manetti recalled at the end of the century, "and wanted to copy and imitate" Brunelleschi's view of the Palazzo della Signoria. "I have seen more than one of these efforts and none was done so well as his." Above all, like Alberti, Brunelleschi transformed an artistic question—how to represent a building or a set of buildings effectively—into a technical problem—how to create a geometrical technique for producing visually convincing picture spaces.[63]

About the success of Alberti's "miracles of painting," we know only what he tells us (and what Giovanni da Fano shows us). But about Brunelleschi's, we know more. From the 1410s to the 1430s, methods like Brunelleschi's were applied to project after project by the very Florentine artists whom Alberti, according to his dedicatory letter, admired most. Ghiberti used them to dazzling effect in his second set of Baptistery doors, Donatello applied them brilliantly in his small stone reliefs, and Masaccio made them the basis of his experimental frescoes in Santa Maria Novella and the Carmine.[64] No wonder that Alberti, having written a geometrical treatise on how to create a realistic illusion of three dimensions in two—and having defined producing such illusions as the artist's central task—chose Brunelleschi as his first and ideal reader, and presumably as his judge and redeemer as well.

The argument about the fall and rise of culture that Alberti put forward in his dedication, for all its classic style, thus replayed discussions with which all literate engineers were familiar. It may well have reflected his effort, once again, to please and interest Brunelleschi. In general, engineers won prestige by introducing new ways of doing things, where craftsmen had won prestige by sticking to tradition. Their competitive demonstrations,

with their elaborate visual rhetoric of innovation, could succeed only if onlookers thought the results amazing. Engineering practice, in other words,
rested on the assumption that some kind of progress in the arts could take
place. Brunelleschi strongly believed this and saw his own work in many
fields as a powerful case in point. He unhesitatingly proposed new ways for
carrying out such enormous, frighteningly difficult projects as the dome of
the Florentine Cathedral. He stuck to his guns even when the servants of
the Operai, the committee in charge of the Cathedral works, twice carried
him bodily out of meetings, since the other masters declared him mad.[65] He
also took out the first patent ever issued for one of his devices, thereby both
securing his intellectual property and creating a still more powerful legal and
social technology at one and the same time.[66] Trademarks and patents developed rapidly in this period.[67] Evidently, intellectual property rights—and
the human ability to innovate that underpinned them—preoccupied ambitious Italian engineers and merchants. In a sense, after all, the assertion that
one could do what one's predecessors had not, and the demand for recognition of one's right to profit from one's own invention were two sides of
the same coin. Enlightened patrons realized this. In 1445, Leonello d'Este
wanted to attract to Ferrara Antoine Marin of Grenoble, a particularly gifted
engineer who specialized in mill wheels. Leonello praised Marin's work, as
"if not superior to that of those ancient makers of wheels, at least equal to
it." And he promised Marin housing, freedom from the gabelle, and a mo-
nopoly both on his wheels and on "any other new devices that he may discover, which do not fall within the normal methods."[68] For Alberti to
address Brunelleschi, on the subject of perspective, was to confront a reader
convinced of, even obsessed by, the legitimacy of the New. No wonder that
Alberti thought that progress in the arts might make a good talking point
with his sensitive, easily offended dedicatee.

Engineers were not the only ones to take an interest in questions of cultural movement and its direction. When Alberti argued that modern intellectuals need not be crippled by the burden of the past, he revived an issue
that had long worried not just Brunelleschi but many other Florentine intellectuals as well. Niccolò Niccoli, as we have seen, notoriously insisted that
no modern, not even Dante or Petrarch, could hope to write anything that
deserved comparison with the works of the ancients, and Leonardo Bruni
and others as notoriously contradicted him. In choosing the realm of technology to assert his counterclaim, Alberti put forward a thesis that other
humanists would defend in the papal curia and elsewhere. The peerless clas-

9. Lorenzo Ghiberti. Gates of Paradise. Baptistery, Florence. Alinari/Art Resource, NY.

10. Masaccio. The Tribute Money. Brancacci Chapel, Santa Maria del Carmine, Florence. Alinari/Art Resource, NY.

sicist Lorenzo Valla, for example, insisted that modern writers must do their utmost to master the syntax and usage of classical Latin, which he laid out in detail; yet he admitted that the escapement clocks, with their large bells, that sounded the hours in many Italian cities were a modern invention for which even he used a nonclassical word: *horologium*. It is at least possible, then, that Alberti learned from other scholars to think of technology as an area where the moderns had achieved more than the ancients.[69]

But learned engineers had already set precedents for Alberti's treatment of these problems—and for his juxtaposition of engineering and the visual and literary arts. Giovanni Dondi dell'Orologio, a close friend of Petrarch, taught medicine and astrology at Pavia and Padua in the fourteenth century. In his writing, Giovanni repeatedly addressed the question of whether the moderns could ever hope to match the ancients. Sometimes he took a positive view. In introducing his account of his planetary clock, for example, he pointed out that astronomy rested both on ancient authority—the work of Ptolemy—and on modern observation—the Arab and Latin astronomers of the Middle Ages.[70] In a letter to the Franciscan Giovanni Centueri of Cremona, however, Dondi struck a radically different pose. Centueri, like Bacon and many other scholastics, had praised modernity, insisting that the hard-edged philosophy and theology of the later medieval university was genuinely superior to anything the ancients had to offer. Dondi struck back, arguing, as a good classicist, that "our minds are of inferior quality" to those of the ancients. No modern poet could match Virgil, no modern historian could rival Livy; even the one limited group of intellects who "were together in one age, and whom Augustus saw" outshone all modern writers. Petrarch himself had admitted as much. Examining a composite manuscript in which his own *Bucolic Ode* was bound with Virgil's *Bucolics*, he remarked pungently, "In this book some grey rags are bound in with scarlet."

"The artistic products of ancient genius," Dondi continued, proved the same point, perhaps even more vividly.

I am speaking about ancient buildings and statues and sculptures, with other things of the sort. When some artists of this time scrutinize the products of that age carefully, they are struck with amazement. I knew a certain well-known worker in marble who was famous for his ability in that art among those whom Italy had at that time, especially in the creation of figures. . . . He used to say that sometimes, passing with his friends by a place [in Rome] where some

images of this sort could be seen, he had held back, looking in astonishment at their rarity, and forgetting his company, had stood still so
long that his companions had passed on five hundred steps and
more.[71]

No one has yet identified the classicizing artist Dondi described.[72] But the
general tenor of the document matters more, for present purposes, than its
truth to life or lack of it. Dondi, the most brilliant technologist of his time as
well as a learned scholar and skilled writer, had raised the same problems
that occupied Alberti half a century later. He had even drawn on classical
texts—in particular, the letters of the Stoic philosopher Seneca, who denounced the building works that he saw all around him in Imperial Rome as
a sign of decay.[73] Dondi's technically informed and erudite expression of cultural despair thus anticipated in many respects the way Alberti would frame
his dedication—though not, of course, the direction in which he would take
the arguments in question.

When Alberti raised issues of antiquity, authority, and creativity in his
letter, he remained within the realm of the professional engineers, one of
whom he claimed to be. Brunelleschi too may have pondered these problems: Antonio Manetti, in his late but sometimes well-informed biography,
explicitly raised the question of whether Brunelleschi "rediscovered or invented" his rules for perspective.[74] Alberti's passionate evocation of the new
art and architecture he encountered in Florence, in other words, was tailored not only to charm a learned réader but also to please a particular
unlearned one.

So was at least one aspect of the way Alberti described his own experiments. In the Italian, but not the Latin, version of On Painting, Alberti specified that he had carried out these "miracoli della pittura" in Rome—that is,
in the curia, rather than in the Florentine Cathedral workshop.[75] Alberti, in
other words, staged his most dramatic demonstrations before the less expert
Roman audience. To Brunelleschi, he described but did not reenact them.
He used them to establish his membership in a community of the technically competent, but he did not try to rival Brunelleschi's famous display
pieces with the Baptistery and the Palazzo della Signoria.

If Alberti saw himself first and foremost as an engineer, a number of features of his work On Painting that have long intrigued and puzzled historians
become much easier to account for. Alberti's effort to create a technical language, in both Latin and Italian, that was capable of describing processes as

complex as setting a vanishing point, laying out a floor or plaza that appeared to recede, and mastering the anatomy of the human body, closely resembled the literary efforts of engineers like Taccola. They also wrote books about their arts, as a way of raising their own status and that of the disciplines they practiced.[76] They worked bitterly hard not only to design particular devices but also to create a terminology that could clearly describe their construction and use.

Engineering and practical arts treatises took many forms, from Taccola's illustrations with brief captions (which were clearly designed above all to advertise his product) to Dondi's dense theoretical treatises (which provided mechanical drawings precise enough to enable his clock to be rebuilt in modern times). So too, the two surviving early treatises on painting, Cennino Cennini's handbook on painting and Alberti's treatise, reflect different approaches within a common enterprise. Cennini finished his book about a generation before Alberti composed On Painting. His work represented, for the most part, the end of the medieval tradition of craftsmen's manuals. He concentrated on the actual processes of painting—finding and preparing pigments and readying a plaster wall for fresco painting. Alberti, by contrast, emphasized the geometry of picture spaces and the rules of aesthetics. Cennini emphasized the role that hard physical work played in painting—as in all the crafts by which men, who inherited Adam's sinful state, had to earn their bread. Alberti saw painting as less laborious—and accordingly more noble—than sculpture, to say nothing of less intellectual crafts. Deeply though Cennini respected the artist's work and calling, he believed that Giotto, a past master, represented the culmination of the art. Alberti knew and admired Giotto's work, but he also held that progress could be and had been made since Giotto's time.[77]

Still, both writers agreed that painters were learned men. Indeed, Cennini underlined precisely this point at the beginning of his work. He argued there that poets, thanks to the knowledge they possessed, had the right to compose and connect whatever elements they pleased, "as their will dictates." In exactly the same way, the painter had the freedom to create a figure that was "half man, half horse, in accord with his imagination (fantasia)."[78] Here Cennini repeated a classical commonplace, the comparison between painting and poetry, and cited a recognizable, even prominent classical source: the Roman poet Horace's Art of Poetry. Like Brunelleschi and Taccola, Alberti and Cennini took different roads, but ones that passed through some of the same points. But Cennini treated painting as one of the many forms of work to which man was condemned after the Fall. His theological views were much closer to Dante's than to Alberti's—as was his emphasis on the supreme importance of "imagination" in poetry and painting.

The comparison with the engineering and practical arts tradition also suggests that Alberti's decision to write two texts, one in Italian and one in Latin, was not exceptional. Taccola, for example, produced his treatise *On Devices* in two versions. The Latin one survives, as Taccola wrote and illustrated it. But he also produced an Italian text. This has survived, not in its original form, but in many full and partial copies, made by artists and engineers who seem to have found it more accessible than the Latin.[79] Many later readers of Alberti, from the anonymous owner of one of his manuscripts in the sixteenth century to the art historian Michael Baxandall in the twentieth, have suggested that he aimed his Latin text primarily at learned readers and patrons of the arts, the Italian one primarily at artists and craftsmen.[80]

One bit of manuscript evidence suggests that the language barrier may not in fact have been high enough to keep out readers who came to the Latin text without a full training in humanist rhetoric. On 11 February 1476, Arnold of Brussels, a student of engineering and perspective, rose before dawn or stayed up all night, at Naples, in order to copy a shorter treatise, *Elements of Painting*, which Alberti drew up somewhat later than *On Painting*. Arnold had the work bound with treatises on optics, perspective and practical arithmetic, weights and measures—clear evidence that he associated the work with the world of engineering and applied mathematics.[81] Other readers who did not write Latin but studied Latin treatises on such subjects—for example, Lorenzo Ghiberti—could then equally well have read the Latin Alberti, especially when he dealt with problems on which they were experts.[82]

Still, it seems all but certain that Alberti wrote the Italian version for painters and other practitioners of the arts. In his prefatory letter to Brunelleschi, Alberti remarked that the architect's dome for the Cathedral proved that he had a "marvellous *ingegno*." *Ingegno*, like the Latin cognate word *ingenium*, had a number of meanings in this period.[83] But in Brunelleschi's world, as we have seen, it had two principal senses: the brilliance specific to the engineer, and the novel inventions that he created. Alberti's carefully chosen terminology reveals the particular set of associations he meant to evoke with the Italian version of his book.

At least one other early testimony confirms that *Della pittura* was meant for artists. Alberti's friend Girolamo Aliotti, a Benedictine writer and scribe from Arezzo who had many Florentine connections, read at some point an anonymous work *On the Art of Casting* in Italian. He asked a Florentine friend to inquire "among your painters and sculptors" who had written the work. Aliotti hoped that his friend might be able to provide a considerably more correct version of the text than the one he had; more specifically, he suggested that the author might have a Latin version. Finally, he expressed a natural suspicion: that the anonymous author might himself be "Signor Battista Alberti."[84] It seems clear that Aliotti believed that this text had much in common with *On Painting*. And that suggested that it might be available in two distinct versions—an Italian one, mostly read in artists' ateliers, and a Latin one, available through the normal humanist book—distribution network. Alberti very probably envisioned his book as circulating, in its two forms, among two different readerships—even if its real reception proved more complex than he had expected.

Further mysteries remain. It is unclear why Alberti—who provided illustrations for *Mathematical Games*, for his work *On Sculpture*, and for a short treatise, parallel to *On Painting*, on perspective—did not equip *On Painting* with the diagrams that would have made its densely technical first book far more accessible.[85] It is also uncertain how Brunelleschi reacted to the book when he read it (a question to which we will return in the next chapter). But it does seem clear that Alberti considered his new allegiance to the world of craft and art a permanent one.

In fact, soon after Alberti completed *On Painting*, with its proud declaration of his own position as a practicing artist, he also completed an artistic project, in which he applied the technical skills he had mastered in the 1430s to one of the tasks that most captivated him: creating a powerful, splendid image of his elusive self. In his autobiography, Alberti praised his own ability not only to paint but to sculpt—again, at a level convincingly accessible not only to the expert but to the uninitiated young:

> He used to invite his friends and have with them endless discussions of literature and philosophy; and to those friends he would also dictate little works while he painted the portrait or made a wax model of one of them. In Venice he modeled the faces of his friends in Florence whom he had not seen for a year and whole months. He used to ask some young boy whether he recognized the image he was painting, and if it was not recognizable to a child, he denied that the

painting was a work of true art. He strove to render his own features and characteristic appearance, so that, by the painted or modeled image, he might be already known to strangers who summoned him.[86]

Once again, Alberti brought off a "miracle" in public. Most historians identify the large portrait plaquette of Alberti now in the Kress Collection of the National Gallery of Art as one of the images he produced with such impressive facility.[87] (See the frontispiece.)

The plaquette is very large, some twenty centimeters high, and an irregular oval in shape. It shows its maker with all the energy of early middle age, with a powerful profile and strongly marked, determined eyes and mouth. Classically dressed, he clearly makes a claim to high social and intellectual status.[88] To the left of his face appears the winged eye that Alberti used as an emblem: to the right, his first initial and the first three letters of his second name, L. Bap, set off by tiny variations on the larger eye. It is, in many ways, a remarkable artistic achievement: the first free-standing self-portrait by a Renaissance artist, the first to clothe the artist as a Roman, and an image far more individual than many portraits by the advanced artists of the time, like those of the donors in Masaccio's *Trinity* fresco. Above all, it appropriates for an artist the form of the profile bust, one "that, for the early Renaissance, encoded majesty and might, suggesting the sitter's personal majesty and the continuity of his dynasty."[89]

· Like Alberti's demonstrations, his portrait medal combines recognizable ingredients in a novel way. Humanists regularly used portraits of themselves as a form of advertising. Set in a large decorative title page, inserted in the first initial of the text, or set out as an independent image, the humanist's portrait asserted his prominence as author even as his position on the page often subordinated him, literally, to the larger and more imposing figure of his patron. Such portraits served exactly the function Alberti claimed for his medal: they made their subjects' images vivid to readers, including potential patrons, who had never seen them.[90]

In choosing this particular classical form for his medal, moreover, Alberti deliberately aimed to please local tastes in Florence and farther north. From the beginning of the fourteenth century, northern Italian scholars had studied Roman imperial coins and gems to obtain vivid images of the heroic and horrific emperors the historians described. The Veronese antiquary Giovanni de Matociis illustrated his history of the empire with stiff but elegant drawings of a great many imperial profiles, derived from coins. Petrarch, a little later, began to compare literary with numismatic evidence. He complained that if Gordian had really been as handsome as the *Historia Augusta* claimed, "he must have had a bad sculptor."[91] Coins and gems deeply interested the Florentine and northern Italian circles Alberti frequented during his early years in Florence and Ferrara. The very influential scholar and translator Ambrogio Traversari was a commanding presence at the Church Council of Ferrara/Florence, which Alberti attended. He discussed coins and gems with the adventurous antiquary Cyriac of Ancona in Venice in 1433—including what Traversari described to Niccoli as a "supremely elegant" image of Scipio the Younger engraved on an onyx.[92] According to Vespasiano, the Florentine intellectual Niccolò Niccoli became a semiprofessional connoisseur of such antiques. No wonder that he was the first to see the value of one of the most celebrated ancient gems in the Renaissance, the Medici cornelian; Ghiberti reset this and tried, unsuccessfully, to interpret it.[93] Alberti's adaptation of a Roman portrait cameo or gem was aptly designed to impress local antiquarian circles, whose members, as Niccoli's case shows, appropriately shared his interest in the work of classicizing artists and engineers.

Alberti's choice of the winged eye as an accompanying emblem was also carefully calculated. He saw symbolic images as encompassing profound messages in powerful, abbreviated form, a notion he developed in one of the Latin works that he circulated among a learned readership as well as in the concrete form of his medal. In a dinner piece entitled "*Convelata*" or "Veiled Sayings," Alberti quoted and interpreted a long series of pithy aphorisms. He ascribed these to Pythagoras and other ancient sages, thus helping to start what became one of the most successful literary fashions of the Renaissance, the effort to collect and comment on short sayings that crystallized central tenets of philosophy.[94] Alberti's glosses on these remarks were clearly designed both to moralize and to display the cleverness of the interpreter, whom he described as a "philosopher"—like himself or Thales, presumably. At one point, for example, the philosopher explains a series of Pythagorean *symbola*, none of which has a very obvious moral sense:

> I interpret the saying "Don't pierce men's footprints with a sword" to mean that we must not tear at a person's memory with hard words. I interpret the saying "Don't place an entire bundle in the fire" to mean that we must not risk all our wealth together in one critical venture. I interpret the saying "When you leave your house, scratch your brow; when you return, scratch the back of your head" to mean

that in the morning we must rouse our caution and diligence for all our undertakings, and that in the evening we must mentally review and criticize whatever we have done during the day.

Alberti recognized that these compressed symbolic sayings could prove obscure. Readers might find it hard, or impossible, to connect the high sentiments the philosopher uncovered with the paradoxical commandments into which he read them. Accordingly, he began his text with a formal defense of such philosophical allegories. In fact, he argued, they were more effective pedagogically than more open teachings. Their striking form could fix them and the morals they taught in the memories of hearers and readers:

> I wouldn't want you to think that such sayings originated in the doting of old men, simply because they seem to smack of superstition. They offer us noble and elegant principles for living which, in my judgment, the greatest philosophers chose to utter in veiled fashion, so to speak. In this way, people would be struck with awe and listen more attentively; and when in their daily life they came across things mentioned in such precepts, they would fix in their memory these erudite counsels of the philosophers. This method of teaching was so highly regarded by the ancients that some of them even promulgated veiled laws. Hence Numa Pompilius, king of the Romans, ordered priests to clench their fists when celebrating rites at a fountain. Imitating the philosophers, he implied that these primitive sacrifices would please the gods most if performed in secrecy.[95]

Here Alberti sketched what would become a besetting passion of many learned writers in the later fifteenth and sixteenth centuries. Practitioners of a "Platonic pedagogy," influential scholars like Erasmus and Andrea Alciati, held that moral teachings cast in a brief, memorable, and slightly cryptic form—like the "Adages" that Erasmus wrote and commented on, or the "Emblems," a combination of picture and words that Alciati devised—would stick to the memories and affect the conduct of the young far more effectively than more open, conventional morality. The poet and scholar Angelo Poliziano and the eclectic, radical philosopher Giovanni Pico della Mirandola devoted long passages to discussing, elucidating—and questioning the use of—pagan mysteries of this same kind. In this case at least, Alberti had developed the foundations of what would become a standard new genre of Latin writing.[96]

Symbols called out for visual as well as verbal embodiment. In the dinner piece that Alberti dedicated to the travails of his counterpart Philoponius, the artist's wares were rejected as "vulgar." The works in question were not texts in any normal sense—not even the sort of "veiled sayings" that Alberti's "philosopher" explained. Rather, they were rings, which Philoponius had both made and engraved with symbols, and which the text described in detail:

> The next ring, of crystal, depicts the vane by which sailors observe the winds. See the letters to each side: AS.IT.BEARS. On the next ring, the fairest of all, there is an unbroken circle. Within it is inscribed YOURSELF.TO.YOU.AND.TO.GOD. Outside the circle, there is a hook and blazing flame.

Counsel (one of the beings who tried to help and guide the frustrated artist) makes clear that here too, Alberti had meant to teach vital lessons about the power of fortune and the limited autonomy of the human will:

> Like sailors tossed amid stormy events and rocky circumstances, we must be cautious argonauts. As the times dictate, we must change the setting of our sails and seek refuge with dignity or chart a safe course through the waves. The sailors' vane is not moved by itself; rather, driven by the winds and breeze, it yields and follows their movements willingly and without resistance. Some winds are breezes, some tempests. We may liken the breezes to our friends' advice and counsels, and the tempests to our grievous misfortunes. Hence, we must not waver or be inconstant. Rather, we must yield without obstinacy to the course of events and to the advice of friends, and we must patiently allow ourselves to be swayed from our pride in our opinions and resolves. Take this ring. There is nothing more capacious, more whole, or more durable than the circle. At every point it is perfectly suited to repelling blows, and its motion is the freest of all figures. We must remain within the safe and free circle of reason, that is, within humanity. For virtue is bound and tied to humanity, and God to virtue, which proceeds from God.

Genius (another counselor) plays the role of devil's advocate, in this case not challenging the allegorical structure that Counsel rears but demanding even more details, which Counsel readily supplies—while at the same time arguing that they are less important than those explicated in the first place:

> You are in too much of a hurry, Counsel. In striving to be brief, you are incomplete. What about the hook and the flame? And on the fourth ring [actually, the fifth], you forgot to explain the meaning of the candelabrum.
>
> COUNS. These are minor details. On that ring, the stable and upright candelabrum inclines toward neither side but shines in all directions, lighting all. Thus, we should not seem to love one person or another more than universal virtue.[97]

In "Rings," Alberti found a way to fuse his belief in visual presentations of profound truths with his affection for provocative puzzles. Here too, he referred to, and perhaps helped to popularize, a newly fashionable way of thinking about antiquity. Just a few years before he wrote, the Florentine traveler Cristoforo Buondelmonti had brought back from the Aegean the late antique Greek text on Egyptian hieroglyphs by Horapollo, which took the Egyptian characters as a symbolic language and offered explanations for a considerable number of them. At the same time, Poggio and Niccoli, working through the newly discovered text of the Roman historian Ammianus Marcellinus, read his detailed description of the Egyptian hieroglyphs found on an obelisk in Rome. As Poggio and others walked the Roman streets, they looked with more and more interest at the curious figures of birds and animals that decorated the fallen obelisks by the tomb of Augustus and speculated about the meanings of this ancient, profound picture language. Taking their cue from Horapollo, they decided that the Egyptians had expressed concepts in a direct, visual way, since each character in their language not only referred to something but represented it.[98] Alberti, in "Rings," evidently set out to create a modern counterpart to the ancient hieroglyphs, a language in which visual symbols, connected with brief, cryptic texts, directly represented moral lessons: an optical language for philosophy.

In adding to his image of himself a winged eye and the mysterious question *Quid tum?* ("What then?"), Alberti once more showed himself a dedicated follower of the most up-to-date intellectual fashion—one he himself had helped to create. The exact meaning of Alberti's emblem remains elusive: the eye could represent, as Alberti suggested in his dinner piece

"Rings," the swiftness, glory and universal vigilance of God, or it could claim as much for the godlike creative artist. Or it could evoke both God and the godlike creator at once, as symbols can, offering the onlooker provocation for continued thought rather than a single message that could be put in words. Alberti's motto seems to be a quotation from Virgil, with which he tried to make light of his illegitimate birth. But it could also be a Ciceronian expression of his own defiance of the opposition he had so often met. In any event, the medal fused classical traditions with Florentine fashions, scholarly and aesthetic, to create a modern symbolic language.[99]

Presumably, Alberti modeled the head in wax and then had it cast: two large flaws, one on the neck and the other running up the cheek past the temple, suggest that errors took place at some point in the handling of the materials. More serious mistakes certainly affected his treatment of his own head. Alberti crowded the image onto its irregularly shaped plaquette, not making it part of a harmonious composition with the eye and inscription, as professional medalists regularly did in the late 1430s and 1440s. He also left its modeling very flat: though the elements of the profile are carefully caught and strongly rendered, the planes of the face and of the skull beneath the skin are not even sketchily indicated. Alberti's ear appears in almost full re-lief—but it therefore strangely dominates the composition as a whole.

These flaws have led some distinguished connoisseurs to insist on the "dilettantish" quality of the medal.[100] Alberti himself might not have ob-jected to this description. In the *Life*, as we have already seen, he explicitly said that he had modeled and dictated at the same time. In *On Painting* he insisted, "Sculpture is easier and surer than painting . . . relief is more easily found by sculpture than by painting."[101] He also suggested that a form of por-traiture that did not emphasize the underlying structure of the face was like-lier to prove attractive than one that delved too deeply into crags and wrinkles. And he reserved special praise for images in which "the surfaces are so joined together that pleasing lights pass gradually into agreeable shad-ows and there are no very sharp angles."[102] These comments suggest that Al-berti did not set out to produce a profoundly revealing image of his own face, in the manner of Donatello. Rather, he produced an exercise in facility—a self-portrait that revealed its creator as much in the rapidity and ease with which he had clearly made it as in the features it depicted. It seems possible indeed that Alberti, the experimenter in vision and reflection, used a me-chanical method to capture his own silhouette. Vasari saw in the house of Palla Rucellai a self-portrait by Alberti, made with the aid of a mirror.[103]

Accounts of artists as self-created (like similar accounts of writers) often distinguish, implicitly or explicitly, between the artist's effort to project a particular image of the self and his actual practices. Alberti's medal challenges this distinction: its making, one might say, forms part of its matching. His *ingegno*—the plaquette—reveals the *ingegno*—brilliance—of the man who was both its subject and its maker.[104]

Alberti's medal clearly anticipated, and may have served as a source for, the portrait medals of princes and scholars that two professional artists he knew well, Pisanello and Matteo de' Pasti, would produce in the 1440s and 1450s. Unlike the later medals, Alberti's portrait had only one side. But it resembled the medals in portraying its subject in two complementary ways: visibly, through his physical portrait, and spiritually, through a carefully chosen emblem, of the sort that appears on the reverse of later medals. De' Pasti's medal for the great teacher Guarino of Verona, for example, represented a scholar in heroic attitude and Roman dress on its obverse, and on its reverse the elegant figure of a naked young man, standing, in a balanced posture, on the top of a fountain. Alberti's emphasis on the profile view as the appropriate one for a heroic head may also have had a powerful impact, on painters as well as medalists. His profoundly impressive silhouette looks forward to some of the canonical heroic images of the mid-fifteenth century, like the magnificent hatchet profile of Federigo da Montefeltro.[105] It also represents the most radical of rebuttals to the vivid, ghastly portrait of the

11. Matteo de' Pasti. Portrait Medal of Guarino of Verona, 1374–1460, Humanist, ca. 1446. Samuel H. Kress Collection, © 2000 Board of Trustees, National Gallery of Art, Washington.

scholar as social leper that Alberti had sketched in his treatise *On the Advantages and Disadvantages of Letters.*

Alberti's medal gave physical embodiment, crisp and novel artistic form, to his and other engineers' and artists' new claims to elevated social and intellectual status. At the time, the known ancient images on coins and cameos represented rulers, not writers; they celebrated courage in their profiles, not erudition and eloquence. So did modern reproductions of them in manuscripts. In deciding that modern intellectuals also deserved to be made eternal in bronze, Alberti gave the ancient form a radically new function. He used it to represent the artist, and the intellectual, as a hero—an example that later artists would follow, both literally and creatively. Yet he also used the emblematic component of his self-portrait to emphasize the impossibility of producing a visual image adequate to representing a scholar's mind—a problem later to be explored by Dürer and many others. He thus gave birth to two of the enduring, paradoxical enterprises of Renaissance art. And he did so by creating a form of art that was both classical and modern, both traditional and innovative.

Alberti's practical work, like his writing, consistently reveals his unwillingness to make a text or image entirely from traditional ingredients. Rather, he combined these with the novelties that he grasped in each of his new environments. In claiming to be Brunelleschi's colleague, he tied the Italian engineering tradition to the particular accomplishments of Florentine artists as well as to his own prowess as an observer and writer. In showing off his own prowess as an inventor, he combined his own work on perspective and the properties of light with the discoveries of Masaccio and Gentile. But in order to explain the significance of what he had done, he crafted an erudite text, building on Dondi's writing and his own classical reading to create a new, powerful set of images about the progress of the arts. When devising the parts he wished to play, Alberti consistently combined the materials he had brought with him with techniques that he had only just encountered.

Even in his most powerful works as technician and artist, Alberti did not seek to rival the artists around him. Rather, he emphasized his own individuality and offered them provocation, at one and the same time. He succeeded, clearly, in both enterprises. Alberti demonstrated his mastery of the Italian technologists' methods and accomplishments by his "miracles of painting"—but he showed these off discreetly, in Rome and Venice rather than in Florence. He established himself less as an artist than as a unique figure in the world of the arts: one who could speak both from the outside and the inside. As he did so, he found that he could move freely in the elevated social and artistic circles where he hoped to remain. The medalists' use of his innovations provides concrete evidence of his success in positioning himself. And positioning, for Alberti, was a creative act, which sometimes changed the very arts that he observed and criticized.

In the end, as Alberti's friend Landino remarked after his death, he was less a lion than a chameleon—a creature whose colors continually changed to match those of the protean backgrounds he explored. When the humanist set out to write about the arts, he did so as one who had tried to learn their nature from the inside. The penetration, brilliance, and originality with which he fitted himself to new environments emerge nowhere more clearly than in the treatise on painting to which his dedicatory letter to Brunelleschi served as a prelude.

I V

ON PAINTING:
ALBERTI AND THE ORIGINS
OF CRITICISM

In late September and early October 1433, the antiquarian Cyriac of Ancona visited Florence. A skillful observer, Cyriac entered vivid records and fresh, awkward drawings of much of what he saw into the "commentaries," or notebooks, that he carried with him on his travels. Cyriac knew at first hand some of the most spectacular works of ancient art and architecture, from Naples and Rome to Alexandria, Cyzicus, and Constantinople.[1] But like the book collector Cardinal Bessarion and other well-informed travelers, he found the built world of his own age equally impressive.

Cyriac saw that the Florence of the early fifteenth century was undergoing a revolution in architecture and sculpture. He took a special interest in the huge new cupola that Brunelleschi was raising over the Cathedral; the architect himself showed Cyriac his work in progress. As a passionate antiquary, Cyriac naturally also visited the Baptistery, which he, like most Florentines, took to be an ancient temple of Mars converted into a Christian church. What struck him most about the building, however, was not its antique structure but its "three very beautifully sculptured bronze doors depicting sacred histories, partly the handiwork of the great artist, Nencio [Ghiberti]."[2]

The choices Cyriac made, as he inspected and recorded the Florentine artistic scene, reveal that he genuinely made an art of traveling. A precise and selective observer, he pulled out and followed two or three threads from the colorful fabric of Florentine craft production; and he chose them in a way that reflected careful thought about what he saw and heard. In later years, Cyriac recounted to his friend Francesco Scalamonti how he had seen "the fine great Church of Santa Reparata lifting its dome to the sky, a marvelous building which he thoroughly inspected under the guidance of the most eminent architect, Filippo, along with its highly decorated marble campanile." And he made clear more than once that his interests had included both ancient and modern art forms—as well as the innovative sculptors who, like him, were involved in a scholarly and artistic effort to reclaim the classics: "He also saw in the houses of Donatello and Ghiberti many statues, both antique pieces and their own modern works in bronze and marble."[3]

Brunelleschi, Ghiberti, and Donatello were far from the only recognized artisans who were producing works of high quality in Florence, and their innovative styles did not win the interest of all well-informed customers. Masaccio and Masolino, working on frescoes in the 1420s, had carried out pictorial innovations that closely resembled the work of the sculptors in crucial respects. Masaccio's fresco of the chapel of the Trinity in Santa Maria Novella, for example, created a powerful illusion of a three-dimensional space, using perspective techniques like those applied by Donatello in his relief sculpture of the 1430s. But other successful painters—like Gentile da Fabriano, who also enjoyed great esteem in the Florence of the 1420s, before he moved to Rome—impressed their clients just as much with very different practices. Experiments in reproducing a great variety of textures and figures, elaborate play with light, and rich ornamentation, rather than the austerely technical innovations of a Masaccio, induced Florentines to appreciate Gentile. This variety in tastes and accomplishments, moreover, was only natural. A generation after Cyriac first saw the city, Florence had 84 specialist woodcarving and intarsia studios, 54 ateliers doing decorative work in marble and other stones, and 44 gold- and silversmiths. (By way of comparison, 70 butchers and 66 spice merchants met the more practical needs of the Florentine population.) Within any given craft, projects and practices varied widely. Painters' workshops, for example, produced everything from enormous, innovative frescoes to modest, readymade painted wooden wedding chests (*cassoni*, a Florentine specialty). A wide range of styles competed, in architecture and sculpture as well as painting.[4] It took a well-informed observer, with a trained connoisseur's eye and an ear open to studio chat, to identify the artists who were making something new by confronting Florentines with the double shock of brilliant invention and radical classicism.

Alberti first came to Florence a few years before Cyriac, in all probability. He returned in the train of Pope Eugenius IV, not long after Cyriac's visit. He too arrived as a well-trained observer with honed visual skills as well as a refined Latin style. And he too, as we have seen, eloquently described the visual impact of the new buildings and artworks that he encountered in the city of his ancestors. It is especially revealing that Cyriac, independently of Alberti, connected Brunelleschi with Donatello and Ghiberti. Apparently, both men reported not their own idiosyncratic views but what they had heard and been shown in the studios. Radical differences in style separate these artists from one another, at least in the eyes of modern viewers schooled in art-historical distinctions. In the 1430s, however, they seem to have been viewed—or even to have described themselves—as members of a single avant-garde. Alberti's canon of new artists was historically grounded, a fact that has important consequences for the interpretation of On Painting. The book can help us see the art of its time through contemporary eyes.

Like Cyriac, Alberti believed that common concerns and interests linked a whole group of especially innovative artists, for all their individual differences. Like Cyriac, he took a special interest in the relation between modern art and classical models. Like Cyriac, finally, he saw in Brunelleschi's dome an achievement of a special kind, a work so staggering in its size and difficulty as to claim primary attention from any informed visitor. Evidently, an elective affinity connected well-informed scholars like Cyriac and Alberti to artists like Brunelleschi and Ghiberti.

But where Cyriac recorded and later described what he saw, Alberti felt inspired to offer a comprehensive historical and cultural interpretation of the Florentine scene. In the letter to Brunelleschi, he treated the work of a set of artists as virtually canonical: as showing that history itself had changed direction. Nature, far from showing signs of exhaustion as the end of time approached, could still produce men—and men things—greater than anything the world had experienced before. In the text that the letter accompanied, the Italian text of Alberti's book On Painting, he did even more: he provided the first modern manual for painters, the first systematic modern work on the arts. The affinity between a kind of art and a kind of observer inspired the writing of a manifesto.

Alberti's little book stands as a crisp and vivid historical monument to one of the legendary moments in the history of art and letters. In the mid-1430s, scholars from all of Italy descended on Florence to read the newest discoveries of Poggio, the manuscript hunter; to hear Traversari's learned discourses; and to see the dazzling range of new buildings, statues, and paintings that Florentine artists had created. The return of Cosimo de' Medici from exile in 1433–34 enabled many other members of Florentine patrician families who had strong interests in the visual arts to come back to their native city. And preparations for the Church Council of Ferrara/Florence, which met from 1438 onward, brought distinguished churchmen and their retinues from Europe and beyond to Florence as well.[5]

At this exciting moment, when Florence's intellectual circuits were already overheated by a surplus of new messages, Alberti used the tools of the humanists to describe, and to try to shape, the work of the artists. He knew very well that he was doing something new. The most elaborate ancient text on the arts was the Natural History of the elder Pliny, an encyclopedic treatment of the marvels of nature and human industry that traced in detail the development of painting and sculpture, and that had been a favorite source for medieval and earlier Renaissance scholars in search of information about the arts (and much else).[6] Alberti brusquely dismissed his ancient predecessor: "I am not writing a history of painting, like Pliny, but a completely new treatment of the art. So far as I have seen, there are nowadays no extant ancient texts on this."[7] Where Pliny had told stories—luscious, pointed stories—Alberti would offer systematic, coherent, and detailed principles of painting (and would steal as he liked from the Natural History anyhow, in order to give vivid examples of what he had in mind).[8] In his treatment of color, similarly, he made clear that he would not offer detailed instructions on where to find the best pigments, of the sort provided by Vitruvius, the Roman writer on architecture—the highly local, practical information that Cennini lavished on his readers.[9] Rather, he offered a theoretical discussion of the scale of colors and their use in painting. No wonder that this first artistic manifesto of the modern world, and the milieu of excited and articulate public debate in which Alberti wrote it, have sometimes reminded modern readers of the critical texts on painting that Baudelaire and others composed in the glass-walled, brightly lit cafés of Paris in the age of Baron Haussmann. Alberti wrote a cosmopolitan text about a metropolitan society and culture. He not only listened to the new art talk and examined the new art; he set out to give both a durable written form.[10]

Yet the analogy between the modernism of Alberti's Florence and that of Manet's Paris has only limited validity. Their aesthetic and professional situations and concerns differed radically. Alberti set out to transform painting from a traditional craft into a learned art. The essence of the painter's work, he insisted, did not lie in the value and elegance of the materials he used— the criterion on which Cennini, who saw himself as aiding the painter to master a traditional craft, insisted.[11] The painter's skilled hand and cultivated intellect, not the expensive pigments on his palette or the gold leaf on his shelves, defined his achievement—an austere dismissal of mere luxury that has many parallels in Alberti's other works of this period on social and moral questions. To train his mind and hand to produce the effects that gold leaf and fine ultramarine could not, moreover, the painter had to master a theory as well as a whole range of skills subordinated to it. As Alberti described them, they became canonical in studio practice and formal training.[12]

The artist's central technical goal, Alberti explained, was to create a particular kind of illusion: "to draw with lines and paint in colors on a surface any given bodies, in such a way that at a fixed distance and with a certain, determined position of the centric ray, whatever you see represented seems to stand out in relief and exactly to resemble the bodies in question."[13] If successful, the painter's achievement would have dramatic effects, especially on his subject: "Painting possesses a truly divine power in that not only does it make the absent present (as they say of friendship), but it also represents the dead to the living many centuries later, so that they are recognized by spectators with pleasure and deep admiration for the artist. . . . Through painting, the faces of the dead go on living for a very long time."[14] To attain these high ends, the painter must carry out a whole series of subsidiary tasks. He must learn, using the rules of optics and a particular set of geometric techniques, to construct a convincingly three-dimensional picture space. Onto this stage he must bring three-dimensional, volumetric bodies, whose skin clearly covers bones and muscles and is covered in turn by garments that move, like real ones, in the passing currents of the air. He must pose these bodies in solid, believable postures, always placing the hollow of a figure's throat, for example, vertically above the ball of the foot on which its weight rests. Finally, he must direct them as they act out spatially, emotionally, and historically consistent stories, which will automatically inspire an onlooker with the proper emotions—emotions that the painter himself has felt beforehand. As always, Alberti found extremes threatening and tried to find a mean.[15] In this case as in others, the ancient language of rhetoric, which Alberti spoke so well, provided the terms and tools he needed. The painter must achieve enough "variety" and "copiousness" to give his picture life and movement, rather than make it simply crowded and confused.[16]

To produce this synthetic treatment of the painter's task, Alberti drew on his own expertise, both as a humanistic scholar trained in rhetoric and as an engineer experienced in dealing with the physical world. He also made an intensive study of the Florentine artists who interested and challenged him most. Alberti did not describe any current work of art in detail—a decision that has disappointed many modern readers in search of period responses to Renaissance art. But he repeatedly drew on features of current artistic practice and existing critical terminology, even as he called for the creation of what would be a new art—one not identical with any form of painting practiced in the Florence he knew. Finally, he devised what amounted to a new social model for artistic life and practice—one appropriate to the standing of the new, learned artist, whom he saw not as a mere craftsman, who followed traditional recipes, but as the practitioner of a demanding learned discipline. In doing so, Alberti imagined the ideal artist as a figure who shared features both with erudite, creative engineers and with the literate, critical milieu of humanist writers and critics. The new artist that he wished to call into existence represented a combination and transformation of existing types.

Alberti, as we have already seen, knew the world of humanist Latinity, the formal art of prose composition, intimately before he arrived in Florence. In a series of classic studies, art historians have shown that he used assumptions and metaphors long established in rhetoric, the central humanist discipline of which he was himself a master practitioner, to reframe the painter's art, and that later critics followed him in doing so. When Alberti insisted that the central value of painting lies in the emotions that it can provoke, he clearly recalled the rhetorical tradition. Writers on rhetoric from Aristotle onward had always emphasized, as Alberti did, the psychology of speakers and listeners. They had always defined good speech as effective and affective: the best speech could move hearers to right action by playing on their emotions. Alberti's definition of painting as an affective art would remain a central theme in writing about the arts, discussed and developed for centuries to come.[17]

The analogies between painting and writing, moreover, were not limited to the general level of goals. Alberti used as one of his models the treatise

The Education of the Orator by Quintilian. This comprehensive, detailed work, written in the first century C.E., had circulated in the Middle Ages, for the most part, in mutilated form. Poggio discovered a complete text in 1416 in the Swiss monastery of St. Gall.[18] In fact, Alberti followed Quintilian, through much of his work, point by point, in order to produce an introductory work on painting as thorough, consistent, and complete as his ancient forerunner's—though he also drew on Cicero's *On Invention* and *Brutus* and on a wide range of other texts from the literary tradition.[19] The ancient writers on oratory had set out to produce what they called a "good man skilled in speaking" (*bonus homo dicendi peritus*), a man both trained in effective political speech and equipped with historical and moral training, one who spoke well and wisely. Alberti, similarly, drew up a manual for the training of a *bonus homo pingendi peritus*, and in it he described the art, its practitioner, and his education in full detail.

Alberti was no purist: he made as extensive use of Horace, who offered rules for the composition of poetry, as he did of Quintilian, and he drew no sharp distinction between the two. But he saw poetry, for the most part, in generally rhetorical terms—as a formal art of composition, with precise rules that each practitioner must learn. In doing so, he followed a tradition well established in his own time, one that grew from deep roots in the culture of ancient schools and commentators. Ancient poets had often made analogies between the verbal and the visual arts: *ut pictura poesis*, wrote Horace, quoting the Greek poet Simonides and quoted in turn by everyone else: "poetry is like painting."[20] Modern scholars from Petrarch onward had adapted this and other texts to fit modern conditions, drawing elaborate parallels between the effects of painting, for example, and those of effective language. Even Cennini, the Florentine artist who devoted most of his work to the discussion of highly practical questions about the preparing of walls and the making of colors, quoted Horace to support the view that an artist had to be able, like nature herself, to create new beings in his imagination—a partial parallel to Alberti's new theory.[21]

One principle of ancient rhetoric in particular played a central role in Alberti's work: that of decorum. Rhetoric, in the ancient world, was an art of the moment and the situation. The orator must always speak in ways that fitted his own age and position, the subject he had to deal with, and the audience he addressed. Words, images, and gestures not chosen in this way, however attractive they might seem in themselves, would not move the audience and achieve the orator's practical end. The effective orator consistently portrayed himself, his clients, and his enemies as recognizable types, whose actions, just or unjust, matched their known identities and characteristics. Persuasion was effected by skillful manipulation of conventions, within a cultural framework, a detailed regime of propriety, that the speaker shared with his audience.[22] Alberti applied this principle to painting—and found it so flexible that it supplied him with much of the framework that gave his work coherence.

Decorum—the term usually used for this canon—required that the painter make each member of a given body fit the rest, in age, texture, size, and color; that each body present in a painting play a part in the story to be told; that each gesture made have the "sweetness and grace" appropriate to the art. When Alberti insisted that the artist know not only the surface of the human body but also its anatomy, he argued that this was required not only by the need to reproduce three-dimensional reality but also by the literary principle of decorum. Failure to observe anatomical correctness would lead to breaches in the coherence of the work as a whole, as the artist assigned inappropriate members or expressions to figures in his work: "In the composition of members, special attention should go to seeing to it that the members correspond neatly with one another"—a principle that, Alberti explained, could be applied only by an artist willing to study not only the surfaces of the body but the bone and muscle beneath them as well. Alberti never sounded more practical, more wedded to the direct study of nature, than when he argued that the artist must treat a human body as a machine. Each motion of an arm, he explained, must be balanced by a countervailing motion of the opposed foot. Even in this case, however, he made clear that the originally literary theory of decorum motivated his demand. Alberti analyzed the body as a mechanism because he wanted to show the artist how to avoid excesses in the depiction of moving arms and feet.

The analogy between rhetoric and painting, in other words, gave Alberti much more than an attractive conceit to work with. It also provided him with an intellectual framework and a formal vocabulary. These enabled him to discuss, in an orderly and coherent way, many problems of representation that would otherwise have been very difficult even to formulate in words—and to describe, in general and abstract terms, the concrete innovations of the artists he knew. In his analysis of the portrayal of motion, for example, Alberti took from Quintilian a classification of the seven possible types of movement that an orator might have to make and that a painter might have to reproduce: up or down, to the right or the left, forward or backward, in a circle.[23] Later, he considered the artistic representation of movement in human hair and garments—inanimate matter intimately connected to the human bodies whose motions artists had to evoke. Here too Quintilian's seven kinds of motion provided Alberti with a basis for classification—but one that his own well-developed pictorial sense and stock of metaphors enabled him to develop in ways Quintilian himself had not anticipated:

> I like to see hair make all the seven forms of movement that I mentioned. Let it move in a circle, striving to form a knot, let it flow like waves, imitating flames, and let it sometimes creep like snakes under other strands of hair, raising itself now in this direction and now in that.[24]

Alberti made clear that this colorful description rested on actual practice, what he "like[d] to see." And in fact, it seems highly likely that he had a particular period form of artistic practice in mind. In the mid-1430s, as Alberti was composing his work, Luca Della Robbia was fashioning relief sculptures for the *cantoria*, or singers' gallery, of the Florentine Cathedral. Donatello, at the same time, was carving his reliefs for the outdoor pulpit of the cathedral at Prato. For all the differences between Della Robbia's meticulously rendered surfaces and Donatello's much rougher carving, they both showed hair and garments, moving in all seven of the ways Alberti vividly described, to endow the figures they represented with life and mobility.[25] The terminology of rhetoric enabled Alberti to find a precise verbal form with which to define what he saw taking place in the artists' ateliers. Like the engineers, Alberti had to create a language in which to discuss new forms of human invention in a clear and concrete way. Unlike Taccola and others, however, he could borrow from the existing stock of rhetorical terms and theories a large part of the verbal equipment that he needed.

By using the model of rhetoric, in other words, Alberti could create both a coherent, systematic manual and a consistent, provocative theory of painting. Often, moreover, he wrote as if he saw himself not as a painter or a practical man but as an orator, using verbal skills to comment on a world of visual practice that was not his own. He eloquently described the pleasure that painting brought him, remarking that he sometimes found, when he painted in his *ozio*, or spare time, that three or four hours had gone by without his noticing—exactly the words one might expect from an amateur rather than a professional, one who saw painting as a fount of delight rather than a painful and sometimes dirty source of income.[26] Writing on the details of optical theory, Alberti pointed out, even more explicitly, that few painters could offer the kind of theoretical analysis of vision and their ways of representing it that he did. He urged the painters among his readers not to reject his advice as irrelevant:

> For if painters are asked what they are trying to achieve in the surface they are painting, they can do anything better than answer about their intentions. Therefore, I beg painters with a serious interest in their art to listen to me. For it was never shameful to learn something worth knowing from any teacher at all.

At the end of his book, similarly, Alberti asked painters to reward him, if they found his book useful, by incorporating his face in their works. When Alberti made this request, he invoked the normal practice of the Florentine artists he most admired. Masaccio, for example, incorporated recognizable portraits not only of particular donors but also of the humanist chancellor Coluccio Salutati and other prominent individuals into his frescoes in the Brancacci Chapel. But Alberti referred to the practice, as he did to the painters' explanations of what they were doing, not as a fellow practitioner but as an outsider, a writer commenting on a craft that was not his own.

For the most part, however, Alberti represented himself not as an erudite writer commenting on the practices of artists, but as "a painter [speaking] to painters, going over the elements of the art of painting." "We painters," as he put it in another passage, "wish to express the emotions of the mind by the motions of the members."[27] Here and elsewhere Alberti sounds very much like the sculptor Ghiberti, who ventured to suggest an alternative to Pliny's famous account of a contest between Apelles and Protogenes to draw the finest possible line, noting with proud self-consciousness that "I speak as a sculptor"—and thus not as a mere scholar.[28] This claim had precise intellectual consequences. Alberti meant—as he made clear in his letter to Brunelleschi—to address the technical methods of the artist as well as his general culture and training. In the beginning of On Painting, when he presented the geometrical concepts and terms he would use in his exposition, he also promised that he would lay out in precise technical detail the geometrical bases of the art of painting. Indeed, he described his first book as "entirely taken up with mathematics."

At the same time, however, Alberti approached the mathematical prob-

lems in question from a pragmatic point of view. Like the engineers, he practiced applied, not pure mathematics: he wrote, as he said, "not as a mathematician but as a painter."[29] Accordingly—as Alberti made clearest in a
short treatise *On the Lines and Points Used by Painters*—he applied even standard geometrical terms not in the normal, abstract way, to merely mental
lines and points, but as painters applied them in the real world, to the lines
and points they drew: "The points and lines used by painters are not those
used by mathematicians, for whom each line may contain an infinite number of points. By our definition, a point is a sign that a painter considers as a
sort of mean between a mathematical point and a quantity capable of measurement, perhaps like atoms."[30] Alberti, in other words, described himself
in characteristically labile terms even when discussing problems in geometry,
an art that normally depended on strictly drawn definitions. Ever the
chameleon, he played both the outside observer and the initiated par-
ticipant in the painter's craft, as a given subject required. This pose fit his
position as an engineer—an innovative practitioner of both intellectual disciplines and practical pursuits—especially well.

Alberti did more than claim expertise: he displayed it. More than once
his work incorporated detailed references to existing techniques. In discussing the ways in which different surfaces take light, he remarked: "I observed that plane surfaces keep a uniform color over their whole extent,
while spherical and concave vary their colors."[31] Alberti may well have observed the phenomenon in question in nature. But Giotto, the one modern
artist whom Alberti explicitly praised, had also observed and employed the
principle that "in the open air there is normally no gradation of tone upon a
planar surface."[32] When discussing the appearance of receding human figures
in a correctly executed painting, as we have seen, Alberti remarked that
their faces should remain on a single level, their feet retracting upward toward their heads as their bodies become smaller with distance.[33] From the
1420s onward, Florentines could see this principle applied in a masterly way
in the Brancacci Chapel, where Masaccio had used it in his fresco of Saint
Peter and the tribute money, to create a visually convincing image of men
standing in a circle. Alberti, in other words, drew on a range of paintings executed over the last several decades for the concrete examples of practice
that he mentioned.

Sometimes Alberti's descriptions and prescriptions were very up to date
indeed. He insisted that the artist become an expert on sketching nude bodies, able to draw the bone, muscle, and sinew beneath the skin and the

naked body under its clothes.[34] Nude sketches by Florentine artists, emphasizing efforts to represent volumetric, coherent bodies, apparently began to appear within a few years after Alberti wrote. Perhaps Alberti's prescriptions, transmitted in writing or orally, helped to change artistic practice. It is also possible, however, that he had in mind such existing analytical exercises in drawing as the sketchbooks of Pisanello and Gentile da Fabriano—or another body of nude sketches now lost.[35]

In book three of *On Painting*, similarly, Alberti told the artist how to compose what he called a *historia*—a complex and controversial term that normally meant a substantial work of art in which several figures appeared:

> When we are about to paint a *historia*, we will first consider for some time the fairest order and method for painting it. Putting sketches down on paper, we will make notes on both the whole *historia* and its parts, and we will consult all our friends about it. In the end, we will strive toward having everything so far worked out in advance that there is nothing in the work we are to produce, the exact placement of which we do not fully understand. To grasp this even more certainly, it will prove helpful to divide our sketches into parallels, so that everything can be transferred to its place in the public work, just as it was taken from our private notes.[36]

Here Alberti elegantly showed how to transfer into the realm of painting a central practice of humanistic rhetoric, as he had learned it in Barzizza's school: the making of elaborate preparatory collections in notebooks before producing a final text. But when Alberti drafted these words in 1435, he also had something highly practical in mind: the production of frescoes and other large-scale, publicly commissioned works. Hence his description of the final *historia* as a "public work," a work immediately accessible to viewers.[37] At almost exactly the same time, Uccello produced a preparatory sketch, now in the Uffizi, for his painted monument to Sir John Hawkwood in the Florentine Cathedral. Its intersecting parallels strongly suggest that he worked from the sketch when laying out his fresco.

The chronological correspondence between Alberti's text and Uccello's images is striking. So is their substantive correlation. Uccello's sketch imposed on the horse that Hawkwood rides a rigid, schematic geometry: its rump, for example, forms a segment of a circle. In the fresco, by contrast, the horse's contours flatten out, offering a powerful contrast to the strong circular form of its head and neck. But Uccello deliberately dissolved the eerie elegance of his sketch into the uncertain naturalism of the final work. The contours of horses clearly fascinated Uccello, who also produced very different, more stylized horses in *The Battle of San Romano* and *The Hunt*. Most likely he found it attractive, when working in the small compass of a sketch or a panel painting, to emphasize abstract geometry. On the vastly larger scale of the equestrian monument, by contrast, he emulated the sculptor's craft, emphasizing the muscular power of the horse's forward movement rather than the austere beauty of his own line.[38]

Alberti did more than describe and name individual techniques. His expertise enabled him to confront, directly, one of the primary innovations created by Florentine artists in the 1420s: the systems for representing the three-dimensional world convincingly, on a two-dimensional surface, that Brunelleschi, Masaccio, Donatello, and Ghiberti had devised and applied from the 1410s onward. Alberti defined the painter's technical task—as opposed to his affective goals—in terms of these new techniques for making a flat, opaque surface or a low relief appear to be something else. "The painter's duty," he wrote, "is to inscribe and paint any given bodies on a surface, with lines and colors, at a fixed distance, and with such a fixed positioning of the centric ray, that everything which you see in the painting seems exactly like the bodies in question, and in the same relief." Both learned and ignorant judges of painting, he insisted, agreed that the most pleasingly painted faces were those "that seem to stand out from their panels, as if they were sculpted"—and not to be merely laid out in outlines. The painter's ability to make the objects he represented seem to stand out from the flat surface, rather than the capacity to decorate the surface with luxurious ornament, provided the chief added value in his work.

More important still, Alberti laid out precise instructions for achieving these ends. The painter must imagine, he counseled, that a pyramid of visual rays extends from the object he wishes to represent to his eye—which is, in fact, the source of the pyramid. A painting should represent exactly what would appear on a window that intersected this pyramid at a given point.[39] To create a painted surface that effectively resembles this imaginary scene, the painter needs to master rules, which Alberti set out. He must set a vanishing point—a point where the centric, or most powerful ray, sets out from the object to meet the viewer's eye. This point he should normally fix at more or less the eye level of the intended viewer. All lines perpendicular to the plane of the picture must converge on it. All lines parallel to it must appear at intervals that decrease according to a set geometric rule. A checked pavement, laid out geometrically, could both enhance the power of the illusion and offer geometrical proof of its validity. If a line drawn diagonally across such a pavement passed through the corners of the tiles shown, then the representation applied Alberti's geometry correctly.

Many questions of scholarship remain open, some of them vital ones. What sources did Alberti draw on when he laid down his rules? "Perspective"—the formal, geometrical treatment of sight—formed part of the learned tradition of scholastic natural philosophy practiced at the University of Padua and widely studied in Florence. Alberti used the conceptual vocabulary of the optical tradition to lay out his theory about the pyramid of vision, which gave his perspective a theoretical foundation. He analyzed the process of vision as one that began in the eye, as rays passed outward from it, forming a cone, to touch each object seen. The "centric ray"—the ray that covered the distance between the center of the eye and that of the object— was stronger than the rest, which perhaps explained its power to define the vanishing point. And a picture represented, in a sense, nothing more than an imaginary slice taken out of the visual cone at a given point: a strikingly clever way to justify Alberti's theoretical emphasis on perspective and foreshortening in mathematical terms. In drawing on technical literature to this effect, Alberti remained within the norms of the engineering and practical artistic tradition. (Ghiberti also read extensively in the medieval literature on optics, on which he drew heavily in his *Commentaries*.)[40]

But Alberti's text did not make a clear and rigorous connection between these theoretical arguments, which provided a further underpinning for the claim that painting was a liberal art, and the techniques actually used to create a convincing picture space. His exposition rested on "only the barest framework, the mathematical skeleton, of the perspectivist theory of vision."[41] And his own early experiments in perspective (which we examined in Chapter 3) were practical ones, designed to produce impressive spectacles rather than to prove old theorems or yield new ones.

On Painting consistently reflects its author's pragmatic orientation in other ways as well—for example, in its insistence on teaching not true but applied geometry. As a craftsman, Alberti had become familiar with a long tradition of technical innovation relevant to the creation of systematic perspective. Practical geometry offered a whole series of techniques for measuring, in rigorously accurate terms, objects too large or distant to reach. The so-called abacus books, which Italian mathematicians had written since the fourteenth century and on which Alberti would himself draw when he wrote a textbook of geometry, often contained sections dealing with the application of geometry to problems of measurement. Alberti's own *Mathematical Games* set and solved many problems related—though not identical—to those that confronted a painter setting out to make a realistic rendering of a physical space. Suppose, for example, that you want to measure the height of a tower, the dimensions of which you do not know but the bottom of which is accessible. Place a vertical staff in the earth, says Alberti. Lie down, with your feet to the staff, and sight past it to the top of the tower; place a piece of wax on the staff where your line of sight touches it. Then the ratio of the distance from the wax to the bottom of the staff, to the distance from the bottom of the staff to your eye, will be the same as that of the distance from the top to the bottom of the tower, to that from the bottom of the tower to your eye.[42] Similar triangles served Alberti again and again as the basis for achieving effective measurement of the real world. Brunelleschi knew the same techniques and seems to have used them as he gradually moved from making ground plans and elevations of the ancient buildings he studied, which were not drawn in perspective, to thinking about the ways in which the onlooker saw such structures. In the end, Brunelleschi designed his buildings with a sharp eye on how perspective shaped the experiences of visitors.[43]

Alberti, like Brunelleschi, very likely moved from using familiar techniques for measurement to applying them to problems of representation. He combined the traditional, vernacular geometry of surveying with the learned geometrical optics he clearly also studied, inferring that if one set of triangles would work for measurement, the many triangles that together formed the optical pyramid would work in the same way. Just as the vertical staff intercepts, and interprets, the triangle of vision that measures off the tower, so the plane that Alberti told the painter to cut through the visual pyramid would intercept and interpret its image of the world—an idea that clearly fascinated some of the artists who read Alberti's work, like Filarete and Dürer.[44] The new perspective represented neither a new worldview nor a way of capturing the three-dimensional world as it really is on a two-dimensional surface, but a brilliant fusion of traditional theories on vision and geometry with practical methods that had evolved since before the last century—and whose limitations and larger cultural meanings were discovered by later interpreters.[45]

The surviving evidence does not allow for a more precise reconstruction of Alberti's work on perspective. But it does show how seriously he concerned himself with this new ideal of what painting should achieve. Alberti knew, for example, how hard the young painter could find it to represent a scene convincingly, as light changed, as wind moved hair and garments, and as models shifted position. Traditionally, artists had circumvented this difficulty, learning their trade by imitating the work of earlier masters. Cennini, for example, recommended this method with great confidence.[46] Alberti admitted that it "is a help to imitate the work of others, because they have greater stability of appearance than living beings."[47] But he urged the painter who did so to copy sculptures—even mediocre ones—rather than paintings, even good ones, since by doing so he would learn not only about making an exact likeness but also about the fall of light on a three-dimensional subject. Even when imitating, the painter must perform his special magic of distilling three dimensions down to two.

More important, Alberti offered the young artist what seems to have been a new way of solving the problem. He suggested that the painter make a net or veil out of very thin thread, which he could hang at a set point between himself and the bodies and objects he wished to represent. By noting which segments of the objects he meant to depict fell in which squares of the veil, he could fix their locations precisely and copy them without making mistakes. This device would enable the painter to keep a clear sense of the ever-elusive spatial relationships among his subjects, and their orientation to him, even as changing light and shadows threatened to confuse him: "you know," Alberti explained, "how impossible it is to paint something that does not continually present the same aspect." More pragmatically still, the veil would enable the painter to fix the position of the vanishing point—and to see how moving it affected the rest of the picture space. It would allow him to locate every part of a subject's body—"the forehead in one parallel, the nose in the next, the cheeks in another, the chin in one below, and everything else in its particular place"—and to transfer them, without possibility of error, to the corresponding places on a squared painting surface. It would even help the painter carry out the hardest of his practical tasks, fixing and transferring in flat paint the round and projecting surfaces he saw. Alberti had used the veil himself: both "judgment and experience," he wrote, had confirmed its usefulness. He may well have invented it.[48] And it certainly became a popular device, one that later writers and artists from Dürer onward applied—though painters may well have understood it in a different way once they began to paint on canvas that shared formal properties with the veil, which was also woven, rather than on wood and plaster.[49]

On Painting, in other words, wove together the literary and the technical strands in Alberti's culture in a text that seemed cogent and accessible to his fellow scholars. And he based it—as he repeatedly insisted—on informed direct study of the way that painters worked. But he had more in mind than simply offering an account of art as it was. Like most later writers of manifestos, Alberti wanted not only to interpret the world of representation but to change it.

Alberti told the painter that he should prepare himself to carry out his "most capacious" and "highest" task: to paint history. As his many complementary references to *historia* and its Italian equivalent *storia* or *istoria* reveal, Alberti had in mind a carefully composed picture, in which a substantial number of characters—ideally nine—appeared. He told the painter how to plan histories in advance, where to find appropriate subjects for them, how to avoid errors of taste, and how to set his aesthetic goals. The term became a central one in Alberti's work. A close examination of what it meant to Alberti reveals exactly how he tried to transform the existing language and practices of art. In doing so he drew on an existing, if inchoate, language of art as well as on the resources of humanistic rhetoric, forming a new and more precise term—one carefully crafted to embody a particular aesthetic program.[50]

The Latin term *historia,* which Alberti used, calls to mind one of the central products of humanistic rhetoric: the written narrative of the origins of a kingdom, or a monarch's reign, or a battle. Cicero described history as *opus oratorium maxime*—"the supreme work of the orator"—and Alberti made clear that he had this definition in mind when he called the *historia,* more than once, "the greatest work of the painter." The normal humanist history, with its great deeds, colorful processions, and exciting battles, all cast in a uniformly classical style and designed to move and instruct the reader, has much in common with Alberti's description of the painted *historia,* at least so far as its ideal style and intended effects were concerned. And the one concrete example of a modern *historia* that Alberti cited—Giotto's *Navicella* in the Vatican, a mosaic of Jesus and the disciples in their boat—represented a pregnant narrative, though a sacred rather than a classical one.[51] Alberti had previously used the term *history* to refer to narratives: for example, when he complained that the existing "histories" of the martyr Potitus were inaccurate, or when he admitted, in his treatise on the uses of literature, that he was not yet experienced and capable enough to write a full-scale history.[52] In applying the term to painting, Alberti once again underlined the analogy between the painter's and the orator's arts.

But history in this classic literary sense does not exhaust the meaning of *historia* in Alberti's theory of painting. The Latin word, like its Greek cognate, can also mean any form of inquiry or narrative, and Alberti used *historia* in this sense when he denied that he intended to produce a "history of art" like Pliny's.[53] In fact, Alberti made clear to the humanist reader of his Latin text that he did not mean to be bound by classical usage. Alberti offered detailed descriptions of what he considered appropriate subjects for a *historia*. One of these referred not to an actual event but to an elaborately allegorical painting (of Calumny by the ancient artist Apelles). In this case as in others, Alberti used *historia* to refer to classical myths, a usage that occurred in Latin poetry but not in prose. Cicero, indeed, had insisted on the absolute distinction between *historia* and *fabula*, while Alberti tended to identify them.[54] Clearly Alberti intended not simply to use *historia* as Cicero had but to endow it with a new range of meanings.

As more than one scholar has recently argued, Alberti certainly had at least one further sense of *history* in mind. In late antique Greek and Latin, as in the Tuscan and French of the fourteenth and fifteenth centuries, *storia* or *istoria* already referred to a kind of work of art. Francesco Sassetti, the fourteenth-century writer, for example, told a story about Giotto in his seventy-fifth novella. Giotto, following the custom, went to San Gallo on the first Sunday of the month with his *brigata* of men and women. There, looking at a *storia* of Our Lady and Joseph, one of his friends asked, "Tell me, Giotto, why is Joseph always represented as so melancholy?" "Isn't he right?" replied the painter. "He sees that his wife is pregnant and he doesn't know who was the father." In this instance—as in dozens of others—*storia* simply referred to the sort of large-scale narrative painting in which Giotto himself specialized.[55] It is only reasonable to think that Alberti had such usages in mind.

But the Latin term *historia* and its Italian cognates had another sense as well in the existing Florentine language of art—one that might well have been the first to come to the mind of a Tuscan reading a text about the visual arts in Latin or Italian. A *historia* could be not only a painting but a relief panel in which several figures appeared. Dante used the word in this sense in canto ten of *Purgatorio*, where he described a series of magnificent *storie* cut into living rock. This sense of *history* remained current in the Tuscany of Alberti's day.[56] It occurred especially often in documents on the actual practice of Florentine artists, where it generally referred to relief sculptures that included several figures: the content, not the style, determined whether they were called *figurae* or *storiae*.[57] The Operai of the Florentine Cathedral, for example, commissioned Della Robbia to produce *storiae* for the singers' gallery. Evidently the term had some currency outside the realm of official contracts as well. In 1434, for example, the gifted but mercurial Matteo degli Organi, a famous builder of musical instruments, sent a letter to the Operai of the Prato Cathedral. In it he defended Donatello, who was taking a very long time to produce relief sculptures for the outdoor pulpit in Prato. Donatello's *storia*, Matteo pointed out, had received enthusiastic praise from expert judges. In saying so, Matteo referred unequivocally to the relief panel Donatello had just finished.[58] Ghiberti played on the term's ambiguity when he remarked, in his *Commentaries*, that the *istorie molto copiose di figure* ("relief panels, very well supplied with figures") in his Gates of Paradise *erano istorie del testamento uecchio* ("were stories drawn from the Old Testament").[59]

Learned humanists like Alberti regularly used *historia* and *storia*, in this postclassical, technical sense, as part of the vocabulary with which they discussed works of art. In 1426 Leonardo Bruni proposed a set of twenty topics for the second set of bronze doors for the Baptistery:

> I consider that the twenty stories, which you have decided are to be chosen from the Old Testament, should have two qualities principally, being both resplendent and significant. By *resplendent*, I mean that they should delight the eye with the variety of their design; by *significant*, that they should be important enough to rest in the memory. . . . It will be necessary for whoever does them to be well instructed about each story, so that he can do a good job of setting out both the persons and the actions that occur in it, and that he has a certain grace, so that he can adorn them well. . . . But I would very much like to be with whoever has the job of designing it, to make sure that he grasps the whole significance of each story.[60]

Bruni's scheme is more conventional than the one Ghiberti eventually adopted, but its vocabulary is revealing nonetheless. Bruni, perhaps the leading humanist in the city, felt ready, ten years before *On Painting* was written, to specify the aesthetic qualities of major works of art. The ones he felt called upon to discuss were relief panels meant to bear representations of narratives. He described the properties he thought they should have, emphasizing—as Alberti would—their effect on viewers, the need for variety,

12. Donatello. The Feast of Herod. Baptismal Font, Baptistery, Siena. Alinari/Art Resource, NY.

13. Lorenzo Ghiberti. The Story of Joseph. Baptistery, Florence. Foto Marburg/Art Resource, NY.

and the countervailing need for decorum in the choice and execution of the figures depicted. And he called these representations, evidently using an established term, *storie*—"histories"—though he also used the term for the narratives they represented.

In short, *historia* or *storia* was a labile term when Alberti seized upon it. It could refer to the work of a painter or a sculptor, just as *pictor*—literally, "painter"—could refer to either sort of artist. Alberti himself tended to argue that painting was superior to sculpture in that it conveyed an illusion of relief, rather than simply producing it. But he too referred, in *On Painting*, to the *historia* as a work that could be painted, molded, or carved.[61] Men who spoke of *historia* hoped, by doing so, to create an aura of knowingness and artistic expertise. It was the sort of word that the merchants and clerics who had served in the Cathedral Operai might use to show that they too understood something about art and artists. Alberti did not create the word, but he enriched its aesthetic potential when he used it to refer directly to the rhetorical theory of painting.

Of the five artists whom Alberti singled out for praise in his letter to Brunelleschi, three were fashioning relief panels during the period from 1434 onward, when he arrived in Florence and wrote his book. As has often been pointed out, the relief panels of the 1420s and 1430s correspond more closely than any paintings of the time—except Masaccio's frescoes—to Alberti's demands. Alberti required that his artist produce three-dimensional spaces. Ghiberti's *Isaac* and *Joseph* panels for the Baptistery doors and Donatello's marble reliefs of Herod and Salome, for all their differences, all included elaborate experiments in creating illusions of perspective—experiments not obviously mandated by the the stories they told.[62] Alberti called on the artist to people his work with anatomically correct, three-dimensional figures, as many as possible in rapid motion: "The painter who wishes his representations of bodies to appear alive should see to it that all their members perform their appropriate movements." He emphasized the importance of using thin garments and hair, both of them moved by the wind, to convey this quality to onlookers. He urged painters not to use too much color and to avoid the use of gold leaf—to employ an economy of means that would yield paintings with much of the look of sculptures. The one ancient piece of art that Alberti cited as exemplary, finally, not on the basis of his reading of an ancient text but from his own inspection of it, was a Roman *historia* or sarcophagus relief depicting Meleager.[63]

Though Alberti praised Masaccio, whom he presumably saw as the only creator of painted "histories" that met his criteria for excellence, he called for the production of a kind of work that even Masaccio did not carry out: secular paintings that embodied the technical innovations found in relief sculptures and that represented mythological subjects like the Calumny of Apelles and the three Graces. The reliefs of Donatello and Della Robbia contained numerous figures that match these descriptions in precise detail, in both style and content.[64] Like Alberti's ideal painter, they adopted a classical style; used hair and garments to reveal the motions of the bodies beneath them; and carefully avoided the dual extremes of excess and poverty, producing works that matched Alberti's prescriptions. They were copious and varied but not crammed with figures or incidents.

Alberti, in other words, did not use the term *history* either in the central, precise sense assigned it by classical rhetoric or in the more general one in which it figured in the Italian vernacular. Rather, he used it to call for the creation of a kind of painting that did not, in his full sense, yet exist: painting that would combine the technical innovations of Brunelleschi and Masaccio, the new three-dimensional space they had learned to represent, with the classical subject matter and classicizing style of the relief sculptors. Like many later manifestoes, Alberti's was as prophetic as it was descriptive. In the course of the next half-century, Mantegna and Castagno, Bellini and Botticelli would produce works that closely corresponded to his requirements.

In the texture of its language, and in both Latin and Italian, *On Painting* drew on existing repertoires of terms. Alberti worked not only with the artistic achievements but also with the verbal resources of the Tuscan culture he encountered in the 1430s. Like his system of criticism as a whole, his critical language rested on a conscious effort to find a classical vocabulary that reflected, as well as reshaped, existing practices—and one that synthesized existing forms of practice and speech with Alberti's high Latinate literary culture. Yet he refused to be limited either by the vernacular or by the classical conventions that he played with. Once again, the way in which Alberti defined and used the term *historia* is revealing. When Cicero distinguished between *historia* and *fabula*, he emphasized not the difference between their rhetorical effects, since either might entertain and improve an audience, but that between their fact contents. The Roman historian Sallust, in a celebrated passage, insisted that the wax funeral masks of heroic ancestors set Romans' hearts ablaze "not because the wax, or their form, has such power in itself, but it is the memory of the events that makes the flames rise in the

14. Luca Della Robbia the Elder. The Cantoria. Museo dell' Opera del Duomo, Florence.
Alinari/Art Resource, NY.

breasts of virtuous men."[65] Alberti, however, saw myth and history as equally appropriate subjects for a painted *historia*; indeed, as we will see, his exemplary *historia* came from the realm of myth. No one had more strongly underlined the supremacy of emotion—and, more generally, effective expression—in defining either oratory or painting. And no educated reader could have missed Alberti's insistence on this point. Context helps to explain the way that Alberti went about writing his book, and the ingredients that he used: but it cannot account for the particularities of his thought or the originality with which he reworked tradition.

In one respect above all, *On Painting* did not resemble the rhetorical treatises usually identified as its models. Alberti described painting as an art not of performance but of production. The painter, in his view, had to work rapidly, with facility. But his product should be designed ahead of time, laid out in detail, in his private notes, before it appeared in the public realm of fresco or panel painting. The actual rendering of the final image merely gave material form to what Alberti saw as the higher work of the artist's intellect. In technical terms, invention (choosing the right subject matter) mattered more than elocution, memory, and action (adorning it with the right images and using them effectively in public).

Oratory—as Quintilian and others described it, in the very works on which Alberti relied—differs radically from painting. The orator speaks in a particular time and place, addressing a particular audience. He must be able to perform spontaneously—when, for example, he must reply to unexpected witnesses or new arguments in a court of law. In order to perform their public tasks, both the painter and the orator certainly have to prepare in private. Like Alberti's painter, who must sketch his way to mastery of nature before he can attack large-scale projects, Quintilian's orator must amass a store of stylistic devices and effective anecdotes in topically organized notebooks before he can rise to his feet and deliver an encomium deploying them. But Quintilian relegated writing to the status of a private, preparatory skill—one designed to make the orator a more effective public speaker, a role that required at least the appearance of spontaneous composition.[66]

In particular, neither Quintilian nor Cicero provided a full source for the passages in the second and third books of *On Painting*, in which Alberti described the way that a painter should define his task and invite patrons and other critics to help him carry it out. Here he characterized the ideal painter as one learned above all in geometry but also in the liberal arts. He should spend as much time as possible in the company of "poets and rhetoricians." These *litterati*, Alberti explained, often have a rich stock of ideas for the sub-

15. Sandro Botticelli. The Calumny of Apelles. Uffizi, Florence. Alinari/Art Resource, NY.

ject matter of paintings—and the choice of subject matter, the *inventio* as Alberti called it, using the rhetorical term, constitutes a painting's chief merit.

In painting, as in writing, Alberti evidently saw antiquity as the chief source from which a painter should draw. In book three he drew on one of his favorite ancient writers, Lucian, to suggest the sort of *historia* that poets and rhetoricians could help a painter invent. Alberti adapted from Lucian a detailed account of a painting by Apelles—one for which the text was his sole source, since the work itself no longer existed:

> The description that Lucian gives of Calumny painted by Apelles excites our admiration when we read it. I do not think it is inappropriate to tell it here, so that painters may be advised of the need to take particular care in creating inventions of this kind. In this painting there was a man with enormous ears sticking out, attended on each side by two women, Ignorance and Suspicion; from one side Calumny was approaching in the form of an attractive woman, but her face seemed too well versed in cunning, and she was holding in her left hand a torch, while with her right she was dragging by the hair a youth with his arms outstretched toward heaven. Leading her was another man, pale, ugly, and fierce to look upon, whom you would rightly compare to those exhausted by long service in the field. They identified him correctly as Envy. There are two other women attendant on Calumny and busy arranging their mistress's dress: they are Treachery and Deceit. Behind them comes Repentance clad in mourning and rending her hair, and in her train chaste and modest Truth. If this *historia* seizes the imagination when described in words, how much beauty and pleasure do you think it presented in the actual painting of that excellent artist?[67]

The lost painting that Alberti described here was an object of lively discussion in the world of learning. The text by Lucian that Alberti paraphrased was a favorite in his circle. Guarino of Verona had translated it early in the century, and Alberti's friend Lapo made a new version in 1436.[68] It does not appear, from Alberti's version of the text, how or if a fifteenth-century viewer, even an erudite one, could have identified the painting's characters—much less decoded its larger message. Even Lucian, after all, remarked that a "guide" had explicated the image for him. Some have found it paradoxical that Alberti's model painting could not have been understood without an accompanying text.[69] But it was not only theorists like Alberti who saw the richly worked allegorical scene it described as attractive. In 1495 Botticelli, who created renderings of ancient myth that challenged comparison with religious painting in their scale and complexity, produced a detailed rendering of the scene, following Alberti's description, detail by detail.[70]

The learned painter, in other words, should learn about appropriate subjects from his even more learned friends among the literati. But he must ask them and others to comment on the way he executed the painting as well. In fact, "while the work is in progress, any chance spectators should be welcomed and their opinion heard." The modern painter must school himself, as the great ancient ones had, to listen to responses to his work and incorporate them into it as it reaches completion:

> They say that Apelles used to hide behind his painting, so that viewers could speak more freely and he could more honorably listen as they went through the flaws in his work. I therefore want our painters to ask and listen to everyone's opinion, openly and often. For this helps the painter, among other things, to acquire favor. Everyone thinks it an honor to express his opinion on someone else's work. And there is no need at all to fear that the judgment of censorious and envious men can detract from the painter's praises. For the painter's merit is public and known to all, and he can call his own well-painted work as a talkative witness on his behalf. Therefore he should listen to everyone and, after first thinking the matter through for himself, make corrections. Then, when he has listened to everybody, he should follow the advice of the more expert.[71]

The painter's work, in other words, was collaborative. His mastery of geometry and anatomy, like the orator's mastery of literature and history, was his alone. But his applications of them, in the form of finished paint, he must subject to the judgment of as many critical viewers as possible. Some of these critics would be experts: he should follow them above all in "emending" his work. The economy of artistic production could not function, Alberti held, without exchanges of opinion as well as money.

When Alberti told the story of Apelles, he deployed a classical source that artists, as well as humanists, might well have recognized: Pliny's *Natural*

History, the very text that he had dismissed elsewhere as a mere history, not an analysis, of the art of painting. Ghiberti drew heavily on the *Natural History* in his own *Commentaries*, in which he sketched a history of painting.[72] In the case of Apelles, Pliny wrote that "it was also his habit to exhibit his finished works to the passers-by in a balcony, and he would lie concealed behind the picture and listen to the faults that were found with it, regarding the public as more accurate critics than himself." Like Alberti's ideal artist, Apelles had invited the "ordinary people" to judge what he had done.

But once again Alberti did not simply repeat his ancient source: he placed a highly personal twist on it. For Pliny had gone on to make very clear that Apelles valued not the aesthetic but the technical judgment of his nonartistic onlookers:

> There is a story that, when a cobbler found fault with Apelles for putting one loop too few on the inner side of a sandal, he corrected the mistake. Elated by this, the cobbler next day proceeded to find fault with the leg, whereupon Apelles thrust out his head in a passion and bade the cobbler "stick to his last," a saying that has also passed into a proverb. The charm of his manner had won him the regard of Alexander the Great, who was a frequent visitor to his studio, for . . . he had issued an edict forbidding anyone else to paint his portrait. But when the king happened to discourse at length in the studio upon things he knew nothing about, Apelles would pleasantly advise him to be silent, hinting that the assistants who ground the colors were laughing at him; such power did his personality give him over a king habitually so passionate.[73]

Pliny left the sovereign painter in command, allowing his critics to suggest minor corrections of technical errors in the imitation of reality—and only those aspects of it that they knew better than he. Alberti, by contrast, emphasized the need for continual interplay between creative energy and critical opinion.

In this discussion, as in his terminology itself, Alberti fused practices and ideas previously kept apart. To some extent, the collaborative world of public art production that Alberti called for actually existed. A document that we have encountered once before, the letter of June 1434 in which Matteo degli Organi defended Donatello, gives a vivid idea of one kind of art talk:

Most dear Sirs, the cause of this letter is that Donatello has finished that *storia* in marble, and I promise you that I know all the experts in this town are saying with the same breath that never has such a *storia* been seen. And it seems to me that he has a good mind to serve you well. . . . He begs me to write to you for God's sake not to omit to send him some money to spend during this [Saint John's] holiday, and I charge you to do so; moreover, he is the kind of man for whom a snack is good as a feast, and he is content with anything.[74]

Matteo—himself a fairly stormy petrel, at least in his dealings with the Operai of the Duomo—conjured up, a year before Alberti wrote, exactly the world described in book three of *On Painting*. The artist working on a major public commission finds himself surrounded by critics. Some of them are identified—or self-identified—as experts, "men of understanding." They discuss everything about him, from his way of life to his artistry. They see him, already, as a likely source of trouble—one born, Marsilio Ficino would have explained a generation later, under the intellectual's star of Saturn rather than the merchant's star of Mercury, and likely to demand too much and work too little. But they also see his individual talent, rather than the materials he uses, as what sets him off from his rivals. Alberti's artist—and the "overcultivated" public whose advice he asked for—already existed when Alberti came to Florence. Some artists described the artistic society they knew in very similar terms. Ghiberti, for example, spoke of the crowd of "experts and scholars of the art of sculpture and goldsmiths and painters" who conveyed a statue of Venus found in Siena, in a sort of classicizing charivari, to the Campo, where they displayed it—only to see it destroyed by ignorant men who thought it unholy.[75]

Alberti, however, added a new ingredient to the mix. Many historians have convincingly argued that he intended, in *On Painting*, to stress the equality of painters—at least the best painters—and writers: to define painting as a liberal, intellectual art.[76] In doing so, however, Alberti did not have in mind an abstract, atemporal ideal of the writer—or even the particular historical figure of the Roman rhetorician, as modern historical scholarship has reconstructed it. Rather, he had in mind a particular literary system—the very one in which he himself struggled, during the 1430s, to attain intellectual mastery. This system, as we have seen, was as collaborative in form, as bound to the assumption that creativity is a social, not an individual, process, as the system for commissioning art to which Alberti connected it.

Like Poggio, Alberti meant his requests literally as well as figuratively. "Emendation" was a process he took very seriously indeed. In his dialogue *Pontifex*, which deals with the life of the clergy and denounces their failings, he explains how the virtuous father of a family should "emend" the conduct of those for whom he has responsibility. The same moralizing use of this literary term also occurs in the writing of his friend Lapo.[77] In his own career as a writer of artistic Latin, Alberti repeatedly asked for help from friends and associates, who "emended" his work. Some of his closest friends, like Beccadelli, became famous for their skills as critics of others' work.[78] Even when he found himself frustrated by particular critical responses—like those of Niccoli—he never lost faith in the idea that a collaborative, social system of literary production would yield better results than a completely individualistic one. When Alberti called on critics to "emend" works of art—and asked Brunelleschi and other artists to "emend" his own treatise—he was not repeating an empty commonplace. Rather, he was trying to exemplify the virtue of intellectual openness, the deliberate vulnerability, that characterized his own efforts as a writer in the same period.

The collaborative system of art production that Alberti designed in *On Painting* rested, in other words, not only on the texts that preserved the classical tradition in rhetoric and poetics in theory, but also on an existing model: the established modern system of humanist book production. When Alberti set out to rework relations between artist and patron, he envisioned the artist as working in a particular mode: as someone who resembled a writer in a very specific historical sense. He also imagined the critic as a particular kind of intellectual adviser. His functions certainly included the provision of iconographical schemes. But they also required him to detect and correct stylistic errors: errors of taste, of consistency, and of finish. Like so many Niccolis, Alberti's critics were to insist on a good *compositio*—in essence, that each work of art obeyed the rules implied by its particular genre and subject matter. Above all, he implied, a good painting, like a good speech, must obey the principle of decorum, showing a perfect correspondence in all its parts to its subject matter. Just as all the words used in a given text must belong to the same stylistic range, so all the members of a given body must fit the sex, age, and character of the person: "It would be ridiculous if the hands of Helen or Iphigenia looked old and rustic, or if Nestor had a youthful breast and soft neck, or Ganymede a wrinkled brow and the legs of a prize fighter, or if we gave Milo, the strongest man of all, light and slender flanks. It would also be unseemly to put emaciated arms and hands on a figure in which the face were firm and plump."[79] The painter, like the writer, must not lack the visual equivalent of Latinity—fluency in a system of expression ruled by strict protocols.

The costume and attitude of individuals, Alberti argued, must obey the same rule of decorum. Niccoli, Poggio's trusted if unkind literary adviser, objected to his assigning the names of his colleagues in the papal curia to participants, his reference to Bernardino da Siena, and his use of medieval and modern Latin translations from Greek texts in his dialogue *On Avarice*, because they represented breaches of decorum.[80] Alberti, in much the same way, insisted that the painter must depict his characters in dress and bearing appropriate to them: "It is not suitable for Venus or Minerva to be dressed in military cloaks, and it would be improper for you to dress Jupiter or Mars in women's clothing. The early painters took care when representing Castor and Pollux that, though they looked like twins, you could tell one was a fighter and the other very agile. They also made Vulcan's limp show beneath his clothing, so great was their attention to representing what was necessary according to function, kind and dignity."

Alberti subjected the "composition of bodies"—the arrangement of the figures in the painting as a whole—to an equally strict regime of decorum. In an unusually vivid and detailed comment, Alberti revealed the radical implications of his criticism for contemporary art: "Something that I see quite often deserves particular censure: that men are depicted in buildings as if they were shut up in a box, which they can scarcely fit into when sitting down and rolled up into a ball. All the bodies must, then, conform in size and role to the subject of the action."[81] The Albertian critic would condemn, out of hand, the popular images in which Gentile da Fabriano and others made no effort to observe period dress or conformity of scale. The glamorous displays of gold leaf with which Gentile and other contemporary artists adorned their work, as Cennino Cennini had advised, found equally little sympathy from Alberti. Using precious materials in this way violated the decorum of the painting, which was meant to represent by artifice, not to present in the solid reality, whatever it depicted.[82] Thanks to his rhetorical training, the critic would be splendidly placed to detect such errors in execution and help the painter or sculptor to correct them. The critic's advice, in other words, would play a major role not only in the conception of pictures but also in their execution.

Such critics, working actively with painters, would become the arbiters of an imaginary republic of the arts, closely connected to the republic of letters. By imposing rigorous standards, they would enable painters, like writ-

16. Gentile da Fabriano. Adoration of the Magi. Uffizi, Florence. Alinari/Art Resource, NY.

ers, to escape error and the ensuing public humiliation—a fate all too likely in a proverbially competitive and critical environment. In recent decades art historians, noticing Alberti's remark that learned men could supply painters with erudite subject matter for their work, have tended to see this as the central role that he thought humanists like himself could play in the production of works of art.[83] In the nineteenth century, however, Aby Warburg, soon to become a pioneer in the study of the afterlife of ancient art, viewed Alberti's work differently. Warburg found his stylistic suggestions—for example, his description of the proper motion for hair and clothing—very striking and argued that the work of Botticelli and other fifteenth-century artists embodied a similar aesthetic. Text and context alike confirm this view. Alberti's imagined community of critics was intended not only to suggest recondite subjects for artists but also to criticize and improve their execution in paint, stone, or bronze—just as they did for one another's Latin compositions.[84] Alberti consistently implied that his vision of collaboration between literati and artists paralleled the existing system of collaboration among writers—down to the conclusion of On Painting, in which he asked future writers on the art to help painters by "emending his mistakes" and "making the art of painting complete and perfect," as orators and rhetoricians had cultivated their art in antiquity.[85]

Like many handbooks of rhetoric, including Alberti's own, *On Painting* offers rules for the most general case, giving only brief examples and assuming that local needs may require deviation from the precept. Nonetheless, some striking correspondences between Alberti's instructions and particular artists' practices have come to light. At one point in his discussion of the *historia*, Alberti argued that when it came to the expression of strong emotions, a strategic omission might sometimes be more effective than an effort at direct representation: "They praise Timanthes of Cyprus for the painting in which he surpassed Colotes, because, when he had made Calchas [a priest] sad and Ulysses even sadder at the sacrifice of Iphigenia, and employed all his art and skill on the grief-stricken Menelaus, he could find no suitable way to represent the expression of her disconsolate father; so he covered his head with a veil, and thus left more for the onlooker to meditate on about his grief than he could see with the eye."[86]

Here, as elsewhere, Alberti cited a famous story and interpreted it in a personal way. Pliny remarked that Timanthes had veiled the father's face "which he could not depict in an appropriate way"; Valerius Maximus, author of a collection of examples from Greek and Roman history, told the story as well and drew the same moral from it about the limits of painting as an art. "When he veiled the head of Agamemnon," Valerius asked rhetorically, "did he not confess that art cannot express the deepest sorrow?"[87] By contrast, the ancient authorities on rhetoric, Cicero and Quintilian, praised Timanthes as a master. Cicero stressed the fact that the painter, like a good orator, had chosen decorous restraint over indecorous violence. Quintilian pointed out that Timanthes had adroitly solved an apparently insoluble technical problem, leaving the father's emotions, too strong to be portrayed directly, to the spectator's imagination. He urged orators to do the same.[88] Alberti followed the rhetoricians, arguing as they had that Timanthes had not failed, but succeeded, in the practice of his art. But he went further. Where Quintilian said merely that the painter had left spectators to "guess" the father's feelings, Alberti explained that he had left them to "meditate"— the verb used in the fifteenth century for the sorts of thought and feeling that a religious image should evoke.[89]

In this case, as in many others, Alberti clearly saw himself as offering stylistic advice. It is all the more striking, then, that Donatello—in late works like his *Lamentation of Christ* (now in London) and his *Crucifixion* (in

San Lorenzo, Florence)—began to veil the faces of figures suffering strong emotion. Alberti's text reflects the practice of the Florentine artist most renowned for his abilities in the representation of gesture and emotion.[90] Once again the technical language of rhetoric enabled him to describe and analyze contemporary practices in a powerful, coherent way.

What the surviving evidence does not reveal is the extent to which Alberti's ideas found readers or listeners among the Florentine artists. A poem ascribed to him, *Venite in danza*, which evokes a charmingly varied group of men and women dancing and exchanging looks around a laurel tree, has been connected with a small Florentine painting (now in the Art Museum of Princeton University) that represents the Garden of Love. In this elegant, lively little painting, twelve human figures and a dog appear, adopting graceful positions. This modest image may well embody one version of the sort of painting Alberti favored.[91]

Perhaps, in the light of the analysis offered here, it might prove more rewarding to look not for Albertian perspective but for Albertian transactions among painters, critics, and others. Alberti, for example, dedicated his book, in its Italian form, to Brunelleschi. And he did so at a moment when Brunelleschi had just suffered legal consequences for attempting to free himself

17. Anonymous.
Garden of Love.
Florence, ca. 1430.
The Art Museum,
Princeton University.
Bequest of Frank
Jewett Mather, Jr.

from the rules recently established by the guild of painters and establish his own legal freedom to act: in 1435, the sculptor actually went to jail in a test case.[92] The Albertian text was offered to an Albertian figure, as when Alberti asked Brunelleschi, characteristically, to "emend" any errors he found in *On Painting*—and thereby acknowledged the architect's social equality or superiority to him. No more Albertian statement could be imagined than this clear reference to Brunelleschi's status as the practitioner not of a craft but of a liberal art, based on geometry and modeled on rhetoric.

Paolo Uccello's case is also suggestive. In May 1436 the Operai of the Duomo commissioned him to paint his fresco monument of Hawkwood—itself an Albertian project, in which the painter's skill in perspective, anatomy, and coloring were to produce something as impressive, but not as expensive, as a bronze equestrian statue. On 28 June, however, the Operai gave instructions to eradicate the fresco, evidently on stylistic grounds: "because it is not painted as is proper." Early in July they told Uccello to paint the work again.[93] Evidently the Operai found his work basically excellent but objected to some major feature of its execution. Uccello seems to have

18. Paolo Uccello. Equestrian Monument to Sir John Hawkwood. Duomo, Florence.
Alinari/Art Resource, NY.

envisioned the fresco, in the first instance, as a demonstration piece for perspective and foreshortening, one that would give a strong illusion of being a three-dimensional statue, on a three-dimensional pedestal, seen from far below. Perhaps, it has been suggested, he originally foreshortened the statue of Hawkwood in a way visually consistent with the pedestal. The resulting image would have been a very quaint one, seen from the floor: one in which the horse absolutely dominated its rider. The Operai, displeased with the resulting image, had Uccello make a new one—one in which he represented the pedestal as seen from below but showed the horse and man, more grandly, in a direct view from the side.[94] This would make a fine case in point of Albertian criticism, applied to a major stylistic decision and resulting in "emendation" of the work in question. But in this case as in Brunelleschi's, the transaction was obviously independent of Alberti's book. The question is not what influence Alberti exercised but what concrete phenomena he meant to describe and analyze in a work devoted, as he explicitly said, not to abstract theory but to the world as it really appears, in all its gross detail and texture.

Alberti's efforts to deflect attacks from his learned Latin writings did not all succeed. He received harsh criticism from the very readers who mattered most to him. The Italian text of On Painting appears to have suffered much the same fate at first. Alberti's dedication did not mollify its recipient: Brunelleschi, ever paranoid about his intellectual property, presumably reacted with characteristic irritation when he saw that Alberti's work contained a long discussion of perspective but did not mention him or his model panels. In the 1440s, describing the contest he had waged with Ghiberti in 1401 over the commission to make the Baptistery doors, Brunelleschi made his tale into a devastating parody of Alberti's republic of scholars and artists.

Ghiberti—so Brunelleschi now told the story—had deliberately consulted with every goldsmith and sculptor in Florence as he created his trial panel of The Sacrifice of Isaac: "he had the idea, as he was a shrewd person, of proceeding by means of hard work and by humbling himself through seeking the counsel—so that he would not fail at the confrontation—of all the people he esteemed who, being goldsmiths, painters, sculptors, etc., and knowledgeable men, had to do the judging." He had gone so far as to redo his work repeatedly in line with their suggestions. Accordingly, they received his work as an incomparable masterpiece, one that even the ancient sculptor Polygnotus could not have surpassed. They praised it enthusiastically to the thirty-four members of the jury who were charged to make a final decision.[95]

Brunelleschi—so Manetti told the story—had "made his panel quickly, as he had a powerful command of the art" and "was not eager to talk about it with anyone since, as I have said, he was not boastful." Hence the experts could not believe that his competition relief was actually better than Ghiberti's, though in fact it was. They proposed that the two men share the commission—a demeaning offer that Brunelleschi naturally rejected. In this case, Alberti's network of critics and artists revealed itself to be nothing more than a cabal. And Alberti's theory of painting was revealed to be, like his work on architecture, a mere tissue of generalities, not a powerful or useful formulation of the theory of the art that Brunelleschi and others had revolutionized in practice.

Over time, however, Alberti's book found readers in many quarters. Scholars like the Milanese humanist Angelo Decembrio read and excerpted his work, which came to be a central source for learned discussions of the arts.[96] So, more remarkable still, did artists. The most articulate painters and sculptors of the fifteenth and sixteenth centuries—Antonio Averlino, known as Filarete; Leonardo da Vinci; Albrecht Dürer—all carried on Alberti's effort to create a theoretical basis for painting and an aesthetic language in which the theory could usefully be couched. Most of them wrestled with the specific issues that he raised—for example, the gnarly question of whether painting or sculpture could claim the higher intellectual and aesthetic standing. And all of them drew on terms and ideas that Alberti had been the first to hammer out.

One more ancient anecdote—the story of Zeuxis and the maidens of Croton—reveals the way in which Alberti's text became the source for a language of art. Alberti told it thus:

The idea of beauty, which the most expert have difficulty in discerning, eludes the ignorant. Zeuxis, the most eminent, learned, and skilled painter of all, when about to paint a panel to be publicly dedicated in the temple of Lucina at Croton, did not set about his work trusting rashly in his own talent as all painters do now; but, because he believed that all the things he desired to achieve beauty not only could not be found by his own intuition, but were not to be discovered even in Nature in one body alone, he chose from all the youth of the city five outstandingly beautiful virgins, so that he might represent in his painting whatever feature of feminine beauty was most praiseworthy in each of them. He acted wisely, for to painters with no model before them to follow, who strive by the light of their own talent alone to capture the qualities of beauty, it easily happens that they do not by their own efforts achieve the beauty they seek or ought to create; they simply fall into bad habits of painting, which they have great difficulty in relinquishing even if they wish.[97]

Alberti crafted this passage in his usual methodical way, cutting and burnishing ancient materials until they became distinctively his own. He found the substance of this anecdote in two of his favorite sources: Cicero's work On Invention and Pliny's Natural History.[98] He set the story in Croton, as Cicero had (Pliny put it in Agrigento); but he had Zeuxis produce his work for the temple of Lucina, following a bad reading in Pliny's text.[99] These texts were entirely appropriate to Alberti's ends: Cicero modeled his own eclectic method, which allowed him to borrow from a variety of earlier rhetorical texts in On Invention, on the painter's eclectic approach to his models. Pliny showed at the start of his work, to which he attached extensive bibliographies, that he too had eclectically drawn on a vast range of Greek and Roman writers. The passage ranks with Alberti's most neatly crafted mosaics: never had he chosen more appropriate stones.[100]

As always, Alberti changed his sources as he fused them. According to Cicero, Zeuxis decided that he should base his work on direct study of the most beautiful young women of Croton. He asked to see them, nude. But the citizens who had given the painter his commission refused this request. They took the painter to the gymnasium where young men wrestled and showed him many handsome boys. They informed him that these boys had lovely sisters—and that he would have to infer their special beauty from the masculine beauty of their brothers. Finally, Zeuxis obtained permission to see the five most beautiful virgins, for just long enough to transform the truth about them into a "silent image." Cicero, in other words, not only justified his practice as a writer with the story, but also told a joke, to enliven the opening of a dry and technical textbook. The Roman orator's story reveals, moreover, his uneasy awareness that to paint a nude, the painter needed to see a naked model. The highest achievements of art might provoke—or require—erotic complications and social inversion.[101] Cicero's story had a sexy edge to it.[102]

Alberti meticulously cleansed the story of every vestige of erotic suggestion. Throughout his work, which defined the painter's task as the expression and generation of emotions, he insisted that a scrupulous regime of decorum must always keep passion within carefully defined limits. Sexual urges were clearly out of bounds. In his view, female nudity had a symbolic value that purged it of erotic content—a point that he underlined in an elegant way. As we have seen, when Alberti set out to describe a sample *historia*, he paraphrased Lucian's description of the elaborate allegorical painting of Calumny by Apelles. Lucian, one of his favorite writers, had described the figure of Repentance as a woman dressed in dark clothing, weeping and looking backward, full of shame, at Truth. Alberti carried out a subtle but deeply meaningful switch of attributes: he described Truth, not Repentance, as "chaste and modest."[103] By doing so, he indicated that he saw Truth "as a naked figure of the 'Venus Pudica' type"—an allegorical figure whose nudity indicated her pure character.[104] He thus brought into being the figure of "Naked Truth"—a personification that would retain her popularity with artists and emblem-makers for centuries.

The inventor of *nuda veritas* hoped to prevent his readers from seeing the nude female body, when portrayed by a painter, as sexually suggestive or ethically problematic. Alberti, in other words, not only adapted but bowdlerized Cicero and Pliny, making the story of Zeuxis, originally a suggestive one, embody his ethical and aesthetic program. Virtually everyone who talked or wrote about the arts after Alberti followed his cue and cited the story as Alberti retold it.

For the painters, the final product usually sufficed: the arrival, not the journey, mattered to men whose use of the classical tradition was basically pragmatic rather than erudite. Alberti's version of the story of Zeuxis became a standard component of studio chat and of artistic literature. Painters cited it regularly, to widely different effect. Sometimes they interpreted it as Alberti did here, as proof of the vital importance of direct study of nature; sometimes, as Alberti did in his later work *On Sculpture*, as proof that the artist has access, thanks to his study of nature, to a universal ideal of beauty that is better than any individual human. Raphael, for example, wonderfully rewrote the passage in his letter to Castiglione, making the "idea" more important than the empirical study that Alberti wanted it to rest on: "In order to paint a beautiful woman, I should have to see many beautiful women, and this under the condition that you were here to help me with making a choice. But since there are so few beautiful women and so few sound judges, I make use of a certain idea that comes into my head."[105] Vasari, by contrast, plastered a more literal version of the story across a wall in the Casa Vasari in Arezzo.

Alberti loomed large in the world of those who talked about art for decades, even centuries, after his own time. But it is not certain that any artist gratified Alberti's wish that his face be preserved in a fresco.[106] It is clear, however, that his brilliant, idiosyncratic book achieved, in the long run, its author's central aim: it made a powerful case for a new art and a new kind of artist, one so powerful that it would become an orthodoxy in its own right. Even those who had no special reason to wish Alberti well, like Ghiberti, seem to have read and learned from *On Painting*.[107] Antonio Averlino, known as Filarete, a highly professional sculptor and architect, drew freely on Alberti's work, not only for the optical bases of perspective, on which he cited Alberti explicitly as an authority, but also for information on everything from color theory to the myth of Narcissus (where he misunderstood what Alberti had to say).[108]

One could even use Alberti, wickedly, against Alberti. When the Holy Roman Emperor Charles V staged his triumphal entry into Antwerp in September 1520, parading between diaphanously dressed women holding torches, the strait-laced Habsburg kept his eyes strictly to the front. Not so the artist Albrecht Dürer, who took the opportunity to inspect the young women as closely as he could. "I," he later recalled, "since I was a painter, examined them a little less modestly."[109] Here Dürer cited the Albertian principle that the painter must study naked female bodies directly—even though he knew, as his telling of the story shows, that in doing so he violated the equally Albertian principle of decorum. In sixteenth-century Italy, as academies formed and aesthetics became a central theme of discussion both for artists concerned with theory and for literary men, something like the republic of the arts that Alberti had dreamed of came into being, and the language he had created from ancient and modern sources became the medium for their discussions. Long after his death, when he was usually read not in his own Latin or Italian text but in later Italian translations, Alberti paradoxically obtained part of what he had always hoped to claim: not a monopolist's mastery of the language in which art was discussed, since this is continually developed and extended, but at least a founder's chief share in what had become a popular and glamorous as well as an intellectually productive enterprise.[110]

V

INTERPRETING FLORENCE:

FROM READING TO REBUILDING

1 January 1404. I know that in this wretched life, our sins expose us to many tribulations of soul and passions of the body, and that without God's grace and mercy, which strengthens our weakness, enlightens our mind, and supports our will, we would perish daily. I also see that since my birth forty years ago, I have given little heed to God's commandments. Distrusting my own power to reform, but hoping to advance by degrees along the path of virtue, I resolve from this day forward to refrain from going to the shop or conducting business on solemn church holidays, or from permitting others to work for me or seek temporal gain on such days. Whenever I make exceptions in cases of extreme necessity, I promise, on the following day, to distribute alms of one gold florin to God's poor. I have written this down so I may remember my promise and be ashamed if I should chance to break it.

Also, in memory of the passion of Our Lord Jesus Christ who freed and saved us by His merits, that He may, by His grace and mercy, preserve us from guilty passions, I resolve from this very day and in perpetuity to keep Friday as a day of total chastity—with Friday I include the following night—when I must abstain from the enjoyment of all carnal pleasures. God give me grace to keep my promise, yet if I should break it through forgetfulness, I engage to give twenty *soldi* to the poor for each time and to say twenty Paternosters and Avemarias.[1]

This irresistible confession by the merchant and historian Goro Dati plunges us into an immediately recognizable social world. A Florentine paterfamilias of the fifteenth century sits in his study, recording his inmost thoughts in a carefully dated series of formal entries. He describes a long, intense series of struggles: the desperate balancing act of a performer on a tightrope, caught in the merciless floodlight of his conscience, propelled in several directions at once by the needs of his body, the problems of his business, and the longings of his soul. He tries to discipline himself by planning and controlling his own use of time, forcing himself to divide the week, as the church demands, into secular and sacred portions. He knows, in advance, that he will fail. And he offers a merchant's remedy: not pretty excuses, but fair payment, for the sins that he can hardly hope to avoid committing. Modernity is upon us.[2]

We recognize the signs of Dati's condition partly because they remained familiar for centuries. But we also see them, at least in this fifteenth-century context, as especially Florentine, because Alberti taught us to do so. His *Four Books on the Family* reached a limited public in his own day: only three complete manuscripts and several partial ones, as well as others containing a later adaptation of the original text, survive. It was not printed until 1843.[3] But as soon as Anilio Bonucci included the work in the first complete edition of Alberti's writings, it attracted attention. Historians who saw themselves as living—as Alberti had—in a pressured, changing social and intellectual environment soon considered it profound—even though they differed sharply about the work's interpretation.

In the age of *Buddenbrooks*, modern techniques spread with breathtaking speed through German industry, relegating the old patrician families of the imperial and Hanseatic cities to the economic sidelines. The most creative German social thinkers confronted the iron cage of modernity with all the fascination Burckhardt had brought to bear on the transformation of his old European paradise of Basel. What made modern capitalism modern? Alberti seemed to shed some light on the subject.

A great student of the origins of capitalism, the economic historian Werner Sombart, found the explanation for the rise of capitalism in a combination of developments: the development of a money economy, the spread of abstract bookkeeping techniques, and the growth of a bourgeois ethos that preached honesty, hard work, and the rational use of time. The Florence of the Renaissance, he argued, was the first locale where all of these concepts and techniques fused. He identified Alberti as "the most perfect type of the 'bourgeois' of those days" and held that "his works provide a mine of information for obtaining an insight into the outlook of that generation of middle-class folk."[4] But Max Weber, the pioneering sociologist and social historian, found in Alberti confirmation for his own thesis that true capitalism came into being only after the Reformation. The new sense of a secular "vocation" created by Calvinism and the "innerworldly asceticism" that Calvin demanded had made the capitalist. As for Alberti, "that great and versatile genius of the Renaissance, who besides theoretical treatises on mathematics, sculpture, painting, architecture, and love (he was personally a woman-hater), wrote a work in four books on household management," he preached a respect for ancestry and the idle country life that "would in the eyes of every puritan have been sinful idolatry of the flesh, and in those of Benjamin Franklin the expression of incomprehensible aristocratic nonsense."[5] Alfred Doren, who pursued both economic and intellectual history and knew the Florentine sources better than anyone, agreed with Sombart: he described On the Family as a "philistine's charter" and treated Alberti as an absolute bourgeois.[6]

After World War II, Otto Brunner, a brilliant, reactionary historian of European society, offered a radically different reading of Alberti's work. In a groundbreaking book that focused on the writings of a forgotten seventeenth-century baron, Brunner emphasized the long history of the European great house, from the Middle Ages through the Renaissance and beyond. For Brunner, On the Family represented not the embodiment of a new economy and a new economic attitude, but one stage in the long history of European thought on the management of the household—a tradition that had begun in classical Greece and flourished in the Middle Ages.[7] Massimo Danzi, one of the leading contemporary students of the text, has found inspiration in Brunner for a new interpretation of Alberti's work—one that ties it more firmly to its time and place of composition than any previous one.[8]

The social historians who in the 1960s and after launched a massive

Franco-Anglo-American-Antipodean invasion of the Florentine archives regularly compared the results of their statistical and anthropological inquiries with Alberti's text. To this day, all scholars interested in the thought and feelings of the families who inhabited Florence's first palaces draw on Alberti's vivid conversations—above all those in book three, in which the characters examine in meticulous detail the ways of maintaining a great family's demographic and economic stability.[9] And to this day, interpretations of the text differ sharply.

Most of Alberti's interpreters, however, now acknowledge the presence, in his characters and in his mind, of dramatic, lifelike contests between opposed values and concerns, of contradictions as powerful as those evoked by Goro Dati. In *On Painting*, Alberti described the aesthetic of a particular generation of Florentine artists; in *On the Family*, he staged the family dramas of the Florentine patricians who fought the city's battles, built its buildings, and—between the 1370s and the 1430s—ran its government. Like a domestic conversation heard through a partly open window, his work compels attention, offering a seductive sense of intimacy with the past. In fact, however, *On the Family* is a highly artificial work, one that represents only one of several stages in Alberti's lifelong effort to come to terms with Florentine traditions, institutions, and urban forms. Once the dialogue is reinserted into its intellectual and biographical contexts, both its value as reportage and its interest as polemic will be much easier to evaluate.

The early history of Alberti's *On the Family*—and of his engagement with Florence itself—is anything but clear. In his autobiography, Alberti states that he wrote the first three books by 1434, before he ever arrived in Florence:

> Before his thirtieth year he wrote, and for the sake of his relatives he did so in his ancestral tongue, so that he might serve those ignorant of the Latin language, his first, second, and third books in Tuscan *On the Family*. He finished these at Rome, on the ninetieth day from when he began them. But they were unpolished and rough, and not in every respect perfectly Tuscan. For he had not mastered his ancestral language, since he had been brought up among foreign nations during the long exile of the Alberti family. It was hard to write elegantly and with polish in a language that he was just then beginning to use regularly. But within a short time his extreme effort and industry enabled him to attain a great success. Those of his fellow citizens who wished to win a reputation for eloquence in the council con-

fessed that they had regularly taken a good many ornaments from his writings to adorn their own speech.[10]

The story seems straightforward enough. Alberti wrote his most elaborate work on Florence before he knew the city well at first hand. He drew his information and his precepts, as he said in the prologue, in part from written sources, "the great writers of antiquity"; and in part from "the excellent customs of our own Alberti ancestors." Though the language gave him trouble, he persisted and completed the work. The earliest manuscripts, now preserved in Florence, generally confirm this account. Both the partial and the complete texts bear numerous signs of revision by Alberti himself—evidence that he did not exaggerate the difficulties he encountered.

Later in his autobiography, however, Alberti offered a more complicated statement about his work's reception by its initial Florentine readership:

He passed his first, second, and third books *On the Family* to his relatives to read, but among all those Albertis, who had plenty of free time on their hands, hardly one was found who thought it worth his while even to read through the titles of the books—and that although foreign nations eagerly demanded those works. This he did not take well. He could hardly avoid feeling rage, moreover, when he saw some of his relatives openly ridiculing both the whole work and the author's futile enterprise along with it. These slanders made him decide that he would burn the three books he had completed, but some men of weight intervened. His sense of duty finally enabled him to conquer his indignation, and three years after he published the first three books [by 1437?], he brought out a fourth for those ingrates, to whom he said: "If you are men of honor, you will love me; if you are dishonorable, your own wickedness will make you the object of hatred." The charm of those books transformed many illiterate fellow citizens of his into eager students of literature.[11]

This account of the book's reception echoes the first in claiming that it eventually found an audience. But it also suggests that Alberti did not simply work hard to produce a fine piece of Tuscan prose, as he originally suggested. Rather, his efforts at revision and expansion represented his response to the ridicule with which his Florentine relatives greeted the book in its first state.

On the Family still shows signs that a highly personal motive inspired its composition. Alberti discussed at length the difficulty of preserving a family's demographic health. And he not only lamented the family struggles that had depleted the Alberti clan and others, but argued that adoption might provide a reasonable solution for the problem. It seems highly likely, then, that Alberti intended the work as a brief on his own case: his passionately nostalgic collective portrait of the Alberti family may have been a plea for formal admission to it.[12] If so, it failed. Alberti seems to have acknowledged this when he entered his symbol, the winged eye, and his motto *Quid tum?* in a Florentine manuscript of the revised text. The question *Quid tum?* occurs in Virgil's tenth eclogue, where the god Pan (or the poet Gallus) describes the companions he wishes for: "So what, if Amyntas is dark? Violets are black, and hyacinths are black."[13] Lowly status, the god insists, does not make an attractive friend cease to appeal. The winged eye (which Alberti elsewhere interpreted as an emblem of divine sovereignty) presumably represented a claim that creative ability could make up for the status that the family refused to award him.[14]

How then did Alberti read and describe the society of his ancestral city? And why did his intended readers find his book so alien? *On the Family* recounts a series of discussions held in Padua on one day in May 1421, as members of the Alberti family attend the deathbed of Lorenzo Alberti, the father of Leon Battista and Carlo. The discussions cover a wide range of topics, from sex and fatherhood to childrearing and careers. They include treatments of many subjects dear to the humanists of Alberti's generation and the one before it—like the best way to rear a child and educate a youth. In the prefatory letter to book three, which he dedicated to Francesco d'Altobianco Alberti, Alberti himself described the work's general movement very well:

> Therefore, Francesco, as you know, I have already written two books, in the first of which you learned how, in the well-conducted family, elders exercise care and discretion in the training of the young, and the young, in turn, behave as they are obliged and duty bound to do toward their elders. There you saw what diligence is required of fathers and mothers in the bringing up of their offspring to good behavior and high character. My second book set forth what are the chief considerations in marrying and discussed the proper occupations for young men. So far, then, we have made the family large and set it on the road to success; now, since economy is reputed to be ex-

tremely important if wealth is to be well enjoyed, here is this third book. Here you will find a description of a proper *pater familias*.[15]

Marriage and childrearing, household management and money were obsessively interesting to the humanists of Alberti's generation, who ransacked the moral writings of Aristotle and others for guidance. But Alberti's gift for characterization enabled him to cut unusual paths into the didactic undergrowth. Though the erudite young bachelor Lionardo takes a leading role throughout, different partners engage him in discussion in each book: his cousin's husband Adovardo in book one, the young Battista himself in book two, and in book three the unforgettable sixty-four-year-old Giannozzo, who insists, in words that adumbrate famous passages in Leonardo and Machiavelli, that *io non so lettere*—"I am uneducated, and have in life tried to know things by experience, not from what people have said."[16] The work as a whole brings before the reader fully realized and individual characters rather than the straw men who sometimes appear in Renaissance dialogues, neatly matched, like American Tourister suitcases of different sizes.[17] And though Alberti treated topics widely discussed in humanist writings on moral and social questions—the purpose of marriage, the proper form of spousal relations, the rearing of children—he did so in a highly vivid, individual way, in a style clearly formed in his difficult times, at his unstable place.

Many individual passages of the work bear a clear stamp of period and place. In book two, for example, Lionardo describes in detail the best way to generate a son. A husband, he counsels, should come to his wife in a calm mood, not troubled "by anger, fear, or some other kind of disturbing emotion" that might infect the child in turn with an evil character. He must be in good health, or his children may emerge "leprous, epileptic, deformed, or incomplete in their limbs and defective." The weather must not be too hot or too cold. Even when all of these conditions are fulfilled, the husband should not approach his wife until "the first digestion is over, when you are neither empty nor full of heavy food." Then he should, if possible, see to it that he is "intensely desired by the woman." This fanciful image of a passionless male having silent, businesslike sex with a passionate woman fit beliefs widely held in Alberti's time, especially by medical men who took a professional interest in such topics. And it fits in with many other aspects of Alberti's great clan, in which males clearly regulated the household with an unquestioned authority that real life might have challenged. Nonetheless,

Lionardo apologizes, twice, for bringing up this delicate subject and discussing it even in a "veiled" and "compressed" way. Up to now, Alberti's
standard of decorum holds.

If sex embarrasses the young intellectual, however, another subject
makes him literally turn red. Arguing that one must compete for success in
this world, Lionardo finds it necessary to discuss, after the generation of
children, the accumulation of wealth. "Perhaps the present moment," he
comments, "as the evening grows dark, is just right for this subject, for no
occupation seems less attractive to a man of large and liberal spirit than the
kind of labor by which wealth is in fact gathered."[18] This passage has puzzled
even perceptive readers: what does sunset have to do with money? But one
of my beloved teachers at the University of Chicago, a German émigré
named Christian Mackauer, explained it with economy and elegance. If talk
of sex moderately embarrassed Alberti and his idealistic persona in the dialogues, Lionardo, then talk of money horrified both of them. The code of
Christian morality, as interpreted in early fifteenth-century Florence, condemned many standard mercantile and banking practices. The feudal code
of honor, to which many patricians aspired, did the same, for other reasons.[19]
Filled with the "uneasiness, self-consciousness, self-defensiveness" that Li-
onel Trilling identified as the characteristic emotions of sensitive individuals
forced to live in a mercantile society, "the sense that one is not quite real,"
Lionardo hesitates to explore the "sordid, hidden reality" of money, until
night cloaks both his blushes and those of his audience.[20] Sex, by contrast,
he had analyzed in broad daylight. Touches like this, as brief as they are
vivid, give On the Family the qualities of high fiction that set it apart from
such competitors as Poggio's genuinely brilliant dialogues On Avarice, in
which one character ventures a dazzling, even phosphorescent defense of
greed as the emotion that makes civilization possible.

The richness and complexity of On the Family make its historical interpretation all the more difficult. Does the book describe the real family life of
Alberti's day, for example, or does it prescribe a return to a lost past? Historians have collated Alberti's description of the Florentine elite with many
other forms of evidence and sometimes established a direct correspondence.
But often their results are ambiguous. Alberti's characters lament the days,
now long gone by, in which whole families lived under one great roof, brothers sharing home and hearth with brothers even after they had reached maturity and married. The economic historian Richard Goldthwaite, working
in the first instance from economic evidence, argued that in Alberti's time

Florentine families were actually fragmenting into nuclear units. The nostalgic tourist's evocation of a lost past reflected real changes in the social order. But F. W. Kent, also an erudite and original student of Florentine great families and their world, reconstructed a very different set of relations, economic and emotional: one in which the ties of fraternity and sorority still bound. The members of the clans he studied wove tight webs of friendship and marriage alliance, built loggias together, and inhabited particular urban zones, even after they no longer lived in one great house. For him, the affective bonds that connected Alberti's characters rang truer, when tested against the historical record, than their cries of regret for change and decay in all about. This generally friendly debate has persisted for a generation without finding a clear resolution, while Alberti has served as a genial expert witness on both sides.[21]

Certainly Alberti incorporated in his work fragments of the proverb-laden language of the male patricians who dominated Florence in the early fifteenth century. Uncle Giannozzo, for example, the practical man whose advice fills so much of book three, offers the young Lionardo some ancestral wisdom. Messer Benedetto Alberti "used to say, and he was a prudent man not in public affairs only but also in every aspect of private civic life, that it was a good sign if a merchant had ink-stained fingers." Lionardo expresses puzzlement, inducing Giannozzo to explain himself more crisply:

> He considered it essential for a merchant or anyone who does business with a large number of persons always to write everything down, to note all transactions, and to keep a record of every item brought in or taken out. As he watches over the enterprise, he should almost always have his pen in his hand. I, for one, think this an excellent precept. If you put things off from today to tomorrow, they elude you or are forgotten, and the agent finds excuses and occasions either for dishonesty or for carelessness like his master's.

Such records, Giannozzo explains, are too precious to show his own wife; he keeps them "locked up and arranged in order in my study, almost like sacred and religious objects."[22] The merchant is not only *homo oeconomicus* but *homo litterarius*, and his skills as writer and enumerator come close to defining his chief functions in the world.

The heads of Florentine families did exactly as Alberti's imaginary elder instructed. They regularly kept memoirs—texts of varying forms that combined elements of the notarial protocol, the family tree, the account book, and the diary. More than a hundred of these texts survive from the fourteenth to sixteenth centuries. They differ in a great many ways but converge in revealing a concern, like that expressed by Giannozzo Alberti, for preserving the details of family business and personal fate for generations to come.[23] And their authors agreed with Messer Benedetto Alberti that the obsessive recording of human and financial details would play a central role in success in the mercantile life:

> Every time you have an official document drawn up, be sure that you have a book ready in which you write the date, the name of the notary and the witnesses, and that of the person with whom you make the contract. . . . Men often play you false, with dangerous consequences. To avoid these you should always keep your documents in excellent order. Keep them in your trunk.[24]

Cosimo de' Medici, who followed these precepts religiously, took pleasure in recording the many ways in which he saved money. He noted, for example, that he would have been willing to give the corrupt official who let him out of prison a far larger bribe, had the man been clever enough to ask.

Alberti evoked a world whose inhabitants were sharply aware of time and its passing, alert to momentary opportunities: the shifting world of the early modern city, in which the solvent power of money corroded traditional values. Like Leibniz's universe, this world was divided into atomic units: the households on whose well-being society rested. At the center of each of these Alberti set a new figure: a paterfamilias blown up, by a magnificent metaphor, into a hulking, almost grotesque figure of control, one vibrantly alert to everything that could affect his house and tautly ready to deal with every difficulty or challenge. Uncle Giannozzo remarks, with a characteristic mixture of irony and respect, that "men of letters" often use analogies with the world of animals to explicate the world of men. Ants make a fine example of providential conduct and care for the future; bees, of obedience and cooperation. "Allow me, therefore," he continues,

> to follow you in this respected and noble custom. You know the spider and how he constructs his web. All the threads spread out in rays, each of which, however long, has its source, its roots or birthplace, as we might say, at the center. From there each filament starts and

moves outward. The most industrious creature himself then sits at that spot and has his residence there. He remains in that place once his work is spun and arranged, but keeps so alert and watchful that if there is a touch on the finest and most distant thread, he feels it instantly, instantly appears, and instantly takes care of the situation. Let the father of a family do likewise. Let him arrange his affairs and place them so that all look up to him alone as head, so that all are directed by him and by him attached to secure foundations. The father of the family should reside, then, in the midst of all, alert and quick to feel and to see everything, ready, whenever there is need of intervention, to provide it immediately.[25]

Lionardo professes to be deeply impressed by the "system and diligence" that this metaphor embodies; yet even he does not take up the images of surveillance and rapid response that Giannozzo's spider also conveys. The text is deeply suggestive, in other words, often in ways that its explicit content does not acknowledge.

Alberti did not set out to write a straightforward work of reportage, and it would be foolish to see in it a simple correspondence between literature and life—if such correspondences ever in fact exist. He omitted whole categories of fact central to the experience of all Florentine families, like the recent transformation of public finances by which the republic hoped to survive in an age of increasingly demanding and expensive warfare. Persistent problems had led, only a decade before he wrote, to the creation of the *catasto* system, a property tax based on a close examination of the assets and debits of every family in Florence. This system replaced an earlier one that used forced loans that were based on rough estimates of the assets in question. It required each family to report its composition, investments, property holdings, and other assets in detail.[26] Burckhardt, with characteristic prescience, treated the statistical consciousness that gave rise to this financial system as evidence for his argument that the Renaissance made the city into a work of art.[27] More recent archival work has shown that the execution of the *catasto* was more haphazard than its conception, as family influence and patronage enabled many to escape their proper burdens. But even a porous tax system required the enlargement of the corps of public officials and an enhancement of the powers of government. Alberti, maintaining the fiction that his work took place in 1421, did not refer to the new Florentine tax system, a clear indication that these fictional conversations, which he set in

Padua, were meant to be seen as taking place in a locale distinct from the Florence in and for which he wrote.[28]

More important still, Alberti stated explicitly that parts of his dialogue formed, among other things, a set of exercises in a familiar style. "You will notice," he wrote to Francesco d'Altobianco Alberti in the preface to book three, "the bare simplicity of the style, and in this you will recognize that I have done my best to imitate the charming and delightful Greek writer Xenophon. You, Francesco, since you have always held me dear and liked my works, will read this good *pater familias* and learn from him how to rule and preserve your own person, first of all, and then whatever you possess."[29] Alberti, in short, adapted a classic Greek text on one of his central topics: the *Oeconomicus*, a dialogue on household management, by Socrates' disciple, the historian and soldier Xenophon. Alberti deliberately set out to make book three of his own text an Italian analogue to Xenophon's, in terms of its stylistic register.

In using a classic work on household management to address the needs of a modern father, Alberti followed humanist fashion. The immensely influential Bruni, for example, produced in the early 1420s a translation of and commentary on the pseudo-Aristotelian treatise on the same subject. Like Xenophon, Aristotle dealt not with economics in the modern sense but with household management: the techniques needed to maintain the household, or *oikos*, which formed the core of ancient Greek society. These techniques included not only protocols for the organization of a house, the definition of gender roles, and ways to acquire and maintain wealth, but also much information about agriculture, since the *oikos* strove to be self-sufficient.[30] Bruni used Aristotle's text to address such vital contemporary topics as the legitimacy of lavish expenditure on one's house and household—and he did so with such a sharp eye for what the Florentine public wanted to read that his work became a best-seller before printing. More than two hundred copies of it survive, their original owners making a good cross-section of the Italian elite, lay and clerical. True, Alberti provided an adaptation rather than a translation of his text. But Bruni often did the same—for example, he adapted, with varying degrees of creativity, Greek originals for his Latin histories of the first Punic War, the wars of Sparta and Athens in the late fifth and early fourth centuries B.C.E., and the Italian war against the Goths.[31] So did Italian humanists of the previous generation, like the Venetian Francesco Barbaro, who reworked a treatise from Plutarch's *Moralia* in his own treatment of the problems connected with marriage (and whose work has been set into its own larger context by the social and cultural historian Margaret King).[32] Alberti, in short, followed precedent when he presented his third book as readymade rather than bespoke. As always, however, he altered his original radically to fit the changed conditions of the modern world. He drew on other ancient sources as well, emending all of them when necessary. Only a close comparison between Xenophon's text and Alberti's reworking of it—as well as other fifteenth-century documents concerned with the same issues—will reveal the full pattern of intentions that guided his efforts and help to clarify the special features of his version of Florentine clan life.[33]

The relationship between Alberti's book and its classical prototype seems at first straightforward. Both recount dialogues at second hand. Both award a principal part to men of experience and weight. Xenophon's Ischomachus, who tells Socrates how to run an ideal Athenian household, resembles Alberti's Giannozzo in many ways. Neither is young, but both are seasoned by their years. Active, even hyperactive, they take regular exercise, oversee their households with the minute attention to detail of the ideal watchman in Jeremy Bentham's Panopticon, and generally embody that type of the prepotent, ageless Mediterranean man which Picasso exemplified for the twentieth century. Both explain how they tamed and trained innocent young wives, making them active but compliant partners in their business. Both design ideal country houses whose rooms are laid out to serve different functions and are to be used in different seasons, while fertile gardens make the family unit self-sufficient.

These resemblances, however, do not make Alberti's work a copy of Xenophon's. Alberti, as we have repeatedly seen, defined creativity not as making something completely new but as reusing a classic idea or theme in a novel way. In an Italian dialogue written early in the 1440s, he compared an eloquent speaker to the inventor of mosaic flooring, who saw that he could not rival those who had created great columns of marble and roofs of bronze:

Therefore, to adorn the floor and distinguish it from the other surfaces of the temple, he took the little scraps of marble, porphyry, and jasper left over from the whole structure. Fitting them together in accordance with the colors and shapes, he composed picture after picture, making the whole pavement splendid. This work gave as much pleasure as the greater ones of the rest of the building. The same has occurred among the literati. The intellects of Asia and especially the

Greeks, over a long period, invented all the arts and disciplines. They constructed in their writings a sort of temple to Pallas.

The modern writer, Alberti's character explains, quarries his materials from the palace of antiquity. If he succeeds in assembling them "in such a way that their colors match a certain preexisting form and painting, and that there is no visible fissure or ugly gap among them, they give delight."[34] The task of the historian, then, is to look for some of the cracks and gaps that Alberti hoped his literary craftsmanship would render invisible.

It does not take long to find some of them. Xenophon's character Ischomachus is both a model active citizen and a model household manager: he inhabits both the public space of the city and the private space of the household, and he sees the two roles as complementary. But in Alberti's work, Ischomachus undergoes fission. He reappears in the double form of Giannozzo, the older, practical merchant who insists that the sensible man avoid the annoyances of public life in order to tend to his family affairs, and Lionardo, the young, book-learned scholar who insists that "glory is gained in public squares."[35] What had been unity in Xenophon appears as duality, even contradiction. Evidently Alberti thought that in his day, unlike Xenophon's, a man would find it very hard to lead at one and the same time the private life of prudence and the public life of honor: the family man's loyalty to relatives and friends had become almost impossible to reconcile with the political man's loyalty to the public interest.

Alberti's characters, like Xenophon's, inhabit a male world. No women speak. In book two, when Lionardo describes progeneration, and in book three, when Giannozzo sketches a Florentine ideal marriage, the voices of Alberti's characters are labeled masculine as clearly as that of their author. Sometimes they repeat, or seem to, the advice of Xenophon's Ischomachus. Both he and Giannozzo tell, for example, at gloating length, how they dissuaded their young wives from using cosmetics. Ischomachus recounts: "Well, Socrates, once I saw that she had made up her face with a great deal of white powder so that she might seem paler than she was, and with plenty of rouge so that she might seem to have a more rosy complexion than she truly had. And she wore platform shoes so that she might seem taller than she naturally was." Ischomachus dealt with these crimes against the codes of proper fashion and conduct in a masterly way. He asked his wife what she would think if he, Ischomachus, pretended to have more wealth than he really had, or used cosmetics and eyeshadow to appear more beautiful than he really was. She replied at once that she preferred his real self to any falsification. He explained that he felt the same way about her. At once she promised never to use cosmetics again.[36]

Alberti's Giannozzo did not accuse his wife of wearing high heels, since these belonged, along with a high, belled hat, to the uniform that the Florentine government tried to impose on prostitutes.[37] But he explained to her, as Ischomachus had, that cosmetics did not really adorn the human face. Giannozzo's wife agreed to imitate the Alberti girls, who kept their complexions sparkling fresh by washing them with nothing but river water. Unlike her Greek prototype, however, she backslid. At dances, her face sometimes seemed too red to be true. Once she even erred at home, covering her face with pumice to prepare for a dinner party at Eastertime. Giannozzo observed her "showing off and being merry with everyone" as they arrived: "I waited till we were alone. Then I smiled at her and said, 'O dear, how did your face get dirty? Did you by any chance bump into a pan? Go wash yourself, quick, before these people begin to make fun of you. The lady and mother of a household must always be neat and clean if she wants the rest of the family to learn good conduct and modest demeanor.' "[38] The ritual of humiliation had its effect. Giannozzo's wife at once began to cry. He let her wash off tears and makeup together, and she never did it again.

The two stories teach the same moral, but their ways of imparting it contrast sharply. In each, the older male explains proper conduct to the younger female. But Ischomachus treats his wife as a reasonable, if inferior, creature, whom he must convince. Giannozzo, by contrast, finding that persuasion fails to make his wife perfectly docile, resorts to the sharp weapon of his formidable sarcasm. He clearly enjoys turning his wife's training into a game of subordination. Fifteenth-century Florentines were not feminists. Crowds poured into the Duomo to hear Bernardino of Siena denounce women for their efforts to seduce men by their tight clothing, lewd gestures, and bright cosmetics. Sumptuary laws distinguished prostitutes and Jews from honorable women, while the fashion police regularly arrested those whose sleeves or gowns exceeded permissible levels of display.[39] Some of Alberti's departures from his classical model certainly resulted from the fact that in his social world, Xenophon's model of two spheres, one for males and one for females but each in crucial ways of independent value, did not seem to apply directly. To some extent, Alberti accurately depicted a changing urban society in which patrician women, confined to their homes, took less and less part even in such fundamental public activities as criminal cases.[40]

But Alberti's adaptation did not simply represent the intensification of Athenian chauvinism to a still more repressive Florentine standard. Not all upper-class male Florentines in Alberti's time viewed women as he did. Giovanni Morelli, in a famous passage in his autobiography, recalled that his sister Mea was "blond and white" of complexion, with "hands that seemed to be of ivory, so well made that they seemed painted by the hand of Giotto." Her gifts were more than physical. "She read and wrote as well as any man, knew how to dance and sing perfectly," and could serve a table of men or women with polish and politesse. An expert in household economy, she was never mean but wasted not and wanted not. And she ran her entire household with a combination of firm discipline and skilled diplomacy, immediately "seeing to any scandal, anger, or melancholy that she had noted in anyone, with words and deeds."[41] Giovanni's evocation of his sister's beauty is not his own composition but a well-chosen passage drawn from the portrait of Elena in the fourteenth-century *Istorietta troiana*. But his careful account of the managerial and diplomatic roles that women played in the social system of the great Florentine clans, overseeing expenditures and healing rifts, reflects realities uncovered by historians from Iris Origo to Sharon Strocchia and Leonida Pandimiglio.[42] Vespasiano, similarly, recognized—like the painters of Florentine *cassoni*, or wedding chests—that unmarried girls appeared in public in ways that the reigning theory did not recognize. At weddings and receptions, for example, girls took an active part: they dressed elaborately and danced with men of appropriate social position.[43]

Confronted with the lively, sometimes contradictory world of Florentine society, Alberti's imagined city sometimes reveals itself to be, like his treatise on painting, not a description of existing customs but a call for their improvement. To portray the female sphere, for example, he used Uncle Giannozzo. And he in turn, despite his claim to be a "man without letters," echoed the author's views. Speaking as Giannozzo, Alberti applied his favorite literary and aesthetic principle, decorum, to the problems of women's conduct. He has Uncle Giannozzo explain that he told his wife to maintain decorum in all things. Decorum required grave speech and gestures, the sort that he had treated, in *On Painting*, as appropriate to women; it called for silence when outside the house and constant, ordered activity within it.

The good wife, like the good husband, must be constantly active: "Altogether avoid idleness, always keep busy." But the busy wife must never become a busybody. Above all, she should never quarrel with servants and others, for if she did so, she would inevitably engage in actions and make gestures inappropriate to her sex and standing. " 'It is an ugly thing,' " says Giannozzo, " 'If women like you, dear wife, who are honorable and worthy of all respect, are seen with wild-eyed contorted expressions, screaming, threatening, and throwing their arms about.' " The ideal mother of the family must take responsibility for as many areas as the father. Here too decorum must reign. A good wife does not simply collect and lock up all the household's goods, from jewels and gowns to flax and baby chicks, as Giannozzo's innocent wife naively proposes. Rather, she sorts everything, putting each household item "where it is absolutely safe, yet accessible and ready to hand, while encumbering the house as little as possible."[44]

Neat, ordered, and inhabited by dignified figures carrying out the tasks appropriate to them, the households of Giannozzo and his like would resemble so many domestic "histories" by Albertian painters. Like the *historia*, Alberti's model family was clearly meant as an ideal pattern, a model for emulation. Real life is messier than high art, and everyday emotion and long-established customs would never allow most families to be ruled as Alberti directed. The artistic version offered an ideal to aim at. When Alberti (through Lionardo) insists that mothers should nurse their own children, for example, he reveals his distance from Florentine realities. Wealthy Florentine children were normally nursed for their first two years or longer, by nurses carefully chosen by their fathers. This system caused endless problems, as nurses became pregnant, quarreled with mothers, or struck for higher pay: it also contributed to high infant mortality. But it was the norm, and Lionardo's discussion of the topic represented a plea for reform.[45]

The treatise on household management that was attributed to Aristotle in the Renaissance—the pseudo-Aristotelian *Economics*, which Alberti also read—offered a more hierarchical version of the *oikos* than Xenophon. In fact, Aristotle was so hierarchical that his interpreters tried to qualify his analysis in crucial ways. Bruni, for example, underlined the limitations on legitimate male power in his commentary: "The man is head of the household, the king, so to speak, of his own house . . . he is not prevented by any ancient law from exercising power over servants and children. But, says Aristotle, the man does not seem to have authority in the same way over his wife. On the contrary, there are certain laws that the man must observe toward his wife. If he transgresses them, he does her wrong." Where Aristotle quoted Hesiod to the effect that a household needed "a house, and a woman, and an ox to plow the field," putting wives and domestic animals on the same level, Bruni insisted that "Hesiod was not thinking of a wife but of a slave-girl." To save the ancient philosopher's credit, Bruni claimed that Aristotle—like Dante much later—had appropriated a poet's line at the expense of distortion. Bruni, in short, made his ancient text more moderate on the very points where Alberti made his more patriarchal.[46] Alberti, in other words, imposed a highly personal framework of interpretation on the materials he deployed.

Other sections of On the Family transposed discussions that took place among the learned humanists of the curia into the Florentine cultural tradition. In the preface to book three, explaining his intentions to Francesco d'Altobianco Alberti, Leon Battista describes On the Family as a massive scholarly and linguistic project. Older members of the Alberti family, he writes, used to discuss in the family's lovely gardens "which was the greater loss, the fall of our ancient, most extensive empire [i.e., the Roman Empire], or the dying out of our ancient, most beautiful tongue [i.e., Latin]." The second seemed the worse; but it was also an inevitable consequence of the first. Barbarian invasions had brought new peoples into Italy: Gauls, Goths, Lombards, Vandals. The need to communicate forced the natives and barbarians to speak with one another, and this "mixing . . . made our originally refined and polished language grow from day to day more rustic and degenerate." Italian, in other words, descended from Latin and contained many barbarian elements that the older tongue had lacked.

Some scholars, to be sure, denied this account, insisting that Italy had always been bilingual. These purists, conscious of how difficult they themselves found it to write Latin correctly, refused to "believe that the women in those days knew things which are obscure and difficult even for the most learned scholars today," like conjugations and declensions. They argued that Latin had always been "an academic and artificial invention, understood but not truly used by many people." Even ancient Roman scholars had communicated with their wives and servants in a second, less complex language, the direct ancestor of Italian. Alberti insisted that these purists were wrong: everyone had used Latin, for all purposes, in antiquity, just as everyone used Italian in his own day: "How many women in those days were highly praised for their good Latin." Even Italian, moreover, had a grammar of its own— one that foreign slaves, for example, found extremely difficult to master. And his own first extended work in the Tuscan dialect—the form used by Dante, Petrarch, and Boccaccio before him—demonstrated that one could use a popular language to address the general public on moral and practical issues of complexity, while drawing on the most subtle and serious classical writers—just as Cicero had done, in Latin, for the Latin-reading and -speaking public of his own time.[47]

In staking out this position, Alberti was not so much presenting a Florentine tradition as taking sides in a learned debate that passionately divided the humanists of the papal curia and the Florentine chancery. In spring 1435, an argument about Latin had broken out among the humanist secretaries who gathered outside the pope's bedchamber. The mendacious, clever circle that Poggio had enjoyed so much, the "chamber of lies," buzzed with original linguistic theories. Leonardo Bruni argued that the ancients had spoken not Latin, a written and learned language, but a second, "vulgar" tongue. Flavio Biondo rebutted this thesis. Others joined in. Before the debate reached an end, Bruni was called away to the pope's side, so Biondo drafted a short treatise in which he argued that all Romans—illiterate women, children, and servants as well as literate men—had spoken Latin. Barbarian invasion and centuries of linguistic and social fusion had turned this originally unified language into Italian over the centuries.[48] Some weeks later, Bruni replied in writing, insisting that even the learned Romans had used a language without a formal grammar when communicating with the unlearned. The large audiences at Cicero's speeches, he suggested, had enjoyed them without understanding the details—exactly as modern Catholics could be carried away by the music and power of the liturgy even though they did not understand it: "the bakers and woolworkers and persons of that sort would have so understood the orator's words as they now understand the Mass."

Bruni and Biondo had some common ground. Both agreed that ancient Latin had survived, to some extent, in zones of society that had escaped foreign invasion. Bruni admitted that Roman women still spoke a purer language than the men did, "a pure and native Roman dialect."[49] He argued forcefully, a year after the debate took place, that "each language has its own perfection and its own sound, and its polished and learned diction"—a clear admission that Italian, like Latin, has a grammar of its own.[50] He even wrote biographies of Petrarch and Dante in Italian to replace what he saw as the trivial ones of Boccaccio. Yet neither man seems to have argued that Italian could provide a proper medium for the sort of learned debates he and his friends carried on in classical Latin.[51]

Alberti, in writing a large-scale work on problems of morality and household management in Italian, implicitly challenged Bruni, offering what he took as more accessible advice, to the same patrician public, on the same questions, but in their own Tuscan dialect. And he did so on civic grounds like those that Bruni had long used to justify his own literary activities: because by writing in the language generally used in his own time, he could profit "the many" rather than "the few." By prefacing his characters' remarks with an attack in his own voice on Bruni's history of the Italian language, Alberti ensured that no one could miss the polemical point of his work.

In one respect, moreover, Alberti went further than the other contributors to the debate. Bruni had argued that the Romans used two languages: a cultivated tongue and a vulgar one. He had not connected the latter with the modern *volgare*, Italian. Biondo had argued that the *volgare* used in medieval and modern Italy came into being after Rome fell, but he had not pronounced on its literary qualities or possibilities. Alberti, by contrast, indicated that the Tuscan language had been "originally refined and polished," and that the barbarian invasions had caused it to degenerate.[52] By so doing, he suggested strongly that the modern vernacular, which Dante, Petrarch, and Boccaccio had turned back into a cultivated language, was not something new, but was the recreation of something old: the revival of the original language of the Etruscans, who had inhabited Tuscany before the Romans did. He thus offered a new pedigree, fashioning an "Etruscan myth" for the Tuscan literary tradition—one that later Florentine scholars would take up and embellish wildly.[53] At the same time, he provided a clear, practical plan for improving what remained of the primeval eloquent speech of the Italians. Direct adaptation of classical originals, he said, would restore the polish of this ancient language. Italian, he both argued and tried to demonstrate, could provide a vehicle for one of the most demanding and Latinate of genres, the Ciceronian philosophical dialogue, as readily as it already had for lyric and epic poetry.

Alberti had arrived at a position of importance and repute in the city. In April 1440, five years after the Italian-Latin debate began, the distinguished scholar Ambrogio Traversari died, literally in the odor of sanctity (lilies sprouted miraculously on his grave). Girolamo Aliotti tried to convince the distinguished humanist Carlo Marsuppini to write a life of the great man. When Marsuppini gave him an equivocal response, he turned at once to Alberti, writing, "It will be, without doubt, a very rewarding work, and one that will enhance your reputation. The subject matter is very broad, and worthy of your gifts." Though Aliotti tried hard to persuade Alberti, nothing came of his proposal. But it illustrates the esteem that Alberti enjoyed as

Latinist—and perhaps as hagiographer.[54] However, Alberti's efforts to attain a reputation in the vernacular would soon shake his arduously attained position among the humanists.

Alberti tried often and hard to make his intellectual enterprises collaborative. In the years 1440 and 1441, as he was putting the final touches to *On the Family*, he turned his work on the Tuscan language into a project for a task force. Alberti had already composed a considerable amount of Italian rhythmic prose and verse, some of it radically experimental, on the traditional theme of love.[55] With financial support from Piero de' Medici, he now organized what he called a *certame coronario*, a public contest, the winner of which would receive a silver laurel crown. Alberti and Piero had in mind the ancient custom of rewarding with a crown of oak or laurel those who did some service to the Roman state, as well as the rich and complex web of legends about poets' coronations that had taken shape in antiquity and grown thicker and more complex in the Middle Ages.[56] But the form of this contest would be nativist, adapted in part from the artists' contests for commissioned works that both fascinated and disturbed Alberti. As in the artists' contests, so in this one, a subject was proposed: entrants had to write in the Tuscan vernacular on the theme of friendship. Many distinguished writers—including not only Florentines, like Alberti's relative Francesco d'Altobianco Alberti, but also non-Tuscans like Cyriac of Ancona—tried their hand.[57]

As Alberti had done when writing on the household, the competing poets ransacked the ancients for myths to evoke, sources to cite, and models to adapt. Antonio degli Agli drew on the late antique Neoplatonist and mystic, pseudo-Dionysius the Areopagite: in that circle whose center is everywhere and which has no circumference, "I saw the holy fount and example of friendship." He used the mythical figures of Medusa and Circe to illustrate how love, when it longed for the wrong object, could descend to the realm of beasts; and he invoked Prometheus, "rapt into the skies," to exemplify the higher, purifying kind of love. Mariotto d'Arrigo Davanzati laid out the opinions on friendship of the pagan philosophers Socrates, Aristotle, Theophrastus, and Pythagoras, then capped the list with the supposed view of Augustine, "the worthy heir of Ambrose, who holds, in the *City of God*, that one should love one's friend as the soul within one"—a misquotation, perhaps drawn from an existing anthology. Alberti's friend Leonardo Dati adapted phrases from Virgil to apostrophize the "temple of Flora" (the Florentine Cathedral), which had the good fortune to serve as the stage for the contest: "O happy place," he wrote, which would become dear to the *celicoli*, the inhabitants of heaven, as the poets who thronged there strove to capture the "hidden thing" that was friendship.[58]

As always, Alberti accorded expert critics a large role in his enterprise. Ten papal secretaries, including several of those who had joined the debate of 1435 about the history of Latin and Italian, agreed to serve as judges—the equivalent of the panel that had chosen Ghiberti's models for the Baptistery doors. On 22 October 1441, the contestants read their poetry aloud in the Cathedral of Santa Maria del Fiore, before an enthusiastic crowd. Copies of the texts—more than two hundred, according to Alberti—rapidly went into circulation, reaching princely libraries and attracting the praise of the learned throughout Italy.[59] A second contest, on the theme of envy, was planned for the following year. Humanist students of the history of Latin and Italian, like Biondo, seemed poised to approve Alberti's effort to classicize the modern language (Tuscan), supporting his challenge to Bruni's enormous cultural and personal authority.

Unfortunately, Alberti's recourse to collective judgment produced sharp debate rather than consensus. The ten judges refused to award the crown to any of the erudite poets. True, they admitted, the contestants had all done well at carrying out the central tasks of rhetoric (which they, like Alberti, saw as very closely connected to poetics): "the invention was very rich, and it was well laid out and well adorned." But the modern adaptations, they insisted, all fell short of the ancient works from which their contents were drawn: "despite their qualities, they were vanquished by some in their arguments."[60] The poets had emptied their notebooks in vain, so it seemed: their Italian verse reworkings of Latin originals added too little value to deserve a prize. The verdict is not altogether surprising. The whole idea of treating the classical theme of *amicizia*, subject of one of Cicero's most widely read dialogues, in Italian and in "barbarous" meters, may have been shocking even to Biondo and Poggio. One could admit that the best spoken Italian contained remnants of good Latin, as Biondo did, without remotely wishing to see the vernacular Tuscan replace the classical language. And many may not have wished to offend Bruni—who had, after all, insisted in public and on paper that many subjects could not be treated fully and smoothly "in the vulgar tongue."

The judges prudently awarded the crown not to an individual but to the Cathedral treasury. Alberti, furious, wrote a magnificent *protesta*, in which he denounced the judges for failing to carry out their job of offering helpful criticism to those who had asked for it, in the best humanistic tradition. He expressed the suspicion that "there is one among you who attacks this literary hegemony of ours, and claims it is unworthy for a vernacular to strive against a very noble literary language, and that such contests should accordingly be forbidden." He scattered much sarcasm over those who had evidently forgotten that "we are all from Jupiter, and we all buy salt, one as much as another." But he also explained exactly how the judges had misunderstood their historical task. Before the Latin language reached a state of high cultivation, he explained, the Romans had been "content with the earliest poets as they had them—clever, perhaps, but with little artistry." Similarly, good modern critics should help their contemporaries to defend and illuminate their language, not denounce the crudity of their first efforts to do so. In literature, as in the world of technology and the visual arts, Alberti had hoped to find help when he asserted the legitimacy of the modern world. But this time he failed.[61]

Alberti's protest made as little impression as most replies to critics have made, before and after. He had provoked Bruni, after all: Bruni, who not only ruled the chancery of Florence but was a man of great wealth and power and a considerable scholar. In a world of manuscript books, he commanded great interest among literate men: 3,400 manuscripts of his works survive, an astonishing number. Giovanni Rucellai recalled that Bruni was held to be the most learned man in Europe. A letter that Bruni sent to one of Alberti's closest friends, Leonardo Dati, suggests how the great man felt about Alberti's enterprise. Dati had produced a work on envy, the theme of the second proposed contest. Bruni commented dryly: "I have seen your text directed against envy, and I praised and praise your genius. But it seems to me that a good bit more could be said against stupidity than against envy. Both are evils, to be sure, but stupidity is the worse one." Alberti ventured to accost Bruni one day in Santa Croce, where he complained about what he described, in an apparent attempt at diplomacy, as the mischief of Carlo Marsuppini, a younger humanist who would succeed Bruni as chancellor. Bruni professed not to understand Alberti's complaint and advised him to avoid literary quarrels; later—after being urged to do so by Jacopo Ammannati—he sent Alberti a cool Latin letter in which he proclaimed his own "simplicity" and urged the younger man not to think so ill of his friends—presumably meaning Bruni himself.[62]

By 1442, in other words, Alberti's attempt to define what was Florentine in Florence, culturally and linguistically, seemed to have fizzled. His public celebration of the Tuscan language had turned into an occasion of humiliation. Bruni had been in the situation that the Cambridge classicist F. M. Cornford described in *Microcosmographia academica*: "From far below you will mount the roar of young men in a hurry . . . They are in a hurry to get you out of the way." Playing every one of his cultural and social cards, Bruni triumphed over the younger man, retaining his cultural capital undiminished. Alberti found himself reduced to the characteristic straits of the humanist in a difficult situation: trying to make himself believe that Stoic canons of self-discipline really provided a therapy adequate to heal the wounded self. In later decades, Alberti's innovative Italian poetry would provoke imitation, both in the Florence of Lorenzo de' Medici and in wider circles in Ferrara and Naples. Alberti, in retrospect, played a central role in the tradition of Italian poetry, modernizing the tradition of Petrarch, with its rich lexicon of oxymorons, in ways that Lorenzo and others found deeply stimulating. But Alberti's place in Italian literary history must even now be reconstructed from quotations and allusions; he could not have known, in the 1440s, that he would later find so many understanding readers.[63]

After husbanding his energies and resources, Alberti returned to the attack—even as he also cultivated court patrons outside Florence. He settled on an expert helper, a jungle guide, who could lead him through the labyrinths of Florentine language and life, in the person of Leonardo Dati.[64] Dati, an expert on the ways of the curia, joined with Alberti in organizing his poetry contest and in many other enterprises. In 1443 Alberti submitted *On the Family* to the scrutiny of Dati and Tommaso Ceffi. Dati was a sharp and expert critical reader, as much a specialist as Niccoli, to whom many submitted their writings. Niccolò della Luna had begged Dati "not just to correct, but to emend" his text on friendship for the *certame coronario*. Matteo Palmieri submitted his massive, heretical Italian poem *The City of Life* to his judgment. Dati's critical bite, like Niccoli's, was every bit as bad as his bark. He even managed to offend Ceffi, his partner in editing Alberti, with the abrasiveness of one of his commentaries. Dati and Ceffi found that in *On the Family*, Alberti badly needed their editorial help. He had quoted too many writers "without mentioning their names, almost as if you had not read their works or were inventing the quotations and leaving a blank." And his "style is too lofty and there is a roughness about it that accords ill with the Florentine tongue and that the general reader may disapprove of; this is particularly evident in the beginning."[65]

Alberti made at least some of the revisions his critics suggested. But he also returned to the study and cultivation of the Florentine dialect—and went so far as to compile the first grammar of Tuscan, arguing that the language actually was, in many respects, Latin, not an illegitimate descendant of the classical language. If he never mapped the city, he did provide the first paradigms of Florentine nouns and verbs. He showed particular ingenuity— as the poet, scholar, and alchemist Giovanni Augurello remarked, a few years after Alberti died—when "he created a new alphabet, taking some letters from Latin and adding others," to represent Tuscan phonetically. He insisted that "those who claim that the Latin language was not shared by all the Latin peoples, but belonged only to certain learned scholastics, as we say today, will, I believe, abandon this error when they see this little work." He made clear that he could provide for Tuscan a grammar exactly like those that "great and learned intellects" had created in Greece, and then in Rome, for the ancient languages. And he compiled a detailed and accurate account of Tuscan usage in his time, often describing relatively recent developments like the substitution of *fussi* for *fossi* and *fusti* for *fosti* in the perfect tense of the verb "to be" (*essere*).[66] It was a remarkable feat of observation and codification, driven, at times, by Alberti's characteristic desire to correct and impose order. Sadly, Alberti's public failure robbed him of credit for his real achievements in the vernacular. This work was forgotten for centuries.

Alberti's efforts to revise *On the Family* eventually bore fruit, at least indirectly. An adaptation of the third book, in which Uncle Giannozzo describes the ideal household and householder, circulated widely among Florentine patrician families—so widely, in fact, that it became detached from its original author and context. Many copies of it reassigned the role of the old man of experience not to Giannozzo Alberti but to Agnolo Pandolfini (though some also bear the name of the Pazzi). The text was not only copied but read: Giovanni Rucellai, for example, transcribed long extracts from it into his notebooks, the famous *Zibaldone quaresimale* (Lenten Soup).[67]

In the final versions of the text, moreover, Alberti pulled off a remarkable synthesis. Returning to the social and moral problems that had troubled him for years, he found a way of describing them in terms that had a powerful local resonance. Ever since the loss of his own great expectations, as we have seen, Alberti had been deeply troubled by the power of fortune: the embodied force of circumstance that had leveled so many noble houses like his own. In more than one of his short Latin *Dinner Pieces*, he had raised the question of whether, or how, men could struggle with fortune. In "Fate and Fortune," one of the most striking, he envisions life as a river, into which all must throw themselves. Some, grasping floats, ride high—only to find themselves dashed against the rocks by the waves, punished for their ostentation. Others, seeming barely to swim, "know when to pause briefly to wait for an approaching boat or for planks borne by the river, and when to use their great strength to avoid the rocks and to fly to shore in glory." Some repair and steer boats for others, winning glory as rulers. Others skim across the water with wings and winged sandals; they are seekers of truth and inventors of the liberal arts. If the allegory seems clear, the lessons that emerge are sometimes puzzling. Even the rulers are constantly confronted by crises, when the lazy members of their ship's crew rebel against their authority or superfluous members must be thrown into the water to save the rest. Those who seek truth and create new knowledge enjoy an unquestioned preeminence. For the rest, though, no one is guaranteed a safe passage. At the end, the philosopher reflects that human virtue and industry are valuable but only partial aids against disaster:

> I observed that Fortune is kinder to those who fall into the river where there chance to be whole planks or a boat. By contrast, I found that Fortune is harsh to those of us who have plunged into the river at a time when we must continually overcome the waves by swimming. But we shall not be unaware that prudence and diligence are of great value in human affairs.[68]

Time and chance, fate and fortune await all, and only the victories of the spirit seem likely to prove permanent.

Alberti here presented a radically agonistic picture of human society, not as a lucid, static, and ordered system but as an arena of strife and competition. The duties of man do not emerge clearly: Should one stick to household management or try to control and save the state? The philosopher's vision provokes questions instead of providing answers. No choice of a practical or political vocation offers certain rewards, in this world or the next.

The Florentine merchants of the 1430s and 1440s were coming to inhabit a world that Alberti's images reflected with striking accuracy. Explanations of the world that were based on traditional social hierarchies could not, by the nature of things, make sense of a city in which those of noble blood had long since been declared "magnates" and deprived of political rights. Religion offered some consolations, but some of its most popular and authoritative voices condemned the basic forms of trade and banking by which Florentines were making themselves rich. The brilliant Franciscan preacher Bernardino da Siena denounced the pursuit of wealth. He agreed that trade carried on "for honest purposes" and on a modest scale, with the aim of maintaining a single family or helping the poor, was acceptable, but he denounced the pursuit of gain for its own sake: "If a man does it to support his family or to get out of debt or to marry his daughters, it is licit. But what shall I say of the man who has no such need, yet toils so much? . . . I say that if he is not doing it for the poor, he is sinning." Though Bernardino had learned from the writings of Peter John Olivi to allow latitude of various kinds for the earning of profits in trade, his rhetoric became fiery when he condemned the lending of money at interest, even when it was disguised as currency exchange or carried on to serve the state itself. His audiences came and listened avidly, even though not one of them was willing to raise a hand when Bernardino asked those "who have as much property as they need" to do so.[69]

Like Goro Dati, with whom we began this chapter, the articulate patrician knew that the basic pursuits on which his social and political power rested seemed to contradict the teachings of his religion. He also knew that nothing was easier to lose than capital (as Alberti too had found out). Success brought problems of its own. The state, and one's fellow citizens, avidly tried to find out one's total worth; prudent fathers urged their sons to plead poverty, dress in rags, and conceal their wealth in the countryside. And no success lasted forever. Royal houses and local power-brokers refused to pay their debts, bankrupting the great banks and ordinary men who had bankrolled their wars and trading expeditions. Political power shifted unpredictably: only alliance with a really powerful family could preserve an ordinary man from disaster, and even that could lead to exile and worse—as happened to many followers of the Albizzi regime, which had dominated Florence in the early fifteenth century, after the Medici returned and expelled them. Even the basic medium of the mercantile economy, money itself, caused terrible problems. "Don't advertise the fact that you are rich," wrote Giovanni Morelli. "Instead, do the contrary: if you gain 1,000 florins, say that you have made 500. . . . And this is quite legitimate, because you are lying not to steal from another but rather so that your property will not be taken from you unjustly."[70] "What is there," echoed Adovardo Alberti, in Alberti's dialogues, "that's more likely to go astray [than money], more troublesome to get back, more easily dissipated, spent, and consumed in smoke? What is there more likely to disappear in all sorts of ways than money? There is nothing less stable, less solid."[71]

The shifting grounds and conflicting commandments characteristic of modern urban life had powerful psychic effects, as Aby Warburg pointed out long ago, on the more sensitive Florentine merchants. Still Christians, they offered their devotions to Dominic and Francis as well as many other saints. But as practical men, they knew that from day to day, the ground—or the sea—could open and swallow them. Even late in life (so the late fifteenth-century merchant Francesco Sassetti discovered after a largely successful career), one might find oneself writing a last will in which one confessed to one's sons, "Where Fortune intends us to make landfall, I know not, in view of the upheavals and the changes amid which we now find ourselves (may God grant us a safe haven)."[72] Next to the power of providence stood fortune: cheerful or jealous, but incalculable in either mode. Sassetti hoped that divine providence would guide him home, but he knew he could not rely on it to do so. Giovanni Rucellai, who eventually became the chief patron for Alberti's architectural work, asked the philosopher and medical man Marsilio Ficino whether human intelligence and industry could counter the power of providence. He received a long, equivocal response, suggesting that one could use prudence and forethought to confront fortune directly; or retire into contemplation, withdrawing from the world and thus from combat with fortune; or simply yield to it, allowing it to rule one's life. Ficino recommended the third course as wisest.[73]

This spiritual conflict was complicated, at the moment when Alberti began to compose his work, by the political change that took place in Florence, as Cosimo de' Medici took control of the city. Over time, the Medici appropriated the city's republican institutions, as they manipulated the electoral system to fill offices with their supporters. They also fostered a more aristocratic style of life, allowing great clan heads like Giovanni Rucellai to display their wealth without suffering financial or political penalties; in fact, they ran the city financially, to a large extent, for the benefit of their supporters. Thus Alberti composed his work at a time when the elements of Florentine social and moral tradition—already multiple and varied—were beginning to shift their forms and positions.[74]

Casting his work as a dialogue among sharply differentiated speakers, Alberti crafted it to mirror, if not to heal, the divided hearts of men like Sassetti and Rucellai. Should the patrician opt, as many had done in the fourteenth century, to live for himself and his family, avoiding the endless entanglements and dangers of political life and trying to win honor by maintaining rigorous honesty in private life? Uncle Giannozzo argues that he should, denouncing public life as one long odyssey of unnecessary business:

"Now you must organize taxes, now expenditures, now provide for wars, now clarify and revise laws; there are always so many connections between various tasks and activities of government that neither you alone nor you with the help of supporters can ever accomplish as much as you want." Or should the patrician opt for the public life, trying to win honor by caring for the public good? Young Lionardo takes this Ciceronian, civic republican line, as did others in his generation. "Fame," he urges with unforgettable eloquence, "is born not in the midst of private peace but in public action. Glory springs up in public squares; reputation is nourished by the voice and judgement of many persons of honor, and in the midst of the people."

Alberti celebrated his elders' successful pursuit of wealth: he made one of his characters boast that over a long period, the Alberti had contributed a whopping one thirty-second of the city's total revenues. He enthusiastically describes the continual energy and willingness to take risks that have enabled them to "buy their empire from fortune with gold and blood." But he also acknowledges that many families as great as the Alberti have seen their treasure "quickly exhausted, and their treasure has, as people say, gone up in smoke, leaving sometimes only poverty, misery, and disgrace." Uncle Giannozzo magically conveys the quality of urban life: "in the city are the workshops of great dreams."[75] But he speaks with still greater eloquence about the decency, cleanliness and good health associated with a self-sufficient life on a farm in the country. Alberti insists, throughout his work, on certain values: he continually stresses the worth of the liberal arts and the need to pursue honor at all times. At the same time, he admits that the best ancient books could not provide guidance for all modern occasions, and that in the chaos and noise of everyday life, the demands of honor are not easy to define. His own dialogue, which recast a Ciceronian debate in unmistakably contemporary language, made clear exactly how creatively one had to use ancient sources to make them fit modern occasions.[76]

Book three of On the Family thus became a theater in which Alberti staged a central drama of Florentine life. He himself espoused neither a private, mercantile vision (which prized gain even over patriotism) nor an idealistic, civic ideology (which set public over private life). But he appreciated the "rich variety of . . . Florentine ideas," the range of views held by Florentine patricians and the degree to which they actually contradicted one another.[77] He dramatized the conflict between them by using the dialogue form. And the adapter who produced the more popular version of book three took a further step: by assigning both positions to the same speaker,

Agnolo Pandolfini, he flattened the conflict that Alberti had wanted to put in relief—but probably came closer to the lived experience of many Florentines, who tried to hold both positions in some kind of creative tension. That, at least, is what Giovanni Rucellai seems to have felt as he copied the passages in question into his notebook.

Not all the views Alberti expressed in book three found assent, not even those he held most dear. The painter, he wrote in *On Painting*, should make only the most sparing use of white and black in order not to diminish the effect of these colors; he must also avoid the use of gold, because "there is greater admiration and praise for the artist in the use of pigments."[78] He should, in short, practice *masserizia*—"economy"; a good painter should be *avaro e massaio*, "greedy and economical."[79] The householder, Uncle Giannozzo argues in book three of *On the family*, should show the same virtues. Excess expenditures on a luxurious house, he argues, are optional at best; waste is to be avoided at all costs, and one should set on the table not "pheasant and capon and partridge" but "a good domestic spread, with no lack of wine and plenty of bread"—ideally, produced on one's own estates.

Alberti often receives credit for reviving the ideal of magnificence in private life. And he did allow Lionardo to argue that family wealth could legitimately be used to adorn public and private buildings, as a way of attaining "fame and authority." As Florentine political and social codes evolved in the age of the Medici, such suggestions bore fruit in architectural patronage on a newly large scale. But these were seeds that sprouted in a changed environment from the one in which Alberti wrote. Alberti's balanced presentation of the uses of wealth, in which Giannozzo powerfully argues the case against conspicuous expenditure on luxuries, showed far less sympathy for conspicuous consumption than did Bruni's commentary on Aristotle. Bruni agreed with Aristotle that wealth, properly used, allowed the paterfamilias to adorn his house and enjoy his life, and he recommended the construction of a house "appropriate to one's riches." True, even Giannozzo praises cloth with "joyous colors" and a fine nap, boasting of the high quality and long life of his garments; then as now, the rich paid less than the poor for items of everyday consumption. But he also insists that well-kept old clothes do honor to their wearers' prudence, and that new clothing should be bought and worn only for feast days. Once again, decorum, not magnificence, was Alberti's ruling principle: "Among first considerations, my very first would be and always has been to keep my household well dressed, each member in accordance with his station."[80] The Alberti who had found the displays of the wealthy so depressing in his years as a poor student was no more inclined to favor them as a mature man.

It was Bruni, not Alberti, who expressed the views of those Florentine patricians who were making their private lives and houses into works of art: Marco Parenti, for example, who adorned the austere chambers of his city house with splendid *cassoni* painted by Domenico Veneziano and gave his wife, Caterina Strozzi, a long overgown trimmed in marten, a silk dress, seventeen shirts, and a garland adorned with no fewer than eight hundred "eyes" from select peacock tails. At this point Alberti did not foresee the boom in luxury consumption that would soon seize Florence, transforming the very meaning of his favorite term, so that *masserizia* came to mean not only "thrift" but "consumer durable."[81]

Alberti's other arguments may have had a deeper impact than the one he made for thrift in family life, notably his plea for intelligence and judgment in the use of artistic materials. When Uncle Giannozzo sets out to instruct his young wife on the evils of cosmetics, he cites a parallel from the arts:

> There was a saint in the room, a very lovely statue of silver, whose head and hands alone were of purest ivory. It was set, polished and shining, in the center of the altar as usual. "My dear wife," I said to her, "suppose you besmirched the face of this image in the morning with chalk and calcium and other ointments. It might well gain in color and whiteness. In the course of the day the wind would carry dust to it and make it dirty, but in the evening you would wash it, and then, the next day, cover it again with ointments, and then wash it again. Tell me, after many days of this, if you wanted to sell it, all polished and painted, how much money do you think you would get for it? Much less than if you had never begun painting it?"
>
> "Much less," she replied.
>
> "That's right," said I, "for the buyer of the image does not buy it for a coating of paint which can be put on or off but because he appreciates the quality of the statue and the grace of the master."

One version of the *Trattato*—the shortened text of Alberti that Rucellai and many others read—incorporates this passage with few changes. It must have been one of the first texts that clearly expounded the view that a work of art should be judged by the skill deployed to make it rather than the materials used. In the second half of the fifteenth century, contracts between Florentine patrons and artists laid an increasing emphasis on the artist's skill, specifying the amount of time he himself must spend or requiring him to paint the faces and hands of the principal figures, rather than demanding the use of especially expensive and durable pigments, as such contracts had done before. It seems more than likely that On the Family and the Trattato helped to give wider currency to an appreciation of artistic skill.[82]

In the 1450s, Alberti finally established himself in Florence as an architect. By then, as we will see, he had developed a highly individual intellectual and artistic style, and the world around him had changed as well. In book four of On the Family, written in the late 1430s, he developed a new understanding of that changed society, one that emphasized the role of patronage and the need for obtaining support from great men. And he put his precepts into practice, finding employment as an architect and consultant on ancient and modern buildings in courts across Italy. In Florence Alberti worked, as is well known, not in a court but as a consultant to a great man, Giovanni Rucellai, transforming sections of Giovanni's Quarter of the Red Lion into one of the classic areas of urban experimentation in the modern world. In the facade of the Rucellai Palace and that of Santa Maria Novella, he imposed the rhythms of classical architecture and aesthetics on the picture of the city as a whole, intervening in a powerful new way in the fabric of the city without producing full-scale new buildings from scratch.

How Alberti and Rucellai came together we do not know. As F. W. Kent has shown, Alberti may not even have been the one who convinced the Florentine merchant to become a connoisseur and patron of architectural projects.[83] But their tastes and beliefs coincided, in ways that show how well Alberti had understood the urban patricians whose mentalities he dramatically portrayed. Alberti held, as his Dinner Pieces show, that symbols and heraldic emblems had a great power to sum up, in an artistically attractive and pedagogically effective way, the lessons of morality and prudence. He also came to believe, as he argued in On the Art of Building, that the facades of major buildings, public and private, should speak to the passerby. Inscriptions, reliefs, myths, and symbols could offer moral as well as aesthetic lessons, as the hieroglyphs of the Egyptians had once done for visitors to their temples.

Fortune, Alberti knew, offered opportunities but also posed dangers with which all men were fated to contend. For all his ambivalence about man's

19. Facade, Rucellai Palace, Florence.
Alinari/Art Resource, NY.

20. Exterior, Santa Maria Novella, Florence.
Alinari/Art Resource, NY.

ability to achieve anything against fortune, however, he dedicated an especially eloquent passage to the space that, he thought, must remain for autonomous human action even in a cosmos ruled by fate. Nothing, Uncle
Giannozzo says at one point, really belongs to anyone—except "a certain
power of will and force of reason," one's body, one's spirit—and time, the
universal, neutral medium in which one can use one's strength of character
to oppose fortune's whims. The most memorable of the speeches Alberti put
in Giannozzo's mouth takes the form of instructions on how to use time
against fortune:

> Do as I do. In the morning I plan my whole day, during the day I fol-
> low my plan, and in the evening, before I retire, I think over again
> what I have done during the day. Then, if I was careless in perform-
> ing some task and can repair the damage immediately, I do so; for I
> would sooner lose sleep than lose time, that is, than let the right mo-
> ment for doing something slip by. Sleep, food, and things of that sort
> I can catch up on tomorrow, and take care of my needs, but the mo-
> ment for doing something that must be done, no.[84]

Uncle Giannozzo, for all his plain speech, great age, and mastery of local tradition, does not regard time as Goro Dati had: as a coherent fabric, divided
by God Himself into secular and sacred segments. Instead, it has become a
modern, featureless continuum, duration without preset divisions, there for
the taking—and exploiting: merchant's time.[85]

Giovanni Rucellai recognized his own experience of time in Uncle Giannozzo's words, which he copied more than once into his *libro di ricordanze*.
He urged his sons to "practice economy with time, because it is the most
valuable thing we have." Only time—or the unremitting use of it—could
combat the fortune that, rather than providence, ruled human affairs as a
merchant saw them. Giovanni took these concepts extremely seriously:
when he suffered reverses, he described himself not as punished by God but
as "struck down by fortune."[86]

When Giovanni and Alberti erected their largest and most elaborate
statements in stone—the Rucellai Palace and the facade of Santa Maria
Novella—they collaborated to insert these lessons into them. Stylized sails
scud along both facades, meticulously executed in the fine decorative
stonework that Alberti loved. And in the courtyard of the Rucellai Palace, a
particularly fine *tondo* (circular relief) makes the lesson clear. Time is portrayed in the classical image of Occasio, a female figure in *contrapposto* with

a forelock and the back of her head bald. (Opportunity knocks only once, and those who fail to grasp her have lost their chance forever.) She serves, in turn, as the mast of the ship of fortune, the sail of which she holds and directs.[87]

Alberti almost certainly designed this vivid visual statement of his central theme. In his dinner piece "Rings," written in the 1430s, he suggested that a sailor's wind vane would serve as an excellent emblem for the lot of men: "Like sailors tossed amid stormy events and rocky circumstances, we must be cautious argonauts. As the times dictate, we must change the setting of our sails and seek refuge with dignity or chart a safe course through the waves."[88] Alberti's patron of the 1440s, the marquis of Ferrara, Leonello d'Este, used a sail or vane, as well as a lion, as one of his emblems, indicating that the soldier of fortune had as precarious a life as the great banker. He may well have done so at Alberti's suggestion. The message of the new buildings challenged the monumentality of their forms—or perhaps gave monumental form to their challenging lesson of the ultimate precariousness of life. A new idea of how the cosmos works—and a new ideal of human heroism—had taken on visual forms of unmatched prominence, as it had taken on verbal ones in On the Family.

Neither Alberti nor his patrons ceased to believe in Christianity. Rucellai, after all, sent his sails scudding along the facade of a great Dominican church (the very one that another patron of the arts and votary of fortune, Francesco Sassetti, abandoned when he was denied his wish to embellish his chapel with Franciscan imagery). In San Pancrazio Alberti built for Rucellai a magnificent shrine of the Holy Sepulchre: but though he adorned it with splendid classical inscriptions and fine inlaid emblems, he did not include among them fortune's sail. Still, patron and architect-intellectual had struck a new path. These men now understood the everyday life of mercantile and political man as taking place in a realm ruled by fortune rather than by providence: a realm where, in a complex, reciprocal relationship, only the man who enjoyed fortune could have virtue, the power to act, while only the power to act could enable a man to oppose the power of fortune and seize the chances she offered. They certainly no longer agreed with Petrarch and Salutati that Christians could use images of fortune only as allegories of divine providence. They were moving, verbally and visually, toward a dissociation of sensibilities, perhaps the first one in modern life. Alberti had felt and expressed this side of Florentine experience in the 1430s; a generation later, he gave it concrete artistic form.[89]

If Alberti never described Florentine buildings in detail and never tried to offer the realistic depiction of Florentine life with which scholars have also credited him, he did express, more plangently than anyone else, some of the deepest fears and aspirations of the male Florentine patricians of his day. His texts and his buildings matched their explanations of the world around them. In 1513 Machiavelli would write the new cosmos, with its capricious ruler and conspicuous lack of providential order, into *The Prince*. But long before then, Alberti had written it into the private memoirs and princely buildings of Florence's great clans.

Vital parts of *On the Family*—parts that meant less to Weber and Sombart than they did to Otto Brunner—reflect Alberti's effort to find security in this dangerous world for clans like his own. Giannozzo, in particular, argues in detail that even an urban family can sustain itself without spending its cash reserves—by buying country estates that can provide such necessities as grain, wine, wood, straw, poultry, and fish. He gives precise economic instructions. To farm efficiently and independently, one must choose a good site—one with slopes exposed to the sun for growing grapes, wet soil for producing hay, and flat fields for cultivating grain. The land in question must be well situated: in a place with pure air, not exposed to floods. The family should buy its country property, not rent it: otherwise the landlord might end up enjoying the improvements and investments the head of the house makes. And it should employ a limited number of peasants, training them to work hard and effectively and learning to avoid their "little tricks" and efforts to cheat their masters. Once bought, finally, the villa should be made into a work of art, in a distinctively Tuscan mode, at once attractive and practical: planted with a pleasing variety of pines and other fruit trees, arranged "in good order and in rows, for they are more beautiful to look at if so planted, they shade the seedlings less, they litter the field less, and the workers have less difficulty in picking the fruit."

Like Xenophon—whose counsels he summarizes—Giannozzo argues that the ideal villa should be in the suburbs, not in the deep country: "I would strive to have an estate in such a location that the fruits and crops could reach my house without too much difficulty, and I would be particularly delighted if the estate could be near the city, for then I could go there often, often send for things, and walk every morning among fruits and fields and fig trees."[90] Such an estate—so Giannozzo and Lionardo, for once, agree— would be a paradise, an endless source of plenty and pleasure, providing gifts without end, from chicken to cheese, and affording opportunities for healthy exercise as well.

This passage of *On the Family* is cast in an optimistic tone, glossing over many practical difficulties in an effort to show that pleasure and profit can easily be reconciled. In another short work, *The Villa*, which Alberti probably wrote around 1438, he gave more detailed instructions for farming, adapted from the tough-minded *Works and Days* of the ancient farmer-poet Hesiod. This severe text begins not by emphasizing the delights of the country but by insisting that one "buys a villa not to please others but to feed one's family," and it describes the farming life as one of acres and pains.[91] But Giannozzo's and Lionardo's duet about the joys of country living also captured something new and vital. In the early decades of the fifteenth century, great families like the Medici, some of them instructed by Alberti himself, began to establish villas of a new kind in the suburbs—houses open, rather than fortified, with ornamental gardens and orchards. Here clans could play, and sometimes even live, the life of autarky that Giannozzo prescribed, in settings that resembled the Roman villas of Cicero and Pliny. Alberti—who eventually resolved the question of whether such estates should be more ornamental or more practical by distinguishing between the plain farms of the middle class and the country seats of aristocrats—captured the new ideology and aesthetic of country life at its time of origin, when even the Medici still expected their properties to yield agricultural produce on a large scale.[92]

Alberti never ceased to concern himself with his family's beloved city. In a dialogue of the 1440s, *On Refuge from Hardships*, his characters begin by praising eloquently the beauty and temperate inside climate of the Florentine Cathedral. But the body of the work concerns itself not with urban settings or with outside temperatures but rather with the inner climate of a single person bent on self-mastery.[93] Alberti set himself to work out rules for mastering the self, for living productively with old wounds and old sorrows, for attaining a kind of Stoic autonomy and discipline. This turn from building a city or a household to building a particular kind of self coincided with a decisive turn in his career. Like many of the artists whose work corresponded most closely to his ideas, Alberti the Florentine by descent and affection would become a courtier by calculation. And in the court he would find new spheres for both artistic and intellectual activity.

VI

THE ARTIST AT COURT:

ALBERTI IN FERRARA

In 1443, Alberti devoted several days to writing a Latin treatise about horses. In some ways, the work reads like a summary—or a parody—of the literary works he had turned out in Florence during the 1430s. As always, he used ancient and modern sources self-consciously. But this time he took care to praise the ancients from whom he drew vital information, listing Greek and Roman writers like Xenophon and Vegetius who had discussed the breeding, training, and medical care of horses "in a learned and elegant way." Modern French and Italian writers like Pietro de' Crescenzi, the thirteenth-century author of a detailed treatise on husbandry, seemed "igno-ble" by comparison: but even they proved "useful and well-informed" after careful study. Alberti explained to Leonello d'Este, marquis of Ferrara, to whom he dedicated the text, that he had drawn up not a radical new mani-festo but a "short summary" of what he found in existing texts—presumably, though he did not make this clear, the ones to which he had access in Fer-rarese libraries.[1]

As in earlier works, Alberti took care to frame this work with introduc-tory passages that identified the public he hoped to address. The text was concise, austere, and pitched at a high level of generality. This level of exposition, he explained, might seem strange in a treatise on so practical a subject, but he had adopted it deliberately, out of consideration for his probable readers: "Those who read this should bear in mind that I was writing not for blacksmiths or shepherds, but for a ruler, and a very erudite one at that: that explains why I wrote in such a concise way, perhaps more so than the ignorant crowd would like."[2] Once again, Alberti had created a new language, in this case one in which he could discuss the genitals and dung of horses with propriety and eloquence.

But the curious resemblance between Alberti's treatise on horses and his earlier works emerges most clearly at the level of content. In On Painting, he had explained how Zeuxis achieved the highest ideal of beauty in a work of art by drawing features selectively from five women.[3] In On the Horse, he showed how one could actually produce ideally beautiful horses by carefully selecting the breeding stock: "See to it that those that you choose for parents and creators of the herd are of an attractive appearance, and of a proper age and one appropriate to the task." He carefully listed the features the breeder should look for, first in the father and then in the mother. And just as he had braved embarrassment in the eugenic section of On the Family to explain the proper way in which procreation should take place, so he now explained in detail how to choose the proper time for horses to mate and how to bring the male to the appropriate level of sexual stimulation. As Alberti had previously explained how to fit the physical and intellectual activities of boys to their ages, so he now showed, in detail, how to train a horse, year by year, as it passed from being a colt to being ready to serve in warfare or the hunt. As he had rejected physical compulsion and excess discipline in the education of boys, so too he insisted that horses were best trained in ways that brought them pleasure rather than pain. Alberti's aesthetic and pedagogical ideals could be realized more fully, it seems, in the world of horses than in the world of men. The painter who emulated Zeuxis could produce, at best, an ideal image of a woman more beautiful than any real human. The breeder of horses, by contrast, could produce an ideal mare and stallion.

As always, Alberti insisted on the need to strike a balance. The horse's emotions must be neither too strong nor too weak to enable him to carry out his functions; his training neither excessive nor inadequate; his humors in equilibrium; his habits regular.[4] At the same time, however, good horses, like virtuous men, must constantly engage in purposeful activity: "If someone asks," he remarked, "what is the first principle to emphasize in the training of horses, for my part it is simply that you exercise the horse well. For our ancestors decreed that horses should have no holidays." Like the ideal merchant, the ideal horse would be "ready for motion of every kind, its body vibrating lightly; its feet striking the ground; its ears eager, attentive, trembling." And like the ideal figure in a painting, the ideal horse would be suited in every feature to its task, as its training would be ideally suited in every way—timing, place, temperature, humidity—to improving its physical and mental constitution. Alberti, who had once proudly applied his erudition and aesthetics to creating a theory of human excellence, now applied them as a prince's consultant on veterinary medicine.[5]

The shift looks like a chapter in a tale of decline and fall. In fifteenth-century society, however, horses mattered deeply, possessing social and cultural status higher than that of many humans. Like other forms of livestock, they were essential to civilized life and were harder to replace than humans. At courts, moreover—and Ferrara boasted one of Italy's most culturally innovative courts—horses mattered more than in most other places. The Este, who ruled Ferrara, rode horses into battle and to the hunt. They bred horses for speed, entering them in the *palio* at Siena and elsewhere, and they had their horses' portraits painted by their favorite artists. As noblemen and warriors, they had to be skilled horsemen. Riding with pleasure and panache helped them to play the role of rulers fittingly at home and, in some cases, to make their way in foreign courts. Francesco d'Este, the bastard son of Alberti's patron Leonello, needed to be a good horseman in order to serve, as he did for many years, in the brilliant northern courts of Charles of Charolais and Charles the Bold, where he took an active part in wars and tournaments.[6] Alberti himself esteemed the beauty of horses very highly indeed. He saw them as the image "of *partitione*: the appropriateness and correspondence of all the parts" that he thought should characterize a well-designed building.[7] In offering advice on horses, suitably attired in neat Latin, he was doing his proper job as a well-placed technical expert at court—exactly the sort of role that the engineers whose company he aspired to join normally played. In fact, Alberti's treatise on the horse and its management reveals his success at finding an appropriate and profitable role, one in which he could deploy his formidable skills for a generous and appreciative patron.

Alberti had worked to make a place for himself in Florence, as we have seen, well into the 1440s. But the republic that his ancestors had served had not proved consistently hospitable. As early as 1437, he evidently began to consider taking another path as well, more or less simultaneously, at one or more of the secular courts whose rulers avidly supported the new learning of the humanists and the new art of the painters and sculptors whom Alberti admired most. A longstanding member of the curia, he already knew how to deal diplomatically with both his superiors and equals. Presumably, he consulted with friends like Leonardo Dati, a connoisseur of patronage relations who knew how to work for others without compromising his own dignity. A letter from Dati to Girolamo Aliotti gives a sense of the frankness and precision with which they exchanged favors for themselves and for others who, like Aliotti, occupied somewhat more marginal places on their mattering maps: "But my patron is aware of this matter, and I think it would be unworthy of my rank to keep bothering him so often. Battista Alberti will be here within the month. I have informed him of the matter, and he has promised that he will speak with him."[8] Like their mutual friend Matteo Palmieri, who had argued for the virtues of the active life in the 1430s but turned in later years to more contemplative and theological interests, Alberti and Dati saw that the world was changing.[9] By the 1440s, the free pursuit of virtue in the piazza and the city had come to seem a distant ideal, compared with the possibilities offered by the patronage of great men who could sponsor original literary and artistic work. Eventually, Alberti drew up an elaborate blueprint for success at court; more remarkably still, he followed it, with precision and discipline. By the middle of the 1440s, he occupied a position of immense cultural authority at the court of Ferrara. More important, he had established a new way of life for himself, as a courtier, which would take him very far indeed.[10]

As a member of the papal curia and the holder of a substantial benefice, Alberti could have undertaken a purely religious career. His *Life of Potitus* had apparently interested and pleased some clerical readers. And from the mid-1430s onward, he and his curial colleagues occupied a privileged position from which they could observe—and if they wished, participate in—the most exciting ecclesiastical developments of the age. Pope Eugenius IV, who had been in office since 1431, had been chased from Rome in 1434 by mob violence and forced to take up residence with the curia in Florence. The Council of Basel, which continued to meet, posed a permanent challenge in practice to his authority, as it also did, in theory, to that of the papacy itself. But by 1437 Eugenius had reasserted his authority successfully in several new spheres. For one, he had presided over the dedication of the finished Cathedral of Santa Maria del Fiore in Florence. For another, after sharp competition with the Council of Basel, he had managed to convince the Byzantine emperor and the patriarch of Constantinople, who desperately needed support against the Turks, to come to Florence or another Italian venue—not Basel or one of the other cities proposed by the council—to try to negotiate a renewed union with the Latin church. By November 1437 the Greeks were on their way, led by their lay and spiritual rulers, the patriarch and the emperor. For the next two years Eugenius conducted negotiations with them in Ferrara and Florence, exchanging arguments both on the overt plane of theological debate (about the divinity of Jesus) and on the less explicit one of symbolic action (about forms of obeisance). Alberti moved with the pope and the curia, first to Bologna, where Eugenius spent most of 1437, and then to Ferrara. In the presence of the many potential patrons who took part in the debates over theology and liturgy, he and others with talents like his could certainly hope to rise.[11]

The society of the papal curia in these years was brilliant, even spectacular. Alberti's friend Lapo da Castiglionchio described it as an earthly equivalent to the celestial hierarchy of angels—perfection, or the closest approximation to perfection that humanity could reach:

> The priests in the curia enjoy the highest measure of dignity that is allotted to mankind. Here we find, first of all, the pope, who holds the place of God and is, after Him, the greatest being whom we have. He is elected not by human decisions but by divine authority and by God, by the voice and authority of God. Next there is the splendid and excellent college of cardinals, who fill out the rank of the apostles. They seem not only to assist the pope in carrying out his functions but also to adorn his curia. Then come the archbishops, bishops, patriarchs, protonotaries, and other ranks, almost infinite in number. When they assemble to perform the mass or any other divine service, and sit in their ranks, with the pope seated in his august pontifical throne, and they sing divine hymns and psalms in their different, varied voices, no one could be so inhumane, so barbarous, so crude, or again so ferocious, so inimical to God, and so irreligious, as not to be moved by such sights and sounds. Religious feelings must dominate the onlooker's mind, as astonishment and sweet delight fill his soul. His eyes must feast on that miraculous spectacle, his ears must be filled with that incredible sweetness and harmony of song. Nothing on earth is more beautiful than this spectacle, or greater, or

more divine, or more worthy of admiration and of being recorded in detail. Not only the men who are present, and who are endowed by nature with the ability to exult and rejoice, but the very walls of the church themselves seem to do so.[12]

Like Shakespeare's Leonardo, showing Jessica the heavenly spheres and describing their harmonies, Lapo represented the curia as perfect, eternal, full of life, and rich with power to inspire.

In actuality, Lapo viewed the curia with far more ambivalent feelings than this single set piece, taken from a long and intricate dialogue, suggests.[13] Alberti, however, knew his own mind and spoke it. A conscious victim of open injuries of class and standing, and a critical observer of what he saw as a corrupt and degenerate church, Alberti was inspired by the preparations for the council to write what amounted to a denunciation of the clergy of his time. Between 13 and 17 October, he composed *Pontifex*, a dialogue between two of his family members: the Franciscan Paolo di Jacopo Alberti and the jurist, bishop, and later cardinal Alberto di Giovanni Alberti. As in *On the Family*, he claimed not to present his own theories but to record family discussions, which he characterized as "extremely religious and full of important points of instruction." The work, which he dedicated to Carlo, ranged over a number of topics, including the virtues and duties of the ideal ruler. But Alberti—whose satirical bent and fascination with all the practical details of life have often led modern readers to see him as irreligious—took care to show, through the speeches he assigned to both characters, that he saw himself above all as a passionately devout Christian. He explored in detail the wiles of the devil, the enemy "who fears neither arms, nor fire, nor force of any kind; whose attack you cannot hold off with a ditch or even a valley; whom even the best-armed guards cannot keep out of the most private part of your court, out of your very closet: the one who hurls men into an abyss of misery." And he made his two clerics—one a member of a mendicant order and the other a "secular" clergyman, a priest who lived in the world and held important jobs—into ideal figures of Christian discipline.

Like Giannozzo in *On the Family*, Paolo and Alberto describe techniques for self-discipline as the best defense against vice. Since attaining maturity and full self-knowledge at the age of twenty, Alberto explains, he has found daily performance of the Mass essential, for it enables him to pray to God for protection against all forms of evil. He scrutinizes every corner of his habitation, where the devil may lurk, before retiring. Paolo the Franciscan's reply makes explicit what Alberto has only suggested: that the good Christian must scrutinize his mind for sin every night, as exactingly as the good merchant scrutinizes his memory for bills unpaid and tasks undone: "For I understand what you are insisting: that I must go over every recess and corner of my mind, where a vice could possibly be concealed, and expunge it."[14] Alberti's asceticism is not just innerworldly: activity and self-control, in his view, should play just as vital a role in religious as in economic life.

But Alberti constructed his protagonists as ideal rather than as typical figures. Both of them, in the course of the dialogue, repeatedly show how hard it is for anyone making a career in the higher ranks of the clergy to preserve his mind and soul from corrupting influences. Like the father of a family, the high ecclesiastic must serve as the master of a large household. Paolo insists, like Giannozzo, that prompt, full payment of salaries is a duty as well as a sensible way to make servants as hardworking and vigilant as their master. But, he continues, the high cleric's household has special qualities that pose special problems. Its members are hired servants, not blood relatives. The cleric has to exercise extreme diligence in order to attract only virtuous men and to discipline them while in his employ. Even then, however, discretion requires him to keep certain matters secret, so that none of them know all of his affairs. Some jobs, moreover, prove persistently hard to fill. Paolo urges Alberto to look among the legendary naked sages of India, the gymnosophists, for someone "wise, temperate, and abstinent" enough to serve as a proper legal representative. Even the most exacting measures cannot prevent the lazy, the tricky, and the self-interested from sneaking in alongside the active and honest.

Perhaps from a distance the curia looked like the angelic choir brought down to earth. But the actual work of the church, at its heart and in each diocese, was carried out by bishops and their staffs. And no one could envy the master of an episcopal household, as Alberto describes him, burdened with all the duties of a secular paterfamilias but deprived of all the aids with which blood ties and family traditions endow the latter:

> Household administration will prove even harder for a bishop than for the head of a family. For the latter has to care for his own kind, born from and raised by him or in his intimate circle, bound to him by love and fidelity. He has many appropriate ways at his disposal to improve his relatives: admonition, correction, threats of cutting them

out of his will. Above all, the paterfamilias can actually take pleasure in leading his own kin, joined by blood, living together, educated in the proper forms of conduct, less stubborn, more obedient to parental words, to virtue. But we bishops face an entirely different situation. For when we first occupy our see, we have to gather men from wherever we can to make up the number of servants we need. The household that takes shape consists of men who speak different languages, follow different customs, and have grown up in different nations. They are eager not to serve you but to win profits for themselves. They fear work, not shame. Neither threats nor promises will readily turn these stubborn souls into docile ones.[15]

The innocence of the exile, who had rarely experienced life with his extended kin, found expression here, in Alberti's idealization of the kin group whose members were linked by blood ties. But his portrait of life in the upper ranks of the clergy has a grim, novelistic realism. The episcopal palace was clearly no place for idealists. The end of the text—where Alberto remarks that the time has come to move to "the main hall, where we may, as is customary, hear our citizens, asking for counsel on their affairs"—emphasizes the secular ties that bound the secular clergy to an unglamorous round of politicking.

More distracting, and potentially more harmful, than any of the specific problems that Alberti's two characters describe was the general style of life that high office imposed on the cleric. As head of a large household, he had to hold open house, not only to servants who wished to enrich themselves, but also to the beggars who thronged his doorway. Hospitality gave rise to social disorder. But it also provided an excuse for high living. Both Alberti characters agree that all too many bishops and other high clerics are as dedicated to the besetting sins of the rich and powerful as their secular counterparts. The most vivid passages in Alberti's dialogue describe clerics whom luxury has corrupted. Though they are priests, these men would not attend a meal unless the costliest rugs had been spread before them, delicacies drawn from every land and sea were dished up, and the table was adorned with the finest gems and vessels. The church had all too many drunken bishops, "their foreheads and faces bright red, their eyes shining like torches from being hung over"; all too many proud bishops, who refused to be addressed except by men in an attitude of adoration, and who gave their answers in a voice pitched so impressively low as to be unintelligible. The higher ranks of the church, as Alberti described them, included many Tartuffes, men who showed off their holiness by walking "with their neck twisted, their shoulders slumped, their hands limp," and few virtuous and holy men.

The church, in short, was more likely to repel than to attract anyone who hoped to make a life that was both successful and virtuous. Its splendor chilled devotion. In particular, it offered little hope to young scholars. Few clerics had either the learning, or the love of it, that their calling theoretically required. Consequently, as Paolo points out at the end, men of letters are left to starve. Alberto agrees with the Franciscan that scholars deserve better. Scholars, he argues, actually do the church more service than "the inviolate purity of virgins, or the tears of widows, or the fastings of the cloistered, or the crowns of the hermits."[16] But he offers no prospect that the situation of the humanists will actually improve.

In this case as in so many others, the dialogue form that Alberti adopted did not reflect any substantive doubts in his mind about the basic principles at issue. Despite their different positions in the church, his two protagonists agree on every important question about the life and discipline—or lack of it—of the clergy. It seems likely, rather, that Alberti chose the dialogue form in order to work out, rapidly and in writing, his own formal decision to pursue success at a secular court. For in the same year that he composed the *Pontifex*, 1437, he added a fourth book to *On the Family*. Here too he wrote a dialogue; and here too, he used the form not, as he had in the early books of the same work, to work out a conflict of basic positions, but to tell a story. Book four begins with a detailed narrative, a tale within the tale, set in the years just before and after 1400, of how an Alberti achieved high position both at secular courts and in the curia. He deftly carries out secular functions, without ever putting his honor in peril, even though serving those masters could easily have forced him to do so.

Just before dinnertime, as Leon Battista stages the discussion, the Alberti, who have already debated how to preserve a family and the nature of success and honor in the city, attack a new topic. Stimulated by the arrival of another kinsman, the witty Buto, they discuss friendship. Their debates touch on many issues, from the qualities that make friendship possible in the first place to the proper way to bring a relationship to an end. But the central theme, for the first half of the book, is friendship between rulers and subjects. A family member who is experienced in public life, Piero, takes on the task of explaining to Battista and Carlo how "to find their way as I did into the secret and private chambers of princes, and to remain there, as they may need or wish to do, thanks to the prince's benevolence and friendship, with no danger of being rejected." From the start, in other words, Alberti's protagonist describes friendship in instrumental rather than emotional terms: as a relation into which one chooses to enter, in cold blood, to achieve particular practical ends.

As a highly directed and purposive activity, friendship—or the winning of it—naturally requires the development and application of sophisticated techniques. Piero promises that the boys "will be pleased to learn of my various and different devices, my devious and seldom-used means, which have rarely been described." These he recommends as "most useful ways to deal with men in civil life." Later in the dialogue, other speakers clarify what Piero has only suggested: that the ancient literature on friendship, which deals with it chiefly in moral terms, has little practical advice to offer about "the actual ways and habits of men" in the world—though the ancient political historians can still provide useful examples of the forging and maintenance of social bonds.

Piero tells compelling stories: tales of how he became the familiar of three great rulers in a row, Giangaleazzo Visconti of Milan, Ladislas of Naples, and Pope John XXIII. These three examples were brilliantly chosen to make Florentine readers attentive. Giangaleazzo and Ladislas had both made war on the Florentine republic that had outlawed the Alberti, the former in the years leading up to his death in 1402 and the latter in the 1410s. Though John XXIII, the Neapolitan who had been forced to resign the papacy by the Council of Constance, retired to Florentine territory in the 1430s, he had been accused of virtually every sin from impiety to sodomy. In arguing that a member of a great Florentine line could honorably serve men like these, Piero—and Alberti—show that talent and energy can lead one very far indeed from native grounds.

Piero admits that he did not find it easy to avoid political trouble when working for Giangaleazzo, or danger when serving at the court of the capricious pope John, whose favor could be won or lost in a moment, so that "from hour to hour, there were universal intrigues to bring hatred and dismissal upon anyone more in favor with the pope than with another." The courtier's lot, as Piero describes it, resembles that of a rock climber—one is continually confronted with new slopes to traverse, each more slippery or crumbling than the last. Only unremitting attention to detail and constant willingness to adapt enabled Piero to keep his high positions. The courtier who hopes to swim in the shark-filled waters of a princely retinue—so Piero points out, choosing a revealing analogy—has to be as continually on his guard, and to refine his skills as exactingly, as a falconer training a wild bird of noble descent. A single slip can bring about his downfall:

> When I was with the duke [Giangaleazzo], I found it burdensome and irritating always to be on the watch, to observe with infinite pains exactly what was going on and come running at once not to be late or miss out on any occasion for coming into his presence. Now with Ladislas, I found it onerous to have almost no leisure and to lack any definite time to devote to my own activities and concerns. It was required of me to wait on him so much, to be nowhere but there, that I well learned the truth of the saying that the cultivation of great men's patronage is like the training of a hawk. One flight may make him wild and strange; one slight error, one mistaken word (as you literary men know by a thousand examples in books), even a single misbegotten glance alone, can be the cause of a lord's falling into a fatal passion against one whom he at first loved very much.

Courtiership, like falconry, requires dexterity and suppleness: the courtier must train a superior and beautiful being, one ruled by an imperious will, without causing the irritation that would spoil his whole exercise in shaping his and his ruler's selves.

For all its dangers, however, the courtier's life also offers great rewards—rewards best savored in repose, at the end of the demanding career. Piero eloquently explains how much he treasures the skills that won him the favor of these very different masters. While his independence and ready wit pleased Giangaleazzo, as he tells the story, his masterly handling of dogs during a bear hunt enabled him to save Ladislas's life. Like Saint-Simon two centuries later, Piero—or Alberti—emphasizes that the courtier must concentrate all his attention on his master's will, that he must always be present, even when doing so demands stern self-discipline. Piero's account of the courtier's creation of a successful self, though less famous than Giannozzo's, has much in common with it:

> I had to exercise great patience and to exert an almost incredible firmness of purpose. Not infrequently, I assure you, I spent a whole day without food, pretending to have other concerns, merely waiting to encounter and greet these persons. I absolutely refused to lose by

lack of diligence any occasion that seemed useful to win me more welcome in their eyes and suited to make me more familiar to them by daily acquaintance. To make sure, moreover, that I never left them with a feeling of surfeit, I never departed their company without giving some promise of things to come; I made sure I was always a happy sight, one who would give some new service, while I also made myself likable by my modesty and reverence toward them.[17]

Piero's stories may or may not derive from the Alberti family's oral tradition. But they do show that Leon Battista nourished no illusions that his life at a secular court would be easy, even as he girded himself to attempt it. Rather, he gathered all his forces and trained himself to become, like Piero, a deft and alert controller of noble air traffic, one whose unwavering attention to courtly bodies in motion would enable him to avert collisions and crashes.

The autobiography that Alberti wrote in 1438 emphasizes his desire to achieve grace in the arts of walking, riding, and speaking—and to do so in such a way that he seems to accomplish it all without effort.[18] Alberti thereby expressed not only his general confidence that he could win glory, but also his particular desire to create a self that could succeed in a new environment, one just as dangerous as, if more promising than, those in which he had already lived. Early in book four of On the Family, Ricciardo tries to define the qualities that help one to win friends. Virtue certainly helps, he argues, as does property, and poverty certainly hinders. But the really central quality is "a certain something for which I cannot find a name, which attracts men and makes them love one person more than another. It is something that resides I don't know where, in the face, the eyes, the manner, and the presence of a man, giving him a certain grace and charm full of modesty. I can't express it in words at all."[19] When Alberti wrote his autobiography, he believed, or wanted to believe, that he had achieved this mysterious state of secular grace—a state very much like the one, achieved without apparent effort, that Baldassare Castiglione would call, a hundred years later, *sprezzatura.*

Alberti had more than a general career path in mind: he also knew where he wanted to follow it. From the 1430s onward, the Este, who ruled Ferrara, in the Po valley, as marquises, had made an ever larger impression both on the Italian political scene and on the humanist republic of letters. Ferrara itself was very attractive: situated handily between Venice and Bologna, on what was then a navigable branch of the Po, it was far smaller than Florence, probably never reaching more than 30,000 inhabitants, and it never became a center of manufacture.[20] But it served as a way station for merchants, ambassadors, and others traveling from northern to central Italy. Surrounded by prosperous farms and pasturelands, rich and well governed, Ferrara played the role of a political as well as an economic intermediary. Known for their ability as diplomats, the Este regularly negotiated peace treaties between the larger warring states to their north and south. Niccolò III, marquis until his death in 1441, reputedly could arrange anything from finding an inn to put up a rival ambassador, to devising those soothing words that make political compromises possible. The Este, in other words, helped to create the new political and cultural Great Game of professional diplomacy, which took its permanent shape in this period—the age of Europe's first resident ambassadors and of the Treaty of Lodi, the first nonaggression pact of modern times.[21] Masters of the new tactics of the day, equipped with a substantial and effective army, hardened by riding, hunting, and hawking, ugly but impressive of feature, prone to rapid displays of terrible violence against their subjects and even their loved ones, the Este were among the most charismatic Renaissance tyrants. They made obviously appropriate hosts—and their city an obviously pleasant venue—for the upcoming council of the Greek and Latin churches.[22]

The Este were also among the first Renaissance rulers—along with Alfonso of Aragon in Naples and Federigo da Montefeltro in Urbino—to provide substantial patronage for innovative artists and scholars. By the time the curia arrived at Ferrara in October 1437, the city could already boast some impressive works of art and engineering. One of the Russians who accompanied Isidore, the metropolitan of Kiev, to the council—and who had already seen such rich and splendid northern cities as Lübeck and Nuremberg—recorded his amazement at the impressive combination of high technology and majestic architecture that he encountered in the center of Ferrara, dominated by the great castle from which the city was ruled:

In the papal palace, there is a large, high tower, rising above the piazza, made of stone and adorned with a clock and a great bell. Whenever it is struck, it is audible throughout the city. At the front of the tower is a porch with two gates. On the hour the bell sounds, and an angel comes out of the tower onto the top of the porch; it appears in full view, as if it were alive; and after it has played its trumpet, it goes back into the tower by the other gate. Everyone who sees the angel and its trumpet also hears its sound. Also, on the hour an angel approaches the bell and strikes it.[23]

In the course of the fifteenth century, the Este would become both the greatest palace builders in Italy and skilled connoisseurs of the visual arts. Even before the council took place, they had become effective patrons of classical education and humanistic literature. In 1429 they succeeded in bringing one of the most erudite and effective humanist teachers, Guarino of Verona, to Ferrara, where he built up a superb and famous humanist school.[24] Leonello spent seven years as Guarino's pupil, from 1431 onward. He learned not only to read classical Latin but to write it, becoming a passionate bibliophile as well.

In the late 1430s, Ferrara boasted an increasingly active university, rich private libraries, and lively, attractive intellectual circles. Private houses offered a sophisticated, pleasant lifestyle, which combined the urban and the rural. Alberti's friend Lapo, for example, describes how he and a friend and supporter, Angelo da Recanate, ate together during the council, deploring the troubles that afflicted the Roman Church, then strolled after lunch in a pleasant nearby garden, "where, having walked some distance amid the trees and vines, and becoming tired, we sat on the grass, and as we sat began to converse as we had before."[25] Ferrarese villas harbored formidable libraries, well stocked and prettily housed, like those of Giovanni Aurispa and Giovanni Gualengo. During the council, so the Milanese scholar Angelo Decembrio recalled, Gualengo invited Leonello and all his courtiers to visit him. After tasting the first figs and washing in the dew that Giovanni had collected the night before in a splendid silver vessel, the visitors climbed the stairway to his library, where he had strewn the floor and bookshelves with fragrant white and purple flowers.[26] The lovely settings apparently promoted lively arguments. In Decembrio's fictional account, the pleasures of the brunch did not distract Leonello and his friends from engaging in a detailed discussion of how to read Cicero.

More prosaic sources confirm that Ferrara harbored a lively intellectual life. The medical man Ugo Benzi offered his guests more bracing hospitality than Gualengo. After giving all the Greek visitors to the council who had philosophical interests a magnificent lunch, Ugo had the tables cleared away and invited them to dispute with him "on all the philosophical topics, on which Plato and Aristotle disagreed in their works, saying that he would defend whichever position the Greeks decided to attack." Though the debate lasted for hours, the Latin Ugo emerged victorious from his contest with the erudite Greeks. The house of Este—as Aeneas Silvius Piccolomini, later to become Pope Pius II, reflected in his account of this episode—"was always friendly to the learned."[27] Ferrara, in short, offered cultural opportunities that could have been custom tailored to fit Alberti's special skills and central interests. The city swarmed with scholars and patrons well equipped to appreciate his subtle, allusive prose and the new ideals of style that undergirded it.

By the middle of the 1430s, Ferrarese and Florentine circles were in regular contact. Leonello himself briefly visited Florence in 1435. In May of that year, his brother Meliaduse and the erudite courtier Feltrino Boiardo, an ancestor of the poet Boiardo, took part in a lively discussion "in the more secret part of the papal curia" in Florence, "with some men of the highest quality." Poggio spoke at length in praise of the Roman historian Livy, arguing that the vast chronological and substantive range of materials that he had covered and the brilliant Latin prose in which he had done so made him the greatest of historians, whatever Plutarch and other Greeks might say. Boiardo agreed. When Poggio, the great explorer of monastic libraries, went on to say that he had heard plausible news of the existence of more books of Livy than the thirty already in circulation, Boiardo demurred at first. But after Poggio reported in detail on the rumor he had heard, that a manuscript with one hundred books of Livy, "written in Lombardic script with an admixture of Gothic," had been sighted in a Cistercian monastery somewhere in Dacia, Boiardo showed interest. He demanded that Poggio transmit the report to his erudite prince.

Like other collectors, Leonello found Poggio's enthusiasm contagious. Two years later, he bought from Poggio an expensive manuscript of the letters of Saint Jerome. This codex had become the subject of another conversation in the curia, this time at Bologna, where the collector Giovanni Aurispa had urged Poggio to sell the book to Leonello.[28] Eventually, Leonello also bought, read, and praised a three-volume set of Livy's history, prepared by the Florentine stationer Vespasiano da Bisticci and adorned on its opening page with interlaced white vine leaves—the most fashionable style of Florentine book produced in this period. For all Leonello's love of the intricate traceries drawn by Ferrarese illuminators, he had to admit that Florence was the richest source of generally well-corrected classical manuscripts.[29] No wonder that this learned prince's fine Latin style and unpretentious love of learning won him Poggio's respect—although he was nettled when Ferrarese scholars and collectors, whose competence he doubted, murmured that he had overcharged Leonello for his Jerome.[30]

Not all contacts between Florentine and Ferrarese intellectuals were friendly, or even polite. In 1435, in fact, a sharp literary dispute broke out between Poggio and Guarino. Poggio was heartily sick of the aggressive foreign policy of the Albizzi regime, which had ruled Florence until 1433. In order to show that he sided with Florence's new and thoroughly modern rulers, the Medici family, Poggio insisted that Scipio, the man of peace, had been the greatest of ancient heroes. Other humanists who wrote in praise of the first Medici to control the city, Cosimo, consistently represented him as a bringer of peace. But Guarino, the servant and teacher of rulers whose military prowess he admired, preferred the other side in Florence and admired Caesar, whose works he read with the young Leonello.[31] The debate continued for some months, in the course of which Poggio produced at least one powerful document—a long letter in which he argued that republican liberty, of the sort represented by Scipio, had played a vital role in fostering literature and the arts in ancient Rome. For the most part, however, the controversy enabled both Poggio and Guarino to show off their considerable rhetorical skills and biting wit—as well as their ability to read whatever modern messages they liked into classical texts. For a time, the contest became so bitter that it threatened the tranquillity of the humanist republic of letters. A scholarly Englishman, Humphrey, duke of Gloucester, commended both Poggio and Guarino's learning but criticized the latter for his "biting, and too slanderous, style of writing." By May 1436, however, peace had been restored, thanks to the intervention of Leonello and a learned young Ferrarese canon, Francesco Marescalco.[32] From this point on, Florentine and Ferrarese humanists enjoyed close relations; in the 1440s, Poggio sent his own son Gian Battista to mingle and study with the learned in Ferrara.

Eventually, Alberti—as book four of On the Family clearly shows—decided that direct approaches were not the best way for a man of no means to approach a ruler. Instead—so he had Piero argue—one should identify an intermediary figure, a man of good will who already stands high in the favor of the prince in question. Such an intermediary has to display the powers with which his position endows him by bringing others forward as well—especially those who can help the prince spend his free time pleasantly. Piero explains, in general terms, that the adroit courtier begins his approach to the prince by tailoring his speech and actions to suit the tastes of the appropriate honest broker: "In order to arrive at the friendship of the duke, I saw that it would be necessary to make use of one of his old friends and present intimates. Such a man would be the path and the means for presenting myself to him at an appropriate time and in a suitable way whenever an occasion offered of the duke's being less busy than usual with the grave public affairs that normally engaged him."

In line with the Alberti family's taste—repeatedly expressed in *On the Family*—for concrete examples, Piero then tells the story, in detail, of how he put this principle into practice:

He [Giangaleazzo] loved good men and was a father to the nobility. Among all those about him, then, I chose one who seemed to me intimate with the prince and of whom I also heard from others that he had more influence than anyone on his secret and private affairs. This was a man whose acquaintance I could cultivate freely without giving offense, a man of a helpful nature, and one to whom the name of our Alberti family was not unwelcome. He was so placed in fortune, moreover, that he would not, in order to hold on to what he had or in hopes of making some later use of me, be slow and backward in mediating for me and in making available to me the valuable generosity of his patron. For you know that some men are so stingy with the presence and the very words of the prince they have some power over that they will hardly give you a chance to see him without forcing you to make heavy payment. Sometimes, too, they avoid making any use of the favor they have with him except for themselves alone. This man, Francesco Barbavara, therefore, a man of intelligence and of noble manners, an intimate servitor of the prince, kind, liberal, and in no way reluctant to grant me his friendship, was the man I assiduously cultivated with my visits and greetings. Since he loved the poets, I used on occasion to recite to him as much as I had memorized of various poets, and especially of our Messer Antonio Alberti. His poems, which are full of sweet ripeness and adorned with touches of much delicacy and grace, delighted this learned man, for Antonio is, like the other Tuscan poets we have, well worthy of being read and praised. From day to day, then, I gradually became

Barbavara's close friend, so that he wanted to help me and to find some way of augmenting my standing and my fortune. Then I opened my heart and mind to him and obtained by his request a welcome, warm reception and frequent access to the prince.[33]

Making friends with an intermediary—making the broker open his purse of favor and dispense some of it—was no easier in principle than making friends with the ruler above him. It required constant thought about how to please: "Even with Barbavara, this friend of ours, as well as with that prince, the duke of Milan, I had to exercise great patience and to exert an almost incredible firmness of purpose." But the game was clearly worth the candle. Just as proper prayer for the intercession of a saint could win a believing Christian divine grace, so proper dealings with a favorite could win an adroit courtier a share of the same favor: "And, as you know, we become great not only through our own diligence and skill but also through the zeal and ingenuity of our supporters, whose service augments at once our authority, dignity, and power." Like most of his contemporaries, Alberti saw himself not as a naked, unique individual, building a career on the basis of personal accomplishments and merits, but as a member of multiple hierarchies who could make upward progress only with the help of those who already occupied higher positions.[34] One prayed for grace, in fifteenth-century Italy, not to God but to a saint; and one prayed for support, not to a prince but to his established servants.

The courtier in this period was constantly exposed to the glare of princes like Federigo da Montefeltro and Alfonso of Aragon. Sunlike beings, whose energies permeated their courts, they could withdraw their warmth from any of their inferiors at any time—as Alfonso, who preferred to wear black, did when he ordered his young men to rub up against a Sienese ambassador and ruin the overly fine brocades in which he came to court.[35] But the sun was not the only planet to exercise influence on earth—as Adovardo Alberti explains in On the Family, in a passage in which he draws an elaborate analogy between the study of friendships at court and the study of astrology, in order to bring out the sheer difficulty of devising an art of courtly life:

Ah, Lionardo, what a mass of further information would be needed before one could really discuss this matter in its breadth and extent. It is as though some student had heard from the astronomers that Mars disposes the force of armies and the outcome of battles. Mercury establishes the various branches of knowledge and governs the subtlety of minds and marvelous skills, Jove controls ceremonies and the souls of religious men, the sun reigns over worldly offices and principalities, the moon precipitates journeys and the fluctuations of spirit among women and mobs, Saturn weighs down and slows our mental processes and undertakings—and so he would know the character and power of each. But if he did not know how to evaluate their effect according to their place in the sky and their elevation, and what favorable or unfavorable effect their rays have on each other, and how their conjunctions are able to produce good or ill fortune, surely that student would be no astrologer. The mere recognition of those bare principles is indispensable to any understanding of the art, but even with them you have only just entered the domain of other, almost innumerable laws necessary if you would foresee and understand the things which the sky tends to produce. Similarly, these very useful and numerous examples and sayings, which you say are so amply provided by the best authors, do not give us all the help we need.[36]

The court, in other words, was not just a world, it was a cosmos, and understanding it called for profound and strenuous intellectual efforts; the courtier must become a cosmographer, his gaze turned resolutely upward toward the blinking stars that give off light and warmth.

Rising to the position of star in this night sky of social hierarchy was even harder than mapping the constellations of power. It was less like climbing a single rope, hand over hand, than like scrambling up and along a complicated cargo net. This, at least, was the form of motion Alberti adopted when he began, in 1437, to move toward attracting Leonello's favor. In doing so—in treating friendship, as his characters advised, as a pragmatic affair, something to be analyzed and exploited—Alberti was certainly not violating his own, or anyone else's, ideals—any more than the astrologer did when he treated planetary conjunctions in the same way. He was simply trying to deal in a constructive way with the forces that ruled his society.

As Alberti looked north and east toward Ferrara, he identified at least four different men as being in a position to make his way straight, and he appealed to each of them. First he befriended Leonello's younger brother, Meliaduse. Their relationship presumably began during Meliaduse's time in Florence in 1435, and it probably involved discussions of classical subjects—like the conversation on Livy that Poggio described, in which Alberti could

have taken part. In 1437, when Alberti dedicated the revised version of his
Philodoxeos fabula to Leonello, he referred to Meliaduse as an intimate personal friend. In his epistle, he made clear that he saw his relation to
Meliaduse, rather than his own attainments, as the key to Leonello's affec-
tions: "I was not so foolish as to believe that my stories would do more to
move you than the desire and judgement of your loving brother."[37] Before
Alberti left Florence, in other words, he had already begun, both through
conversation and by letter writing, to weave connections with the Este
court.

Poggio made an equally appropriate and effective broker. A prominent
and respected scholar and a benevolent older friend of Alberti's, he presumably knew (as Alberti did) that not every book offered to Leonello found acceptance in the prince's chaste, select personal library.[38] Accordingly, on
12 October 1437, he wrote a letter to Leonello, in which he praised the "elegance and charm" of Alberti's play as well as the author's personal devotion
to Leonello.[39] Alberti had every reason to believe that the classically educated young prince would be inclined to greet his reconstruction of the ancient stage with interest and enthusiasm.

As Alberti moved with the curia from Florence to Bologna, only twenty
miles from his goal, he came into closer contact with a third natural intermediary: Poggio's once and future friend, the great teacher Guarino. During
1437, while Alberti lived with the curia in Bologna, he was increasingly
troubled by the worldliness of the priests and prelates around him. He took
refuge in writing, producing not only the dialogue *Pontifex,* in which he
vented his spleen directly, but also further short works, ironic and satirical in
form, in which he showed his distaste for men by expressing his love for animals. In a eulogy for his dog, for example, Alberti praised the animal for
possessing qualities no human could match. Able to learn any language
quickly, brave, energetic, and self-disciplined, Alberti's dog was more virtuous than any of the ancients, each of whom had had a fatal flaw. Aristotle
was greedy, Plato lascivious, Cicero ambitious, Caesar tyrannical, Cato lustful; Alberti's dog, by contrast, had all the virtues and none of the vices. He
even embodied the ideal beauty that had never manifested itself in any single human body. While Zeuxis had had to examine five virgins to produce
one ideal representation of a goddess, "my dog was of so handsome a counte-
nance, that Zeuxis would have found it easy to draw from its lineaments all
that beauty and grace in painting that he derived from the Crotoniates."[40]

The Greek writer Lucian, master of irony, helped inspire Alberti to work
this satirical vein. And when Guarino, now nearby, produced a Latin ver-

sion of Lucian's mock-eulogy of the fly, Alberti thanked him for the work with bubbling enthusiasm. This incomparably witty text, he declared, had not only cured him of an illness but had inspired him to write his own extravagant praise of flies—a firework of a eulogy, in which he praised the insects for such unexpected attributes as their piety (since they were always the first to attend sacrifices), their bravery (since they were always willing to attack other creatures, however large and strong), and their intelligence (since they had anticipated the mathematical achievements of Pythagoras and provided, with their gaily decorated wings, the model for the cartography of Ptolemy). Alberti's *jeu d'esprit* publicized his taste, which he shared with Guarino and others, for the witty, sometimes over-the-top Greek rhetoric of the first and second centuries C.E., the so-called Second Sophistic.[41]

Alberti's fourth honest broker in Ferrara—and the one whom he approached in the most original way—was a canon, Francesco Marescalco. Marescalco did not himself produce elaborate texts in Latin, but as a student of Guarino, he enjoyed the prestige of an expert in literary style. Rather like Niccolò Niccoli—whose correspondence with Poggio he eagerly read, after Poggio dedicated a collection of their letters to him—Marescalco collected newly discovered or translated classical texts, taking advantage of Poggio's detective skills and acquaintance with skilled scribes to add to his library.[42] Like Niccoli, too, Marescalco edited texts written by moderns. His opinion carried much weight: as late as 1457, when Poggio was a very established author indeed, even a mild expression of disapproval on Marescalco's part could worry him:

> I received your letter, in which you indicated that you had read my little books [*The Variability of Fortune*] in one night, and that a sleepless one. And you say further that you find it entirely excellent, except for one point, which I may find problematic as well. For it seems foolish to sow in a sterile field, since one loses both the seed and one's labor.[43]

Poggio had intended to dedicate *The Variability of Fortune* to Sigismondo Malatesta, the tyrant of Rimini, but Marescalco apparently advised against this course. No longer young, Poggio still wanted to win the approval of an editor he respected before he let a substantial piece of his Latin writing go into public circulation.

As this story suggests, Marescalco's interests—and his social authority—

extended outside the field of pure scholarship and rhetoric, into that of conduct as well. Scipione Mainenti—the Ferrarese scholar with whom Poggio
had been discussing the historical and moral assessment of Scipio and Caesar—assured Poggio, in a conversation at Florence, that Marescalco was not
only erudite but "endowed with the most pleasant of characters and with
virtue."[44] Over the years, Marescalco took care to remain on warm personal
terms with Poggio, writing to congratulate him very affectionately on his
marriage and maintaining contact with him for decades thereafter. And he
willingly helped Poggio's young friends, like the schoolmaster Filippo Tifer-
nas, gain an entrée into Ferrarese society in the 1440s.[45] Like the Milanese
courtier Francesco Barbavara, whom Piero Alberti praises so warmly in Alberti's dialogue, Marescalco evidently saw his role in real life as that of opening the Ferrarese favor bank to deserving foreigners whose scholarly gifts
he respected. This course of action was, of course, neither innocent nor
quixotic: the favor that someone like Marescalco enjoyed had to be expended to become visible.[46]

Accordingly, Alberti chose Marescalco to be the recipient of one of his
most distinctive gifts. In four days in December 1437, while still working in
the papal curia in Bologna, he composed a set of one hundred fables. In a fictional letter to Aesop, the Greek who had supposedly originated the genre,
Alberti asked for a critical comment, a "judgment." More or less by return
mail, he received it. Aesop observed, in a short reply, that anyone who read
Alberti's fables could see that those who maintained that the Italians had no
brains were wrong—even though few mortals actually could boast of any intelligence. Those who condemned Alberti simply failed to realize that his
irony and wit were actually virtues. The work in question clearly formed a
move in a learned game: from the start, the reader was confronted with the
question of how to read Alberti's work for tone as well as content.

Alberti presented his fables, and his prefatory exchange with Aesop, to
Marescalco. His dedicatory letter described the work as a bouquet of flowers,
perhaps picked too soon but nonetheless likely to please a man of Marescalco's learning and taste. He apologized, in particular, for one aspect of the
fables, their brevity. But the terms of his apology are suggestive:

If my fables seem a bit obscure to you at times, you will have to par-
don me for this brevity, which I worked very hard to attain. For, as
they say, brevity is always liable to be obscure: and I thought that fables should be particularly brief. But since they are so short, they will
not bore you much even if you reread them again and again. I ask

you, accordingly, to be willing to put in the bit of work needed to understand them: once you have done so, I think, you will find immense pleasure in them.

As in his work on horses, Alberti was writing for a reader, or a small group of readers, who were as learned and as quick on the uptake as he was himself. He meant his book, like the rings engraved with emblematic designs that he described in his dinner piece "Rings," to pique and provoke the curiosity of those who encountered it, to force them not just to read but to decipher its message. This was coterie literature, aimed at the members of a learned court.

The body of Alberti's work more than bore out the promise of its prefatory letters. To be sure, some of his little stories were nothing more than jokes, of the kind that Poggio and his learned friends had exchanged in the 1420s in the "chamber of lies" in the curia at Rome. "A lame man," so goes one of Alberti's stories, "had part of one of his feet cut off, where it was too long, so that he could walk more evenly. Once it was cut off, he found himself lying on the ground, rendered incapable of walking at all." "The brass asked that it be considered the equivalent of gold"—so starts another. " 'Well then,' asked the silversmith, 'can you stand up to the heat of the fire, to which the gold has been subjected so often?' 'It's not that important to me,' answered the brass, 'to have so high a valuation.' " Stories like these made up the common coin of humanist joke collections, with their emphasis on human stupidity and their taste for humiliating those who tried to raise themselves above their proper status. Cleverer—but no more profound—was the sergeant's complaint to the flag. Why, the soldier asked, did the flag always seem to be retreating when carried into action against the enemy, only to flap toward the enemy, apparently praising him, when the regiment ran away? The flag replied, snappily, that though it was not a traitor, it preferred to applaud the victor—a vivid story, but not one that clearly concealed a complex lesson.

In other cases, however, Alberti's fables were more subtle. They turned into miniature versions of the dinner pieces, and like the dinner pieces they taught basic lessons about morality and prudence. Alberti took special pleasure in his own eighty-eighth fable:

A lake turned pale with fear when clouds rose from the mountains into the air and lowered above its head, for it thought that they were mountains, and might collapse on it. Finally, when the clouds turned

into water, ran off as rain and made the lake larger, it said: "How foolish I was to fear what was really to my great benefit."

Like this story, several others emphasized, in related ways, the folly of excessive ambition, the weakness of the intellect, and the fallibility of the
senses—for example, the fable of the boy who tried to catch a ray of sun between his palms, until he was told by the shadow that "divine things can
never be held in a human prison."

Alberti's interests and obsessions found compressed and provocative expression in this new form. For example, the eternal need to watch the passage of time became the subject of a joke about a virgin eating a pear. When
she complained that the fruit had tasted bitter when it looked most deli-
cious, only to become hideous-looking when it actually achieved a state of
ripeness, the pear replied: "Do you think it's easy to work out what age has to
do with ripeness?"[47] Alberti's hatred of religious insincerity inspired a series
of fables, like one in which a captain, after bringing his ship safely home
from a dangerous voyage, decided to dedicate some part of it to the gods, as
an offering in the temple. The keel, the mast, and the anchor all asked him
to honor them by choosing them: but he took the rudder instead, since it
was the cheapest.

Most provocative of all were the numerous stories that treated nature itself as red in tooth and claw, not as a harmonious whole but as a war of all
against all: "The worm devoured the nut in which it had been born. 'What
an ungrateful wretch you are,' said the nut, 'to bring ruin on me, when I
made your existence possible.' The worm answered, 'If you brought me into
being so that I could die of hunger, you did me wrong.' "[48] In stories like
these Alberti's mordant sense of evil expressed itself in an almost Darwinian
vision of a universe in constant conflict.

Alberti found ways to refer to painting and sculpture in his fables. In On
Painting, he had argued that the myth of Narcissus was an allegory of the origins of painting: as the beautiful boy had tried to hold fast the image of himself that trembled on the surface of the water, so the painter tried to catch
the ever-changing image of the world he saw. One of Alberti's fables neatly
turned the myth—and its account of painting—on its head: "A fish desperately desired to climb a tree; impelled by that wish, it leaped through the
trees painted on the surface of a pond—and thus destroyed the painted trees.
'Are you so insane,' asked the trees, 'that even imaginary trees run away
from you?' " Another dramatized an artistic dilemma: Did the great artist

create something that not only seemed alive but really was so? Or was he a human craftsman who worked with ordinary materials and made and corrected mistakes? "When a statue of Venus, which Praxiteles had made, kept looking at him in an improper way, he asked again and again, trying to urge, persuade, beseech, and finally threaten her into correcting the fault in her eyes. Finally he decided that he himself had to remove the flaw with his chisel." Still other fables revealed Alberti's knowledge of the natural processes that led silt and plants to build up in waterways and made different substances behave in different ways when heated.[49]

In a Renaissance court, the riddling, provocative style that Alberti adopted had a clear function. The Este and their courtiers—like practically everyone else of similar rank in fifteenth-century Europe—cultivated a taste for heraldic emblems. Leonello, for example, used the lion, the leopard, and the blindfolded lynx as personal devices on his coins and medals. In content and form alike, these images of noble descent and status called for decipherment:

> The bandage over the eyes of the feline beast, streaming and fluttering in the wind, recalls Leonello's *impresa*, the famous *vela*, a word having the double meaning of "veils" and "sail." This symbolic word, dark and ambiguous as *imprese* were wont to be, appears to have influenced the choice of the motto, "*Quae vides ne vide*" (shut your eyes to what you see).[50]

Alberti, who kept his fables brief and cryptic, used them to show, in the most effective possible way, that he had a skill the Este valued. In a world that esteemed the clever manipulation of symbols above many other skills, he was an expert on symbolism. To an audience that prized riddles, he offered riddles without number.

None of Alberti's riddles were more striking—or more carefully pitched to attract attention in Ferrara—than the fables in which he himself appeared, in the transparent guise of a lion, engaged in struggles that recalled his own. Told that another lion had been granted the right to enter heaven, he wrote, a lion, "burning with the desire for glory," carried out "every task of the highest difficulty to perfection" in order to surpass all the other lions. Asked by an envious bystander why he was working so hard to attain a fate that had already been determined, he replied (with Alberti's characteristic will to attain glory and sense that the virtuous generally did not succeed),

"For me it will be enough to have earned the highest place." Another lion, led by a slave through the streets and shops of Rome, gave direct expression to Alberti's view of his critics. Asked why, when it could outrun Pegasus, outleap leopards, and overcome bulls, it lowered itself to serve a mere man, the lion answered that it both helped its friends and despised those who barked slanders at it. Yet another leonine fable crystallized Alberti's sense of himself as a performer. A lion amazed the audience in a theater by its ability to throw a marble disk, make a huge marble ball revolve, and play delicately with an egg. A critic objected that all three things that the lion manipulated were round and accordingly easy to use. "Yes, o expert in these matters," answered the lion, "it is as you say: but you should note that what I am playing with is not a ball, little man, but a round egg."[51] Like the marquis of Ferrara, Alberti had found in the animal world a creature that could express his own sense of self—and do so in an original, provocative way. The animal, moreover, was a lion—and thus a reference to Leonello's name as well as to Leon Battista's. Under the smooth Latin prose, one hears the whisper of a forgotten language of male courtship.

Alberti's pincer attack worked formidably well. He spent time in Ferrara, not only during the council but in the 1440s as well, though he always alternated his stays there with periods in Rome and elsewhere. He convinced the Este, Meliaduse and Leonello alike, that he had uniquely valuable services to offer them. At the same time, however, he shaped his own work, as engineer, connoisseur, and writer, to show that he appreciated their particular needs and interests. By 1450, when Leonello died, Alberti had had a powerful impact on tastes and practices in Ferrara. And his own career had taken what would become its definitive direction.

Alberti established himself in Ferrara, in the first instance, as the author of *On Painting*: a connoisseur of the visual arts, deeply knowledgeable about how ancient painters and sculptors had gone about their work and how ancient rulers had used their work to good aesthetic and civic effect. In 1441—immediately after Leonello succeeded Niccoló as marquis—two painters of great eminence, Pisanello and Bellini, competed, in the Florentine manner, to paint his portrait. Angelo Decembrio, writing long after the event, made Leonello describe their rivalry in some detail, showing that he saw it as something like a failed attempt to institute in Ferrara Alberti's ideal system of collaboration among artists and critics:

> In . . . ancient times, painters and poets were rewarded and praised
> with almost equal generosity. Artists would show their work to each

other and then correct it, whereas nowadays, as we know, they are consumed by rivalry with one another. You remember how Pisanello and Bellini, the finest painters of our time, recently differed in various ways in the portrayal of my face. The one added a more emphatic spareness to its handsomeness, while the other represented it as paler, though no more slender; and scarcely were they reconciled by my entreaties.

Clearly, the social system of artistic patronage had not functioned as Alberti hoped: rivalry had led to injurious, rather than constructive, criticism. Equally clearly, however, the Ferrarese court and its artists—if not necessarily Leonello himself—had become familiar with Alberti's book and its central theses. Leonello (at least as Decembrio represented him) had a critical vocabulary at his disposal that enabled him to compare the two portraits in a subtle way, if not to explain which was better.

Later in the same work, Leonello argues in detail, in the purest Albertian language, that a skilled artist must know the internal structures of the human body, lay out the figures he means to portray in a detailed preparatory sketch, and ensure that even the bones and muscles that do not appear in his painting are accurately accounted for under the visible surface:

> There are some painters, though not many, who do try to imitate the ancients. First they carefully work out all the measurements of the body they are going to represent, so that no part of it may be nearer to or further from another part than the rule of nature herself ordains. Then, no less skillfully, they consider which parts of the body should be tense and contracted, and which relaxed and sunk into it so as to be almost hidden: so that, whether the figure is standing, sitting, or lying down, there may finally be a natural aptness in the representation of any of the body's movements. And then, last of all, they add clothes and the body's outer covering. If, for instance, you were going to paint Ajax and Hector fighting with each other, you would have to portray them quickly and skillfully in the nude, and then, following your sketch, dispose the costume and armor only after you had worked out the position proper to the heroes' actions.

Ferrarese aesthetics (even as Decembrio made Leonello describe them) were not purely Albertian. Alberti saw the portrayal of hair and costume as crucial to the painter's task of representing motion. Leonello, by contrast, insists (according to Decembrio) that the greatest works of art represent nude bodies; costumes change, after all, eventually coming to look ridiculous, while "the artifice of nature is supreme, no period fashions change it." Decembrio's portrait of Leonello as critic, for all its highly plausible detail, was not wholly true to life. His Leonello denounces the "tapestries from Transalpine Gaul you see hung on walls," not because Flemish weavers lack skill but because "the weavers and designers are far more concerned with the opulence of color and the frivolous charm of the tapestry than they are with the science of painting." In particular, they frequently depict apocryphal scenes from ancient history—like the medieval legend about the discovery of Trajan's head, "its tongue still pink and living"—or distorted figures from classical mythology: "they represent Bucephalus, Alexander's horse, not with the jaws of an ox, as Curtius describes him . . . but rather as some hell-horse of Pluto's or Charon's, or like Jason's fettered fire-breathing bulls. And so it goes on, wherever one looks, through the folly of these northern people." Alberti may well have denounced Flemish tapestries as frivolous and indecorous—as images that failed to live up to his sere standards of composition and purpose. The real Leonello, however, collected them eagerly, and at considerable expense.[52]

Alberti did not take the city—or even its massive, well-fortified castle, where he was a welcome guest for many years—entirely by storm. His advice, though it influenced Leonello, did not determine all of his decisions by any means. The court remained eclectic. Leonello's favorite artists included innovative painters whose work closely fitted Alberti's stylistic ideals: for example, Piero della Francesca and Andrea Mantegna. But his favorite painter of all, Pisanello, cultivated a graceful mixture of Italianate and more traditional style. Decembrio's portrait of Leonello, though not fully accurate, corresponded to historical reality when it represented the prince as having learned from Alberti but also having developed tastes and interests of his own.[53]

If the part Alberti played at court was not dominant, it was still significant. Over time, Leonello and his subjects assimilated Alberti's ideals and some of the actual Florentine practices that had inspired them. In 1443, for example, Leonello decided to carry out a public artistic project, on a far larger scale than the simple portraits over which Pisanello and Bellini had gone to war. The city of Florence had for many years devoted central public spaces to works of art that carried powerful religious and political charges, like the Baptistery doors. Some of these public artworks were explicitly meant to celebrate great political and military actors of the city's past. Paolo Uccello's great painted monument to the English mercenary captain John Hawkwood, for example, still dominates the nave of the Florentine Cathedral. With this work Uccello revived the classical equestrian monument, known to all visitors to Rome from the monument to Marcus Aurelius which then stood near the Lateran. Donatello later transported this form to Padua, where he executed a free-standing equestrian monument in bronze to the mercenary officer Gattamellata.

In 1443 Leonello decided to enter the same cultural sweepstakes: he commissioned a bronze equestrian monument to his father, to be placed on a structure modeled on a Roman triumphal arch. It would stand immediately in front of the Este palace, looking toward the cathedral.

It is certainly possible that Alberti helped Leonello, or even inspired him, to conceive of the project. He was already establishing himself in Ferrara as an expert on architecture and engineering. In *On the Art of Building*, he emphasized the vital role of public statues, urging that figures exemplifying "the greatest excellence and perfection" be set up, at communal expense, in prominent places—like piazzas—where they could help to inspire and educate the citizens. He took a special interest in the placement of triumphal arches, which he saw as a visually dramatic device for defining the point at which a road debouches into a public square. The carved decoration on the completed triumphal arch in Ferrara, moreover, resembles that of Alberti's first major architectural project, the Church of San Francesco in Rimini. This was carried out by Matteo de' Pasti, an illuminator, sculptor, and architect who also worked regularly in Ferrara. It seems altogether likely, then, that the project design as a whole reflected Alberti's thinking.[54]

In any event, a competition was declared. As in the competition for the Baptistery doors in Florence, several artists evidently submitted entries at a preliminary stage. Two drawings in Jacopo Bellini's London sketchbook, for example, represent equestrian monuments that bear the eagle, another heraldic animal associated with the Este.[55] They may well reflect his plan for the statue. Two Florentine artists—Antonio di Cristoforo and Niccolò Baroncelli—were apparently selected as finalists. As Brunelleschi and Ghiberti had done for the Baptistery doors, they created "images"—presumably three-dimensional models. Neither entry was obviously better than the other: "many spoke in favor of each of them, one finding one of them better, and the next man the other." A choice had to be made.

But the simplest criterion, that of the statue's likeness to its object, did not suffice to settle the question, as an official document confessed with some embarrassment: "Each resembles the aforesaid prince, and both are very handsome, so that the judgment as to which of them is more appropriate and better can be made only with great effort and by experts in painting." On 27 November 1443, eleven of the twelve members of the committee of the Savi, who were responsible for making the choice, met to consider the two models, at Leonello's request. Given white beans (to indicate support for Antonio) and black ones (to indicate support for Niccolò), the Savi voted six to five for the former.[56] It was too close to a draw for comfort.

At this delicate point, Alberti's expert help was requested. In fact, he explained in the introduction to his treatise On the Horse (which the contest inspired him to write):

> The citizens had decided to place an equestrian statue of your [Leonello's] father, made at vast expense, in the forum, and the best craftsmen had competed for the project. At your orders they chose me, since I take much pleasure in painting and sculpture, as an adviser to the judges. After repeatedly examining the works of art, which were made with extraordinary skill, I thought that I should write a work of some seriousness both about the beauty and form of horses, and about their nature and habits more generally.[57]

Alberti's intervention had to do, then, both with his expertise on the arts and with his knowledge of nature—or at least of horses.

The actual outcome of the competition suggests the form that his advice took. Though Antonio had won more votes, he and Niccolò collaborated on the statue. Antonio executed the man, Niccolò the horse. It seems highly likely that Alberti suggested the compromise, arguing that Niccolò's model horse was superior. By negotiating a settlement less rancorous than the Florentine one that had so embittered Brunelleschi, he established himself as a dominant figure, the expert critic.

Niccolò was portrayed as a truly grand figure, equipped with the beret and baton appropriate to his office, riding as Leonello did when he carried out his formal possesso, the ceremony by which he took command of the city. The grandly decorated arch bore an inscription in Latin that commemorated Niccolò's skills as a diplomat, calling him "three times creator of peace in Italy," and it stressed the direct line by which power had been transmitted from Alberto d'Este to Niccolò and from Niccolò to Leonello.[58] The fact that the competition took place at all—and the nature of the opinions expressed—probably reveal the impact of Alberti and of the Florentine models for artistic life and work that he brought with him. All members of the Savi committee were consciously trying to identify the artist who could most successfully achieve ideal beauty and produce a convincing likeness of the particular individual—fulfilling Alberti's two conflicting commands to the artist. When the judgment proved difficult, all agreed that the intervention of someone acknowledged as an expert on the arts was required. Alberti's description of the event in his treatise and that in the archival document recording the deliberations of the Savi do not agree in all respects. Moreover, the documents do not mention Alberti. But the impressive presence of his new vision of the arts—and its impact on their practice—are unmistakable.

Alberti also seems to have played a vital role in the creation of what became a very popular new form of art in Ferrara in these same years. In 1438, Pisanello produced a bronze medal, which bore on one side a portrait of the Byzantine emperor John VIII Palaeologus, who came to Ferrara for the council, and on the reverse an equestrian portrait of the emperor, dressed for hunting, praying before a wayside cross. This work drew on several precedents well known in scholarly and artistic circles, especially among antiquarians. From the fourteenth century on, scholars interested in Roman history had collected coins that bore the images of Roman emperors. Leonello, for his part, eagerly collected ancient gems and coins: he seems to have been the first Italian prince to do so. Decembrio did not depart far from the facts when he represented the marquis as giving an intelligent and appreciative little speech about the way that such material remains of the ancient world complement the textual record: "I often take great pleasure in looking at the heads of the Caesars on bronze coins—bronze having survived more commonly than gold or silver—and they impress me no less than the descriptions of their appearance in Suetonius and others. For the latter are apprehended by the mind alone."[59] It seems likely in general terms, then, that Pisanello saw his medal as a modern counterpart to such classical objects—at once the revival of an ancient art form and an appropriate way to record, for a posterity centuries to come, the appearance of a genuine Greek emperor.

A great deal of evidence supports the view that Alberti helped to inspire the creation both of this medal and of the many others that Pisanello and others wrought in the 1440s. From the start, Pisanello's medals bore his signature, boldly executed. The reverse of the medal for John VIII, for example, declared in both Latin and Greek that it was "the work of the painter Pisanello."[60] In claiming that he, as a painter, could preserve his model for posterity, Pisanello performed exactly the historical role Alberti had ascribed to the artist in *On Painting*.

But the connections are even tighter than this correspondence of artistic practice with theory. Alberti, as we have already seen, had created a self-portrait in the form of a large medal or plaquette, itself probably modeled on an ancient portrait gem. It seems highly likely that he fashioned this image as part of his approach to the Ferrarese court. Like his fables, the portrait emphasizes the connection between Leon Battista Alberti and Leonello d'Este. It gives the artist tightly curled "leonine" hair, which was one of the Ferrarese ruler's most distinctive features.[61] The portrait medal also uses an emblem: beside the artist's face, and formally echoing the knot that holds his classical cloak on his shoulders, appears a winged eye carried by a raptor—a provocative and puzzling device that reappears, in part, on the portrait medal of Alberti later done by Matteo de' Pasti and in Alberti's own manuscripts. And Alberti, like Pisanello, signed his work in classical capitals: "L. BAP." Though not identical with Alberti's plaquette, Pisanello's first medal seems to represent an experimental move in the same direction.

In the course of the 1440s, as Pisanello and de' Pasti made the medal into a standard form, they modified Alberti's precedent in further, vital ways. Like the medal for John VIII—and unlike Alberti's self-portrait—later specimens were circular in form. Though many medals, like Alberti's, bore both a portrait and an emblem, they normally appeared not next to one another, as on his plaquette, but on opposite sides of the piece. But the precedents Alberti had set remained basic, and individual medals often seem to reveal his direct participation, at least as the iconographer behind the artist. In 1443, when Pisanello made a series of some eight bronze medals for Leonello, Alberti was in Ferrara consulting on the statue of Niccolò III. One of the medals that Pisanello made at this point has on its obverse a portrait of Leonello, and on its reverse a lion being shown music or taught to sing by a *putto*—a combination of motifs dear to Alberti. Behind the lion appears an inscribed stone tablet, with the date of the medal, 1443, and another symbolic image close to Alberti's heart: the sail or weathervane that, as he had pointed out in his dinner piece "Rings," nicely represents the need to adapt to circumstances. As sailors trimmed their sails in stormy weather, in order to find a safe haven or at least a safe path through the waves, so the prudent statesman must adjust his course whenever political tempests endangered him. If this medal praised Leonello's political astuteness—and gave him what became a favorite emblem—a second one taught him a moral lesson. Alberti argued in his *Teogenius*, an Italian treatise on morality that Leonello encouraged him to write, that the wise man must realize how pitiful and helpless he is. A being who came naked into the universe, he must learn that his body—and all the wealth and splendor that may surround it—are nothing more than an empty vessel. In his second portrait medal, Pisanello used as the reverse for Leonello a naked male figure, lying on the ground, before what may well be a vision of a great metal vessel containing flowers— another Albertian lesson crystallized in visual form.[62]

Matteo de' Pasti, similarly, followed Alberti's precedent by dedicating a medal not to a ruler but to a scholar: Guarino, whom he represented on the obverse with a fine, beetling forehead. Like Alberti—and unlike the secular rulers whom both Pisanello and de' Pasti immortalized on medals—Guarino wears Roman costume. On the reverse, the medal bears the artist's signature on the rim, and in the center a splendid fountain, surmounted by a statue of a boy in a strikingly elegant pose, armed with shield and mace—another provocative, and as yet undeciphered, image.[63]

The fashion for medals spread rapidly through the Italian courts, from the Malatesta of Rimini to the Gonzaga of Mantua and beyond. Pisanello and de' Pasti—whose work, like that of most court artists, was a movable feast, which they offered to many patrons—presumably carried it with them. In doing so, they were almost certainly carrying on a development begun by Alberti in Ferrara, drawing on both his humanistic scholarship and his artistic skill to create what would eventually become a vivid historical record for his own age, when that had turned into antiquity, in the distant future. The antiquaries of the future would need to have all their wits about them to unravel Alberti's emblems; but at least they would know for certain which medals were the work of Pisanello and which of de' Pasti and would not have to speculate, as Cyriac and Traversari did, about possible attributions to Praxiteles, which rested on no documentary evidence at all.

The most revealing of all the works that Alberti produced for his Ferrarese patrons was *Mathematical Games*, which he dedicated to Meliaduse, sometime before the latter's death in January 1452 and probably also before

Leonello's death in October 1450. This short treatise was Alberti's most direct contribution to the literature of practical mathematics and engineering.
Here he tried to attain a different set of stylistic effects from those he had
used to appeal to Marescalco and Leonello. He wrote in Italian, not Latin,
liberally glossing and repeating himself. As he explained, "I did my best to
write as openly as possible, but one must remember that these problems are
extremely subtle. It is almost impossible to handle them in so clear a way
that the reader does not have to bring his full attention to bear in order to
understand them." At the end of the work, he confessed that he had omitted
many fascinating problems and methods that he had found in "ancient"
writers on engineering "solely because I could not find a way to say them as
clearly and accessibly as I hoped to say them." His exposition was so simple
as to be almost colloquial at times. Occasionally, he addressed problems in a
way that suggested that they had literally come up in conversation: "Let us
return," he says at one point, "to what you asked me about." "I recall," he
says at another, "how I showed you the way to aim a bombard when you cannot see the point that the stone is meant to strike."[64] Unlike the Sienese engineer and writer Taccola, who repeatedly stated that his diagrams and
captions would be cryptic except to expert readers, Alberti did his best
throughout Games to write on a level that a nobleman without special training could follow without great effort. When he had addressed the learned
Francesco Marescalco, Alberti had deliberately made his prose difficult and
provocative. Discussing horses, one of Leonello's central interests, he had
kept his work brief because his reader was already expert. But he made
Games far more accessible—more accessible, in fact, than practically useful.
Evidently, Alberti wrote less as an engineer than as a court servant, playing
with the terms and techniques of engineering without taxing his patron's patience.[65]

Despite this self-imposed limitation, Alberti found plenty of "very rare
things" with which to delight Meliaduse. He chose the topics that he covered using at least three criteria. First, he selected problems that could be
clearly presented and solved relatively simply. He equipped the book with
diagrams, line drawings to which he referred regularly in the course of the
text, remarking again and again that a particular technique appeared "here
in the illustration." It seems very likely that Alberti used drawings to instruct Meliaduse in the surveying and military techniques he described in
the Games. Describing one method (among several) for measuring the
height of a tower, Alberti apparently represented in his diagram a man mea-

suring the height of the Vatican obelisk.[66] Angelo Decembrio, writing in the 1450s or 1460s, recounted a courtly conversation in which Guarino—probably standing in for Alberti—discussed the measurement of the obelisk, as well as the monument's composition and origins: a conversation that a diagram like Alberti's would have clarified in every way. It seems legitimate to imagine that Alberti's book derived from a series of informal lessons, in which he presented and explicated particular images, diagrammatically, to his pupil.

Alberti selected not only topics that could be visually presented, but also ones that could be solved by a pupil who did not have an extensive set of techniques at his disposal. Meliaduse apparently understood the geometry of similar triangles before he began work with Alberti. Accordingly, Alberti reduced problems of measuring the height of buildings, the width of rivers, the depth of wells, the areas of fields, and the distance of targets, among others, to similar triangle problems that Meliaduse could solve without undue effort. Again and again the answers to these different problems converged on the same simple theorems; and even then Alberti apologized when he felt that a problem had become "laborious to understand."

Pleasure, as well as ease of solution, played a role in Alberti's choice of problems: as he said at one point, he "had resolved here to explain only pleasant things to you: so let us leave those subtleties on the side." Accordingly, he spent considerable time and space on problems that seemed particularly enjoyable, like how to draw a map of Rome or another city, a task that he described as "very delightful." He recounted the witty tale of how Archimedes had weighed a crown in air and water in order to prove that a goldsmith had tried to cheat Hero of Syracuse: "you will get much pleasure," Alberti observed, "from what the ancients wrote about Hero." A water clock, which used air pressure to produce a constant spray of water for a set period, seemed a "most delightful game"—and his discussion looked forward to the many hydraulic devices that would be secretly installed in Italian gardens of the late fifteenth and sixteenth centuries to play organs and drench visitors.[67] Science as surprise, technology as treat: Alberti had a good reason for calling his manual of courtly applied geometry a set of games.

The central motive for his choice of topics, however, was the appearance of practicality. Alberti addressed, for the most part, problems that were genuinely likely to confront the ruler of a small warfare state based in a river delta: how to measure fields that changed shape; how to survey and measure roads in the territory between Ferrara and Bologna; how to prevent the water in rivers and canals from eroding their banks; how to tell time with an impressive public clock.[68] Alberti, in sum, gave Meliaduse entertaining, and sometimes sophisticated, solutions to the very problems about which he and his brother were most likely to need an engineer's advice. Here, as in his treatise on the horse, Alberti played the role of a technical consultant to the Este: a consultant who combined expertise in many fields that were directly relevant to court life with an ability to present his recommendations attractively and painlessly.[69] It seems unlikely that this instruction can have been intended for practical use: but it presumably established Alberti's credentials and acquainted Meliaduse with useful terms.

At least once Alberti referred explicitly to his combination of skills. Describing methods for building aqueducts, he advised Meliaduse that he had treated this complex problem at full length in his treatise *On Architecture* (later changed to *On the Art of Building*), which he had written at the direct request "of your illustrious brother, my Lord, messer Leonello."[70] Alberti had developed, in the course of his time in Ferrara, more than a part-time interest in the problems he covered briefly in *Games*. He had become not just an observer of engineers and architects but one of them. In this capacity—which he, like others, saw as complementary to his work as humanist and antiquary—he forged a position and a self fully worthy of his highest early aspirations. His new skills made him useful and welcome in several courts, and eventually won him a stronger position in the curia and at Florence—and evidently without compromising his strong sense of what his honor as an Alberti demanded of him. Alberti not only wrote the script for advancement at court but acted it. The author of *Philodoxeos fabula*, the lover of glory, had become at last the star of his own play.

VII

HIS LOST CITY:

ALBERTI THE ANTIQUARY

No one appreciated the bright sun that shone near Rome on 15 July 1535 more than the military architect Francesco De Marchi, for it enabled him to see in what might otherwise have proved difficult conditions. After putting on a diving apparatus designed by an associate, De Marchi lowered himself into the shallow waters of Lake Nemi, a small, clear body of water picturesquely located in a crater in the Alban hills, not far from Rome. Peering through a crystal "the size of a palm," which the designer had thoughtfully inserted in his helmet, he saw crowds of tiny fish, which the water magnified to near-monstrous size. The apparatus worked: De Marchi stayed under water for half an hour, and when he returned to the surface, the top of his white shirt and his silk hat, adorned with white feathers, were still dry. His jubilant companions snatched the plumes, which they kept as souvenirs.

The first dive was not altogether a success. De Marchi's ears hurt under water—so severely, he remarked, that it seemed as if someone had driven a needle through his head. He bled copiously at the nose and mouth, spoiling the otherwise dry white shirt. The fish posed the worst problem of all, even though De Marchi knew they were not so huge as they looked under water.

He had once seen a fisherman drown in the Arno when his breeches snagged on a tree root, so while preparing for the dive, De Marchi had removed his breeches. But he did more than strip. Since he came from Bologna, he knew that he might survive half an hour without breathing, but not without eating. So he made himself a sandwich of bread and cheese. When the stale bread crumbled, the crumbs attracted fish. And the fish immediately attacked De Marchi "in the part of the body that anyone can imagine." He tried to beat them off with his hand, but the fish, "who were, so to speak, in their own home," paid no attention and continued to investigate his naughty bits. De Marchi's first experience of underwater exploration would have discouraged a less determined man.

But De Marchi persevered. Later, binding up his mouth and ears, he returned to the depths of the lake. There, as he knew he would, he found a precious submerged monument: the remains of two Roman ships, which the famous antiquarian Flavio Biondo had described almost a century before. Staying under for an hour, De Marchi stared and prodded. He examined nails made of iron, which were deeply corroded, and of bronze, so fresh that they seemed to have been forged the day before. He investigated the hull, which the Roman shipwrights had built up of several kinds of wood and covered with layers of lead plate and cloth, and attached a rope to it. Workers on the surface, turning a windlass, managed to bring up, not the ship as a whole, but enough of it "to load down two strong mules."

De Marchi also saw, but did not venture to explore, "certain dark parts" of one of the ships, which he took to be the remains of "the palace that had been built upon it"—a structure that had turned it into a grand houseboat. De Marchi, in short, made a bold and thorough job of this early venture in underwater archaeology. Unlike Guillaume of Lorraine, the designer of the diving bell who had also explored the ships, he did not venture to swim into the wrecks themselves. Accordingly he could not confirm Guillaume's belief that he had observed metal beams inside the hull. But in its way, De Marchi's adventure in the heart of underwater darkness compares with the sculptor and goldsmith Benvenuto Cellini's memorable nighttime trip to raise devils in the Colosseum. A loyal exponent of the heroic tradition of the fifteenth-century engineers, De Marchi interpolated a long account of his adventure into a treatise on military architecture, most of which dealt with quite different subjects.[1]

The two Roman ships sunk in Lake Nemi were pleasure barges that had belonged to Caligula, just over seventy meters long and astonishingly well preserved. During the eighteenth and nineteenth centuries, their remains stimulated any number of fantastic attempts at reconstruction, and they yielded spectacular bronzes to a diver who explored them in 1895. Both vessels were finally raised between 1928 and 1932. One of the great enterprises of Fascist archaeology, it required lowering the surface of the lake as a whole. Sadly, both ships were destroyed by the Germans as they retreated toward Rome in May 1944. The full records made of them in the 1930s, however, remain vital sources of information about shipbuilding in antiquity.[2]

De Marchi—as he knew—was following in the watery footsteps of Leon Battista Alberti when he arranged empty boats on the surface of the lake to support lifting machinery. His dives were also homage to his predecessor, whose earlier effort to plumb the depths of the lake had been only one, though the most dramatic, of a wide range of archaeological projects. Alberti had made himself over the years into a deft "service professional" for great men, and one of the services he offered was expert advice on antiquities. In doing so, he helped to define a discipline that had developed in the course of the fourteenth and fifteenth centuries: antiquarianism. Its proponents explored the ancient cities they inhabited. They tried to identify the ruined buildings and works of art that had once adorned them, to reconstruct their forgotten customs and institutions, and to sort out the history of their foundation and early development. Dry and technical in content but sometimes splendidly illustrated with copies of inscriptions and miniatures of ancient sites, their works assembled a vast range of details about the lost social and cultural practices of the ancient world. This approach to antiquity fascinated Alberti, who pursued it for more than half of his lifetime and did much to give antiquarianism the shape it would retain for centuries to come.

The antiquarian enterprise grew directly from the European landscape— in particular, the ruin-strewn landscape of Italy, where every acre of urban ground was a historical palimpsest.[3] Throughout the Middle Ages, Roman aqueducts and sarcophagi, bridges and baths, temples that had metamorphosized into churches and arenas that had been redeveloped into neighborhoods provoked the curiosity of residents and travelers. The city of Rome in particular had been the center of the world, *caput mundi*, and it remained the most massive single collection of romantic ruins, a vast nostalgic landscape somehow rendered three-dimensional. The past was present in every Roman street: the great feudal families that fought to control the city made their strongholds in the Colosseum and the ruins of Roman *insulae* or apartment houses. Guides to the marvels of ancient Rome directed visitors to the

Colosseum and the Pantheon, the Spinario and the Vatican obelisk, about which they told divertingly improbable stories. But accurate information circulated too. Even the miniatures of Roman buildings that decorated the manuscripts of medieval French romances reflected some direct knowledge of the monuments. By the fourteenth century, many writers on Roman history and visitors to the city had realized that Trajan's column and the arch of Constantine, with their reliefs of ancient soldiers and their weapons, were literally "histories" in stone.[4]

From the fourteenth century onward, innovative scholars like Petrarch began to look systematically at the built and sculpted past. Instead of retelling traditional stories about individual sites long associated with Roman heroes, they tried to imagine what the city as a whole had looked like at particular times in its history. Petrarch inserted a detailed description of the republican city, marred by some anachronisms, into his epic *Africa*. Instead of passing on information gleaned from the writings of earlier collectors, the Renaissance antiquaries tried to work directly from the monuments. Poggio Bracciolini, as we have seen, stood at the center not only of the intellectual life of the papal curia but also of Alberti's circle of friends and patrons. He also helped to shape antiquarianism. Poggio filled his house with fragments of ancient statuary. He intrepidly deciphered and copied down ancient inscriptions, even when doing so required him to brave the Italian midday sun and to endure the teasing questions of young women. Between 1431 and 1448, he wrote a large-scale treatise on the ruins of Rome, which took the form of a dialogue between himself and another papal secretary, Antonio Loschi. *The Variability of Fortune* gives a good sense of the culture of antiquarianism as Alberti first encountered it.

Poggio made his book a charter of the new scholarship. He began with a panoramic evocation of Rome's ruins, as seen from the Capitoline, describing the Forum and the Palatine, once the heart of the republican and imperial capital, but now transformed by time's passage and human invaders into a wilderness of fallen beams and columns. Then he narrated his own heroic efforts to sort through the rubble and identify the places where high history had once been made. More than once Poggio showed his independence, not only from the modern Romans who were destroying the urban fabric, turning perfectly preserved buildings into quarries for stone that they burned to produce lime, but also from his intellectual predecessors. For all Petrarch's learning, he had accepted the traditional description of the pyramid of Cestius, a well-preserved stone monument of the first century B.C.E. that still stands near the Protestant Cemetery, as the grave of Remus, even though the inscription that named the builder and identified the structure as his own memorial was still extant.

"I believe," Poggio has himself say in his dialogue, "that Petrarch followed the common opinion, not considering it very important to search out the inscription, which was covered with bushes. In reading it, those who came after him have shown less learning but more diligence." Loschi, Poggio's partner in this not-very-convincing fictional exchange, replies by praising his modest friend. Poggio may not rival Petrarch's erudition or eloquence, he concedes, but by assembling the materials and making them available to a wider circle of scholars, he has transformed the study of ancient Rome, turning an individualistic quest for details into a collaborative form of interdisciplinary research: "I am most impressed, Poggio, by the meticulous care and precision with which you have assembled the inscriptions from private and public structures, inside and outside the city, in a small volume and made them available to scholars."[5] Poggio thus established a new criterion of accuracy: personal inspection of the evidence. At the same time, he created a new kind of text: a written work containing apparently firsthand reports on material facts, arguments, and evidence drawn from stones and inscriptions that were thousands of years old. And he suggested that this sort of scholarship—unlike the writing of narrative history—must rest on the work not of a single gifted and experienced individual, but of a community whose members collaborated with and corrected one another. Antiquarianism, as Poggio practiced it, seemed to have been given a firm new set of standards and a well-developed set of methods, which would undergo refinement as each generation corrected and improved upon the work of the last.

In fact, most antiquaries, in the fourteenth and fifteenth centuries, used direct inspection of the monuments as only one tool among many. Everyone knew that the ruins were obscured by a blanket of interpretive confusion and error even thicker than their coat of ivy and brambles. Yet Poggio and his colleagues still drew information regularly from medieval guidebooks, from earlier collections of inscriptions, and from the oral traditions that lived on among the few thousand inhabitants who still haunted Rome's narrow, porticoed streets. Accordingly, they repeated their share of traditional legends. Poggio thought that a temple of Tellus had stood, as the books on Rome's wonders had claimed, in the Forum, and he misidentified a round structure by the Tiber as the Temple of Vesta. And he was an expert, a specialist. Ordinary Romans eagerly handed out misinformation to all comers, identifying every large building in the city as a bath.[6] Even an antiquary as proficient as Biondo, who devoted long, erudite books to the institutions and topography of ancient Rome, could say little about the earlier uses of those parts of the city that were still thickly inhabited, like Trastevere. Only chance discoveries—like the fragments of Augustus' great sundial, which were turned up, some decades after Alberti's death, by a barber digging a latrine—shed light on such major features of the ancient city as the Campus Martius. Few large-scale excavations were carried out in the Renaissance. The basis of most scholars' knowledge of ancient topography and other central fields remained more textual than empirical. Some of the most expert modern students of the Renaissance antiquaries have given largely negative verdicts about their efforts to reproduce exactly the ruined buildings, shattered works of art, and fragmentary inscriptions that they explored and excavated.[7]

But any simple description of this lively, rapidly developing discipline does violence to its complexities and contradictions. Antiquarianism, like most new fields of study, grew from existing practices of many kinds. Its creators included craftsmen and scholars, artists and editors of texts, who often regarded one another with a distrust made more severe by the social distance that separated them. Antiquarians of all sorts, moreover, exaggerated their claims to novelty, applied problematic methods, and made unjustified assumptions. But these errors are hardly surprising. The makers of new kinds of scholarship and science always launch several *Hindenburgs* for each *Spirit of St. Louis*. Historians must judge their success or failure in charting and analyzing the ancient remains, but they should also seek to understand the interests that drove them to work as they did, leading them to attack particular problems and notice certain points and omit or miss others. One way to do so is to examine their practices as they took shape in the work of pioneers like Alberti.

Alberti described himself as a model antiquarian, one who learned from direct work on the monuments. In *On the Art of Building,* he argued more than once that only the rapidly disappearing relics of ancient structures could offer good models for modern architecture:

Examples of ancient temples and theaters remained that could serve as the best possible teachers on many points. But I saw—not without sorrow—these very buildings being despoiled more each day. And those who happened to build nowadays drew their inspiration from inept modern nonsense rather than proven and much-commended methods. Nobody would deny that as a result of this a whole section of our life and learning could disappear altogether.[8]

Fortunately, Alberti had dedicated himself to a systematic effort at rescue archaeology, mastering the principles that underlay the built monuments before they disappeared:

No building of the ancients that had attracted praise, wherever it might be, but I immediately examined it carefully, to see what I could learn from it. Therefore I never stopped exploring, considering, and measuring everything, and comparing the information through line drawings, until I had grasped and understood fully what each had to contribute in terms of ingenuity and skill; this is how my passion and delight in learning relieved the labor of writing.[9]

Alberti, in short, claimed that his work on architecture rested as much on close examination of the monuments as on close reading of the texts. More than once he remarked that he had learned "more from the works of the ancients than from writers" like Pliny and Vitruvius—not surprisingly, since most of the ruins he knew directly belonged to buildings raised in the Imperial period, after Vitruvius's death.[10] He peppered *On the Art of Building* from beginning to end with detailed observations about everything from the surface of Roman roads to the pitch of Roman roofs. Alberti's antiquarian study of ancient ruins thus underpinned the new architectural theory into which he poured his most ambitious effort as both scholar and writer.

The first readers of Alberti's text immediately grasped his commitment to the imitation of ancient models and his confidence in his own expert knowledge of them—even when they denied his claim to authority in the field. The Florentine scholar and writer Antonio Manetti seems to have interpreted the bold passages just quoted as directed against his own hero Brunelleschi, whose biography he wrote. Probably because of these lines, he portrayed the Florentine architect, rather than Alberti, as the first master of Roman archaeology. "For hundreds of years" before Brunelleschi's time, Manetti remarked, no one had paid attention to the ancient art of building: "if certain writers in pagan times gave precepts about that method, such as Battista degli Alberti has done in our period, they were not much more than generalities." He then described how Brunelleschi and Donatello, not Alberti, had pioneered the study of ancient architecture in the first decade of the fifteenth century.

Curiously, this polemic against Alberti supplements Alberti's own works, making clear, indirectly but helpfully, how Alberti must have developed his antiquarian craft. After Brunelleschi refused to share the commission for the second set of Baptistery doors with Ghiberti—so Manetti told the tale—he and Donatello had gone off to Rome. Untroubled by their greedy, ambitious wives, unconcerned for respectable dress and conduct, they had become what the journalists of a much later time would call bohemians. And they had devoted themselves to antiquity as fervently and austerely as nineteenth-century noncomformists like the French caricaturist and photographer Nadar and his fellow "Water-Drinkers" would dedicate themselves to art. The two Florentines spent all their time, and all the money they earned as goldsmiths, making plans, elevations, and surveys of every ancient site in the city.

> Together they made rough drawings of almost all the buildings in
> Rome and in many places beyond the walls, with measurements of
> the widths and heights as far as they were able to ascertain [the latter]
> by estimation, and also the lengths, etc. In many places they had ex-
> cavations made in order to see the junctures of the membering of
> the buildings and their type—whether square, polygonal, completely
> round, oval, or whatever. When possible, they estimated the heights
> [by measuring] from base to base for the height and similarly [they es-
> timated the heights of] the entablatures and roofs from the founda-
> tions. They put strips of parchment on top to square off the pages,
> using Arabic numbers and symbols that Filippo alone understood.[11]

These activities seemed so strange to the Romans that they mistook the two ill-dressed and unsociable young Florentines, who spent all their money on excavations, for treasure hunters. Manetti's account of Brunelleschi's accidental travels often has been called into question, and parts of it may not record real events. Paradoxically, however, it seems to describe Alberti's practices as a student of ancient ruins quite accurately.

The one surviving architectural drawing by Alberti, which represents a bath, is not a study of an ancient structure but a plan for a modern one, perhaps for the palace of Federigo da Montefeltro at Urbino.[12] Nonetheless, this plan—and the few early sketches of monuments that survive, for the most part in copies—give us a sense of the sort of ground plans and elevations that Alberti must have drawn in some bulk before he produced On the Art of Building. He continued to treat such drawings as vital tools for antiquarian study until the end of his life. As late as 1471, when he showed Bernardo Rucellai around the city of Rome, they jointly produced a plan of the foundations of the baths of Caracalla. Rucellai claimed that he could demonstrate with a "picture" that "men and women had different places for themselves in the Baths of Diocletian and Antoninus," and he drew other sites as well.[13] Alberti, in short, presumably compiled a notebook or notebooks containing views of ancient sites and objects. These were very likely plans and elevations, for the most part, rather than perspectival drawings of buildings, of the sort often made by later antiquarians and artists like Maarten Heemskerck, and were perhaps interspersed with drawings of figures or designs from sarcophagus reliefs.[14]

Alberti studied the material remains of the ancient world intensively, then, from the beginning of his career as a writer and scholar. He did so, moreover, in the company of experts of many kinds, from whom he derived characteristic interests, skills, and sensibilities. Like the device of the framed perspective veil that Alberti described in On Painting, the technical training he brought to bear both sharpened and limited his abilities to perceive. It determined both which remains he noticed and how he evaluated them. On Painting shows how Alberti had learned to see aspects of antiquity through others' eyes. "They praise," he wrote,

> a relief in Rome, in which the dead Meleager is being carried away, because those who are bearing the burden appear to be distressed and to strain with every limb, while in the dead man there is no member that does not seem completely lifeless; they all hang loose; hands, fingers, neck, all droop inertly down, all combine together to represent death.[15]

It takes some analysis to reveal the identity of the nameless ones Alberti cited here as authorities. Alberti singled out this example, the Meleager sarcophagus, because it fitted a literary type: in Purgatorio, Dante had written that the ability to distinguish life from death was the sign of great art. Alberti thus had a literary motivation for singling out this work.[16]

Alberti was not the only antiquary to take an interest in reliefs. The

Byzantine scholar Manuel Chrysoloras, who taught Bruni and Poggio their Greek, underlined the unique historical value of the reliefs on the arch of Constantine and Trajan's column: "it is possible to see clearly [in them] what arms and what costume people used in ancient times, what insignia magistrates had, how an army was arrayed, a battle fought, a city besieged, or a camp laid out. . . . Herodotus and some other writers of history are thought to have done something of great value when they describe these things; but in these sculptures one can *see* all that existed in those days among the different races, so that it is a complete and accurate history."[17] And Biondo warmly praised the modern *historie* that the sculptor and architect Antonio Averlino, better known as Filarete, had crafted to adorn the silver-covered bronze doors he made for the Basilica of St. Peter. Filarete displayed such "exquisite" craftsmanship with these reliefs, Biondo noted, that he had fully earned his fee, even though it came to four times as much as the cost of the bronze and gold used for the doors.[18] Filarete's work thus exemplified one of Alberti's central tenets: that the artist's skill, more than expensive materials, gave a work its true distinction.

But Alberti showed more appreciation than Biondo for the craftsmanship of the reliefs he discussed. In the ancient Roman Meleager sarcophagus, he analyzed in graphic detail the contours of the figure of Meleager, the "drooping" members that paradoxically reproduced, to the life, the appearance of death. Chrysoloras too had appreciated "the skill of these representations," which he thought comparable to that of Nature itself: "one seems to see a real man, horse, city, or army, breastplate, sword, or armor, and real people captured or fleeing, laughing, weeping, excited or angry."[19] But Chrysoloras said nothing precise about the means the ancient sculptor had used to achieve these visual ends. Alberti, by contrast, traced the modeled muscle and bone, flesh and hair, contour by contour, and found words to express what he saw. For him, Rome was not—or not only—a three-dimensional memory of the past, documented by stone that did not decay so quickly as parchment: it was a work of high art to be appreciated.[20]

Using words rather than pictures, Alberti in this passage came strikingly close to doing what the artists, in the first decades of the fifteenth century, were doing with pen and brush: capturing not only the outlines but the expressive capabilities of ancient sculpture. Unfortunately, few of the drawings from the antique that artists made in this period survive. But the sixteenth-century artist and historian of the arts Giorgio Vasari preserves a highly relevant story, one that suggests what sorts of materials Alberti may have seen and produced. According to Vasari, one day early in the fifteenth century, Donatello was talking with Brunelleschi and other craftsmen in the piazza before the Florentine Cathedral. Recently, Donatello said, on his way back to Florence from Rome, he had passed through Orvieto in order to examine the marble facade of the cathedral there. He had also paid a visit to nearby Cortona, where he had seen "a marble relief" (something that "was rare in those days," Vasari remarks, "since the great quantity that has been unearthed in our time had not yet been dug up"). Brunelleschi, fired by Donatello's account, left immediately for Cortona, dressed as he was and telling nobody where he was going. There he "made a pen drawing" of the sarcophagus in question—probably one still in Cortona that bears a relief of Dionysus in India—and returned to Florence. Such "love of art" astonished even his friend and colleague Donatello.[21]

Within a few decades, artists were certainly playing the new role of connoisseur, just as Vasari described it in this case. Ghiberti and Donatello collected ancient statues and discussed them with scholars like Cyriac and Niccoli. At the end of the 1420s, an anonymous artist (sometimes thought to have been Gentile da Fabriano) made a series of figure drawings based on Roman reliefs. He freely altered the originals and filled in missing pieces, but he showed the same interest in contours and motion that would inspire Alberti. Similarly, when Cyriac traveled to Greece in the 1430s, he made rough sketches of the "extraordinary images" he saw in the friezes of the Parthenon. When he returned to Italy, he found a number of artists who were able to imagine and convey at least something of the aesthetic effects he had directly experienced. Cyriac employed these men to produce more refined drawings of the sculptures and buildings he had surveyed, which he could then present to patrons who shared his taste in antiques.[22] Alberti's brief comment on the Meleager sarcophagus suggests something of what he had learned—probably from the very artists he praised in his letter to Brunelleschi—about how to look and what to look at.

A second antiquarian passion of Alberti's was his love for ancient and modern inscriptions, for monumental words symmetrically carved in stone, a passion that emerged from the projects he built in the 1450s and after. In *On the Art of Building,* he dedicated a chapter to inscriptions, revealing how much he learned from Poggio and Cyriac. He expressed his own strong approval for dedicatory inscriptions in chapels and urged that the texts carved into the walls of a church should teach "philosophical"—moral—messages. In this connection, he devoted some attention to what he, like Poggio and others, saw as the symbolic language of Egyptian hieroglyphs. Following the recently discovered late antique text of Horapollo—another find made by the antiquaries—Alberti mentioned the images of the eye, the vulture, and the bee with which the sage priests had denoted god, nature, and the king.

Another mysterious set of documents carved in stone were the Etruscan inscriptions that Alberti had seen in the ruined towns and mortuaries of Tuscany: "Their letters resemble Greek ones," he wrote in the chapter on inscriptions, "they resemble Latin ones too; but no one understands what they mean."[23] In this case, Alberti's antiquarian interests coincided with those of Florentine scholars he knew: ranging from Bruni, who found consolation for the fall of Rome in the fact that it had liberated the social and cultural energies of Etruscan and other Italian towns that Rome had conquered, to Leonardo Dati, who examined with fascination a text he had found in the town of Montepulciano, which was known for its antiquities. This text described "in the ancestral language" how Bachus Piccolomo, "that excellent and vigorous man," joined Porsenna to make war against the Romans. Dati translated this text into Latin and presented it, not coincidentally, to Pope Pius II—born Aeneas Silvius Piccolomini—who no doubt read with interest of his Etruscan forefather's heroic deeds.[24] Alberti, for his part, gave the Etruscan inscriptions a concrete and precise mythic form, to which he continued to add features as time went on.[25] The Florentine antiquarian did more than dispel old myths: he also helped to create new ones, evoking a strange, unknown antiquity that had existed before the Greco-Roman one and that was in some ways more profound. Unlike Poggio, Alberti did not identify the sources from which he drew his knowledge of the inscriptions, or recount his own efforts to collect and verify the texts. But he had clearly learned much from Poggio and his other learned friends: these erudite men were also aesthetes, who shared his interest in the form as well as the content of ancient words inscribed on stone.

The inscriptions on the facades of Alberti buildings from the 1450s and after tell a fuller story about his contacts with other antiquaries. The Malatesta Temple in Rimini, the shrine of the Holy Sepulchre at San Pancrazio in Florence, and Santa Maria Novella, also in Florence, all bear long, prominent, and distinctive inscriptions in capital letters. Though artists, scribes, and scholars had widely experimented with new forms of capitals before Alberti set to work, they normally found use in manuscripts, on sculptures, or in reproduced inscriptions. Alberti's capital letters imitated ancient ones directly, by virtue of their placement on works of architecture. These enormous inscriptions—the letters on the facade of Santa Maria Novella are some fifty centimeters high—prominently placed on entablatures, were the first ones of the Renaissance that visually challenged comparison with such prominent ancient inscriptions as the one commemorating Agrippa on the Pantheon. Public script, in other words, did much both to determine and to express Alberti's sense of the classical style, as it would for later antiquaries deep into the eighteenth century.[26]

Modern critical judgments of the form of Alberti's letters vary. Giovanni Mardersteig—himself a great type designer as well as a profound student of the history of letter forms—has emphasized the care and intelligence that Alberti devoted to these problems. The letters on the Holy Sepulchre, for example, reveal a lucid underlying geometry and are identical—clear evidence that the stonecutters used set patterns or stencils, themselves based on precise manipulation of compass and stylus, to lay out the forms they cut. Though Alberti's letters were too thin in relation to their height to match Roman models, their inspiration was palpably classical: he was trying to wed the forms used in Roman inscriptions with constructive geometry. No wonder that Luca Pacioli, the artist and mathematician who devised the first formally constructed model alphabet to reach print, paid warm retrospective tribute to the time he had spent living with and learning from Alberti.[27]

But Armando Petrucci, one of the greatest contemporary experts on the history of writing, has analyzed Alberti's capitals and considers them Florentine, rather than classical, in inspiration: an original all'antica version of a Tuscan tradition.[28] Not all of the forms Alberti used harked back to classical models. His narrow E's and wide O's deviate from ancient precedent. So, even more strikingly, does the suspension sign that he used in the Santa Maria Novella inscription, which reflected the practices not of Roman stonecutters but of Christian scribes. In order to save space, work, and time, they made a practice of turning the nasal consonants m and n into horizontal lines above the vowels that preceded them, making am into ā. For Petrucci, Alberti's work was a Tuscan outlier from the grand lines of development in capital letters carried out by northern Italian antiquaries like Giovanni Marcanova and artists like Andrea Mantegna.[29]

None of these scholars raises what seems an obvious question: Where, when, and how did Alberti begin to study ancient lettering in the first place? Capital lettering mattered to antiquarians in the fifteenth century. A modern collector of inscriptions like Poggio could not have avoided thinking about the proper forms of capital letters, even if he himself wrote them fairly casually, taking more interest in the content than the form of the inscriptions he copied out. Alberti was on intimate terms not only with Poggio, who collected the inscriptions of Rome, but also with Cyriac, who attended the Council of Ferrara/Florence and took part in Alberti's own *certame coronario* in 1441. Cyriac took as strong an interest as Alberti himself in ancient sculpture and architecture, studying them with a sharp eye for differences of style and period; but he also specialized in interpreting inscriptions. In his eyes, they offered vital information that was rarely if ever found in literary works: information about the original forms of place names and the true identity of the early inhabitants of cities. The ancients spoke most directly and reliably to the modern world, he believed, through the carved public messages that had once made whole cities into texts and that still offered up fragments of "venerable antiquity" to those with the erudition and intelligence to decode them. When an ignorant priest interrupted Cyriac as he copied an epitaph in a church at Vercelli, he gave his most eloquent definition of antiquarianism. His calling was not only scholarly work but also a form of divination, turned to the past rather than the future: "On the spur of the moment I replied that I had learned amid the oracles of Apollo to revive the dead from the underworld. Once I had said this, I left him behind there, ignorant, confused, his mind quite boggled: but I thought I certainly should not leave my art behind."[30] Inscriptions were clearly of more than antiquarian interest to this founder of the antiquary's art.

Enough examples of Cyriac's own script remain to show how he transcribed and interpreted Roman inscriptions. His copy of the Roman emperor Trajan's inscription in Ancona (now in Berlin) has a number of distinctive features—notably an E that is often far narrower than the A; a very wide, almost circular O (both in violation of Roman epigraphic practice); and an M whose central point touches the baseline on which the letter stands (following classical precedent). All of these forms reappear in Alberti's inscriptions on the Malatesta Temple and in Florence.

Other evidence ties Cyriac directly to the Malatesta Temple in Rimini, for which Alberti created a new facade in the 1450s. Cyriac visited Rimini in 1449 and played a part in the temple's design. The Greek inscription that appears on both side walls of the church is an adaptation of a famous Greek inscription from Naples, which Cyriac himself must have interpreted—and which seems to be carved in a partial imitation of his Greek script.[31]

All this evidence yields a set of related conclusions. Alberti's interest in classical lettering took root in the later 1430s. Cyriac's notebooks determined his first notion of the form classical letters should take. And Alberti's own later experiments built on Cyriac's precedents. The visual evidence of Alberti's letters, in other words, ties him as firmly as do his verbal discussions of relief sculpture to specific period practices. And these, in turn, reveal something about Alberti's contact with and sense of the past. He studied antiquities not only by direct inspection but also in the virtual forms produced by colleagues like Cyriac and Poggio, and like most of his colleagues he made no firm distinction in practice between these two forms of knowledge. Similarly, the naturalists of early modern Italy studied with equal zeal and equal faith real specimens of life-forms collected from forests and oceans, artist's images of plants and animals drawn in principle from life, and crude prints and drawings of imaginary monsters. Alberti's antiquarian practices closely resembled those employed by Ulisse Aldrovandi in his Bolognese museum a century later.[32]

Before Alberti returned to Rome in the 1440s, he prepared himself well, in both the field and the library, to map and excavate Rome's fields of ruins. Many of his colleagues shared his interests, especially members of the curia—Poggio in the lead—who devoted themselves to the study of Roman ruins. Debates raged. Biondo and Maffeo Vegio, for example, both expert students of the history of Rome and the papacy, argued at length over the location of Saint Peter's crucifixion. Biondo placed the event near the Vatican itself, not far from the Castel Sant'Angelo. Vegio set it high up on the Gianicolo, the huge hill that looms over and dominates the papal district of Rome, across the Tiber from the ancient center. Their debate was incorporated into artistic endeavors: Filarete embodied both men's theses in the crucifixion panel of his Porta Argentea. He placed the prominent landmarks that Biondo had used to locate the event—the Castel Sant'Angelo, a turpentine tree, and a fantastic tower representing the *Meta Romuli*—in the foreground. But he took sides with Vegio when he staged Peter's crucifixion on the Gianicolo and placed the classical palace, adorned with Bacchic reliefs, from which Nero watched the event, above the bend in the Tiber. The most elaborate and expensive sculptural project carried out in the Rome of

Eugenius IV thus reflected up-to-date and technical scholarly discussion. Antiquarian expertise, in this environment, had clear contemporary relevance.[33]

During the early 1440s, Biondo gave Alberti his entrée into this lively social and intellectual world. An immensely erudite student of Roman buildings and institutions, Biondo produced the first synthetic works on both Roman antiquities and Italian history. Like Alberti, he maintained close relations with the Este court at Ferrara, which he saw as a center of good classical taste. In a lively and eloquent letter to Leonello d'Este, Biondo described a Roman dinner party given by Prospero Colonna for Sigismondo Malatesta in the so-called "gardens of Maecenas"—gardens thought to have belonged to the wealthy contemporary of the Emperor Augustus whose patronage the poet Horace had celebrated. Biondo himself had been invited not, as he had thought, to eat with the guests but to discuss Roman antiquities with them; the academic expert has always walked a rocky road in high society. But the realization that others saw him as a player, not as a gentleman, did not dim Biondo's enthusiasm.

The setting, after all, could not have been more exciting for an antiquarian. Colonna's party passed through a piazza and up a road on which Colonna had excavated and restored a pavement of tessellated marble. Probably they sat near the Torre di Mesa on the Quirinal, a building destroyed in 1625. Following local tradition, Biondo identified this as the tower from which Nero had watched as Rome burned. It was, he said, "the only place in Rome from which one can attain a view of the whole city."[34] As the guests conversed, Sigismondo described Leonello's decision to issue what he described as "coins after the manner of the Roman emperors"—that is, medals that bore Leonello's own image. (Though Biondo knew that their obverses showed Leonello's name and image, he could not remember what stood on the reverse.) Colonna, Biondo reported, eloquently praised Leonello's "brilliance" and his "imitation of an ancient custom." Modern medals and ancient customs, Ferrara and Rimini—all came together in one conversation, as they did in Alberti's life.[35]

All this expertise in Rome presented Alberti with both opportunities and challenges. He could walk the streets in extraordinarily well-informed company. But if he hoped to take an active part in the conversation, he needed to possess some special expertise of his own. To this end, he struck out in new scholarly directions. Alberti displayed technical and scientific skills of a kind that antiquaries had not previously applied when he drew a

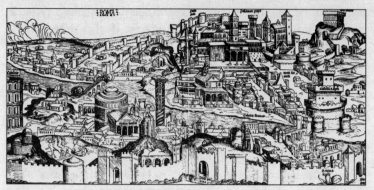

21. Panorama of Rome. Hartmann Schedel, *Nuremberg Chronicle*. Department of Rare Books and Special Collections, Princeton University Library.

rigorously accurate *pictura,* or plan, of Rome. And he cast his results in the form of a short Latin work, the *Panorama of the City of Rome.* What had been a jumble of towers and rooftop *loggie,* fallen columns and proud churches, Alberti transformed into a neat set of tables and map coordinates. Just by reading his work, he claimed, "anyone, even if of only modest intelligence, can make a lovely and appropriate painting [of a city] on whatever surface he wishes."[36] Taken together, the language and substance of the text make its intended readership clear. In at least one similar text, the Latin version of his *Elements of Painting,* he made a similar claim: this short, unillustrated manual, he bragged, would enable even "unskilled and incompetent" men to produce the sort of paintings "that the most learned scholars approve of." He dedicated *Elements* to another member of the curia, Theodore Gaza—and referred to it as a basic text in *On the Art of Building,* yet another work aimed at intellectual readers rather than practitioners. Evidently, then, the *Panorama* represented Alberti's bid to offer his colleagues in the papal service the particular expert service that he saw as his own special creation.[37] As he had taught Meliaduse d'Este about surveying and hydraulics, now he taught his fellow inhabitants of the curia about cartography.

But the *Panorama* was more than a plan. It was the culmination of a series of efforts at observation and recording data, during which Alberti drew on both the engineering tradition and the exact sciences to develop a new cartographic method. One engineering technique, perhaps the earliest, was relatively simple. In his *Mathematical Games,* Alberti had depicted an instrument that, he said, had originally been designed for aiming a projectile weapon called a *trabocco*, or trebuchet, at a target. He then showed how to use it for the more "delightful" end of making "a picture of a territory, as I did when I made my portrait of Rome." Take a wooden disk, Alberti suggests, with its circumference marked off in 48 *gradi* or degrees and 192 minutes, and a plumb line attached to its center. Place it firmly on a flat place from which you can see many other places, such as a tower or campanile. Use the plumb line to determine the direction at which you see a given structure, like a gate. And record the angles in a table. "Do not move the instrument," Alberti warns, "but move yourself, and look at the angles."[38] By doing this from three separate places, one can derive enough data to produce the "painting of the city." After laying out the city plan on paper, the scholar places three small graduated disks on it, in positions corresponding to those of the original observation points. Using his tables, he then draws lines from each of them to the points that correspond to the main buildings. The point where the lines from any two of the three disks intersect locates the structure in question; if a question arises, the third set of data will settle it.

Alberti's method for drawing a plan drew heavily on existing instruments and techniques. The horizon—the circular instrument that he used to take measurements—resembled an astrolabe, a traditional astronomical instrument, trained on the earth rather than the sky. Alberti was hardly the first to use this surveying technique: Taccola's notebooks swarm with images of surveyors using similar instruments to measure the earth's surface. And the plan that Alberti described closely resembled the highly practical charts used by navigators in his day—the so-called portolan charts, which had become Europe's standard, highly effective navigational tool in the thirteenth and fourteenth centuries. These outline maps offered sailors not a rigorous set of cartographical coordinates that located the ports they wished to reach, but rather the angular directions they should follow when sailing to them. A little like the official map of the London Underground system, in other words, they did not claim to represent the actual shape of the world as a whole. But they offered precise representations, first of the Mediterranean coastline and then of others, and they gave the traveler practical instructions for moving from point A to point B with the aid of his compass. It is not yet clear on what underlying cartographic system, if any, these highly practical works rested, or indeed exactly where and how they came into being. But we do know that they developed continually over time, as chartmakers received reports and corrections from ships' masters and travelers. Accordingly, they were a splendid example of practical, useful mapping techniques in action.[39]

Alberti himself used a maritime analogy for his mapmaking. One who drew lines from a given tower to a given landmark, he said, marking them as 20 degrees and 2 minutes or 32 degrees exactly, should work so that if "one had to sail a ship from that tower to this point, one would sight by that same wind marked 20, 2, or 32, 0, or the like."[40] Sailors and their cartographic technologies were well known in curial circles. Poggio, who wrote an elaborate work on India, and Biondo, who planned to write a history of Portuguese explorations in the Atlantic, both had direct contacts with up-to-date mariners. So, in his own way, did Alberti. But if he was not alone in conversing with sailors and pilots, he seems to have been the first to apply their chartmaking methods to the problem of mapping a city, rather than an ocean or a landmass. In doing so, he creatively fused two existing applied sciences in a highly inventive way, obtaining an approximate but highly effective plan.

In composing the *Panorama*, however, Alberti devised a far more ambitious and mathematically far more distinctive cartographic technique, using a complex version of his favorite surveying instrument. It consisted of a disk with a graduated rim, and a movable and graduated ruler affixed to a single point at its center. This device was to be placed at only one observation point—the Capitoline. The observer should record the positions of walls, gates, and other structures, noting both their angular distance from a zero point (marked on the rim of the disk) and their relative distance from the center (as marked on the ruler, which also had a zero point at its center). By doing so, he could record the relative distances that separated every gate, church, or bridge in the city from the Capitoline and from one another. Each point, in other words, received a precise location within a single polar coordinate system. Taking the Capitoline as the reference point, any user of the *Panorama* could lay out a roughly circular plan of the city in which all sites and buildings found their proper places. In an age when maps inevitably underwent change and distortion every time they were copied, Alberti had found a way to transmit securely, not a particular vision of the ancient city as a whole, but the abstract mathematical data from which a scholar or an illuminator could restore the whole lost world to flickering, schematic life.[41]

Many students of the *Panorama* have pointed out that this second, more sophisticated measurement technique resembles the cartographical systems described in one of the best-selling luxury books of the early fifteenth cen-

244 # LEON BATTISTA ALBERTI

tury, Ptolemy's *Geography*.[42] This work, written in Greek during the second century C.E.., was one of the most original achievements of ancient science. It contained elaborate maps and tables of geographical coordinates, like Alberti's, for almost eight thousand locations. Reconstructed and equipped with splendid maps by the scholars of fourteenth-century Byzantium, Ptolemy's text had been translated into Latin in the early fifteenth century by a Florentine scholar, Jacopo Angeli, who dedicated it to Pope Alexander V. It became one of the learned best-sellers of the time. Poggio evoked in one of his dialogues the attraction that this splendidly illustrated book exercised on the most discriminating connoisseurs of books and images: "Following my custom, in the summer [of 1435], when Pope Eugenius had just left Rome for Florence, I went to visit the distinguished gentleman Niccolò Niccoli, whose house was the common resort of scholars. There I found that very learned man Carlo Marsuppini and Cosimo de' Medici, who was both the leading figure in our state and an outstanding citizen. They were examining Ptolemy's *Geography*."[43] Alberti himself knew Ptolemy's atlas well. In his *Praise of the Fly*, a mock-encomium composed in the early 1440s, he wrote appreciatively about the colorful maps that accompanied the *Geography*. The beautiful patterns on the wings of flies, he suggested ironically, had served as the ancient geographer's model: "they say that Ptolemy the Mathematician drew his picture of the world from them; for they say that the Ganges, the Danube, the Nile, and the Po are splendidly depicted on the wings of flies, showing the mountains from which they flow to the sea and the peoples whom they flood, beautifully depicted in triangles, rectangles, and hexagons, with intersecting parallels drawn perpendicular to one another."[44] The ancient cartographer's world maps probably served as the model for Alberti's city plan—and Ptolemy's precise coordinate-based discipline of geography served as the model for Alberti's precise polar coordinate system.

Here, too, Alberti combined scientific methods that had previously been separate. When he laid out his measurements for the walls of Rome—obviously a difficult graphical problem—he provided coordinates for what he called their *anguli*, the points where straight stretches of wall intersected, and their *auges*, the points where they curved farthest away from the Capitoline. Alberti's curious terminology offers subtle but powerful evidence about his methods and the date at which he developed them. *Aux* (plural *auges*) is a technical term, nonclassical in origin, from the language of Arabo-Latin astronomy. It refers to a planet's apogee—the point at which it reaches its greatest distance from the earth. Alberti, who applied the term to a curving wall's farthest distance from the central point of his map, the Capitoline, used it in a very elegant extended sense—suggesting, to alert readers, that the "mathematical instruments" and methods that provided his data might come from the world of astronomy.

Alberti's measuring instrument resembled, as we have seen, the standard astronomical instrument of his time, the astrolabe. He himself, moreover, was a proficient astronomical observer, one who earned the respect of the most adept astronomers of his day. From 1461 to 1467, the young German mathematician Johannes Regiomontanus worked in Rome with the support of Cardinal Bessarion, studying Greek and Latin texts in astronomy and mathematics and engaging in discussions with his Italian colleagues. In a long letter to the Ferrarese astrologer Giovanni Bianchini, he discussed some of the central astronomical problems of his time: in particular, the nature and rate of the precession of the equinoxes, and the closely related problem of the obliquity of the sun's path (the angle at which the sun's path crosses the celestial equator). The latter, in turn, was determined by the maximum declination of the sun—the maximum angular distance that the sun reached north and south of the celestial equator. In his letter, Regiomontanus also discussed various theories about change in the sun's maximum declination, including that ascribed in his time to the Islamic astronomer Thabit ibn Qura. According to Thabit, the sun should reach a maximum declination of 24;2° in the mid-fifteenth century. In fact, however, Regiomontanus and his teacher Georg von Peuerbach had found the maximum to be only 23;28°. Moreover, he remarked, "I have often heard Master Paolo [Toscanelli] of Florence and [Leon] Battista Alberti saying that they themselves had observed carefully and did not find it greater than 23;30°."[45] Regiomontanus was the greatest Western astronomer of the fifteenth century. He laid the technical foundations on which Copernicus would build. And he engaged in multiple conversations on observational astronomy with Alberti and Toscanelli. Regiomontanus regularly subjected his contemporaries to sharp criticism when they misunderstood ancient texts or misapplied mathematical techniques. He helped to humiliate another denizen of the curia, George of Trebizond, for the errors in his translation of and commentary on Ptolemy's handbook of astronomy, the *Almagest*. But he evidently accepted Alberti as one of the few members of the community of competent astronomers.[46] Alberti also knew Toscanelli: he dedicated book one of *Dinner Pieces* to him, with a warmly affectionate letter characteristically asking for "emendations" of his work.[47] The anonymous *Life* of Alberti mentions further letters that he directed to Toscanelli, in which he predicted the immediate future of Florence and the papacy. Evidently the two men exchanged both technical information about astronomy and astrological forecasts of the future.[48]

In his late treatise *On Sculpture*, Alberti referred indirectly to the connection between his work as an astronomer and the nonastronomical uses of the instrument he recommended in the *Panorama*. He showed how to use the methods laid out in the *Panorama* to reduce the outlines of a sculpture to numbers, again following a system of polar coordinates. The same methods, he remarked, would work in astronomy:

> The man who possesses them can so record the outlines and the positions and arrangement of the parts of any given body in accurate and absolutely reliable written forms that not merely a day later, but even after a whole cycle of the heavens, he can again at will situate and arrange that same body in that very same place in such a way that no part of it, not even the smallest, is not placed in space exactly where it originally stood. For example, if you are pointing with your finger at the rising planet Mercury or at the new moon just appearing, and you wish to record the position of the ring on your finger or the angle of your elbow or such like, you could do it with our instruments so that there would not be the slightest error nor any doubt that this is the way things are.[49]

The *Panorama*, in other words, marked a second stage in Alberti's work, one in which he fused methods drawn from two of the most sophisticated quantitative disciplines of the Roman imperial age, astronomy and geography, to serve the needs of his fellow antiquarians.

This circumstance, in turn, helps to explain one point on which many scholars have commented: Alberti's choice of a polar coordinate system and a circular form for his city plan. Older circular plans of Rome, like the circular world maps of the Middle Ages, had that shape for iconic or symbolic reasons rather than cartographic ones. They embodied Rome's claim to be *caput mundi*, the capital of the world: they represented not the city's actual physical form as a historical settlement, but its symbolic form as a microcosm of the universe. Accordingly, they could not have served as models for the precise polar cartography of the *Panorama*, any more than the polygonal maps in Ptolemy's *Geography* could have done so. But astronomers, as Alberti well knew, regularly inscribed the results of their observations in circular maps, showing constellations of the northern and southern celestial spheres. The first modern circular sky maps that reflect sustained efforts at observation were drawn up in Vienna around 1440—the period when Alberti was at work in Rome.[50] It seems highly likely, accordingly, that Alberti had in mind this cosmic but quantitatively precise model as he plotted, with such precision, the most cosmologically overdetermined of Western cities.

We do not know for certain when Alberti devised either of these two cartographical techniques—the simpler one described in *Mathematical Games* and the more complex one in *Panorama*—or which of them came first. He had certainly created the simpler one before 1452, since he described it in *Mathematical Games*. And he could not have devised the more complex version until after 1439, for the *Panorama* included coordinates for the Church of San Onofrio on the Gianicolo, which was built during the 1440s.[51] Both techniques, which came respectively from the tradition of practical mathematics and that of mathematical cartography, were known to him by the 1430s. It seems possible that he began by creating the approximate technique, which was based on more conventional methods and was far easier to describe than the more complex technique presented in the *Panorama*. It also seems reasonable that he collected the full quantitative data that he tabulated in the latter work in the course of his periods of sustained residence in Rome in the 1440s and 1450s. But the details of how Alberti developed this particular piece of mathematical equipment remain obscure.

What is clear is that Alberti made his impact as an antiquarian in the Rome of the 1440s in much the same way that, years before, he had made his first strong impression as a painter. He applied technical skills—in this case, Florentine as well as north Italian ones—to the dramatic, public solution of technical problems. He thus offered the members of his intellectual community something genuinely new and undoubtedly impressed many of his contemporaries. Though the *Panorama* offered rules for making plans, not views, of the city, artists could certainly apply them when they decorated walls or manuscript pages with visions of the monuments of Rome. At least one of the most dramatic early views of the city applied both Alberti's method and his data. In 1457, moving the point of observation from the

Capitoline to the Vatican gardens, the artist who illuminated a Latin Euclid offered a dramatic view of Trastevere and the center of Rome beyond the Tiber. His work rested on Alberti's findings, down to repeating his mistakes: he followed Alberti in placing next to the Tiber a clock tower that actually stood at a short distance from it in the Campo de' Fiori.[52] The precision of Alberti's mapping efforts, and the unique knowledge base they gave him, remained deeply impressive for decades, even as other antiquaries worked in their own ways. In 1471 Bernardo Rucellai, himself a serious antiquary, still paid special tribute to the unique knowledge of "the location and measurement" of Rome's walls that Alberti had acquired by using "mathematical machines."[53]

Alberti's bravura demonstration of his mathematical and technical skills probably won him the most dramatic of all his opportunities as an antiquary: the commission to raise one of the sunken ships from Lake Nemi.[54] As early as 1444, Cardinal Prospero Colonna had told Biondo about a sunken ship, showing him cypress planks and bronze nails extracted from it by local fishermen.[55] Colonna realized, eventually, that the lake in fact contained two ships. But all efforts by the locals to pull them from the water, either with their fishing nets, which accidentally became tangled in the hulks, or with ropes deliberately attached to them, had failed. Reasonably enough, the cardinal wanted very much to know what "big ships were doing in a little lake surrounded on all sides by high mountains." And so, Biondo explained, in 1447 "he hired for that task my friend Leon Battista Alberti, the outstanding mathematician of our time, who wrote most elegant books *On the Art of Building.*" The term that Biondo—and Colonna—used is revealing: Colonna hired Alberti as a "mathematician." His demonstrations of his scientific prowess, in short, won him both Biondo's collaboration and Colonna's support.

Alberti set to work enthusiastically. He placed rows of empty wine barrels across the lake to serve as flotation devices for winches, dropping ropes with hooks from them into the lake.

> Some workers more like fish than men were hired from the seagoing capital Genoa. It was their job to swim downward into the deeper parts of the lake, to find out how much remained of the ship and in what state of preservation, and to use the hooks let down on ropes to dig into and capture [the ship].[56]

More skillful technicians, remaining on the surface, would then use the machines to bring the wreck up.

The description of the enterprise in On the Art of Building corroborates many details of Biondo's account. Much to the regret of later scholars, however, Alberti never finished the separate work, provisionally entitled Navis, The Ship, in which he hoped to discuss his results in detail.[57] But he did describe, on his work on architecture, techniques for building a harbor defense raft that rested, like the machinery he used at Nemi, on empty barrels. He also discussed methods for working below water level on bridge abutments, which may well have drawn on the same experiences. And he mentioned, at one point, a man who had been able to clear a hidden rock from the entrance to the port of Genoa because he could stay under water for a very long time without breathing—evidently a story Alberti had heard from one of the Genoese, "more like fish than men," who dived for him at Nemi.[58] Apparently Alberti took the time not only to give his crew instructions but to ask them questions about their special skills, showing exactly the sort of interest in craft skills of which he had boasted in his autobiography.

When zero hour came, the whole curia made an expedition to the lake's romantically rocky shore to watch. Cardinals and humanists stood by as Alberti's workers strained at the winches. The ship rose, slowly—but then broke apart under the pressure exerted by the crew. Only the prow rose to the surface. Still, "all the men of noble intellect in the Roman curia," according to Biondo, diverted themselves in seeing how this fragment was constructed. The analysis was not simple. The hull of the ship consisted of wood waterproofed with tow, which was smeared with minium (red lead). This was overlaid by a thick woolen stuff impregnated with waterproofing, on top of which were sheets of lead held in place by vast numbers of bronze nails.[59] The chances of reading this technological palimpsest were slim, but Biondo and Alberti tried to reconstruct in some detail the series of processes that had gone into making the ships so water- and fire-resistant.[60]

Alberti noted that the Romans had used wax as a binder for their pigments, and compared their technique to the modern one of using linseed oil to protect paint.[61] Biondo marveled at the perfect state of preservation of the bronze nails that the Roman shipwrights had used, "so intact and so bright that they seemed to have just come from the blacksmith's anvil." And both men discussed another find made by the divers on the bottom of the lake. Biondo described leaden pipes, two cubits long, very solid and thick, which could be combined, as they mated one another with interlocking parts, to any length desired, however great. Elegant letters were inscribed on each of them, indicating, so I thought, that Tiberius Caesar was the creator of the ship. Leon Battista thought that the very plentiful and clear spring waters that bubble up at the town of Nemi, where they nowadays turn mill wheels, were brought all the way to the middle of the lake through a long series of these pipes, to be used in the very large and spacious houses that, we think, were placed on top of the aforesaid ships.[62]

Alberti also discussed the way in which pipe sections should be joined and offered instructions on how to lay them across a lake bottom as the Romans had.[63]

Nemi long continued to attract erudite visitors in search of pleasant woods in which to hold elegant picnics. Bernardo Bembo, for example, recorded a visit to the lake, appropriately in the margin of his copy of On the Art of Building.[64] The wooden beams from the sunken ship remained at the lake shore, where they underwent more than one inspection. In the spring of 1463, Pius II visited the lake and examined the remains of the ship "with a good deal of pleasure." Like others interested in antiquities, Pius found Biondo's and Alberti's efforts to explain the construction of the ship implausible. But he listened with interest to an anonymous informant who compared the houses that had rested on the sunken ships to the water-borne pleasure palaces that Borso d'Este had floated on the Po, Ludovico Gonzaga on the Mincio, and the German electors Palatine on the Rhine. The guide also told the pope something that neither Biondo nor Alberti had revealed in writing: "The divers who went to the bottom of the lake say that in the hold they saw a chest of iron or copper fastened by four hoops and a clay water jar with a cover of gilded bronze."[65] It seems highly likely that the pope's informant was Alberti himself, since he accompanied Pius on at least part of this antiquarian ramble through the Alban hills. Very likely he learned of the metal objects in the ship from his Genoese divers but kept them secret to avoid attracting treasure hunters to the wreck. Discussion never wholly ceased.[66]

This catastrophic experiment in underwater archaeology reveals a great deal about antiquarianism as Alberti and his contemporaries practiced it. It shows, in the first place, that the most spectacular archaeological investi-

gations were systematically planned and dramatically staged. Evidently
Colonna brought as many members of the curia as possible out to the lake to
witness Alberti's equivocal triumph over the powers of time and water—just
as Pope Sixtus V, a century and a half later, would stage the moving of the
Vatican obelisk as a public triumph of the Christian God over the solar
deities of the Egyptians.[67] The story also reveals that as early as the mid-
fifteenth century, antiquarians collaborated, complementing one another's
work. In studying the way the ship's hull was made, the bonds between the
pieces of lead pipe, and the forms of the letters on them, Biondo—whose
forte lay in the analysis of texts—adopted an object-oriented approach. It
seems altogether likely that he reported, in such passages, exactly what Alberti told him. It also seems probable that Alberti inspired Biondo's effort to
compare modern ships with those of the Romans in his later *Rome Tri-
umphant*. The Romans, Biondo remarked there, had had ships of ten thou-

22. Antiquaries study the
Vatican Obelisk. Giovanni
Marcanova, *Sylloge*.
Department of Rare Books and
Special Collections, Princeton
University Library.

sand amphorae in capacity; but at present Aragonese and Venetian galleys of as few as four thousand amphorae "were taken as miracles." "Everything has changed, then: the ships and the terminology": not only the words used to designate different kinds of ships and their components, about which Biondo had expert knowledge, but shipbuilding technology had undergone a transformation, in this case for the worse.[68] But the intellectual traffic between the two men went both ways. Alberti borrowed some erudition from Biondo when he quoted a passage from Suetonius to describe Julius Caesar's abortive effort to build a villa at Nemi. Biondo had already recalled and applied the passage in question.[69] Throughout the fifteenth and sixteenth centuries, antiquarianism would retain something of this interdisciplinary style—for example, in the work of the specialist antiquarian Pirro Ligorio, a man chiefly trained as an artist rather than a humanist, who wrote in Italian and worked with more highly educated scholars whenever he could, but who was also a scholar in his own right and read, criticized and reworked the textual record himself.[70]

Finally, the episode confirms that fifteenth-century Roman antiquarianism was not only a scholarly but a scientific and technological enterprise. The antiquarians applied the most sophisticated engineering and materials analyses then known to their objects—and for sharply practical ends. They not only studied the remaining evidence about ancient ships but also tried to build new ones. In 1525–26 the humanist Vettor Fausto cited the evidence discovered at Nemi, as well as a Roman relief, in order to convince the Venetian government to create a modern quinquereme. His experiment proved so successful that Fausto, a Greek scholar whose erudition was his only claim to expertise about ships, became a sought-after consultant naval architect.[71]

The records of Alberti's adventure at Nemi yield a strikingly vivid, three-dimensional account of his investigation of a particular fascinating archaeological site. Other sources, though not so full or detailed, show that in the 1440s he carried out equally intensive examinations of other sites, many of them in the city of Rome. A long passage in *On Literary Refinement* by the Milanese humanist Angelo Decembrio, for example, describes an inspection of the obelisk that stood, in the fifteenth century, next to the old Basilica of St. Peter. By Decembrio's account, the investigator who explained this legend-haunted monument to the court of Ferrara dismissed with contempt the whole rich body of medieval myths that had accreted about it. This seems a shame, since these Wrong But Romantic tales included not only the widely accepted story that the ashes of Julius Caesar were preserved in the brazen ball at its tip, but also the ingenious legend that the poet Virgil had used his magical powers to move the monolith to Rome from its original place in Solomon's Temple at Jerusalem. Decembrio's investigator mocked unnamed rivals who scraped the sides of the obelisk in a vain effort to determine how it had been made, insisted that its shaft was hollow, and even claimed that they could move it, still upright, to another position. Analyzing word by word the inscription that appeared on two sides of the square shaft, he showed that it mentioned not Julius Caesar but Augustus and Tiberius. With unusual candor, he admitted that the text did not reveal what purpose the obelisk had served in ancient Roman enterprises.

In Decembrio's account, the investigator of this Roman site was the Ferrarese teacher Guarino of Verona, who had a speaking part in many other passages in his text as well. But the historical Guarino took little interest in the antiquarian enterprise. He ridiculed Niccolò Niccoli for his interest in such absurd questions as the height of the obelisk—but Decembrio's fictional Guarino was interested. Decembrio also inserted materials from Alberti's works, which enjoyed great popularity at the court of Ferrara, into other passages in his book. It seems highly likely that this passage too is his adaptation of a lost text by Alberti—a site report, based on investigations that Alberti carried out in the 1440s or 1450s.[72]

The smooth classical style of On the Art of Building begins to show seams and fissures when inspected in the light of these preparatory studies. Again and again the outlines of sunken ships, of reports on particular sites and buildings that were never separately published, break for a second or two its smooth Latin surface. Describing the Circus Maximus, for example, Alberti wrote despairingly that "it is so dilapidated that it does not offer the least impression of its original appearance"—an impression shared by Pirro Ligorio in the next century. Ligorio confessed that he had had to measure other comparable sites, which he did not name, to work out the normal dimensions of a circus's central area.[73] But when Alberti took Bernardo Rucellai and some other distinguished Florentines around the city in 1471, he demonstrated that those who were willing to "dig down to the bottom" of the Circus could "easily see very large fragments of Numidian stone, almost buried"—the fragments, that is, of the Flaminian obelisk, which was soon lost again, not to be rediscovered until 1587.[74] Evidently Alberti had done more work in this wasteland than his brief comment in *On the Art of Building* suggests. His curt comments on a vast range of ancient building practices very likely rested on close visual inspection, and occasional excavation, of Roman roads, foundations, drains, aqueducts, arches, walls, mosaics, porticos, and marble facings.

Particularly striking are Alberti's comments on the Pantheon. He consistently described this temple as uniquely beautiful, a brilliantly skillful application of expensive materials: "In the portico of Agrippa there remain to this day trusses composed of bronze beams forty feet in length: you do not know what to admire more about it, the vast cost or the ingenuity of the builder." He examined the literary descriptions of the temple as well, noting Pliny's reference to the gilded bronze tiles that once covered the roof, and regretting that no ancient source explained the methods used to produce the great coffered expanse of the dome. And he showed special admiration for the architect's structural work:

> Anyone who thinks that extremely thick walls lend a temple dignity
> is mistaken. For who would not criticize a body for having excessively
> swollen limbs? Besides, thick walls restrict the light. For the temple of
> the Pantheon, since the walls needed to be thick, the architect very
> commendably employed nothing but ribs, rejecting any form of infill.
> He used spaces that someone of less experience might have filled in,
> for niches and openings, thereby reducing the cost, while resolving
> structural problems and contributing to the elegance of the work.[75]

When Alberti set out to crown the Church of San Francesco in Rimini with a dome, he expressed his admiration for the Pantheon yet insisted on his independence from any single model: "I for my part have more faith in those who built the Baths and the Pantheon and all these noble edifices, than in [one of his critics], and a great deal more in reason than in any man."[76] For the Pantheon, as for the obelisk, Alberti had probably drawn up an elaborate site report from which he continued to draw details in later years.

It may even be possible to identify the occasion, in the 1440s, when Alberti began inspecting the Pantheon. Biondo recorded, in his *Rome Restored*, that

> By your intervention, O Pope Eugenius, and at your expense, the
> Pantheon's stupendous vault, torn in antiquity by earthquakes and

threatened with ruin, was restored. The curia rejoiced to see it covered with lead sheets where they were lacking . . . That splendid church, clearly superior to all others, had had the lofty columns that support it hidden, for many centuries, by the nasty little shops that surrounded it. These have now been completely cleaned off, and their bases and capitals, laid bare, reveal the beauty of this wonderful building. Its beauty is enhanced by the Tiburtine paving of the *area* of the temple and the road that leads to the Campus Martius in our time.[77]

These emollient words of praise smoothed over what must have been a controversial restoration process. The Pantheon was one of the most prominent of Rome's built features. Throughout the Middle Ages, cobwebs of legend grew over it, as Romans explained that it had been constructed by devils, who heaped up a vast hill of dirt and built the temple, with its huge free-standing dome, on top of it, then told the locals that buried treasure lay underneath—thereby unleashing a gold rush that resulted in the clearing of the building's central space.[78] The piazza in front of the building, moreover, became a battleground. The priests who belonged to the church's chapter and profited from the markets and dice games that disfigured it, struggled with the municipal magistrates in charge of the city's streets, who tried, with papal support, to keep the piazza orderly, clear, and handsome. In 1442, at Eugenius's orders, and again in 1457, the magistrates tore down the shops whose displays of tripe, olives, and wine obscured the columns—only to encounter both passive and active resistance, and to see the shops restored.[79] Biondo mentioned none of these conflicts.

Biondo did not mention Alberti either. Yet it still seems likely that Alberti carried out his study of the Pantheon in the course of this process of restoration and even as one of those who planned it. The two men's evaluations of the building correspond closely. Both of them described its fabric in unusual detail. It seems likely that they examined it together. Perhaps—though the documents do not state as much—Alberti was already serving as an expert consultant to the curia on architectural projects that involved ancient buildings. And it seems clear that he at least witnessed Eugenius's restoration of the Pantheon, and probable that he took the opportunity to survey its structure in detail. The Pantheon became the object of Alberti's detailed scrutiny, ranging from its foundations to its dome and aiming at uncovering both the reasons for its beauty and the secrets of its construction.

Many other sites that Alberti only touched on in his book must have been the object of comparably detailed surveys, if not of his restorative efforts. Multiple traces of these studies, never mentioned in his works, adorn his architecture.[80] No one did more to call the lost city of the ancients back to life. "Come back, come back, o glittering and white"—so Alberti may well have thought, again and again, as he watched the pigs browse where Roman senators had walked.

Like other antiquaries, Alberti worked at times under the zodiacal sign of nostalgia. "The landmarks of some bygone era," he knew, and "records of the times and events to fill the eyes and mind with admiration," made a region especially beautiful, like the ruins of Troy, which were vividly pictured in Cristoforo Buondelmonti's dramatic description of the Eastern Mediterranean, The Book of the Islands of the Archipelago.[81] When Alberti described the large stones used for constructing the walls of Athens, he may well have had in mind the "great fallen walls on all sides" that Cyriac of Ancona saw on first entering Athens in 1436—an experience that Cyriac reported in manuscripts that later circulated widely and that were reworked, both visually and verbally, in a curious novel of the late fifteenth century that became Europe's first romantic evocation of the pleasure of ruins, the Hypnerotomachia.[82] Alberti's discussion of the form of the ancient temple "at Athens," the Parthenon, probably also derives from his reading of Cyriac's report. He could savor the beauties of fallen columns as plangently as anyone, and very likely he did so not only when he walked through the forum, but also when he read Cyriac's codices.[83]

Poggio and his friends meditated on ruins and mutability, but they also made fun of those who became too depressed about them. Cyriac of Ancona, no doubt the victim of a professional deformation, seemed to mourn the fall of Rome with excessive emotion. Antonio Loschi compared him to the man at Milan who began to cry when he heard a cantastorie, or public storyteller, sing "of the death of Roland, who perished seven hundred years ago in battle," went home still in tears, and was still weeping inconsolably at dinnertime because "Roland, the only defender of the Christians, is dead."[84] Like Poggio and Loschi, Alberti had too sharp a sensibility to spend a great deal of time and energy on mourning the distant past. His study of the built record extended outward to pasts not visible in Rome and down to very recent times. As he reached backward into the distant past, trying to reconstruct the form of Etruscan temples, he developed a conjectural history of the origins of architecture, in an erudite, original excursus that attracted the attention of two of his most articulate early readers, Filarete and Manetti.

Equally remarkable is the passage, less often discussed, that reveals how Alberti saw the urban fabric of his own time:

> Watchtowers provide an excellent ornament, if sited in a suitable position and built on appropriate lines; if grouped tightly together, they make an imposing sight from afar. Yet I cannot comprehend the mania prevalent two hundred years ago for building towers even in the smallest of towns. It seemed that no head of a family could be without a tower; as a result, forests of towers sprouted up everywhere. Some think the movement of a star may influence men's minds. Thus between three and four hundred years ago there raged such religious fervor that man seemed to have been born for no other purpose than to construct religious buildings. To give but one example: we have just now surveyed over two and a half thousand religious buildings in Rome, although more than half are in ruins. And what is this we now see, the whole of Italy competing for renewal? How many cities, which as children we saw all built of wood, have now been turned into marble?[85]

This condensed but vivid evocation of the Italian cityscape shows that Alberti saw the urban fabric as a palimpsest, the historical layers of which he tried to separate, date, and analyze. His classical tastes clearly did not prevent him from investigating later strata. He identified the characteristic forms of townscape that had developed in medieval Tuscany and elsewhere, and he surveyed medieval buildings as thoroughly as ancient ones—even if he deplored the excesses to which tower building had led, in San Gimignano and elsewhere. Alberti even provided, at second hand, a historical explanation for the building history that he established: The "movements of the stars," by which he surely meant the great conjunctions of Jupiter and Saturn that take place every twenty years, were invoked by astrologers and great ecclesiastics in Alberti's day to explain the Great Schism and by heretics to predict the fall of the papal Babylon in Rome. Some had suggested that these astral events could explain the fashion for towers in the Middle Ages and for renovation schemes in the Renaissance with equal neatness.[86] Once again, natural philosophy fused with philology in antiquarian practice.

"All that remains is memory"—these sad words, always the antiquarian's refrain, apply with special force to Alberti today, as so much of his archaeological work has fallen into the same oblivion as the marbles and mosaics that he studied. Even the Malatesta Temple—which brilliantly fused Alberti's passion for the monumental arch, his interest in later building forms, and his preference for reliefs that represented limbs and hair in motion—remained unfinished. And yet he created something else that was more lasting. Alberti practiced both the technical and scientific reading of the built past and the philological reading of the textual record; he combined the direct study of antiquities with their creative reuse in modern works of art; and he served as an expert consultant to wealthy men, whom he conducted on antiquarian pilgrimages. Pius II, himself an antiquarian of parts, paid tribute to Alberti's astute discovery of hidden ruins in the Alban hills. Giovanni Rucellai, who came to Rome for the Jubilee of 1450, spent his mornings in church and his afternoons touring the city. It seems highly likely that Alberti guided Rucellai as he inspected antiquities in the gardens and houses of Roman citizens, showing him the splendid columns and architraves of the baths of Diocletian and calling his attention to the fine columns and bronze beams in the portico of the Pantheon. Alberti, who wrote appreciatively in *On the Art of Building* about the flowers and plants depicted in the surviving fragments of Roman mosaic floors, may well have pointed out the "delightful animals, birds and foliage" that Giovanni admired in the brilliantly colored ceiling mosaics of the late antique Chapel of Santa Costanza. Giovanni's son Bernardo later remembered with pleasure how he, Donato Acciaiuoli, and Lorenzo de' Medici had argued cheerfully about the interpretation of Roman inscriptions when they toured the city with Alberti in 1471.[87] Such men celebrated Alberti, in Pius's words, as *vir doctus et antiquitatum solertissimus indagator*—"a scholar and a truly expert antiquarian."[88]

Alberti thus made himself the ideal "counselor in antiquity" to the erudite patrons of building whose palaces he frequented.[89] He carried out all the tasks assigned to the supposedly new professional antiquarians of the sixteenth century—like Fra Giovanni Giocondo, who collected inscriptions, edited Caesar and Vitruvius, and built bridges with equal flair and skill, and whom his friend and patron Guillaume Budé praised as "an outstanding architect, and above all an antiquarian."[90] The technical content of Alberti's antiquarian work must for the most part be inferred from tiny, revealing details in *On the Art of Building*. But a dozen complementary sources locate it in its historical context. Alberti created something more lasting than a collection of drawings and inscriptions. He became the first model for a social type that would remain prominent for centuries, in Renaissance courts,

Baroque academies, and Enlightenment salons—at once a service professional needed by every court and an erudite scholar who had much to offer the scholars, architects, and artists who shared his specialized interests. These men consistently tried, as Alberti had, to combine philological and technical expertise, the scholar's learning and the connoisseur's eye. The Alberti who parted the waters of Lake Nemi lived on not only in the daring dives of Francesco De Marchi but in the cautious lives of a thousand later antiquarians, whose technical practices and professional formation were as "Albertian" as those of any architect or painter.[91]

VIII

ALBERTI ON
THE ART OF BUILDING

Flavio Biondo found modern Rome as fascinating as the ancient city. One day (as he later recounted in a long letter to Leonello d'Este) he joined a hunting party led by Cardinal Prospero Colonna, a chaotic daylong drama of racing men and dogs, best imagined as a surrealist mélange of human and animal limbs in the style of Uccello. When the hunters climbed a tower in the Alban hills and looked down on all of Latium, Colonna "showed [us] how the city of Rome, twelve miles distant, seemed to lie at our feet, pointing out its uninhabited towers, monuments, and fortifications, which fill the whole area so thoroughly that it resembles a forest of towers or castles"— an eloquent verbal counterpart to the painter Benozzo Gozzoli's near-contemporary views of the city.[1] Alberti emphasized, in *On the Art of Building*, the speed with which towers came to dominate the medieval Italian cityscape. By contrast, Biondo used the powerful image of a forest to convey the visual impact of the medieval city, which had grown up like a vast dendral parasite over the ruins of its ancient predecessor but was now deserted and disordered.[2]

This effort at description was not uncommon for Biondo, who made a specialty of examining buildings and their contexts in a critical way. Walking one day down the splendid stone stairs that Pius II had erected in front of the Vatican, he encountered the architect who had designed them, Francesco del Borgo. Biondo sharply criticized the pope's decision to put the statue of Saint Peter to the right of someone descending the stairs, and that of Saint Paul to the left. The "right" side of a piece of paper, Biondo pointed out, corresponded to the right eye and hand of someone writing on it. Buildings should be read in the same way, from the standpoint of those looking at them from the front, not of those leaving them. Peter should appear to the right "as we cross the bridge over the Tiber from the city of Rome, the work of the emperor Trajan, pass under the monument of Hadrian, the Castel Sant'Angelo, and, going to the Basilica of St. Peter, encounter the marble steps below the vestibule. These present themselves to our sight, as we are about to climb [the steps], exactly as pieces of paper present themselves to those who intend to write something."[3] Biondo lost the argument, but the letter to Leonello in which he described it remains one of the most vivid accounts of what it felt like to walk the streets of early Renaissance Rome. Biondo grappled seriously not only with the objective achievements of contemporary architects but also with the subjective impact they had on those who approached them.

Architectural commentary of this precise and scrupulous kind was an art widely cultivated in fifteenth-century Italy. Cyriac of Ancona, for one, had almost as much to say about the Italian cities he visited as about the monuments and inscriptions he found in them.[4] But no one did more than Alberti to forge a language for discussing the built world and to found it on rich theory and observation. In the course of the 1440s and 1450s, he set to work on what became the first independent architectural treatise of modern times, On the Art of Building. Drawing on his experience as a humanist, archaeologist, and connoisseur of the ancient and modern arts, he devised a challenging set of theories about buildings, their makers, and their functions. And as an architect, he put his theories into practice, creating some of the most original private and public edifices of the fifteenth century.

Alberti's connections to the painting and sculpture of his time must be reconstructed from fragments of evidence, assembled with the eye-straining attention to detail and painfully held breath of a watchmaker. By contrast, his own most extensive treatise, a number of archival documents, and a set of structures that he designed all record the origins and progress of his work as an architect. The situation seems, at least, more promising. But for all the richness—or relative richness—of the documentary record, Alberti's architectural career remains the object of sharp controversy at every point. Scholars fall out even over what would seem the simplest of problems: how to interpret the aesthetic and urbanistic ideals that Alberti espoused at eloquent length in the first modern treatise on architecture.

At least two Albertis are reflected in the fun-house mirrors of the modern scholarly literature. One of them came into existence, appropriately, in the high age of modernism. This Alberti devised a totalizing theory, based on a limited, coherent set of what the brilliant and influential German émigré scholar Rudolf Wittkower called "architectural principles." He framed a series of theorems, cosmological in origin and stated in geometrical ratios, that laid out the simple, legible forms that should govern all public buildings. This Alberti described the architect as a godlike figure who imposed a mathematical order on unruly matter. In the ideal case, he could create whole cities from nothing. He would choose a perfect site and divide the population into neighborhoods segregated by occupation and class. He would use the mathematically perfect forms of sphere, arch, and dome as templates to frame buildings harmonious enough to serve for public affairs and public worship. And he would deploy a spatial rhetoric of broad piazzas, raised platforms, and massive roads to ensure that these structures dramatically impressed those who saw them. Alberti thus highlighted the architect's role as an impresario of society and space. Some scholars treat this Alberti as the first in the great series of humane utopians that stretches from Leonardo da Vinci in his own era to Robert Owen and Peter Behrens; others treat him as the first in the grandiose series of tyrannical dystopians that runs from Tommaso Campanella more or less directly to Le Corbusier and Robert Moses.

The second Alberti has emerged in the last generation of scholars, in an age of vernacular styles and sympathy with built environments. This Alberti stands for close attention to context, for deep commitment to the histories of sites, buildings, and cities, for love of tradition. His work looks forward not to the monolithic unity of the modern housing project but to the varied historicism of the last fin-de-siècle and to the suppler post-historicism of ours: he is the ancestor not of the planners who ripped and tore the modern city, but of European and American city walkers like Franz Hessels, Alfred Kazin, and Jane Jacobs, the respectful readers of urban space.

Two kinds of visual evidence capture this opposition very well. Three famous painted panels of the fifteenth century (now kept in Baltimore,

23. Ideal City. Galleria Nazionale delle Marche, Urbino. Alinari/Art Resource, NY.

Urbino, and Berlin) and a painting by Piero di Cosimo (in Sarasota) represent the totalizing Alberti (who, some scholars think, actually designed them).[5] They depict symmetrical buildings that flank empty, splendidly paved squares. Their blankly elegant facades, carried out on a large scale and in a uniform style, seem literally to be pushing aside the smaller, varied house types of the medieval city. The panels vary in important ways—the Urbino panel "stresses the volume and solidity of the structures" it depicts, while that in Baltimore emphasizes the vast scale of the forum it apparently represents. The Berlin panel, which forces the viewer to peer through a low loggia that dominates its foreground, conveys the real visual impact of a Renaissance city more convincingly than the other two. But all three of them "depict visions of an urban setting," in which columns, arches, and massive ancient monuments set off the ceremonial core of a great city. They powerfully evoke the hard-edged world of architectural principle.[6]

By contrast, the realized ideal city of Pienza, which Pope Pius II raised in record time from his ancestral village of Corsignano, has been used more than once as an example of the second Alberti's attention to local knowledge and aesthetics. The public buildings that flank the dazzlingly theatrical space of its central square are not cast in a single stylistic mold. Instead, their diverse, distinctive period styles reveal historical connections to their functions. The cathedral refers to the far bigger one in nearby Siena, the style of whose facade it emulates. The medieval city hall harks back in style, as well as in political role, to the independent city-states of medieval Italy. And the Piccolomini Palace, which faces it across the finely paved central square, attests to the new power and wealth of Renaissance princes like Pius II. The old, narrow, winding roads that debouch on Pius II's new square make its impact more dramatic than larger, straighter ceremonial roads could have. Pienza represents, in this analysis, not a new world of forms suppressing an old one but the harmony of opposites in stone.[7]

Not one Alberti, in other words, but two: and the relations between these two creations of modern historians and the buildings on which the historical original actually worked are just as contentious. Some scholars associate Alberti, often on weak grounds, with every fifteenth-century building project that loosely corresponds with a line of *On the Art of Building*. Yet no documentary evidence shows that he had anything to do with Pienza, for example. Estimable students of Renaissance culture often write as if his supervisory role in creating Pienza had been established beyond doubt, yet the connection in fact rests only on comparisons—some of them quite plausible—between the city as it took shape and passages in Alberti's treatise on architecture. Others consider it unlikely that Alberti could ever have worked wholeheartedly under the direction of overbearing Renaissance patrons like Nicholas V.[8] The first Alberti plays the role of a fifteenth-century Michael Graves, imposing a personal style and coherent design principles on projects of the most wildly varied kinds. The second remains in the shadows like a Renaissance Groucho Marx, refusing to join any club that would have him as a member. The two silhouettes are not easy to reconcile with each other.

Neither of them, moreover, receives much support from some of the most original recent work by architectural and urban historians. Film criticism long ago demoted the once-proud director from *auteur* to one collaborator among many on an art form that no single individual could decisively shape. Similarly, new forms of urban and architectural history attribute to the architect far less autonomy, less creative space, than he once received—and challenge readings that take account only of the aesthetics of a given building or buildings. The architectural and military historian Nicholas Adams, for example, has shown that Pius II used drastic legal and financial means to reorient the center of Corsignano into a ceremonial city. He and his cardinals expelled longtime residents from their homes by compulsory purchase, while the catering requirements of the pope and cardinals transformed the traditional agricultural economy of this country town and strained it to the breaking point. Viewed from the outside, facade by facade, Pienza looks like an early version of Vienna's Ringstrasse: a capsule cultural history of the West in built form, the work of someone with deep respect for the past. Viewed from the archive, however, in the light of the radical changes Pius wrought in landholding patterns and food prices, it looks like a revolution in stone, an ideal grid imposed by force on an alien environment. Even if Alberti had a hand in laying out Pius's hilltop utopia, in other words, the nature of his achievement remains anything but obvious.[9]

On the Art of Building is, by a long margin, the longest and most learned as well as the most influential of Alberti's works. Many scholars have interpreted it, shedding light on Alberti's use of sources, ancient and medieval; his discussion of particular types of building and ornament; and the relation between the book and Alberti's experience of cities and sites. But not all of them have done justice to the magnificent jumble of contents that surprises, and sometimes disappoints, readers. The classical lucidity of Alberti's language and his sincere, and partly successful, promise to supply an orderly and systematic modern book do not fully prepare first-time visitors for the book's close-packed, chronologically divergent layers of content. Perhaps an approach that emphasizes the origins, development, and complex character of *On the Art of Building* as a whole—one that seeks to show how it took shape, and where and when—may help to clarify Alberti's intentions and achievements.

To begin at the level of biography: When, where, and why did Alberti actually write the book? External evidence is scanty. In his *Mathematical Games*, as we have seen, Alberti told his dedicatee, Meliaduse d'Este, that he had written on architecture "at the request of your illustrious brother, my lord messer Leonello."[10] Meliaduse died in 1452, Leonello in 1450. Accordingly, this passage seems to tie the book's composition to the 1440s, and to explain it as part of Alberti's normal work as a service professional at court: a far longer and more systematic treatment of some of the issues already touched upon in *Games*. Some confirmation for this possibility comes from Biondo, who a few years later described the book as finished, and from the Pisan chronicler Mattia Palmieri, who wrote that Alberti "presented" his book to Pope Nicholas V in 1452, while persuading him to abandon his plan to enlarge the Basilica of St. Peter.[11] Great authorities, accordingly, have argued in recent years that the book must have essentially reached completion by midcentury, and that Alberti put the final touches to the project that he had undertaken in Ferrara as part of his service to Nicholas—the first of the Renaissance popes to make building campaigns a central feature of his pontificate.[12]

Plenty of evidence confirms Alberti's long-term interest in the problems taken up in *On the Art of Building*. He seems always to have enjoyed visiting cities and examining buildings. Early in the 1430s, while writing *On the Advantages and Disadvantages of Letters*, he complained that the study of texts deprived the humanist of the time needed "for a pleasure which is most excellent, and most worthy of a free man: wandering through cities and provinces, examining many temples and theaters, walls and buildings of every kind, and visiting both places that are by nature most pleasant, delightful, and strong, and those that the hand and intellect of man have made both beautiful and safe against enemy attacks."[13] The young humanist resented his earnest, time-consuming study of texts because it kept him from walking in the city. One could hardly "drag books along on journeys, or do a great deal of regular reading while deeply involved in coming to know new regions." Even in his mid-twenties, in other words, Alberti wanted to see and think about the built world.

Alberti's letter of 1435–36 to Brunelleschi, presenting the Italian text of On Painting, provides a specimen of his discriminating reactions to the core of a city. Singling out the new cupola of the Duomo as the greatest achievement of modern humanity, Alberti explained how the intelligent traveler should look at it and think about it. In Mathematical Games, finally, a work probably begun soon after On Painting but finished a generation later, the flâneur turned into a surveyor. Here Alberti offered instructions for studying urban sites scientifically. The first problem in the book begins: "If you wish, being at the top of a piazza, to measure the height of a tower at the bottom of the piazza, by sight alone, do as follows."[14] Many passages in On the Art of Building refer, implicitly or explicitly, to architectural projects that he saw carried out in the 1430s and 1440s. He enthusiastically describes the near-perfect state of preservation of the ancient cypress doors of St. Peter's at the time when Filarete replaced them in 1443, for example, implying that he witnessed the installation of the Porta Argentea; he had also evidently experienced the restoration of the Pantheon.

The work also touches on many technical problems of the sort that interested the young Alberti in his role as consulting engineer. In book five, for example, he describes a device for transforming the gangways of ships instantaneously into hedgehogs bristling with spikes, rendering them impossible to board. A second, related invention would enable the crew of an invaded ship to make the entire deck collapse at the touch of a hammer, depositing the enemy helpless in the hold.[15] These comical-sounding destructive engines belong to the infernal world of military technology inhabited by engineers like Taccola and Roberto Valturio, who devised real and fantastic war engines and devoted hauntingly imaginative books to describing them. The mature author of On the Art of Building remained loyal to the young inventor who had astonished the curia in the 1430s with his "miracles of painting."

Alberti's most ambitious book thus drew on interests and experiences that he had cultivated since the 1430s. In particular, his experiences as an antiquarian and archaeologist, which occupied him from the 1430s onward, taught him an enormous amount about ancient buildings. But at least two other factors helped to focus his and others' attention on the problems of architecture and urban layout. One was the development of urban form and architectural practice. True, Italian cities did not witness such obviously radical transformations in the early fifteenth century as in the previous century—especially before the Black Death struck in 1348, when the urban population had reached its peak, walls grew to their largest extent, and great churches and public buildings rose to dominate city skylines. But many of the massive, resource-gobbling urban projects begun in this period of demographic and economic expansion, like the enormous Florentine and Milanese cathedrals, remained incomplete in the Renaissance. In some cases, their completion posed extraordinary technical problems. And these, in turn, raised urgent questions about what it meant to be an architect.

At Milan in 1400, Jean Mignot, an expert consultant from northern Europe, insisted on applying complex geometrical principles to the design of the cathedral's buttresses. He argued passionately that only high flying buttresses—a rigorous solution based on *scientia*—could yield a stable structure: "mere craft [*ars*] without rigorous knowledge [*scientia*] is useless." The locals replied, with equal passion, that their own traditional methods, the "tacit knowledge" they had acquired through the practice of their craft, could produce a structure that would be both beautiful and durable—as indeed proved to be the case (though they too cited learned opinion in the course of the wrangling that ensued). These debates, though carried on by professionals, had to be settled by the lay members of the Operai who presided over the cathedrals. Like the debate over the Baptistery doors, the arguments over the Milanese and Florentine cathedrals dramatically raised the question of what sort of practitioner an architect was.[16]

Private structures also posed new challenges—if not in the realm of engineering, then in those of ethics and aesthetics. As early as the fourteenth century, Italian princes and lords began to consolidate urban properties and transform them into increasingly splendid palaces.[17] In the first decades of the fifteenth century, classical models began to play a larger role, and decorative schemes became increasingly ambitious. Cardinal Giordano Orsini, who erected a splendid palace on the family stronghold of Monte Giordano in Rome, employed Masolino, one of the most innovative fresco painters of the period around 1430, to decorate its hall.[18] His frescoes included a panoramic view (now lost) of the city of Rome itself. Giordano not only undertook an individual building project but cultivated a sense of the larger urban scene in which it fit. In the 1430s and 1440s, these projects attained a new scale, as the heads of great clans built the first of the huge palaces, as large as a modern city block, that eventually came to define the Florentine and much of the Roman cityscape. Writing around 1450, Biondo declared that none of the ancient Roman palaces whose remains were among the city's ruins had been "more magnificent" than the Medici Palace begun by Michelozzo in 1444.[19] These new architectural forms demanded new intellectual as well as architectural foundations. In a society in which even moderate preachers routinely denounced the greed and vaingloriousness of great merchants, palatial buildings required convincing justifications, both visual and verbal. Writing in 1457, in the midst of Florence's first wave of palace building, Giovanni Rucellai—himself a connoisseur, a man who saw building as the most intelligent single way to dispose of wealth—professed his unbounded admiration for Giordano Orsini's "very lovely hall, with its frescoes full of excellent figures and with certain windows made of alabaster in place of glass."[20] Comments like these—which treated the new palaces as exemplary exercises in "magnificence"—began to multiply, as scholars searched the works of Aristotle and Cicero for justifications.[21] Alberti himself, as we have seen, admitted in On the Family that a certain level of luxury was not out of place in the houses of the great.

At the same time, a vital ancient text began to exercise a more and more powerful influence both on its own and as the attractive, powerful center of groups of related texts that clustered around it. The On Architecture of Vitruvius—a Roman practitioner of the first century B.C.E. who worked for Caesar, among other patrons—had circulated fairly widely in the Middle Ages. But most readers had not been in a position to decode the densely technical and deeply corrupt Greek vocabulary of technical terms for architectural forms and elements. The humanists made intensive efforts to decipher and apply what the ancient master had to say. Petrarch, for example, carefully annotated his manuscript of Vitruvius with explanatory notes and cross-references. He took a strong interest in the Roman writer's use of Greek terms for aesthetic qualities, eurythmia and simmetria, that had mystified earlier Latin readers and that he also knew from Pliny's Natural History. Petrarch's disciples—the engineer Giovanni Dondi as well as literati like

Boccaccio—read the text with equal fascination and profit.[22] In the fifteenth century, more technical sections of the text began to command attention. Pier Candido Decembrio, a scholar who served in the Milanese
chancery, compiled definitions of the Greek architectural terms that Vitruvius used, like *xystus* for part of a garden. He also followed early medieval
precedent when he drew and labeled diagrams of Doric and Ionic capitals,
and an entablature part by part.[23]

As Vitruvius became more accessible to scholars, they were challenged
to look harder at the built world around them. For he offered them not only
a treasury of details about ancient building methods, forms of warfare, and
natural philosophy—rich with concrete data even if hard to construe—but
also a guide to thinking about buildings. Vitruvius provided a detailed aesthetic terminology and, more remarkable still, precise instructions for applying it when describing the effect of a given building on its visitors. Both
general architectural principles and the local situation must always be taken
into account, in his view. The appropriateness of an individual style to a
building, for example, depended on its likely effect on those approaching it:
"Correctness of tradition will be expressed if, when buildings have magnificent interiors, their vestibules have been made equally harmonious and elegant, for if interiors were outfitted elegantly, but had entrances deficient in
dignity and respectability, they would lack correctness." When a real city
was planned and built, Vitruvius acknowledged, history and custom necessarily intersected and interfered with aesthetic principles and high style. The
Romans, for example, could not take over the square shape of the Greek forum along with the colonnades that surrounded it, since "from our ancestors
we have inherited the custom of giving gladiatorial games in the forum."
And he also showed, simply and clearly, that urban and rural families, craftsmen and farmers, men and women needed different kinds of houses and
rooms—spaces differentiated to fit their functions. Anyone who worked his
way through On Architecture learned to see the city as a delicately paradoxical work of art, lived in, moved through, and continually judged by inhabitants aware both of what artistic tradition demanded and of what social
usage allowed. Vitruvians were more than readers: they became alert and informed viewers of the built landscape. Vitruvius schooled them to examine
buildings as he had, as the nodes where an intelligent architect adapted general prescriptions and principles to the conditions of a particular site and the
needs of particular users.[24] Alberti was never more Vitruvian than in his
central enterprise: to hold in creative tension the two apparently opposed

ideals of universal, mathematical proportion and local, site-specific adaptation.

Vitruvius was rarely read in isolation. The humanists generally compared and contrasted ancient texts, noting parallels and using information given in one to supplement another. When a major work on a new subject, like *On Architecture*, became more accessible, other texts were charged with new energy and relevance as well. Vitruvius provided in book six, for example, detailed discussions of Roman private houses in both the city and the country. Material and textual evidence shows that his learned readers soon connected these discussions with the many passages in the letters of the younger Pliny in which he described two of his villas, one in the Apennines and the other on the shore of Lake Como.[25]

In the 1420s, Cardinal Branda Castiglione erected what his biographer called "a whole circle" of innovative buildings in the country village of Castiglione Olona, near Varese, some twenty-five miles from Milan.[26] The complex included a small centrally planned church, its simple proportions visually highlighted by the pilasters that framed the segments of its facade; two palaces; and a larger collegiate church. The patron and his architect clearly drew not only on Vitruvius, in their emphasis on symmetry and classical building forms, but also on Pliny, whose own villa on Lake Como had not been far away. They displayed their Vitruvian erudition with the porticoes and colonnades that adorned the larger collegiate church, which was placed in a dominant position, on a hill, and in the splendid atrium that served as the main entrance to the bishop's palace. And they showed their sympathy for Pliny by laying out spectacular gardens—into one of which the doors of the palace guest room opened directly—and by orienting the whole complex so that its inhabitants looked out on ravishing prospects of cultivated land and running water, where brooks babbled and deer virtually offered themselves up to be hunted by men and dogs. Like Vitruvius, they understood the town as an impressive scenographic whole (and they equipped it—as he recommended—with strong defenses). And like Pliny, they tried to place "no rigid barrier . . . between the real and built worlds," to "blur the distinction between interior and exterior."[27]

Even before all of Branda's buildings had reached completion, the perfect observer materialized as if on cue. In December 1431, Francesco Pizolpasso, a cultivated bibliophile from Bologna who served as archbishop of Milan, stayed with Cardinal Branda for a week.[28] The long letter in which he described what he had seen to Juan Cervantes, another cardinal, amounts to a brilliant urbanistic essay, elaborated in conscious imitation of the literary sources from which Branda and his architect had worked. Pizolpasso owned copies of both Pliny's letters and Vitruvius.[29] And he hurled every relevant adjective he could find in either of them into his description of the natural and artificial wonders of Castiglione Olona. He took care to show off his mastery of technical architectural terms by praising the Doric columns of the collegiate church. (Actually, the church's columns and half-columns have medieval capitals.)[30] But his careful use of the same texts that had inspired Cardinal Branda shows that both were the inheritors of a substantial architectural culture couched in Latin. The long epistle in which Pizolpasso described what Branda had wrought, moreover, was clearly meant not as a personal letter to an individual reader but as a literary work in its own right, one designed to obtain publicity. The care Pizolpasso took in composing it emerges from a second letter, in which he asked the advice of the Neapolitan humanist Antonio Panormita about some of the technical terms he used in the first. He dispatched the finished work to a major figure in the papal curia.[31]

Experiments in building and research in ancient texts had thus already begun to shape and interfere with one another before Alberti set to work. In the prologue to *On the Art of Building*, Alberti described architecture as a central subject of fifteenth-century conversation, an art that patrons and architects were taking to a new level of cultivation, while others simply enjoyed commenting on the creations:

> But how congenial and instinctive the desire and thought for building may be to our minds is evident—if only because you will never find anyone who is not eager to build something, as soon as he has the means to do so; nor is there anyone who, on making some discovery in the art of building, would not gladly and willingly offer and broadcast his advice for general use, as if compelled to do so by nature. It often happens that we ourselves, although busy with completely different things, cannot prevent our minds and imagination from projecting some building or other. Or again, when we see some other person's building, we immediately look over and compare the individual dimensions, and to the best of our ability consider what might be taken away, added, or altered, to make it more elegant, and willingly we lend our advice. But if it has been well designed and properly executed, who would not look at it with great pleasure and joy?[32]

This passage suggests that the other members of Alberti's circle discussed building with the same mixture of practical experience, theoretical sophistication, and critical acuity that the "overcultivated" denizens of modern cities bring to the discussion of food, films, and ballet.[33]

As a scholar interested in building, Alberti naturally had to confront Vitruvius, as his colleagues already had. In fact, he had begun to study Vitruvius as early as the 1430s. In On Painting, he had used the Roman writer as a source for ancient views on both human proportions and natural pigments.[34] His own On the Art of Building, not surprisingly, took off from the great example of On Architecture, and Alberti took care to highlight this connection. Like Vitruvius, Alberti cast his work in ten books, which described cities and individual buildings, fortifications and private houses, structural elements and ornamental details, and he provided a detailed evaluative terminology for discussing them as well as technical instructions for fashioning them. Like Vitruvius, he offered a great deal of information about the natural environment in which buildings had to stand, tracing the long-term effects of sun, rain, and wind on structures and those who inhabited and used them. Like Vitruvius, he had an eye not only for individual building types but also for the larger contexts in which they stood and for the way in which a human moving through the city would encounter any given facade or open space.

Richard Krautheimer, a magnificently wide-ranging émigré historian of ancient and modern cities and their builders, suggested long ago that Alberti may even have begun his work as a sort of extended commentary on Vitruvius, a point-by-point critical survey of the same materials.[35] At least one parallel can be cited from the same period. When Georg von Peuerbach and his brilliant pupil Johannes Regiomontanus decided to make the densely technical astronomical textbook of Ptolemy, the Almagest, accessible to a larger public, they cast their work not in the standard form of a chapter-by-chapter commentary but in that of an epitome. This critical survey explained Ptolemy's principles and models, offering new diagrams and technical corrections and additions drawn from the work of more recent Islamic and Western astronomers. Their work proved enormously successful: Copernicus was only one of the many sixteenth-century astronomers who learned their art from the Epitome rather than from the original text.[36] It seems quite possible, accordingly, that Alberti began work with the intention of producing something similar. And he too wound up producing both a fiercely mathematical set of principles and a sensitive account of the visual impact of site on buildings and buildings on site.

Alberti, however, rarely if ever produced a simple imitation of an ancient work. By his own account, as he came to know Vitruvius better, he found himself repeatedly confused, bemused, and enraged by the numerous scribal errors that made the text hard to read: "almost the sole survivor from this vast shipwreck is Vitruvius, an author of unquestioned experience, though one whose writings have been so corrupted by time that there are many omissions and many shortcomings." The form in which Alberti received the text—or so he claimed—put a certain distance between him and its contents. Even more disturbing were the numerous substantive errors that made the author himself, once properly understood, seem less than reliable. Ever the connoisseur of styles, Alberti objected forcefully to the Roman architect's Latin prose as well. Above all, he disliked what he saw as substantive flaws in Vitruvius' work. On the one hand, Alberti rejected the Roman architect's demand that the architect develop an encyclopedic knowledge of the arts and sciences: in many areas, even in the art of drawing, a modest acquaintance with the basic techniques would suffice. On the other hand, Alberti insisted that Vitruvius' work lacked a clear conceptual order.

Accordingly, Alberti adopted a particular set of imitative tactics known by a classical name, emulation.[37] Even as he quoted and followed the ancient master builder, he also challenged his authority, proclaiming that Vitruvius' "very text is evidence that he wrote neither Latin nor Greek, so that as far as we are concerned, he might just as well not have written at all, rather than write something that we cannot understand." Alberti criticized Vitruvius, implicitly or explicitly, on many other grounds as well. Vitruvius praised water as the source of human society and culture. Alberti, by contrast, emphasized over and over that water is the enemy as well as the savior of mankind. A well-built house, he repeatedly insisted, must act like a machine for the dispersal of water. Pitched roofs, solid tiles, and effective gutters, in his view, were essential for all civilized life, since water had the power to take advantage of any hole in a fabric, however small. This he described with the horrified fascination of a Machiavelli denouncing treasonous aristocrats. Here and elsewhere Alberti drew on a massive experience of practical problems as well as exposure to practicing architects.

More important, Alberti imposed on his work an order radically different from that of his ancient model. Vitruvius' book moved from one kind of task to another, taking building types and other architectural projects as its chief organizational principle. Alberti, by contrast, structured his book around three leading concepts, *firmitas*, *utilitas*, and *venustas* (construction, function, and beauty of design), separating his discussion of the forms and structures of different kinds of building, which he analyzed in the first part of his work, from his discussion of ornamentation in the second.[38] And he used the model of Quintilian's treatise on the orator to give form to his work as a whole. Where Quintilian discussed the topics that an orator must use in "invention," Alberti described the forms that an architect must manipulate. Where Quintilian laid out the different ways of organizing a speech that constituted "disposition," Alberti analyzed the ways in which architectural forms should be applied in individual cities and buildings. And where Quintilian treated "elocution," the stylistic adornment of a speech, Alberti offered a detailed study of "ornament," the adornment of buildings. For all the differences and inconsistencies that appeared in the course of his exposition, it seems clear that Alberti once again found in rhetoric his fundamental model for a discipline.[39] Alberti's work was, in effect, a large-scale critique of the one predecessor without whom he could not have written it: a manifesto even more churlish to its ancient sources than On Painting.

Many of Alberti's objections to Vitruvius rest on the inspection of ancient buildings he had carried out in the 1440s. "Examples of ancient temples and theaters," he remarked, "remain that could serve as the best imaginable teachers."[40] And he made clear that he really had carried out such a program of minute observation, its objects ranging from the mausoleum of Theodoric at Ravenna to the aqueducts outside Rome. Drawing a precise analogy with the systematic reading required of a humanist who wanted to become the master of the classical written corpus, Alberti told the architect to base his practice on a collection of drawings. Like the humanist's notebook bulging with methodically organized extracts from ancient texts, the drawings in the architect's notebook must be organized for easy retrieval and effective re-use. He must record the "order," the "places," and the "genera," as well as the measurements and proportions, of every major architectural work.[41] These recommendations gradually entered into standard architectural practice, though no notebook of Alberti's own survives. Here too Alberti reached backward to his early years. As early as the 1430s, borrowing from humanist practice, he had told the painter to compile notebooks of volumetric nudes and body parts. The intellectual origins of On the Art of Building lie in Alberti's early years as technologist, critic, and antiquary.

Origins are not everything, however. Much of the book's content took shape in Rome in the late 1440s and early 1450s—some of it well after the date now accepted for its completion. Elaborate, long-term literary research continued for many years, as Alberti strove to outdo Vitruvius in scholarship as well as conceptual clarity. Vitruvius drew not only on his experience as an architect but also on a wide range of written sources, especially when he discussed technical subjects vital to the architect but outside the boundaries of his discipline, like the virtues and defects of different kinds of wood. In his analysis of the desirable qualities for water, for example, Vitruvius wrote that "I have seen some of these things myself, and I discovered the rest recorded in Greek books, and these are the authors of these texts: Theophrastus, Timaeus, Posidonius, Hegesias, Herodotus, Aristides, and Metrodorus, who, with great powers of observation and boundless zeal, declared in their writings that the properties of places, the characteristics of waters, and the qualities of the regions of the heavens have been distributed in this fashion because of the inclination of the cosmos."[42] Alberti rejected Vitruvius' encyclopedic program, according to which the architect had to be an authority on a vast range of subjects. But he displayed his own erudition again and again by citing similar lists of authorities and compiling anecdotes drawn from them, on every subject from the best kinds of stone to the worst kinds of tomb. "We shall now deal," he promised at one point,

> with the materials suitable for constructing buildings, and we shall relate the advice handed down to us by the learned men of the past, in particular Theophrastus, Aristotle, Cato, Varro, Pliny, and Vitruvius: for any such knowledge is better gained through long experience than through any artifice of invention; it should be sought therefore from those who have made the most diligent observations on the matter. We shall proceed, then, to gather this information from the many, varied passages in which the best authors have dealt with the question.[43]

Alberti's claim to authority, in other words, rested as firmly on textual sources as on drawings of ancient monuments. He insisted that he always compared what he read with what he saw. Occasionally, as in On Painting, he dismissed ancient authority as irrelevant or inferior to direct study: "We could mention many other fascinating anecdotes recorded by the ancient historians on the properties of water and the good and bad effects it may have on man's health, but they are curious ones that would serve to show off our erudition rather than illustrate our arguments."[44] Still, the texture of On the Art of Building as a whole is that of a quilt, not a tapestry: a compilation from multiple sources, not a seamless composition—a fact many readers implicitly acknowledge when they skip the patches of recondite erudition in question.

Consider one passage among many:

> The Spartans prided themselves on not having walls around their city: trusting in their military prowess and the strength of their citizens, they thought their laws sufficient protection. The Egyptians and the Persians, on the other hand, felt that their cities ought to be defended with extensive walling. For example, Ninus and Semiramis, among others, planned the walls of their cities to be wide enough to accommodate two linked chariots being drawn on top, and to be more than one hundred cubits in height. Arrian recalls that the walls of Tyre were 150 feet high. Clearly some were not content with one set of walls: the Carthaginians surrounded their city with three. Herodotus mentions that Deioces surrounded the town of Cebatana with seven walls, despite its elevated position.[45]

Here Alberti has juxtaposed passages from a whole series of Greek writers, most of them even less known in his time than they are now, and few of them directly relevant to a modern builder's tasks. Presumably he had already assembled the relevant extracts in a notebook, under the *locus* (place heading) "walls." When he composed a chapter, he began by setting out the materials he had collected, often modifying them, as he had in other works, to make them fit his purpose.[46] *On the Art of Building*, in other words, not only models architectural scholarship on the relentless excerpting, collating, and compiling practiced by humanists: it also rests on the standard humanist methods of close reading, textual summary, notebook making, and artful adaptation, the "self-perpetuating cycle of textual commentary" that formed the core of learned practice in the fifteenth and sixteenth centuries.[47]

The sources on which Alberti drew, moreover, identify with near certainty the place and circumstances in which he worked. Even a partial list of the Greek texts that he cited, usually several times, contains a number of long, difficult works:

Arrian's *Anabasis*, a history of Alexander the Great, written in the second century C.E.

Diodorus Siculus' *Historical Library*, a massive compilation of materials on geography, ethnography, and mythology, assembled by its erudite author in the late first century B.C.E.

Herodotus' *Histories*, a vast survey of the Mediterranean world and
narrative of the Persian wars written in the middle of the fifth
century B.C.E.

Plato's *Laws*, the great philosopher's strange, dark blueprint for an
ideal state

Theophrastus' *History of Plants*, the massively detailed and technical
work on botany of Aristotle's best pupil, who died early in the
third century B.C.E.

Thucydides' *Histories*, the profound and detailed contemporary history of the *Peloponnesian Wars*[48]

This imposing list reveals much about the nature and chronology of Alberti's work on his book. Some of the texts had received Latin translations
fairly early—like Diodorus Siculus, whom Alberti read in a Latin translation
by Poggio, the first draft of which went back to the 1430s (though the final
draft was not completed until 1449). Other texts, however, did not become
available in Latin until much later—until, in fact, humanists at the papal
curia translated them at the prompting, and with the financial support, of
Eugenius IV and Nicholas V.[49]

George of Trebizond, for example, translated Plato's *Laws* and Eusebius
in 1450 and 1451. Lorenzo Valla finished working on his Latin Thucydides
in 1452, began Herodotus in 1452, and did not complete the latter task until after Nicholas's death. Theodore Gaza made his rendering of Theophrastus in 1453–54. These texts were not easily available even in Greek before
the middle of the fifteenth century. Nicholas had to make exemplars of a
number of them available to his translators. Some of the works in question,
moreover, were immensely difficult. Valla, a more proficient Hellenist than
Alberti, complained bitterly about the notoriously difficult speeches in
Thucydides.[50] Though Alberti certainly knew Greek, he regularly worked
from translations. The intimate knowledge of Homer that he revealed in
more than one work of the period around 1440 rested on a close study, evidently carried out in Alberti's mature years, of the fourteenth-century Latin
translation of the *Iliad* by Leonzio Pilato.[51] And he showed great enthusiasm
whenever a new text reached him in the accessible Latin form with which
one of his friends had endowed it.[52]

In the 1450s, Rome—and only Rome—boasted a place where a scholar
could read the whole range of texts Alberti used, in translations commissioned by the popes. Nicholas V founded the Vatican Library as a reference

collection for all members of the papal curia, one meant to rival the ancient Alexandrian library in scale and quality. He provided a suite of rooms for the collection, which Masolino decorated with splendid frescoes. It became the model for all later libraries divided into public and reserve reading rooms.[53] The translations Nicholas commissioned, as well as the Greek originals, were placed in this collection: Lorenzo Valla deposited the manuscript of his Latin Thucydides there in 1452, to serve as a standard against which other copies could be corrected. Members of the curia in good standing (as we know from records kept a few years later) had the right to borrow books from the library, along with the chains that normally attached them to their benches—a stern reminder that the book in question was borrowed. It seems all but certain, then, that Alberti did the book-based research for On the Art of Building as a curial intellectual—and that he carried out much, if not all, of it after 1452.[54]

On the Art of Building reflects Alberti's experience in the curia—and perhaps that of the popes themselves—in another crucial respect as well. He had spent most of the 1430s in Florence. And the Florence he knew was the product of conscious design decisions that stretched back deep into the fourteenth century. From the fourteenth century on, the Florentine state had deliberately transformed itself into a theater of urban power. The Florentines had reared great buildings, like the Cathedral and the Palazzo della Signoria. They had framed them, whenever possible, according to a simple system of proportions, making them symmetrical in form, keeping their parts uniform, and maintaining their contours in simple, easily legible ratios of height to width.[55]

Aesthetics played a vital role in these decisions. Handsome streets and splendid buildings increased a city's prestige, both at home and abroad. One fourteenth-century statute directs construction of an "absolutely straight road" from one of the city's gates to give access to the goldsmiths' church, Or San Michele, "to enhance the beauty and practicality of the city of Florence." But politics mattered as well. The structures and spaces chosen for visual emphasis normally carried a particular ideological charge. As early as 1330, a statute called for the repaving of the Piazza della Signoria, "because this piazza should be more beautiful and level than any other square or street in the city." The open area in front of the beetling square fortress that embodied the power of the commune—the space where foreign monarchs and ambassadors were to receive their impressions of the city's wealth and power, and where native journeymen were to be overawed by the power of the great guildsmen who employed and exploited them—had to have the formal beauty appropriate to its high political function.[56]

Most remarkable of all, the Florentines seem to have realized, as early as the fourteenth century, what Vitruvius and Alberti stated in general terms: that the point of view from which one sees a building determines its effect. The cathedral's Operai took perspective explicitly into account as early as July 1339, when they proposed that if the Corso degli Adamari (now the Via dei Calzaiuoli) and the piazza between the Baptistery and the Cathedral were lowered, "the beauty of the aforesaid churches would be greatly enhanced, and the churches would appear considerably higher."[57] The architectural historian Marvin Trachtenberg has argued convincingly that such considerations determined the layout of the great piazzas and the buildings that dominated them. Careful consideration of the angles of vision, vertical and horizontal, that would be formed by the facade of the Cathedral, the Church of Santa Maria Novella, and the Signoria itself determined where streets were made to open into the squares where they stood. Like Giotto and other contemporary painters, the laymen who controlled the great Florentine building programs of the later Middle Ages knew about the geometry of surveying and the elements of optics. Like the painters, moreover, they had thought hard about the impressions that structures make on viewers.[58] The Florence whose urban geometry inspired Brunelleschi to create his perspective panels and that filled Alberti with high emotion on his first visit was already, in the most literal sense, an art city, before either man was born. To explore it was, almost by definition, to develop an informed eye for the straight streets, uniform facades, and deliberately chosen viewpoints that state action, though necessarily limited, had hacked through the crowded, meandering alleys of the older city.

The members of the papal curia were in a specially privileged position to understand these lessons. For they took part, in 1436, in the consecration of the Florentine Cathedral, a ritual of great splendor that concentrated the attention of all who participated in the city that served as its stage. Many of those who attended shared Alberti's interest in architecture and had schooled themselves to describe in words a variety of architectural forms and their emotional impact. One humanist—perhaps Giannozzo Manetti, perhaps Alberti's friend Lapo da Castiglionchio—who wrote a detailed account of the consecration, deployed a polished and effective Latin rhetoric to explain how the Florentines and the pope had collaborated to present it.

The writer began by describing the permanent elements of the setting. Then he examined the Cathedral itself with minute care, doing his best to read the hidden logic of its form:

> After repeated examinations, I have decided that the wonderful edifice of this sacred basilica more or less takes the shape of a human body. First of all, anyone who looks closely will see the resemblance between the form of a human body, from the chest down to the feet, and the rectangular space of our basilica, as it stretches from the doors to the end of the vault. But the rest of the space, which lies within the circumference of the vault, is clearly very close to the upper part of a human body, from the head to the chest. And to make this comparison work, put someone in the upper part of the church, orienting his body so that his head points to the east, his arms are extended in opposite directions, one to the north and one to the south, and his feet to the west. And once you have laid a human body out in this way, you will be unable to doubt that this comparison fits perfectly. If, then, the form of our church is like a human body, no one of sound mind can deny that it has been endowed with the most noble and lovely appearance possible, since it is obvious that the human body is superior to all other forms.[59]

The writer not only looked but measured and evaluated what he saw. He admired the great dimensions of the church. He appreciated the fact that its main divisions were clearly marked: how, for example, the "great columns of stone, squared off," divided it "into three naves, more or less." And he descried in Brunelleschi's dome, as seen from below, visual allusions to both the perfection of the sphere and—because it was longer than it was wide—the shape of the cross. In other words, he clearly understood the building as a text written in the languages of arithmetic, geometry, and ornament. The classical anecdotes he had stored in his own notebooks now came to his aid. Parallels abounded. As the Athenians had gloried in their arsenal, the writer urged, the Florentines could glory in their great church.[60] This commentary may shed little light on Brunelleschi's actual intentions, but it clearly formed part of the larger context within which Alberti worked.

Urban design, in fourteenth- and fifteenth-century Italy, normally did not involve the creation of whole new cities—like realized versions of Filarete's symmetrically planned utopia, Sforzinda. Rather, it called for the reconfiguration of existing buildings and the opening of dramatic, straight new roads through old neighborhoods, where lanes twisted, arcades obscured house facades, and only a meter or so of foul air separated the two sides of a street. The Florentines, as he explained, took the consecration of the Cathedral as their pretext for dramatizing a new path across their city. They had already paved with "milky and polished stones" the straight road that led from the Dominican Church of Santa Maria Novella, where the curia was lodged, to the Cathedral. Now they built a wooden causeway, raised three feet above the ground, that stretched all the way from one church to the other. Decked with every kind of fragrant leaf and adorned with the papal arms, this enormous structure provided a magnificent stage for the musicians, the magnificently dressed members of the Signoria, and the pope, clad in purple and gems, to cross the city together, as state and church militant, so that Eugenius could inaugurate the Cathedral.

By this informed account, the authorities, urban and papal, had collaborated to produce an urban spectacle that would overwhelm any onlooker, wherever he might choose to stand or walk:

> The basilica . . . was decorated with every conceivable kind of ornament, and the causeway was also built in a splendid way and endowed with decorations of every imaginable sort. Nothing was lacking to complete this extraordinary display of all the royal, imperial, pontifical, and divine wealth of our time—except to have the walls of the street covered as well with cloth hangings of various kinds and brilliant tapestries. This was done so splendidly that it seemed, to all those who saw it, to represent the absolute summit of all kinds of ornament. This was all carried out in so public and open a way, moreover, that whether onlookers walked on the causeway, or ambled along the street, or wandered through the basilica itself, they were stimulated by delights of all sorts, seeing and smelling at the same time, and were filled with many kinds of pleasure.[61]

The great spiritual event of the Cathedral's opening was accompanied and intensified by a massive assault on the senses—which continued inside the building, where the spectacular polyphonic music stunned all hearers. Contemporaries generally agreed with the writer's estimate of the effectiveness of these measures. No one who saw the magnificently robed and jeweled procession crossing the great footbridge that cut through the heart of the city, underlining the relation between the great church and the Cathedral, between the Roman curia and the Guelph citadel of Florence, ever forgot it.

Leonardo Bruni, who described these events at length in his autobiographical *Commentaries*, found them more engrossing than Brunelleschi's dome.

The lessons of all this grandeur and its effects were not lost on Eugenius IV or on the Tuscan cleric Tommaso Parentucelli, who became Nicholas V. The members of the curia returned to Rome determined to reconfigure parts of its cityscape in the same way. When Alberti—service professional and curial adviser, friend of artists, expert surveyor, engineer, and antiquary—formulated the lessons of Florentine urbanism and architecture in *On the Art of Building*, he was doing what came more or less naturally. Both popes knew that they needed exactly the sort of intellectual and aesthetic counsel that Alberti could supply.

Alberti, in other words, wrote his great book as one of the numerous scholars who thronged the Vatican and the Castel Sant'Angelo in the late 1440s and early 1450s, studying the classics, bickering, and now and then engaging in fisticuffs, or sending a pair of murderers to deal with a rival (in those days, tenure fights were really deadly). Alberti not only did his research in this particular intellectual milieu, he also addressed himself to particular intellectuals who worked there, speaking to their overriding concerns.

For example, he complained bitterly about Vitruvius' Latin style. It was so clogged with unintelligible expressions, he claimed, most of them Greek, as to have lost both its identity as Latin and its clarity as prose: "What he handed down was in any case not refined, and his speech such that the Latins might think he wanted to appear a Greek, while the Greeks would think that he babbled Latin. However, his very text is evidence that he wrote neither Latin nor Greek."[62] Alberti repeatedly emphasized the difficulty of finding proper Latin terms for technical things, and he sometimes found it necessary to coin new ones. Discussing columns, for example, he wrote:

> Words must be invented, when those in current use are inadequate; it will be best to draw them from familiar things. We Tuscans call a fillet [*nextrum*] the narrow band with which maidens bind and dress their hair; and so, if we may, let us call "fillet" the platband that encircles the ends of columns like a hoop.[63]

But he insisted nonetheless that he, unlike Vitruvius, wrote "in proper Latin, and in proper form."[64]

Earlier humanists had seen Vitruvius as a classical as well as an ancient writer: Petrarch did not see why the Roman architect had felt the need to apologize for the crudity of his prose.[65] Alberti, claiming to reach a high standard of Latinity and insisting at the same time on his right to invent new technical terms, took his stand by one of his colleagues in the curia, Lorenzo Valla, who dedicated much of his life to establishing the rules of good Latin syntax and usage on the basis of direct study of the classics. He laid down the results of his work in a massive, influential book, *The Elegancies of the Latin Language*, which he prefaced with the powerful claim that good Latin was "a great sacrament"—an outward sign of inward intellectual grace, or at least the perfect verbal embodiment of correct ideas. Like a fifteenth-century ancestor of the Viennese critic Karl Krauss, Valla insisted that close adherence to honest, accurate speech would do away with thousands of confusions and abuses—for example, the practice of applying the term *religious*, which had originally referred to all pious Christians, to members of orders alone. But he also acknowledged that innovation demanded new words. Modern technical inventions like the clock and the bell had not existed in ancient Rome. Accordingly, rather than use classicizing circumlocutions, one must devise new terms for them: *horologium* and *campana*. Having made this case at length, Valla passed on a draft version of his arguments to another curial humanist, Giovanni Tortelli, who published it in his own massive lexicon, *On Orthography*.[66] In his effort to hold a balance between purism and creativity as in his desire to display his learning, Alberti spoke the normal language of the Roman humanists he knew—the same language that he had spoken in defense of a cultivated Italian. There is every reason to take him at his word, to accept that the pleasure he felt at the fine Latinity of his book mattered deeply to him.

These facts, in turn, suggest something about the larger destination of Alberti's work. At times he insisted that he offered practical knowledge—even that he spoke "as a craftsman."[67] In fact, however, he wrote in an elaborate literary Latin, which few craftsmen could have read without help. Moreover, he saw himself as addressing, in large part, individuals who came to architecture not only from the technological milieu but from the world of learning as well. Alberti told the reader of *On the Art of Building*, "Of the arts, the ones that are useful, even vital to the architect, are painting and mathematics," and he insisted that only precise visual renderings or models could reveal the errors in an architect's first version of a project. But the architect need not be a master painter, he explained. His drawings and models should be honest, flat precise renderings of what he hoped to build, not deceptive exercises in perspective, and his skills in drawing could be quite basic. "I would not expect him to be a Zeuxis in his painting, or a Nichomachus in arithmetic, or an Archimedes in geometry," Alberti wrote. "Let it be enough that he has a grasp of those elements of painting of which we have written."[68] The reader who needed help could simply read Alberti's own textbook, *Elements of Painting*. Working from that slender foundation, he could master the art of building perfectly well.

The *Elements* is a short text, consisting of numbered propositions, originally written in Italian, without illustrations: Alberti translated it into Latin for a fellow member of the curia, Theodore Gaza, to whom he described it as a sort of Famous Artists' manual—a short book that could turn even those totally unskilled at painting into competent draftsmen.[69] The book reached a wide public—including the subtle philosopher Cardinal Nicholas of Cusa, whose copy of it survives in his famous library.[70] The juxtaposition of this text to *On the Art of Building* seems highly suggestive. Neither text was aimed at practitioners of drawing and related arts whose skills were already honed. Both, instead, were intended for educated readers: as Alberti put it in a revealing passage in *On the Art of Building*, "this book has been written not only for craftsmen but also for anyone interested in the noble arts. I shall therefore take pleasure in intermixing here some anecdotes intended to amuse."[71] Some of those whose sense of humor he hoped to tickle might be men who, like Alberti himself, undertook supervisory roles in large-scale architectural projects. Others, presumably, would belong to the large class of architectural commentators to whom Alberti referred again and again, as when he rightly pointed out that everyone, however uninformed, enjoys criticizing buildings. Still others, to judge from the early circulation of the work, were advanced patrons.

On the Art of Building grew to be a large and expensive book—so large and expensive that stationers, to produce copies of it, sometimes resorted to the traditional methods of the medieval university book world, assigning one set of pages to each scribe, who could reproduce it rapidly. Most of the early copies that survive were custom made, as luxury items, for the little group of rulers who built the first Renaissance palaces and surrounded themselves, in the *studioli* or closets that were the jewels at the heart of these huge lotuses, and that were adorned with magnificent perspective views in intarsia of cities, landscapes, other books, and scientific instruments. Federigo da Montefeltro, for example, had a copy specially illuminated for his library. Lorenzo de' Medici, some decades later, found the prospect of obtaining a copy of the first printed edition of the text, which appeared in 1486, so exhilarating that he read it gathering by gathering, as it came from the press, rather than waiting for the whole book to be sewn together and bound. Alberti's intention in writing the book was, at least in part, the same one that inspired Machiavelli to produce another masterly Renaissance treatment of an art, *The Prince*: he wanted employment as an architectural adviser, and he used his physically splendid, stylistically impeccable book as proof of his competence.[72]

To sum up: *On the Art of Building* took many years to compile. It contained materials and reflected influences not only from Alberti's early years in northern Italy, Florence, and Ferrara, but also from the Roman milieu of the 1440s and 1450s. And it addressed not professional builders so much as the rulers, clerics, and intellectuals who hoped to direct their work. One inference at least seems legitimate. Any notion that Alberti produced his work in a single impulse, or to argue for a single program, is unlikely to hold much water.

On the Art of Building is not one book but a whole series of them—some of them so much in tension with the rest that the strain is almost palpable. Yet as the canonical text about classical architecture, its elaborate, coherent treatment of building forms and parts proved so useful to generations of architects and builders that they would go on updating it until the eighteenth century. Imposing order on and glossing the apparent incoherences of Vitruvius, Alberti established the classical style as the ideal and explained in detail what that meant. For all the adaptations they made in practice, architects for generations would judge their work against his insistence that good structures reveal their qualities in the classical forms that expressed their purposes and in the simple ratios of length to width and height that gave them harmony.

Alberti plunged his reader into an imagined classical world, a city of porticoes, triumphal arches, temples, and theaters, of streets lined by facades of uniform height and style and squares with colonnades where old men could take counsel and nurses could oversee playing children. He gave clear instructions on how to distinguish Doric from Ionic columns and temples from basilicas—instructions without which almost no one had been in a position to read either Vitruvius or surviving ancient buildings. He identified the

central quality of a good building as *concinnitas*: the possession of such harmonious and mutually complementary parts that nothing could be added to
or removed from it without spoiling the whole.[73] Unlike Vitruvius, whose
work moved from subject to subject as experience suggested, he organized
his work to show how every aspect of building, from the large scale of the
city as a whole to the small one of the individual room, should follow from
the same principles. And he made clear that an ideal city would be one for
which a single ruler and a single designer chose the site, laid out the plan of
streets, and assigned the proper spaces and positions to every structure from
the prince's palace to the sewers—to both of which Alberti devoted considerable attention. He suggested—though he did not insist on the point—that
this city would institute residential segregation, assigning practitioners of
each craft and members of each social group to a particular neighborhood.
And he envisioned private residences in which public and private, male and
female, spaces were to be strictly divided by their assigned functions and
users—a form of residence that gradually materialized, in Rome and elsewhere, over the next two or three generations.[74] Readers react to this set of
ideals in different ways, depending on the assumptions they bring with
them, but no one denies the power of Alberti's Neoclassical vision—a vision
still capable of inspiring builders and patrons in the age of Winckelmann
and Jefferson.

Yet large sections of Alberti's work do not reflect, in either content or
style, the classical ideology with which he is so often identified. Like Vitruvius, and often in more detail, he discussed many questions from the realms
of natural philosophy, botany, and geology. What unifies these discussions—
so far as anything does—is Alberti's insistence that buildings should reshape
those who inhabit them. Good houses, he argues in his *prologus*, have saved
"honorable families" in Florence and elsewhere. Buildings should work not
only as hydraulic devices, engineered to throw off rainwater and release
sewage, but also as therapeutic machines, designed to promote good health.
The rooms set apart for counsel chambers at the center of a palace should
preserve the energy of the *seniores* who meet there. Cloisters should give
light and air to the solitary monks and nuns who pray in them, hospitals to
the sick, farms to their animals. The pleasant gardens, walks, and porticoes
of country villas promote good health in the entire family; the paintings on
the bedroom walls of city palaces can help women who sleep with their hus-
bands to bear handsome children and invalids to recover from their fevers.[75]
"By their fruits shall ye know them": the test of a building, Alberti indicated

over and over again, lay not only in the style of its decorations but above all in its impact on those who see or live in it. Even beauty, Alberti admitted, depended on effect. *Concinnitas*, like health and eugenics, was in the eye of the beholder.

These two notions of architecture—the purist and the therapeutic— were necessarily in tension with each other. On the one hand, Alberti praised the unique qualities of a particular style; on the other, he insisted on the absolute importance of context, of each structure's function and situation. To hold these two sets of requirements in balance, he invoked for architecture, as he had for painting, an intellectual model: the sister arts of rhetoric and poetics. Like the painter, Alberti explained, the architect played a basically intellectual role. His job was conceptual, not practical (in fact, Alberti recommended that the architect avoid taking sole responsibility for the construction of his projects, lest he incur all the blame for errors and delays). And its essence lay in adapting principles to situations.

Like the writer, the architect must collaborate with his critics, showing his sketches and models to as many of them as possible and correcting his errors on the small scale of design rather than on the enormous—and expensive—scale of the full building. Like the writer, the architect must master an elaborate hermeneutics (a subject to which Alberti regularly returned). Reading the site involved a vast range of skills. The architect must learn how to interpret the earth itself, to ensure that it will hold the foundations of his project. (Alberti mentioned a "certain Spaniard" who reputedly had such "power of eyes and understanding" that he could see the veins that carried underground water as clearly as aboveground streams.)[76] When building a bridge, the architect must scrutinize the flow of water in order to place the abutments in areas where it is relatively calm and where obstructions will not pile up. When digging a well, he must recognize the "clues" that indicate the presence of hidden water. When building a villa, he must read the climate of the locality. And when repairing an existing building, he must interpret the cracks that indicate damage and their causes.

A building's physical setting matters so much, Alberti explained, not only because it underpins the structure's solidity and the well-being of its occupants but also because it largely determines the building's effect. The architect, Alberti explained, must lay out every structure so as to best enhance the impression it makes. By placing palaces and temples on high, separate sites, the architect gives them *dignitas*. By doing the same for country villas, he ensures that they will afford their dwellers healthy views of mountains, hills, and gardens, of "meadows full of flowers, sunny lawns, cool and shady groves, limpid springs, streams and pools."[77] But he also ensures that they will affect their visitors in the proper way:

> A place close to a town, with clear roads and pleasant surroundings, will be popular. A building here will be most attractive, if it presents a cheerful overall appearance to anyone leaving the city, as if to attract and expect visitors. I would therefore make it slightly elevated, and I would make the road leading up to it rise so gently that visitors do not realize how high they have climbed until they have a view over the countryside.[78]

Roads should be built on raised causeways, so that they impress and divert travelers by affording them a changing spectacle.[79] The very last paragraph of the book reiterates the importance of perspective for enhancing or diminishing a building's effect.[80] And effect, for Alberti, serves as the ultimate test of a building's quality: "so that anyone who saw it would imagine that he could never be satiated by the view, but looking at it again and again in admiration, would glance back once more as he departed." The slack-jawed gawk of onlookers unable to find a single flaw in a building, like the breathless hush of listeners unable to find a weak point or dull passage in a speech, confirms the mastery of the creator.

In order to achieve these effects, the architect—like the writer—must constantly bear in mind more than the physical setting in which he builds. He must also understand the social functions of the building and its occupant and adapt the work to fit them in its scale, its style, and its decoration. In architecture as in painting, Alberti stressed the vital role of decorum: "The greatest glory in the art of building," he explained, "is to have a good sense of what is appropriate."[81] The architect must apply this sense constantly: when choosing the proper site for a forum, a theater, a gymnasium, or a temple; when deciding whether a ruler is a king, whose palace should adjoin the city's other buildings, or a tyrant, whose palace should remain grimly separate; when choosing the proper scale for the house of a ruler or a private person; when selecting the subject matter for the images in a church or allotting the parts of a building to their seasonal and social functions.

Decorum determined the proper scale of a project as a whole. Alberti disapproved of the enormous tomb that the courtesan Rhodope of Thrace built for herself, since her calling did not merit so great a monument. But he refused to criticize the equally lavish one built by the brave queen Artemisia for her husband, since her social position made it legitimate.[82] And the same literary economy should govern the details of the design process. Alberti invoked a passage from Horace's *Art of Poetry*—a work familiar to all scholars and many artisans—in order to emphasize the importance of making every part of a building fit the position in which the architect set it:

> When even the smallest parts of a building are set in their proper place, they add charm; but when positioned somewhere strange, ignoble, or inappropriate, they will be devalued if elegant, ruined if they are anything else. Look at Nature's own works: for if a puppy had an ass's ear on its forehead, or if someone had one huge foot, or one hand vast and the other tiny, he would look deformed.

And he invoked the rules of oratory to define the architect's task as one bound in countless complex ways to the immediate situation in which he worked:

> He must ponder the nature of his task, what skills he might offer, and what impression he would like to give: he must calculate the size of the project and the amount of praise, remuneration, thanks, and even fame he will achieve, or conversely if he embarks on something without sufficient experience, prudence, or consideration, what contempt and hatred he will receive, and how eloquent, how obvious, patent and lasting a testimony of his folly he will leave his fellow men.[83]

The computation of probabilities replaces the generation of absolute ratios; in architecture as in other human affairs, the choice of any given element depends on its situation and its emotional effect on others.

Alberti's principle of decorum enabled him to make both his classicism and his situationism flexible. He often praised frugality and declared—as he put it once, echoing Horace again—*Odi sumptuositatem,* "I hate excessive luxury." But he also celebrated the appropriate magnificence of ancient structures like his beloved Pantheon. He saw no reason why temples and triumphal arches should lack magnificent decorations, as long as they served their proper functions of teaching philosophy and celebrating heroism. The principle of decorum ensured that the architect would not employ luxurious materials in excessive amounts or for inappropriate objects. Similarly, Alberti's recognition that a building's situation included not only its natural setting but also its existing built environment radically modified his insistence on placing every structure in an ideal setting. Destroying older buildings to make space for a new one would alienate their owners, he recognized, perhaps unnecessarily. Moreover, a building must often be designed to mitigate the unfortunate qualities of its immediate environment. Alberti's principles, in other words, included a basic deference to audience response that radically moderated their severity and uniformity. His large book, which took so long to write and incorporated such diverse experiences, offered readers not only aesthetic principles of presumably universal validity but also highly context-contingent ways of accommodating these principles to the endless variety of real life.[84]

Alberti's work incorporated the results of many years of thought on his part about the issues that he treated. It did not simply repeat the lessons of a single authoritative text, or base itself on a single body of urban architecture. Even the massive heritage of town planning in Tuscany, which Alberti knew so well from his time in Florence, provided only general inspiration rather than specific tenets. Traditionally the Florentine government saw long streets, straight as a rope stretched between two points, leading the walker to a distant, spectacular landmark, as ideal. Alberti, by contrast, preferred winding ones that gave the walker partial views that flickered and changed until he reached the unexpected, dramatic point from which he could see the whole.[85]

Often, moreover, Alberti wrote more as a prophet than as an observer. The early fifteenth century saw the political authority of the two states that mattered most to him—Rome and Florence—greatly expanded. The great cities began to develop civilized hinterlands, estate country where cardinals and merchants could escape the city's heat, noise, and violence and provide for the needs of their artificial or biological families. This sort of villa life had only just begun to develop in the 1450s.[86] Nonetheless, Alberti gradually developed the belief that every city household needed a country seat. Drawing on Pliny and his own aesthetics, he laid out what became the classic ideal form of the modern villa: the country house, devoid of fortification and surrounded by gardens, placed high to attract the eyes of visitors and please those of residents. When, after his death, Rome and Florence became centers of villa and garden culture, the patrician exurbanites were putting into practice principles that Alberti had devised decades before. The walker in the city was also the prophet of the garden suburb. Alberti put many theses forward implicitly, in the form of examples, which his reader could judge—and, in judging, form his own taste. He could do so—and argue for holding what seemed like contradictions in a fruitful tension—since he addressed himself, in his stately, universal Latin, to an imagined posterity as well as to his contemporary patrons.[87]

As a service professional, Alberti offered brilliant words that proved immensely fruitful among later practicing architects, from Francesco di Giorgio and Filarete down to Palladio and Serlio. They seized upon the genre that Alberti had revived and made their own tremendously important additions to it. And they transformed the genre as they did so, adding detailed practical information and minute, superb illustrations as Alberti had not. In architecture, as in painting, Alberti created an intellectual institution—but one that reached its highest development after his death, and that really took shape only when his work and that of Vitruvius paradoxically reached print together.[88]

Interpretations of Alberti's principles, accordingly, will probably always differ widely in both substance and emphasis. But one set of interpretations seems especially significant: the material one crafted by Alberti himself, in the form of the several buildings that he helped to create between 1450 and his death. He could indeed design buildings, repairing or reusing existing structures and rearing new ones from the ground up. The author of the controversial treatise On the Art of Building also practiced what he preached— or tried to. We now turn from Alberti's most sharply contested book to the even more controversial realm of his sermons in stone.

IX

THE ARCHITECT AND

CITY PLANNER

One of the very last texts that Alberti wrote, a letter of 1470 to Ludovico Gonzaga, the ruler of the northern Italian city of Mantua, resounds with the voice of the practiced designer-entrepreneur-builder. Alberti appealed as deftly to economics as to aesthetics as he pushed for his own design for the Church of Sant'Andrea:

> Now I have recently learned that your highness and your citizens were considering a project here at St. Andrea, and that the central intention was to have a large space that could enable many people to see the blood of Christ. I saw that model of Manetti's. I liked it, but it doesn't seem to me to fit your intentions. I thought about it and worked out what I am sending you. This will be more capacious, more durable, more worthy, more happy: and it will cost a great deal less. The ancients called this sort of temple an Etruscan shrine.[1]

This letter, with its dizzying economy of argument and its proud appeal to an ancient model that Alberti himself had reconstructed, reveals him, as an old

24. Alberti. Facade. Sant'Andrea, Mantua. Alinari/Art Resource, NY.

man, still working: submitting plans to a patron who had employed him for over a decade and proposing to realize high aesthetic values at a satisfyingly low price. The student of ancient architecture, Greek, Roman, and Etruscan, still hoped to find new practical uses for his theories about the past.

The letter leaves no room for doubt: Alberti saw himself as a practicing architect—and one whose expertise extended to details of construction technique. Archival documents and early reports identify some of the specific buildings that he designed, or helped to design: the Church of San Francesco in Rimini; the Rucellai Palace, Santa Maria Novella, the shrine of the Holy Sepulchre in San Pancrazio, and the tribune of Santissima Annunziata in Florence; San Sebastiano and Sant'Andrea in Mantua. Contemporary and later observers have connected him with other projects as well, such as Nicholas V's largely unrealized design for the rebuilding of the Vatican complex and the Borgo in Rome. Many scholars believe that he played a role—often a major one—in the design of Pius II's ideal city Pienza, though no documents tie him to the project.[2] To be sure, controversy blooms about this central sphere of Alberti's activity: serious students of Renaissance architecture have denied that he had much of a hand even in the churches attributed to him by contemporary documents, like San Francesco in Rimini.[3] But most still identify him not only as the influential author of *On the Art of Building* but also as the active creator of a radically new style, classical in inspiration, that gradually transformed large sections of Italy's cities for the next century and more.[4] Little is simple in the life and work of this theorist of classical simplicity—even in the area of his greatest fame.

Alberti, as we have already seen, was at work on *On the Art of Building* by the late 1440s. He did basic research for it in Rome, where he examined ancient and medieval buildings and scoured the texts that had recently become available, thanks to the patronage of Eugenius IV and Nicholas V, in the Vatican's matchless collection as well as outside it. For around a century, most scholars believed that Alberti undertook this immense theoretical project in tandem with a practical career, and that both took off in the same Roman environment, in the same period. As Georg Dehio, a pioneering historian of Renaissance art—and one not afraid of venturing bold theses— pointed out more than a century ago, Nicholas V, who became pope in 1447, not only assembled gifted scholars and collected books but also rebuilt—or wanted to rebuild—the city of Rome itself.[5] Money came from the influx of pilgrims who arrived in Rome to celebrate the Jubilee of 1450; ambitious plans soon followed. The Florentine humanist Giannozzo Manetti, in his biography of Nicholas, described in detail how the pope had "constructed many great edifices" both in Rome and elsewhere. The church and the city, Nicholas reasoned, needed defense from the attacks of outside powers like Naples, which continually threatened Rome, and from the terrifying civil disturbances that had forced his predecessor to flee the city in a small boat, pursued by showers of stones. The church, however, also needed the symbolic majesty and reinforcement to devotion that focused architectural works could provide. Accordingly, Nicholas rebuilt the city's walls, restored the forty "stational" churches that pilgrims traditionally visited to obtain indulgences, and moved the curia from the Lateran, where the popes had traditionally based themselves, to the Vatican, across the Tiber from the core of Rome. This region of the city had prospered in the fourteenth century, but fell on evil times in the fifteenth. Even in the vicinity of St. Peter's, little business took place. There Nicholas "founded"—so Manetti claimed, in the heightened language of panegyric—"a new quarter," which he fortified, building a papal palace that was both defensible and spectacular. Finally, he planned to rebuild the Basilica of St. Peter itself.[6]

In the Borgo, Manetti wrote, Nicholas planned to create nothing less than a magnificent new urban complex, one that stretched from the Castel Sant'Angelo to St. Peter's. Like Bridget of Sweden, the mystic whose visions of Rome as holy city seem to have impressed Nicholas deeply, he imagined a small but splendid ideal city materializing within the sprawling, largely ruinous real one. Drawing on the Tuscan models of town planning that he had known since his youth, the pope decided to build an ordered public space. Three stately streets were to connect two great piazzas, one of them at the north and one at the south end of the district. Systematic occupational segregation would give each street a character and a social level. Nicholas planned to locate the nobler businesses, those of the bankers and cloth merchants, along the central street. On one of the side streets, in more or less identical houses, the middling artisans would ply their crafts; in the other, the lesser ones. Architectural uniformity would ensure that the whole picture of the city never fell into disorder. The shops would be uniformly located in the ground floors, with living space above them. Six colonnades, one on each side of each street, would both adorn the area and protect passersby from rain and sun, while allowing light into the shops and domiciles of the residents. In the center of the piazza before the new St. Peter's, a colossal sculptural complex would celebrate the role of the church as a new Solomon's Temple. The obelisk that had stood throughout the Middle Ages by the Vatican, resting on bronze statues of the four evangelists, would dramatize the main entrance of the Basilica of St. Peter.[7]

Heading this whole enterprise, governing the supervisors that Nicholas appointed, stood the great architect Bernardo Rossellino, who accepted a summons to the papal court in 1451 and appears in the documents as Nicholas's chief builder. Nicholine Rome failed to reach completion, as one disaster followed another. Nicholas managed to realize only a fragment of what he planned. Yet he did deliver an impassioned speech before he died, in which he explained his policy to the cardinals. After first defending the vast sums he had spent on architecture, he then evoked the larger vision that had inspired him. These expensive works, the pope argued, were more than an expression of his own desire for "pomp and empty glory." Rather, great buildings sustained public piety. They offered those who could not read, and therefore could not use books to learn about the origins and history of the Roman Church, "something like perpetual monuments, and almost eternal testimonies, made, so to speak, by God himself"—unshakable evidence that would conserve and enhance their devotion. At the same time, the fortifications he had reared were needed to protect the church "against the foreign enemies and local rebels who continually conspire, hoping to destroy, and rising, in a way that causes serious damage, against the authority of the church."[8] The pope had expected his ideal city to buttress the faith in the literal as well as the spiritual sense.

Alberti, as Dehio noted, worked as a curial official under Nicholas. His book on architecture called for city planning on a grand scale and of a systematic kind. Accordingly, Dehio inferred that Alberti served as Nicholas's architectural and urbanistic consultant. Had Nicholine Rome been completed, it would have amounted to the first great modern experiment in urban planning. Even with only a fragment completed, however, it became the prototype for later popes' efforts to rebuild the ceremonial parts of Rome. And Alberti's own work *On the Art of Building*, which took shape in the midst of these eminently practical efforts, was not only a great systematic treatise but a manual of practical urbanistics.

In the century and more since Dehio wrote, the study of Nicholas's Rome has become a scholarly cottage industry. Recent research has added so many lines and shadows to the picture of Rome's cityscape at midcentury that Dehio himself would scarcely recognize it. True, fifteenth-century Rome recovered from the misery and disorder through which it had suffered during the hard period of papal residence in Avignon, from 1309 to 1377, and the papacy's subsequent battle to reestablish a permanent presence in Rome. From the pontificate of Martin V onward, the curia's more and more sustained residence in Rome stimulated economic growth and intellectual activity. Educated visitors were appalled, as they had been for centuries, by the state of the city: "The hilly part is empty of inhabitants," wrote Pier Paolo Vergerio, "only the plane and the part adjacent to the river is inhabited. There weak new houses rest on the great foundations left by the ancient ones that have collapsed." The population expanded, very gradually, from a low in the twenty thousands. Urban order, as understood by the papacy, was restored only haltingly. The level of crime continued to be high, great noble families still warred on one another, and raids by feudal barons, rapes of women, sackings of houses, and burnings of family vineyards remained common.[9] Every papal initiative, moreover, met with resistance from the neighborhoods and churches that benefited from ancient privileges; their messy, ardent commercial life was as hard to stamp out as weeds, and just as vital.

The Jubilee of 1450, which brought enough pilgrims into the city and enough money into papal coffers to make the papacy debt free, marked a turning point, albeit one of many. Nicholas clearly played a central role in this long, collaborative drama, through which Rome regained its traditional place in Western Christianity, as the goal of pilgrimages and stage for religious celebrations, and the papacy gained a new control over the city. When his biographers emphasized the apocalyptically radical character of his plans, comparing him to the sun, they expressed something of Nicholas's sense of himself: as a martyr pope, one of a succession of such martyrs, who was reestablishing the eternal order of things when he hunted down the radical Fraticelli.[10] But the city's extended, complex process of recovery would not culminate until much later, in the very different ages of Sixtus V, Urban VIII, and Alexander VII. Nicholas, like most of his successors, achieved far less on his own than historians have sometimes imagined.[11]

As a Tuscan, born in Pisa, Nicholas knew how the governments of Florence and Siena had shaped squares and situated buildings into dynamic hieroglyphs of piety, wealth, and public order. His predecessor, Eugenius IV, had already invested in architectural and artistic projects. And many members of the curia had witnessed the opening of the Florentine Cathedral, with its intense celebration of the city's sacred and political spaces. In the middle decades of the fifteenth century, Roman humanists and artists came to see their city too in a new light: not as a rubble-strewn shadow of its former self, a melancholy, barren garden sown with broken columns, but as a coherent, organic, living city, one that already had working traffic arteries and nodes of rapid growth and needed more of both.[12]

These ideas had dramatic material and institutional consequences. On 31 March 1425, papal authority renewed the powers of the "masters of the streets" (magistri viarum), the magistrates responsible for keeping the city's streets open and ensuring that the facades of houses reached a minimum height.[13] They faced formidable challenges. The bull with which Martin V set them to work spoke eloquently of the city's ruinous condition. But the pope—himself a Colonna and hence a member of one of the city's ancient ruling families—faced up to the challenge of reviving Rome's commercial life as well as reestablishing papal authority. He used his intimate knowledge of the city to appoint, as masters of the streets, "noble men" who had carried out important public duties in the recent past. He charged them, revealingly, with the duty of restraining the "butchers, fishmongers, tailors, skinners, and other craftsmen who inhabit different places and workshops in the city, and practice their crafts there: they make a habit of throwing and concealing viscera, tripes, heads, feet, bones, blood, as well as skin and rotten meat and fish in the roads, streets, piazzas and other public and private places."[14] This comprehensive, legalistic directive, as schematic as any statute, nonetheless vividly evokes the soft objects that crunched under the feet and appalled the nostrils of Roman visitors, not only in the 1420s but for decades to come. Rome, the city of symbols, spoke of more than the ancient glory of empire and the primitive piety of the early church. A forest of street signs decorated with the heads of eagles and lions, advertising pens and ink, aids to prayer, and other goods, obscured house fronts. The open, individual porticoes that projected outward into dozens of Roman streets—many of which were no more than a meter or two wide—badly impeded the circulation of traffic and called the attention of visitors, embarrassingly, to the city's messy, unattractive complexion.[15] As late as 1475, when Ferrante of Aragon visited Rome, he pointed out to Sixtus IV that he could not claim to be master of the city so long as its streets were blocked by porticoes or so narrow as to be impassible.[16] And an ancient tangle of traditional rights protected businesses and landlords who saw their own activities as vital to Rome's lively, neighborhood-based life—and resisted fiercely when higher authorities tried to clear them away in order to realize new ideals of order, austerity, and cleanliness. The merchants who earned their livings the hard way, selling fish at the tables that flanked the columns of the Pantheon or flogging holy articles to exhausted tourists outside St. Peter's, were not amused by efforts to empty their working spaces in order to give better visual access to Rome's monuments.[17]

Despite immense practical difficulties, papal government reasserted itself, in corners of the city's built space as well as in its society. The pope was in no position to rebuild the city as a whole, but he would mark strategically chosen places with his symbolic presence. Nicholas rebuilt the ramshackle municipal complex on the Capitoline Hill, adding impressive windows to the Palace of the Senator and placing on its corners towers that soared massively over the ruins of the Forum, even though only one of them reached completion. The papal arms embossed visibly on the towers identified them as his work and as an expression of the papacy's new power and authority. Almost as impressive was the Palace of the Conservators, which Nicholas built on the same piazza, at an angle to the Palace of the Senator. This complex—which found imitation in a number of other cities—powerfully asserted the pope's role in urban government.[18] By 1462, when Pius II renewed the authority of the *magistri viarum*, the new bull was not only cried through the city but also affixed "to the gates of the Capitoline," so that no one could claim unawareness of its provisions.

Papal power had spread outside the Lateran palace, where medieval popes had resided. In Trastevere a rebuilt Castel Sant'Angelo, surmounted by a sculpted angel, and fortified gates at the end of the Ponte di Adriano (which connected the ancient city center to the new papal Rome) prominently defended the entrance to the papacy's new home in the Vatican.[19] A splendid papal apartment in the castle afforded both a refuge in time of siege and a spectacular vantage point from which to view—and show off—the city.[20] Most of the city, to be sure, remained empty. Pigs and sheep still roamed the Forum, as they would until the twentieth century, and only a scattering of gardens and summer houses occupied the hills. Inhabited areas retained much of their traditional disorder, providing until long after Alberti's time a stage for a streetcorner society in which conversation never ceased and crime was poorly controlled.[21] Local opposition to papal efforts, formal and informal, gathered strength after the death of Martin, last of the Roman popes. But in the more thickly settled ancient center and in the Borgo, as in Florence, a network of impressive buildings and improved roads and bridges traced the outlines, dimly visible even to the hopeful eyes of Nicholas and his cronies, of a new urban system of symbols—one that already made it possible to stage more impressive processions and that would prove of special importance when popes died, foreign rulers visited, or masses of pilgrims arrived. Nicholas's plans extrapolated the city's grand future not implausibly from this promising present. At key moments—like 1452, when the Holy Roman Emperor Frederick III appeared in Rome to be crowned—the pope seemed the master of affairs. When Frederick was halted outside the city, to view the spectacle of Rome from the best vantage point, the pope did not emerge from the Vatican to greet him. The emperor could only admit that nowadays the pope had more power than he, and play along. In the city, impressed by the splendor of the procession that greeted him, he inclined his head to the cardinals and doffed his hat and embraced the senator, the official sent out to meet his party—clear signs of the respect that the city's fitfully present grandeur could now evoke.[22]

Yet these changes were not so uniform, so grandiose, or so successful as the flamboyant rhetoric of Nicholas's biographers suggested.[23] Urban historians have subjected his policy to a detailed critical examination, scrutinizing the scattered and often inconclusive archival documents that survive in the hope of determining whether Nicholas was actually involved in the major projects of his period, and if so to what extent. They have argued convincingly that the pope's projects—and the meaning that he and others read into them—changed over time. And they have shown that he did not personally initiate all the projects once attributed to him. The Florentine banking and mercantile community in the quarters of Ponti and Parione, situated in the bend of the Tiber across from the Castel Sant'Angelo, planned and carried out some fairly dramatic urban renewal—very likely with Nicholas's support and perhaps with subventions. Collaborations—labile, slow-paced interventions in the urban fabric—were more common than radical individualistic enterprises.

Nicholas's own projects, moreover, have emerged from close scrutiny as less radical than the rhetorical tradition suggests. He had studied the city's tightly woven social and political textures, and when he tried to change them, he did so for specific reasons. When he created the first Trevi fountain—a modest, square basin with outlets and a commemorative inscription—providing fresh spring water from the Aqua Virgo to residents and restoring one of the ancient functions of Roman government, he demonstrated papal benevolence.[24] At the same time, he made symbolic gestures of another kind. The Castel Sant'Angelo and its crowning statue became charged with a new, threatening meaning in 1453, when Nicholas hanged the rebellious Roman who challenged him, Stefano Porcari, from its battlements.[25] He seems to have tried to achieve a rapprochement with the

Colonna family, allotting property that had belonged to the Porcari conspirators to Angelo Colonna, brother of Cardinal Prospero.[26] Even his plans for the Vatican and its surroundings not amount to a complete transformation of the city. Roman streets and districts were already segregated to some extent by wealth and occupation as well as by family loyalty. The uniform workers' houses and long, splendid porticoes that he planned to build represented an effort to regularize and improve on normal Roman building practices, not to replace them: to preserve the combination of shops and living spaces and open fronts that characterized the Roman streetscape, while opening rooms to sunlight and enabling traffic to move. The whole project can be seen as a rational response to the disastrous economic situation of the Borgo as well as to the political weakness of the papacy's position, both of which became manifest in 1453.[27]

The extent and nature of Alberti's role in Nicholas's activity have become equally controversial. Strong circumstantial evidence suggests that he took an active part in the projects. He expressed a passionate interest in the provision of water, for example, in both *Mathematical Games* and *On the Art of Building*.[28] These works offer powerful indirect support for the sixteenth-century report that he served as an adviser for the Trevi fountain project.[29] Alberti's long-term fascination with the Ponte Sant'Angelo is even better established. In a note that he entered, characteristically, in his copy of Cicero's dialogue *On Old Age* and other works (now preserved in Venice), he recorded a terrible event of the Jubilee year of 1450.[30] On Saturday, 18 December, toward sunset, as pilgrims tried to enter and leave the Borgo on the bridge, the crowding became so extreme that almost two hundred were crushed to death, while another hundred or so, pushed into the river, either drowned or died of the wounds they sustained. "The number of those killed was too great to be believed," Alberti noted: "boys, mature men, and old men, mature women, girls, the noble and the plebeian, people of every age, sex and condition died. An event worthy of being remembered."[31] He carried out elaborate surveys of the bridge's structure and foundations, which he described at length in *On the Art of Building*. He called it "the sturdiest of all the works of man," deplored the fact that only "its carcass"—by which he meant the piles and span—survived, and recalled that it had once had a beamed roof.[32] Giorgio Vasari, never prodigal with praise of Alberti, remarked that

he could demonstrate his ideas quite well with his drawings, as can be seen in some sheets in his hand included in our book; in these sheets are the plans for the Sant'Angelo bridge and the covering, which he designed like a loggia to protect it from the sun in the summers and from the rains and the winds in the winters. This he was commissioned to do by Pope Nicholas V, who had intended to build many similar projects throughout Rome before death interrupted his plans.[33]

There seems every reason to conjecture, then, that Alberti played some role in plans for the rebuilding of the bridge and the area around it—whether he was commissioned to do so by Nicholas, by the Florentine merchant and investor Tommaso Spinelli (with whom he shared a lawyer), or by both.[34]

The most famous relevant document, however, is equivocal. A passage in the chronicle of the Pisan writer Mattia Palmieri connects Alberti with Nicholas, in a way that suggests that his advice played a role in the pope's thinking—but not necessarily a positive one:

> The pope, having undertaken to surround first the Vatican Hill and then the papal palace with a strong wall all the way to the Tiber and the Mole of Hadrian, so that he might keep his people safe inside it, completed the bulk of this work.
>
> The pope, wanting to make the Basilica of Saint Peter more splendid, laid deep foundations and erected a wall of thirteen *braccia* (roughly ten meters). But he stopped this great work, which is comparable to that of any of the ancients, on the advice of Leon Battista, and then an untimely death cut short this enterprise.
>
> Leon Battisa Alberti, a scholar endowed with a sharp and penetrating intelligence and adorned with learning and the arts, showed the pope the learned books on architecture, which he had written.[35]

This short text, probably written from memory and certainly set down many years after the events, has proved fertile ground for hypotheses. Ludwig von Pastor, the learned and prolific historian of the papacy, saw it as the piece that had been missing from Dehio's jigsaw puzzle, arguing that Alberti's *On the Art of Building*—which Nicholas read immediately on receiving it in 1452—inspired the pope's grand design. Carroll William Westfall, who wrote a pioneering and still indispensable study of fifteenth-century Rome, agreed that Alberti had advised Nicholas. But he also noted that Alberti had been in Rome for some years before 1452, which made it unlikely that Nicholas did not know his work before he read the finished *On the Art of Building*. Most probably, Westfall argued, Nicholas had devised his building program when he took his throne in 1447, and Alberti provided designs that others altered and executed—even though the pope and his biographers, who did not grasp Alberti's notion that architects were creative thinkers, gave him no credit in public for doing so.[36] More recently, the late Manfredo Tafuri, a brilliant, encyclopedically erudite student of the whole millennial history of Italian architecture, took Palmieri's text as the springboard for a counterargument. Tafuri followed Eugenio Garin in underlining the dark side of Alberti's thought, his tendency to mockery and satire. He found in Palmieri and elsewhere reason to suspect that Alberti was an outsider in Nicholas's curia and an opponent of Nicholas's plans for the city.

As Tafuri developed this thesis, he brought off a feat highly unusual in any branch of scholarship. He rethought Alberti's role in midcentury Rome from the foundations, looking again at all the documents, many of which no architectural historian had previously taken into account. Citing the passages in *On the Art of Building* in which Alberti criticized colossal statues and other grandiose projects, Tafuri argued that he could not have devised—or even approved of—Nicholas's project for the Borgo and St. Peter's Basilica. And that, Tafuri insisted, explains why Alberti had first advised the pope against rebuilding St. Peter's and then shown him his book. He was trying to educate the pope in his own aesthetics of austerity; and he hoped not just to prevent particular errors of taste but to explicate the principles a patron should follow.[37]

More provocatively still, Tafuri argued that two of Alberti's works show his active opposition to Nicholas's rule over the city. Traditionally, historians of fifteenth-century Rome have treated the pontificate of Nicholas as a silver if not a golden age in literature and the arts. His lavish patronage made possible, as we have seen, the translation of an impressive series of Greek texts, most of which had been unknown in the Latin West through the Middle Ages, and the founding of the great collection of secular and scientific literature that became the Vatican Library. *Literati* competed to praise his beneficence and learning. The book dealer Vespasiano da Bisticci, whose gossipy, detailed lives of his customers and authors rest on detailed personal knowledge, emphasized his learning and piety. Nicholas, according to Vespasiano, did more than build up the largest library since the fall of the ancient one in Alexandria. He also carefully read and annotated in his own hand the works translated for him—like Traversari's elegant new version of the works of pseudo-Dionysius the Areopagite, which, Nicholas said, was clearer, even though it came without any commentary at all, than the medieval versions, with their thick coating of glosses.[38] Nicholas, accordingly, has often received the bulk of the credit for the larger cultural revival in which Alberti took part.

Tafuri and other historians have now floodlighted the other side of the medal. Nicholas's predecessor, Eugenius IV, already supported innovative scholars like Alberti's friend Flavio Biondo and George of Trebizond, both of whom actually fell into disfavor under Nicholas. Alberti, too, Tafuri insisted, found himself a curial outsider in the period when Dehio had placed him at Nicholas's side.[39] Two major literary works that Alberti wrote in the 1440s and early 1450s—his *Momus*, a long, wildly imaginative satire, and his *On Porcari's Conspiracy*, a short, dramatic, but fact-based account of Stefano Porcari's plot to reestablish freedom in Rome—both reveal, according to Tafuri, the author's smoldering discontent.

The *Momus*—a rich, dark allegory about the Olympian gods, written in the 1440s—borrows both its general approach and many of its characters from Lucian, a favorite of Alberti's. It tells at length the story of Momus, "the god of mockery who by turns plays the role of disaffected outcast and dissimulating courtier."[40] Disgusted by the sycophancy of the other gods, Momus plans to overthrow Jupiter but fails and is expelled from heaven. On earth, Momus succeeds in convincing humans to cease making offerings to the gods and rapes the goddess Praise, producing a monstrous offspring, Fama ("Rumor"). Propitiated and recalled to heaven, he gives a brilliant, characteristically Albertian speech at a banquet, denouncing philosophers and praising beggars. When he proposes to Jupiter that he rebuild the universe, the king of the gods accepts his advice, against the advice of Hercules and Juno. Momus suffers further indignities: eventually he is castrated by the Olympian goddesses and chained to a cliff over the sea. The human race tries to appease the gods by building great temples for them and depicting them with statues. They celebrate the new building with a magnificent set of rituals, described in detail and with relish by Alberti: "the ranks of citizens and then flocks of matrons and young women purify the city. Torches are brought, and the dark night made bright. Virgins, standing in the colonnades, adorn the city, and venerate the gods with poems, songs and choral dances."[41] The gods, attracted by the humans' ceremonies, come down to earth. In the great new theater they take the places of their own statues.

Jupiter, charmed and amazed by the theater, exalts architects as the true masters of the universe, far wiser than philosophers. But the winds of Aeolus, released, create a great storm that overthrows the gods, injuring and mutilating them: Cupid lands on Hope, breaking off one of her wings and suffering damage in return, while Jupiter falls on his head, his feet in the air, and breaks his nose. Sadder, and perhaps wiser, they return to heaven; and only there does Jupiter remember that Momus has given him tablets with a code for just rule.[42]

Scholars have long suspected that Alberti meant this elaborate allegory, with its many passages freely adapted from Lucian and others, to convey a serious message. The alternate title, found in both an early manuscript and one of the printed editions, On the Prince, seems to instruct readers to look for serious positive principles. Some of these appear in the text. Momus, in the tablets that he gives Jupiter, advises that the king "display magnificence in public and seek parsimony in private."[43] And Alberti's sixteenth-century Spanish translator took such hints when he cut the work into chapters and equipped it with a political commentary.[44] But others have argued that it is foolish to look for straightforward instruction in this cynical, negative set of interlocking stories.[45] From the fifteenth century, moreover, when some readers identified Momus as the Neapolitan humanist and courtier Bartolomeo Facio, other scholars have tried to create a key that would enable them to read the work not only as a treatise on politics and morality but also as a roman à clef. They have identified Jupiter, for example, with both Eugenius IV and Nicholas V, and his ambitious, doomed plans with both the Council of Ferrara/Florence and the rebuilding of Rome.[46]

In On Porcari's Conspiracy, a breathless short account of the 1453 plot against the pope, Alberti treats Porcari himself with more sympathy than one would expect him to show the devil. This brilliant, tormented man came from an ancient Roman family—one so old that some of its members, who claimed direct descent from Marcus Porcius Cato, called themselves Portius rather than Porcarus.[47] The Rome of the 1450s did not yet boast great "antique" palaces like those beginning to rise in Florence. Families like the Porcari lived in modest city houses, their arms emblazoned on the walls.[48] But they remembered, as Romans always did, the freedom and power that the city had once possessed. Porcari—who served as an important official in Florence and elsewhere and knew the local traditions of Ciceronian republicanism at first hand—felt particularly acute pain at Rome's subjection to papal tyranny. He tried repeatedly, after the death of Eugenius IV in 1447, to convince the Romans to take up arms and regain their ancient liberty.

Nicholas, hoping to conciliate an able man, appointed him to a governorship outside the city. But when Porcari next returned to Rome, he attempted to turn the public carnival regularly held in the Piazza Navona, a lively occasion in which the streets became a theater for unconventional public behavior, into a revolution. Sent away again, this time to Bologna, Porcari organized an armed conspiracy against the pope and returned to the city, where his few hundred followers thronged his modest house, ready to take direct action. But the conspiracy was betrayed. Soldiers stormed the Porcari stronghold, and Stefano himself, though he escaped at first and was hidden in a chest by his sister, was captured, interrogated, and rapidly hanged.[49]

On Porcari's Conspiracy was a Latin letter devoted to this dramatic episode, in which Alberti told the story, as the popular Roman historian Sallust had told that of the conspiracy of Catiline, in tight, even melodramatic prose.[50] Like Sallust, Alberti did not comment elaborately himself, but let his speakers do so.[51] And like Sallust, he showed a surprising amount of sympathy for the devil. Stefano makes a heroic appearance, denouncing papal tyranny in a magnificent speech to his followers and arguing in the best classical republican way that the dominance of priests and foreigners has made it impossible for Romans to lead the virtuous lives of their ancestors:

> And when, for a little while, he had given signs, through facial expression, gesture, and sighs, of the deep pain that he felt, he stretched forth his hand and asked, looking around, if anyone in this throng of excellent citizens felt satisfied either with his own condition or with the state of his fatherland. Was there anyone who could consider the common suffering of all without shedding tears? True, one could learn to tolerate poverty, subjection, mistreatment, insult, and the like, so long as one had the freedom to stay, while mourning, in one's native land. But those who claimed to be the exemplars of piety had invented a new kind of cruelty: they did not allow the Romans to be citizens. Rather, they condemned, expelled, and killed the innocent. All Italy was full of the throngs of exiles, and the city itself had been emptied of its citizens. Only barbarians appeared in the city, and anyone who dared to profess his patriotism was condemned as a criminal.[52]

Long a critic, from the inside, of the curia and the church it ruled, of the materialism and pride of its great clerics, Alberti now combined—or made Porcari combine—that revulsion with a republican's demand for liberty—

which, like Bruni, he treated as the precondition of a virtuous life.[53] By scholarly magic, Tafuri transforms Alberti, long celebrated as the prophet of modern urbanism, into an incisive critic of its grandiose pretensions and its threat to the traditional liberties that preserve society from the inroads of a tyrannical state. This interpretation has found extensive support, especially, though not only, from Italian scholars.[54]

Tafuri's thesis not only sets Alberti outside Nicholas's efforts to rebuild Rome but convincingly explains some paradoxes that older interpretations did not: for example, why archival documents bearing on Nicholas's building program never connect it with Alberti but always with Rossellino. It also helps to make sense of many passages in *On the Art of Building*. Alberti found many occasions in that work to praise the virtues of austerity and parsimony. He evoked the "frugality" that had characterized the buildings of the ancients, public and private, with at least as much enthusiasm as he showed elsewhere for grandeur in structure and ornament. And he recalled, with special poignancy, the simplicity of early Christian liturgy and churches:

> In ancient times, in the primitive days of our religion, it was the custom for good men to come together and share a common meal. They did not do this to fill their bodies at a feast, but to become humbler through their communication, and to fill their minds with sound instruction, so that they would return home all the more intent on virtue. Once the most sparing of portions had been tasted rather than consumed, there would be a lecture and a sermon on divine matters. Everyone would burn with concern for the common salvation and with a love of virtue. Finally they would leave an offering in the center, each according to his means.[55]

Alberti made clear that he preferred the grave, simple churches of early centuries, with their single altars and austere services, to the cathedrals of his own day. The voice of the author of the *Pontifex* still sounds in many passages of *On the Art of Building*—passages deeply out of sympathy with Nicholas's belief that crenellations, gold leaf, and grandiosity would bring the flock of Christians back to God.

Though immensely suggestive, and invaluable as a corrective to earlier exaggerations and oversimplifications, Tafuri's arguments require some qualification in their turn. True, *Momus* does take aim at the pretensions of papal planning. Alberti presents Jupiter's creation of splendid homes for the gods, decorated with statues, gems, and a cornucopia of other delights, as part of a scheme to make them contented by humbling the human race—an effort that Jupiter reinforces by making humanity mortal and liable to illness at the same time. But the argument against creating a new world (or city), which Alberti puts into the mouth of Hercules, is addressed as much to architects as to patrons:

> If one seeks by rebuilding to please the multitude, or seeks no other recompense for these great expenses than popular acclaim, there will always be those who do not entirely approve of your enterprises, and there will always be some very honorable ones among the gods who take more pleasure in the things they are used to than in new ones. And then those great ancient architects who fashioned the world we have with such artistry have disappeared in the course of time, and the whole race of craftsmen denies that anything more elegant, more splendid, or more durable can be built than the one we have, which gives such satisfaction. If you want to try new architects, it is clear enough how good they are: take, for example, the arch of Juno. The popular saying that they apparently built this merely to have it collapse seems quite just.[56]

This is the self-mockery of an artist who firmly believes that the voice of his critics is the voice of God, who holds that even the most ingenious new building must be a failure if it does not fit the existing environment it is designed for, and who knows that even his best creations will stand or fall by the judgments of others.

When Alberti satirized the imaginary arch of Juno, he may have been poking fun at the real Torrione of Nicholas V—the vast circular structure, known as "the new tower," that Nicholas began in 1447–48, in order to protect and to enhance the dignity of the old papal palace and the new one that he was about to construct. On 31 August 1454, this tower collapsed, causing more than one death, and had to be rebuilt—an awkward fact that Manetti tried to smooth over, in his biography of Nicholas, by saying that the pope, who had originally wanted to raise a tower more than a hundred cubits (roughly fifty meters) tall, had decided on architectural grounds to make it much shorter.[57]

But other passages seem to mock Alberti himself. Momus, like his Lucianic model, makes fun of one of Alberti's central concepts, the principle of decorum. He argues that oxen could be improved by adding eyes to the ends of their horns, so they could strike more effectively, and houses by setting them on wheels, so they could move rapidly to escape dangers. He also plays with Alberti's cherished story about the choice of Zeuxis, teaching young women to pray for divine plastic surgery that would remove all of their faults and make them all equally beautiful. And he instructs young women in self-adornment, showing them how to give their faces a rosy color and make their hair wavy—an art that Alberti had condemned, through the mouths of other characters, more than once.[58]

Alberti's self-parody reaches its most acute when Momus makes a magnificent speech on the art of the beggar—which he represents, in a bizarrely Brechtian passage, as the best of all the arts, the only one whose practitioners need not work and can rely on the rest of society to support them.[59] Momus argues, paradoxically, that only beggars can really enjoy public space:

> I will not even grant that kings can enjoy the use of their wealth more than beggars. Beggars possess the theaters, the porticoes, everything that is public. Others will not dare even to sit in the piazza, much less to argue in a slightly raised voice. Fearing censure, in their public actions they dare not do anything that is not in accordance with law and custom, anything merely willful. You, oh beggar, will lie on your face in the middle of the piazza, you will feel free to shout, and you will do for pleasure whatever you feel like doing.[60]

Alberti, in short, conjures up the sturdy beggar as a specter at Alberti's own feast—the ghost whose obtrusive presence disrupts the calm order of his ideal city, whose body interferes with the clean lines of the stone platforms on which his temples stand, and whose voice breaks the public quiet. It is hard to see this comment as directed more against Nicholas than against the ideal urban order evoked in *On the Art of Building*. *Momus*, like Alberti's earlier *Pontifex*, mocks the proud, intolerant denizens of the curia, but like most complex Renaissance satires, it has many other objects as well. It has recently been argued that Alberti based the figure of Momus partly on that of Prometheus, the demigod who stole fire for mankind from the gods and suffered eternal punishment for doing so. Aeschylus had told the story powerfully in his tragedy *Prometheus Bound*. This difficult source, not as yet translated into Latin, was well known to Byzantine scholars but hardly ever referred to by his contemporaries; if Alberti turned to it, he was making use, once again, of a Greek text to which he had access thanks to his position in the curia. He also emphasized, more strongly than ever before, his own ambivalence about the role of technology and invention in human life.[61] Alberti—who knew full well that he had chosen the courtier's career and genuinely feared that human efforts to master nature by throwing up vast buildings and other projects might lead to disaster, even though at times he also praised them—never exempted himself from his own biting irony.

Nor does *On Porcari's Conspiracy* fully support Tafuri's interpretation. Porcari's speech, on which Tafuri relies, is explicitly attributed to a rebel whom the author of the text condemns. Alberti's attitude toward Porcari was certainly complex. He claimed to have written the work just after the events it recorded and insisted on his inability to come to a final judgment. In fact, he adopted the characteristic humanist way of dealing with difficult questions in pragmatics and morality: he staged a disputation *in utramque partem*, on both sides of the question. To achieve this, Alberti brought a series of speakers to his imaginary podium. Foreign members of the curia, shocked and grieved, denounce the threat that Porcari poses to urban order and to themselves. Some natives then contradict them, arguing that Rome remains a stable political and cultural center. Still others worry that the rebellion is not over and that not even Nicholas's vigorous repression of it will keep others from imitating Porcari. Alberti—or his persona—makes clear at the end that he does not know which argument to accept. Unsure whether the *majestas* of Nicholas V or the rage of his opponents will triumph, he disapproves of both papal tyranny and violent opposition to it.[62] The text could be the work of an outsider to the curia, as Tafuri argues—or of a critical insider bitter at the compromises he has had to make.

Like Alberti's works, the context in which they took shape was more complex than Tafuri suggests. As time went on, Nicholas V became, like many rulers, in some ways more suspicious and arbitrary. His curia was a dangerous place for humanists, who had to walk the perpetual tightrope of papal favor. But it was also rewarding. Poggio was only one of Nicholas's beneficiaries who remarked that the pope's predecessors, including Eugenius, had "nodded when it came to supporting and adorning the intellects of scholars."[63] Under Nicholas the curia never degenerated into the dark panopticon described by Tafuri, a system as centralized as a spider's web, overseen by the single power-mad black widow at its center. Some artists and humanists did not enjoy under Nicholas the direct papal favor that Eugenius had accorded them. While new patrons—notably such powerful cardinals as Prospero Colonna and d'Estouteville—offered them support, they still carried out projects that they hoped would please the pope and that they dedicated to him in the hope of returning to the papal bosom. Biondo, for example, fell from favor soon after the start of Nicholas's papacy, but he remained, for the most part, in and near Rome, drawing support from Prospero Colonna and the Este. And he still dedicated his *Italy Surveyed* to the pope. Thus Alberti did not have to be a papal favorite to continue his part-time work as one papal service professional among many.

Under Nicholas, moreover, the curia encouraged a measure of intellectual debate among its inhabitants. Nicholas himself loved no religious text more than the works of pseudo-Dionysius the Areopagite, the late Neoplatonic treatises on the order of the cosmos and the church that were alleged to be the work of Saint Paul's Athenian convert, though they were really written in the sixth century. Lorenzo Valla had denounced the works of Dionysius as forgeries, yet Nicholas still hired him to serve as a papal secretary. Valla found further encouragement for his critical views in Nicholas's curia. Theodore Gaza, one of Alberti's friends, shared Valla's views, gave him new evidence from Greek sources in support of them, and expressed his own critical viewpoint, with supple indirection, in a dedicatory letter to the pope.[64]

The midcentury curia, in short, was no prison house of language or ideology, where intellectuals dared not speak truth to power. Like other contentious coteries of humanists—like the court of Alfonso of Aragon at Naples, where humanists cut one another to verbal ribbons at the king's fabled "hours of the book"—the curia witnessed many bitter quarrels. In this birdcage of the Muses as in others, favorites regularly fell from their perches. But debate was never entirely stamped out. The worst consequence of loss of favor, in most cases, was not death but rustication to a country farm or relegation to a less civilized and lucrative court—the fate met by George of Trebizond.[65] Nicholas had tried to deal with Porcari in the same way, by sending him out of the city, and resorted to force only when he had to.

We have already seen that Alberti compiled the scholarly portions of *On the Art of Building* in Nicholas's new Vatican Library. General arguments that Nicholas's plans for Rome did not mesh with Alberti's urbanistic ideals—for example, because Alberti stressed the importance of choosing a healthy site, while the low-lying Borgo was a well-known fever swamp—rest on a misreading of Alberti. No prisoner of general principles, he always expected the architect and patron to adapt his principles to fit existing environments and contexts. He certainly would not have suggested that the pope refound the Vatican on Elba. The argument that an outsider could not have been an insider, finally, does not stand close examination.

What, then, did Alberti have to do with Nicholas's plans? It seems quite possible that he served as a consultant, both on the ancient buildings that Nicholas hoped to preserve and on new projects like the Trevi fountain. *On the Art of Building* shows that Alberti took a passionate interest in foundations and walls. He made extensive studies of the old Basilica of St. Peter. He examined the damage done to its wall by perpetual exposure to the north wind, explained how the "numerous chapels" helped to support the basilica and divert moisture from it, and offered a detailed proposal to shore the building up "when sections of colonnading were leaning away from the vertical and threatening to bring the roof down."[66]

Alberti may well have examined the Vatican obelisk, which stood near the threatened walls, at the same time that he studied the chapels. He mentions that other architects had proposed to move the shaft, still standing upright, and ridicules their plans ferociously. Perhaps Alberti had in mind Aristotile Fioravanti, who specialized in transporting large columns. Certainly he heard, and probably took part in, debates about Nicholas's project for the Borgo.[67] Alberti may have exaggerated his own role in retrospect. But the evidence, taken together, offers Palmieri's account genuine support—and suggests that Alberti could have served as an adviser and at the same time counseled against continuing with the rebuilding of St. Peter's.

The same evidence also supports a second, more radical proposal: that Alberti rhetorically praised and supported Nicholas's final, almost apocalyptic vision of Rome as a new Jerusalem—the vision that formed so central a part of the cosmic language in which Manetti and other biographers fervently praised the pope's cultural enterprises after his death.[68] True, Alberti condemned excessively grandiose and expensive projects more than once, and he made fun of those who thought they could move the obelisk. But he also acknowledged repeatedly that splendid materials and large structures had their place: he showed nothing but respect for the columns of Trajan and Marcus Aurelius and for the Pantheon (though he ridiculed Egyptian pyramids).[69] And he seems to have exchanged ideas with Manetti, who drew on Alberti's technical vocabulary in order to describe and praise Nicholas's plans for Rome.[70]

One particular coincidence between Alberti's text and Nicholas's projects, which has received little attention up to now, deserves some thought.

Alberti described a plan for what might now be called zero-tolerance polic-
ing of the streets:

> Some princes in Italy have banned from their cities anyone . . .
> ragged in clothes and limb, and known as tramps, and forbidden
> them to go begging from door to door: on arrival they were immedi-
> ately warned that they would not be allowed to remain in the city out
> of work for more than three days. For there is no one so handicapped
> as to be incapable of making some form of contribution to society;
> even a blind man may be usefully employed in rope making. Anyone
> suffering a more serious illness would be assigned by the magistrate
> who is in charge of arrivals to one of the districts, to be cared for by
> lesser clergy. As a result, they would not need to beg in vain from
> their pious neighbors, and the city would be spared their loathsome
> presence.[71]

This passage would have sounded radical, not conservative, to Alberti's
readers. In the late fifteenth and early sixteenth centuries, the most idealistic of Europe's humanists, Erasmus, More, and Vives, all described the expul-
sion or confinement of sturdy beggars as a vital step in the construction of a
just social order. They recognized the need to provide work for the destitute,
and they argued that crimes resulted as much from deprivation as from natural iniquity. But they thought that confining the dangerous poor to work-
houses, where they could earn livings and not endanger others, was a
promising remedy for the dangers that attended Europeans in city streets.
Alberti, the lover of continual activity and industry, would have agreed.[72]

More to the point, Alberti's passage referred to concrete events. On 30
May 1450, the Florentine prelate Rosello Roselli wrote to Cosimo de'
Medici, "I want to tell you our news. This land is a robbers' den. . . . You
know that in the road that goes to St. Peter's, there by the wall, there were
many little shacks for the poor people. . . . Among the poor people who were
there was one with no legs who went on the ground on his bottom; this vil-
lain had killed six men at night with his own hands, and took what they
had."[73] The Borgo itself, in other words, swarmed with deformed and frightening beggars who threatened the pilgrims coming for the Jubilee and endangered good order and papal revenues. Nicholas took radical action to
eliminate this peril, as Roselli also reported: he had the shacks burned down,
executed the legless killer, and put his fellows to flight.[74]

Alberti transformed this drastic solution into a theory of urban order, giving the pope credit for an economic rationality not obviously attested by his actions. He may well have had considerable sympathy not only for the pope's desire to clear out the Borgo but also for his large-scale vision of a holy city on earth: indeed, he may well have collaborated in their realization, whatever his personal feelings about the pope or the grandiose in architecture. Nothing, after all, is more likely to inspire ethical and aesthetic discomfort than collaboration, viewed in hindsight. As a younger man, Alberti had seen collaboration as the way to socialize artistic practice, to remove the possibilities of injury that competition implied. In middle age, he probably came to appreciate that collaboration also has its discontents.

Alberti's urbanism thus reflects both the practical expertise and the practiced flexibility that he recommended at such length in *On the Art of Building*. His own architecture, by contrast, has seemed to many critics to embody his classical principles much more fully than any of the building done in Nicholas's Rome. In his buildings—so Rudolf Wittkower and many others in his wake have argued—Alberti put his classical theory into rich and sophisticated practice, raising grand buildings that stood out, in most cases, from the buildings around them, with facades and proportions that embodied the simple geometry he loved—and thus expressed the cosmic harmonies that should underpin great architecture.

Interpretations like this harbor certain dangers. The first is that of envisioning Alberti's architectural work as something he undertook alone, as though he thought or hoped that his buildings could embody his principles simply and directly. In fact, however, he regularly worked—as *On the Art of Building* suggests—in collaboration with others. Alberti's projects rested, of course, on funds provided by patrons: Sigismondo Malatesta, the brilliant mercenary soldier who defeated the hard-bitten Alfonso of Aragon in 1448 and may have begun his celebrated Malatesta Temple in Rimini in part to celebrate his triumph; Giovanni Rucellai, the Florentine patrician and connoisseur of the arts who funded a whole set of projects, public and private, in his own quarter of the city; and Ludovico Gonzaga, the ruler of Mantua. These men sometimes paid Alberti for his work. They also lodged, fed, and entertained him as a member of their entourages, welcoming him, once again, as a highly skilled professional who could provide them with needed services.

Though every one of the projects associated with Alberti poses problems of reconstruction as well as evaluation, decades of research have established a rough chronology. At some point in 1450 or thereafter—possibly as late as 1454—Alberti began to work for Sigismondo Malatesta, lord of Rimini, papal soldier, and ruler of legendary brutality. Sigismondo fortified Rimini with a magnificent stronghold and decorated it with inscriptions that celebrated his generosity. He also transformed the Church of San Francesco, in the city's center, into something like a temple (hence its informal name, the Malatesta Temple). The grand, severe facade that Alberti designed, the six interior chapels decorated with dynamic sculptures of dancing figures, presumably by Agostino di Duccio and Matteo de' Pasti, and the magnificent tomb of Sigismondo's beloved Isotta Nogarola made the church spectacular, even legendary—like the love between Sigismondo and Isotta that it commemorated.[75]

Vasari had no doubt that Alberti designed the exterior of the church, or that it represented a stunning achievement. "Leon Battista," he wrote,

> went to serve Lord Sigismondo Malatesta of Rimini, where he constructed the model for the Church of San Francesco and especially for the facade, which was built of marble, as well as the vaulting on the side facing south, which contained large arches and tombs for the illustrious men of that city. In short, his fine workmanship so changed that edifice that it became one of the most famous churches in Italy.[76]

Alberti wrapped the old brick church of the Franciscans in a brilliantly devised shell of Istrian stone. He covered the old facade with a restrained, severe new one, divided in its lower half by four half-columns adapted from the nearby arch of Augustus. And he flanked the structure with two long side walls, perforated with niches that enabled light to reach the old windows and provided space, on the south side, for the sarcophagi of scholars and men of letters like the Byzantine Platonist Gemisthus Pletho and the military engineer Roberto Valturio. The ensemble was cast "in a style more overtly classical than that of any Renaissance building constructed up to that time"—an astonishing achievement for a novice who had not grown up in the craft.[77]

Many details remain obscure. Work on the interior of the church began in 1447, while Alberti's involvement began later, in 1450 or even in 1453—perhaps because Sigismondo was inspired by the Jubilee to undertake works on a grand scale. It is not clear how much control, if any, Alberti had on the interior design, though its sculptures, as has often been remarked, clearly embody his taste for bodies in motion and for the expressive use of hair and garments. Sigismondo could not complete the whole structure Alberti had planned. It would have included a massive dome, the second largest in Italy, while the facade would have been flanked by scrolls designed to conceal the roofs of the chapel (the shape of which is also the object of debate). The documents do not prove that Alberti meant to pierce the facade, as many scholars have thought, with niches containing sarcophagi. Yet Alberti, working with a number of local artists and craftsmen, confronted with many practical difficulties, and forced to rely on a patron who obtained building materials by stealing them, in cartloads, from Ravenna, still created a temple of the sort he had described in On the Art of Building: a structure that dominated its surroundings, inspiring awe even in its incomplete form. No wonder that it made him a reputation.[78]

Within a few years Alberti was at work in Florence. Here the wealthy woolen merchant Giovanni Rucellai employed him to design a facade for his own great house, a new facade for the church of Santa Maria Novella, and a tiny model of the Church of the Holy Sepulchre in Jerusalem for the church of San Pancrazio. As it took Rucellai a long time to acquire and combine all the buildings that he wanted, Alberti's facade was designed and built in two stages—and even then it had to be left incomplete. Santa Maria Novella and the Holy Sepulchre represented more finished work, dazzlingly crafted of Florentine marbles and profuse with visual references to older Florentine buildings.[79]

In these buildings, Alberti brought off a bravura feat of adapting universal principle and ancient example to concrete circumstances. The Rucellai Palace was only one of the clan headquarters that went up in Medicean Florence, whose thick, rusticated facades proclaimed their status and guarded the privacy of their inhabitants.[80] But Alberti, though hampered by the need to work in a relatively narrow street, set a clear stamp on the Rucellai Palace by his use of a severely classical system of pilasters and beams, perhaps adapted from the Colosseum. Filarete, writing as early as the 1460s, called attention to its "facade made up of worked stones, entirely made in the antique manner."[81] And in the facade of Santa Maria Novella, with its simple proportions and phosphorescent decoration, he produced a triumphal arch that, even according to Vasari, pleased the highly critical Florentine public when the project finally reached completion, several years after Alberti's death.[82]

Alberti no doubt made other design proposals as well—for example, to his close friend Federigo da Montefeltro in Urbino. But Ludovico Gonzaga of Mantua turned into the chief patron of Alberti's later life. For Ludovico, he reared two highly original buildings: the centrally planned Church of San Sebastiano, work on which began in 1460, and the massive, centrally located Church of Sant'Andrea, the facade for which, with its deep coffered arch and finely carved pilasters, rivals that of Santa Maria Novella for magnificence, though in an entirely different idiom. Ludovico also supported the massive circular tribune that Alberti designed for the Florentine church of the Annunziata.[83] By the 1470s, Alberti enjoyed a unique status in Ludovico's eyes. The patron defended his architect against all critics. He insisted that those who disapproved of his design for the Annunziata had simply failed to understand that a circular design was more beautiful than the traditional cruciform one. When he could not fully understand Alberti's design for Sant'Andrea, he urged the architect to come to Mantua and explain it to him.[84]

Alberti provided a range of services for his clients. The exact nature of his contribution to the projects on which he collaborated is never clear: working, as he generally did, for lords whose power rested on their personal abilities as statesmen and commanders, rather than their mastery of bureaucratic procedures, he may often have provided unofficial advice rather than working, always, on a fixed contract and to a clear rhythm. But certain points are clear.

Alberti, first of all, saw himself as competent to design buildings. In *On the Art of Building*, he noted that he would

> always commend the time-honored custom, practiced by the best builders, of preparing not only drawings and sketches but also models of wood or any other material. These will enable us to weigh up repeatedly and examine, with the advice of experts, the work as a whole and the individual dimensions of all the parts and, before continuing any further, to estimate the likely trouble and expense.[85]

A good model should have certain qualities, he maintained. Unadorned and uncolored, plain and simple, devoid of decoration and the devices painters used to give a false impression of relief, it should emphasize "the ingenuity of him who conceived the idea, and not the skill of the one who fabricated the model." Alberti himself, in other words, would have designed, but not crafted, his models. But he expected them to reveal his intentions not just about the general plan but also about every significant detail in the design. It should, in fact, make it possible "to form a clearer and more certain idea of the design and quantity of columns, capitals, bases, cornices, pediments, revetment, flooring, statues, and everything else relating to the construction of the building and its ornamentation."

Like painting and writing—but even more manifestly—architecture was a social and collaborative art. Alberti envisioned an architect who engaged others to "emend" the faults in his original conception: "It is advisable then to construct models of this kind, and to inspect and reexamine them time and time again, both on your own and with others, so thoroughly that there is little or nothing with the work whose identity, nature, likely position and size, and prospective use you do not grasp."[86] It was easy to go wrong, he pointed out, by building on too large a scale or covering a facade with inappropriately rich ornamentation. To avoid such breaches of decorum, as well as to avoid technical mistakes in the pitch of a roof, he recommended collective scrutiny of the model: "Using scale models, reexamine every part of your proposal two, three, four, seven—up to ten times, taking breaks in between, until from the very roots to the uppermost tile there is nothing, concealed or open, large or small, for which you have not thought out, resolved, and determined, thoroughly and at length, the most handsome and effective position, order, and number."[87] Like the painter, the architect could work at his best only with the help of a community of critics—a community that included both professional builders able to translate a plan into working drawings and other architects competent to criticize the plan's underlying aesthetics.

As we have seen, the evidence does not tell us exactly when Alberti began to work on the earliest project clearly connected with him, the Malatesta Temple in Rimini, or exactly what he hoped the finished church would look like. One point, however, emerges clearly: Alberti made a model that embodied central features of his plan, which in turn became the object of discussion between the patron, de' Pasti, who served as the builder, and others. On 18 November 1454, Alberti wrote to de' Pasti from Rome, to discuss several details of the form of the church. He made clear at once that he approved in principle of the debates that his model had provoked: "Greetings. Your letters were most welcome for more than one reason, and I was particularly pleased to hear that my Lord was doing as I had hoped he would, and taking good counsel with everyone."[88] But he went on to defend his model against the criticism of one "Manetto," who claimed that cupolas must be twice as high as they were wide. Both Alberti's antiquarian expertise and his original aesthetic came into play as he argued: "I for my part have more faith in those who built the baths and the Pantheon and all these noble edifices, than in him, and a great deal more in reason than in any man."[89] Reason, in turn, meant aesthetics based on mathematical principles that regulated the relations among the parts of the building. Any change in the "measurement and the proportions of the piers," for example, "would make a discord in all that music." Alberti, in other words, mustered all of his formidable intellectual resources, played all the cards that his erudition and theoretical apparatus put at his disposal, in order to gain his point. With equal asperity and determination, he defended the pilasters in his facade design, the scrolls with which he hoped to conceal part of the roof, and his refusal to add round windows.[90] A collaborative approach clearly did not imply a willingness to concede on every point.

In fact, Alberti submitted some highly ambitious proposals—even radical ones. He wrote to Ludovico Gonzaga in February 1460, for example, to tell him that he had completed designs for "San Sebastiano, San Lorenzo, the loggia and Virgil"—a comprehensive plan for the redesign of Mantua's Church of San Lorenzo and the square adjacent to it. Alberti's vision included a statue of the city's ancient poet, Mantuan Virgil, and a colonnade flanking the square, of the kind he described in On the Art of Building.[91] At least when working for a secular patron, he did not shy from planning on the grand scale.

Some of his contemporaries held that Alberti wanted to transform the style—the basic look—of the urban centers in which he worked by reviving the lost style of Roman building. Filarete portrayed Alberti as one of the masters of the new art of classical architecture, although he gave Brunelleschi the main credit. In literature, Filarete argued, a stylistic revolution had taken place in his own time, thanks to the revival of the classics: "Ancient building, to give an example, compares to modern as literature does: that is, as the style of Cicero or Virgil compares to that in use thirty or forty years ago. Today, writing is generally practiced in a better way than it was in the past. After several centuries, prose has once again become eloquent. This has been accomplished only by following the ancient style of Cicero and of other worthy men." The same, he argued, had taken place in architecture. To prove his point, Filarete mentioned, among other evidence, the new facade of the Rucellai Palace. Alberti's work thus served as an example of architecture that followed "the ancient practice"—an exact parallel to the work of the literary humanists.

The advocate of a new style, Filarete recognized, did not necessarily find the going easy. He might have to educate his patron. Filarete goes on to present a dialogue in which a lord asks for aesthetic help: "It is true that I do not have a real grasp of these differences. Yet I see some things that I like better than others, such as some columns, and also certain arches, doors and vaults." In reply, the architect asks the lord which columns please him most. And when the lord reveals that arches "that are round please me much more" than pointed ones, the architect explains that his naive prejudice rests on a correct intuition. The sweeping line of the Roman arch, which does not impede the eye, is more beautiful than the jumpy, broken form of the Gothic arch—and, Filarete insists, just as strong, as the ruins of Roman baths clearly show.[92]

The real Alberti sometimes played the same role as the architect in Filarete's attractive fiction: he too tried to give his patrons some aesthetic education, or at least strained their tolerance for radical innovation. Piero de Tovaglia, who carried out Alberti's design for the circular tribune of Santissima Annunziata in Florence—a design that won out in competition against proposals for a more conventional Greek cross form—wrote that "Messer Battista continues to say that it will be the most beautiful construction ever built, and that the others cannot understand it because they are not used to seeing such things, but that when they see it built, they will say that it is much more beautiful than a cruciform plan." Ludovico Gonzaga's son Francesco, a cardinal and a passionate bibliophile, knew a good deal about "the ancient style." But he found Alberti's centrally planned Church of San Sebastiano in Mantua unintelligible. He admitted that it was "in the ancient manner" but qualified this remark by adding that that was "after the fantastic vision of Messer Battista of the Alberti" and that "I could not tell whether he meant it to look like a church, a mosque, or a synagogue."[93] Alberti, in other words, sometimes found that his clever models and arguments did not immediately persuade those who paid the piper and expected to call the tune. Lest they be puzzled or displeased when they visited the building site, all the better that he built a stage of modeling, discussion, and incorporation of feedback into his design process.

Alberti did not supervise the construction of his buildings on site. A builder always intervened between the design and its execution. Matteo de'

Pasti and others executed Alberti's plans, so far as they reached completion at all, for the Malatesta Temple. Giovanni di Bertino, a Florentine *marmorarius* (mason specializing in marble), cut the dazzlingly precise sails, stars, geometrical patterns, and wreathed vines that decorate the facade of Santa Maria Novella. But distance did not mean disinterest. As a member of the curia, Alberti normally could not make more than irregular visits to construction sites in Florence, Mantua, and Rimini. Accordingly, he supplied the builders who carried out his plans, not only with wooden models that laid out the buildings' general lines but also with designs for significant details. In some cases, Alberti collaborated with these men on multiple projects, evidently in a highly practical way. In 1454, for example, during one of Alberti's visits to Rimini, he and de' Pasti took the opportunity to work together on another project, the fortification of Sinigaglia. De' Pasti described Alberti's drawing for one of the charming composite capitals, decorated with stone faces, which he designed for the Malatesta Temple, as "most beautiful."[94]

Alberti may well have laid out with equal precision many other features of his buildings. He had studied the coffered ceiling of the Pantheon with great care, *On the Art of Building* reveals. In fact, he had even devised a way to duplicate its elegant texture cheaply and efficiently. In Sant'Andrea, his last great church in Mantua, the underside of the arch that covers the entrance is coffered—very likely a practical application of his study of the Pantheon.[95] For all its collaborative character, Alberti's architecture reflected his own convictions and his particular combination of historical and technical skills.

Another factor that was outside Alberti's control shaped the outcome of his projects: context—the existing environment in which each of his buildings had to sit. In only one case, so far as we know, did Alberti design and execute a project with little or no reference to existing structures. The tiny, gemlike marble shrine of the Holy Sepulchre that he built for Giovanni Rucellai, wholly inside the existing Florentine church of San Pancrazio, had to be modeled in its general shape on the original Church of the Holy Sepulchre in Jerusalem. Alberti presumably drew on pilgrims' reports and drawings when he laid the building out and equipped it with its curious, off-center canopy. But the larger design he followed for the facade of the little structure—with its strikingly busy overlays of Gothic and classical forms, Florentine colored marbles and classical inscriptions—was his own choice, not dictated by neighboring buildings or required by the function of his own new construction.

25. Alberti. Facade. San Sebastiano, Mantua. Alinari/Art Resource, NY.

Alberti sometimes found himself tightly constrained by existing structures or by technical problems that arose in the course of his work. In building the Rucellai Palace, he had to take into account the scenographic
problems posed by the site, which made it hard to view the facade from a
distance, and by the owner's own relatively slow progress in acquiring all the
houses he wanted to combine. In designing the Malatesta Temple in Rimini
and the facade of Santa Maria Novella in Florence, he had to accommodate
classical shapes to existing, medieval structures and to make their decorations fit local architectural traditions, which differed radically in standards
and emphasis. In rearing San Sebastiano in Mantua, he found that water
rose through the walls by capillary action from the ground under the church,
permeating the structure with so much dampness that he had to alter his
original plan radically, inserting a crypt with windows to allow air to circu-
late and help the building dry out.[96]

Resources—or the lack of them—could pose as serious a problem as context. In Florence, Alberti worked with an outstanding mason, one who could realize his most delicate and original ideas in marble, shaping brilliant, carefully chosen stones with dazzling precision until they embodied Alberti's vision of fortune as a filled sail. In Rimini, by contrast, skilled workers and fine materials were not to be had. Sigismondo Malatesta simply looted churches from the surrounding area—notably one of the surviving late antique glories of Ravenna—to obtain the fine stone that he needed for his temple. Accordingly, the half-columns that decorate the Temple's Istrian stone facade were crudely pieced together. Worse still, Sigismondo ran out of money long before Alberti's full design was complete, so that neither the second story that Alberti had planned for his facade nor the magnificent lead-roofed dome that he had planned to raise at the east end of the church was ever built.

Taken together, these constraints pushed Alberti in one direction, as a practicing architect—and made him deviate, in a significant way, from his theoretical principles. As a theorist, Alberti had eloquently evoked the organic character of the well-designed building. The facade, he argued, should serve a building as skin serves an animal: as the covering naturally suited to

26. Alberti. Facade. Malatesta Temple, Rimini. Alinari/Art Resource, NY.

the structure of bones and muscle beneath. The whole building, moreover, must also be designed to keep water out, to bring sunlight in, and to offer a range of private and public, open and closed spaces: to serve as a coherent mechanism for promoting the good life.[97]

In practice, however, Alberti was above all an artist of facades—a creator of exteriors that radically altered the appearance of a building but did not directly express its internal organization as an organic, living system. The building histories of Alberti's works present many mysteries that cannot be solved here. But a close look at his facades may shed some new light on the way that Alberti applied "architectural principles" in everyday practice. From the start of his active career—the years around 1450, when he set out to rebuild San Francesco in Rimini—he chose as his favorite form for church facades the recognizably classical structure of the triumphal arch. He wrapped one of these around San Francesco, decorated another with magnificent colored marbles at Santa Maria Novella, and perforated a third to celebrate the relic of Christ's blood at Sant'Andrea. In making this strong aesthetic choice, Alberti expressed to some extent his classicism: his commitment, as Filarete would have said, to reviving an "ancient style" of ornament closely parallel to the "ancient style" of Latin that he employed as a humanist.[98] Certainly Alberti found the major components of his stylistic lexicon in the ancient buildings he had studied so hard. Certainly, too, he sometimes deliberately substituted these classical elements for the vernacular ones preferred by some of his rivals. Michelozzo and others had already established what would become the standard Florentine palace facade when Alberti set to work on his great house for Giovanni Rucellai: a heavily rusticated stone front, three stories high, punctuated horizontally by three rows of bays, each containing an odd number of windows. Such facades vividly expressed the wealth and power that set such patrician families apart from ordinary Florentines—especially as the open shops that had once given entrance into the palaces' ground floors made way for barred windows and solid, closed doors, which separated the few inhabitants of these block-sized monuments to private life from the noisy Florentine street life outside them.[99] Alberti, determined to give his own twist to the problem, found a model for a different sort of grand facade in the Roman Colosseum, with its rows of arches flanked by solid pilasters. His "ancient style" came directly from one of the grandest and most widely discussed of antiquities.

But the choices that led Alberti to impose a triumphal arch on the most visually prominent side of his churches were necessarily more complex. Alberti knew Roman temples from direct inspection, and he was familiar with the Parthenon and other Greek ones from Cyriac's reports and drawings. He knew perfectly well, accordingly, that the ancients put porches supported by colonnades where he set triumphal arches, on the fronts of temples—and that the Athenians had used free-standing columns where he insisted on engaged ones or pilasters. Triumphal arches, by contrast, were just that: prominent, free-standing, barrel-vaulted structures designed to commemorate particular military achievements. Alberti recommended that their faces be covered with *historiae*—reliefs representing the events they celebrated.[100]

A paradox emerges. Alberti certainly believed that his architecture consisted of classical components. Instructing Matteo de' Pasti to stick to the plans laid down in his model for San Francesco in Rimini, he underlined his faith "in those who built the baths and the Pantheon." The front of the Malatesta Temple, as has often been remarked, seems to refer directly to a local antiquity, the arch of Augustus; that of San Sebastiano, perhaps, to the arch of Orange, drawings of which circulated in the fifteenth century. Yet these references, for reasons already clear, seem out of place. Why superimpose a pagan triumphal arch, be it well known or local, on the main entrance to a Christian church?

One set of reasons was surely practical. Alberti believed, as we have already seen, that the architect must work with the existing structures on his site: in Rimini and Florence, the existing conditions prevented him from adding more than a facade. He also advertised himself as able to produce work more cheaply than his rivals. In making this claim, he could consider himself well within the classical tradition. More than once in *On the Art of Building*, he explained how the ancients had made their work not only beautiful but economical. That was why they had carried out the finish work on capitals and moldings only after they had erected their columns; why ancient marble workers, even though they had fitted vein to vein and color to color with meticulous care, had not bothered to polish sections that would be too distant from the eye for the omission to register.[101] A colonnade like that at the Pantheon—to say nothing of the Parthenon—would surely have cost far more than the walls adorned with columns and pilasters that Alberti actually erected. In Rimini it would hardly have been possible to create a colonnade. The triumphal arch may well have attracted Alberti first and foremost, then, because it expressed his own, peculiarly economical classicism so well.

But arches, like all other shapes, had symbolic meanings—as Filarete

27. Triumphal Procession. Giovanni Marcanova, *Sylloge*. Department of Rare Books and Special Collections, Princeton University Library.

showed in the dialogue in which an architect convinces his patron of the superiority of the round arch. The triumphal arch, in particular, celebrated the achievements of a great man. Antiquarians associated arches, reasonably enough, with the triumphal processions that they imagined passing under them—jubilant crowds of Roman soldiers, heavily armed and carrying spoils looted from the enemy dead. In imposing this form—and in inscribing celebratory inscriptions to his patrons—on his church fronts, Alberti turned them into tiny modern equivalents of the Forum of Augustus: celebrations in stone. The Albertian church celebrated its patron, lavishly.

At the same time, however, the arch had a second, urbanistic meaning: in *On the Art of Building,* he defined it as "a gate that is continually open." It should stand "at the point where a road meets a square or a forum, especially if it is a *royal* road."[102] Arches, that is, should provide architectural punctuation, dividing one public space from another. In the fifteenth century, churches were public spaces—as much so as roads or piazzas. Open all day every day, they not only resounded with liturgical chant but buzzed with the gossip of the many people who used them as meeting places or thoroughfares. It seems at least possible, then, that Alberti saw the triumphal arch as appropriate to his churches because it fitted the way they were used: because the all-important principle of decorum supported its use.

Yet a problem remains: The arch symbolized the classical world as well, as is unmistakable in the work of the two greatest classicists among fifteenth-century artists, Jacopo Bellini and Andrea Mantegna. In Bellini's Paris sketchbook and Mantegna's lost Paduan frescoes, arches appear regularly—overpoweringly huge ones in Bellini's case, terrifyingly cold and geometrical ones in Mantegna's. They not only offer backdrops to the lives and sufferings of John the Baptist, Christ, and his disciples, but they also stand as emblems for the classical world as a whole. The arch represents empire, paganism, Roman justice, as they impinged on the life and orchestrated the death of the Savior. These uses of the classical triumphal arch in religious art have a theological clarity and legibility that Alberti's application seems to lack; they almost look like criticisms of his architecture.

And yet no evidence proves that contemporaries disapproved of Alberti's choice. Pius II hated Sigismondo Malatesta, hated him enough to damn the man, while still alive, to hell, assuming that the papal ability to name saints must be accompanied by its opposite. He condemned the Malatesta Temple, too. But Pius did not object to Alberti's use of the triumphal arch. Sigismondo, he wrote, "so filled" his church with "pagan works of art that it seemed less a Christian sanctuary than a temple of heathen devil-worshippers," and he erected a tomb, with an inscription "in the pagan style" that read "sacred to the deified Isotta." For Pius, then, the sculptures of classical gods and zodiacal signs by Agostino di Duccio and the epitaph on Isotta's sepulchre defiled the church. But he agreed with Sigismondo about the "due magnificence" of the building itself: it was a "noble temple." For Pius, the church that Malatesta's indecorous use of ornament defiled was an unproblematically splendid one.[103]

What may have led Pius to read the building this way is the relationship—long remarked—between its facade and the nearby arch that Augustus had erected in 27 B.C.E. Anyone entering Rimini through its main gate, on the ancient Flaminian road, passed through Augustus' arch into a large, oval piazza. The Church of San Francesco stood to the right of it. When Alberti reused forms from the arch on the church, he suggested a connection between the two. And that, to a practiced fifteenth-century reader of architecture, presumably called to mind another connection as well. Anyone who knew Rome—as Alberti did—knew that the emperor Constantine had reared not one but two great triumphal arches. The first, free-standing one, encrusted with reliefs, spanned the Triumphal Way near the Colosseum, commemorating his great military victories. The second, which stood at the enormous crossing of the Basilica of St. Peter, celebrated the still greater victory of Christ. The first Christian emperor—as he was understood in the Renaissance—had used the form of the arch for purposes of both state ceremony and Christian religion, to emphasize his reordering of his capital city.[104]

Sigismondo Malatesta, though later excommunicated by Pius II, was at midcentury a papal vicar. He had led the troops of the papacy against the count of Urbino and another branch of the Malatesta family as early as 1432. Later he took part in the consecration of the Florentine Cathedral, and in the years leading up to 1450 he worked closely with Nicholas V, who issued a bull in 1447 permitting Isotta to endow a chapel in San Francesco, enabling it to be restored. In connecting his newly rebuilt church with a Roman triumphal arch, Sigismondo may well have seen himself—as Alberti and even Pius may well have seen him—as insisting on his own status as a Christian emperor. Augustus was certainly no Constantine. But he had ruled the world, justly, at the time of the birth of Christ. The connection was hardly far-fetched.[105]

The arch, then, offered Alberti and his patron more than attractive formal properties and an effective divider of urban spaces. It tied the building on which it was superimposed to another local structure, itself laden with historical and symbolic meaning. Alberti's radically classical facade, erected in the center of a city proud of its Roman arch and bridge, told a story about tradition and connection to the ancient past. In a similar way, the radically different version of the triumphal arch that he added to Santa Maria Novella referred, through the polychrome splendor of its decorations, to the Baptistery and other buildings central to the Florentine cityscape.

The visual language of Alberti's architecture, then, strikingly resembled the verbal language of his literary works. It too represented a tissue of creative allusions, deft reworkings of traditional forms to serve new functions. Like Alberti's literary work, too, his architecture may have harbored strains and contradictions. In the one extensive passage of *On the Art of Building* devoted explicitly to churches, as opposed to temples, Alberti joined his acquaintance Lorenzo Valla in denouncing the oppressive grandeur of the churches of his day. He evoked with nostalgia and a sense of irreparable loss the early Christianity whose practitioners met in small groups, without hierarchy, to engage in a simple service and Lord's Supper and give money for the needs of the poor rather than to collect donations and feast.[106] The passage stands out like a sore appendix in the optimistic mass of Alberti's text, but he did not remove it. Perhaps it was his acknowledgment that rhetoric, for all its powers, was not enough. Or perhaps it was simply a characteristic indulgence in the irony from which the master builder never exempted himself or his most ambitious creations.

EPILOGUE

"Once," Alberti recalled in his late work *On Codes*,

> it so happened that I was with Dati in the pope's garden at the Vatican. In our usual way, we were discussing literary matters. As it happens, we agreed that we approved very warmly of the German inventor who has recently made it possible, by making certain imprints of letters, for three men to make more than two hundred copies of a given original text in one hundred days, since each pressing yields a page in large format.[1]

The two men's enthusiastic discussion of technical innovation soon changed focus to another recent invention, cryptography. Short though it is, the passage makes clear beyond doubt that, at some point not long after 1465, when two German clerics, Sweynheym and Pannartz, established the first printing press in Italy, Alberti saw or heard about the new invention. Now old, he still felt as much enthusiasm for the new technology that these barbarians had introduced to his environment as he had felt half a lifetime before for

Brunelleschi's dome. The aging scholar remained faithful to the ideals of his early time of hope—including the positive view of man's innovative energies that had dispelled his original cultural pessimism.

Alberti, in his Indian summer, retained his energy, his curiosity, and his long-established interests. Down to his death in 1472, he kept on investigating the technical subjects that had fascinated him as a young man. In his work *On Ruling the Household*, a set of moral dialogues written in Italian, he—or his spokesman in the dialogue, who bore his name—insisted that the pursuit of virtue took precedence over all other studies. But he also praised painting and sculpture as worthy arts. He ascribed to the practical pursuits of the engineers a considerable practical value: "since it is not possible always to exercise the intellect, no one will be blamed for doing some work on a project that is honorable and gives him pleasure, like—for example—devising a mathematical instrument or creating a device that can be useful to the state for expeditions on land or sea, or the like." And he pointed out that anyone constructing an argument should emulate the expert hydraulic engineers who did not open up a watercourse before establishing that they had chosen the most direct and open path for the water to flow down.[2]

These references were not merely theoretical. Alberti not only continued to practice as an architect until the end of his life but also retained his interest in the theory of the arts. In the 1460s, for example, he published a complement to his treatise *On Painting*: a short work *On Sculpture*, which he may have begun around 1450.[3] As in his earlier work, so here Alberti paid little or no attention to the materials from which statues were constructed or the techniques used to carve or model them. Instead, he took up a question that he had dismissed as a young humanist: the origins of the art under discussion. All arts that aimed at creating images that resembled real objects, Alberti argued, arose from the spontaneous efforts of nature itself. But all of them rested, in the end, on human efforts that improved on what nature had to offer:

> I believe that the arts of those who attempt to create images and likenesses from bodies produced by nature, originated in the following way. Probably, they occasionally observed in a tree-trunk or clod of earth and other similar inanimate objects certain outlines in which, with slight alterations, something very similar to the real faces of nature was represented. They began, therefore, by diligently observing and studying such things, to try to see whether they could not add,

take away, or otherwise supply whatever seemed lacking to effect and complete the true likeness. So by emending and refining the lines and surfaces as each object required, they achieved their intention and enjoyed doing so. Not surprisingly, men's efforts at creating likenesses eventually reached a stage where, even when they found no help from half-finished images in the material to hand, they could still make the image they desired.[4]

Ancient writers, above all Pliny, had noted the existence of "images made by chance." Some Renaissance painters, like Leonardo, supposedly found inspiration at times in aleatory practices that imitated nature: throwing a sponge at a wall, for example, in order to work from the chance images and resemblances suggested by the splotch that resulted.[5] Alberti, however, did not emphasize the fantastic or the imaginative element in either sculpture or painting.[6] Here, as in *On Painting*, he drew terms and images from the ancient tradition of writing about rhetoric. He thus suggested that sculpture, like the art of speaking, could not only develop over time, as skillful practitioners cultivated it, but could also claim a high intellectual and social status.[7] Concentrated effort by men—including, as always, collaboration and "emendation"—perfected nature. A work that achieved a close resemblance to its subject was a product of one of Alberti's ideal communities of creators. Sculpture evolved because sculptors developed a sense of what each subject required and a set of principles for evaluating each other's work.[8]

As in *On Painting*, Alberti refused to treat his subject as a philosopher, even though he admitted that he himself was no sculptor. He wrote, again, as an outsider, one who hoped he could help his "painter and sculptor friends." Resemblance itself, he acknowledged, was complex and difficult to define, since it rested on a mysterious inborn property that "remains always constant and unchangeable in relation to the species," even as features and bodily contours changed. But he refused to devote an excursus to this subject, since he considered it irrelevant to practice. Like *On Painting*, then, *On Sculpture* was designed as a practical work, even though its author was not a professional practitioner. Once again, Alberti portrayed himself as a critic with practical experience—and once again, he suggested that the ideal community for sculpture would include such articulate individuals as well as practitioners.

Sculptors needed to achieve two kinds of resemblance, he argued. Some tried to produce images that looked generally "like a man, though a completely unknown one." Others set out "to represent and imitate not simply a man but the face and entire appearance of the body of one particular man, say Caesar or Cato in this attitude and this dress." Both projects demanded great effort, since the parts of each body and their relation to one another altered with every change in posture or movement. Accordingly, Alberti provided detailed instructions for two complementary ways of gathering empirical data, for which he once again devised new technical terms: *dimensio* (the measurement of the parts of the body) and *finitio* (the recording of its curves and lines).

The sculptor, Alberti argued, should establish the proportions of each body he examined, using a wooden ruler and a square, which he divided into "feet"—divisions of one-sixth of the body's length from head to foot. By doing so, he could arrive at a full and precise proportional record of its dimensions. Recording the shapes and variations of individual limbs and joints was, of course, far harder than simple measurement. But Alberti applied his favorite engineering device—the circular "horizon," a disk with a graduated rim, a straight pointer that rotated about its center, and a plumb-bob hanging from the pointer on a string—to this challenging task. Working in two dimensions, he had used the horizon instrument to map Rome. Working in three, he now showed that it could also be used to fix the position of any part of the body—even "the hollow between the shoulder blades at the back"—in a coordinate system, so precisely that one could use the data so obtained to duplicate the body in question, or to make half of a statue in one place and the other half in another and then to assemble them.

The sculptor's chief problem, in other words, had an empirical solution: close study of the body, in three dimensions rather than two and based on measurement rather than schemata. Alberti encouraged him, accordingly, "to work from a live model in order to make a figure artistically and methodically." Indeed, he himself had gone still further. He provided a table of measurements that, he claimed, derived from empirical analysis of many individuals' bodies, carefully selected, in a sort of quantitative recasting of the original choice of Zeuxis:

> I proceeded accordingly to measure and record in writing, not simply the beauty of this body or that, but, as far as possible, that perfect beauty distributed by nature, as it were in fixed proportion, among many bodies; and in doing this I imitated the artist at Croton who, when making the likeness of a goddess, chose all the remarkable and

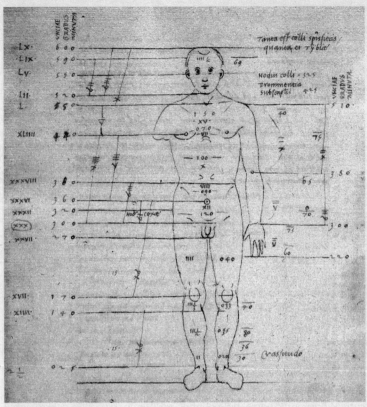

28. Anonymous. Sketch of human proportions, illustrating Alberti, *De statua*. Oxford, Bodleian Library.

elegant beauties of form from several of the most handsome virgins and transferred them into his work. So I too chose many bodies, considered to be the most beautiful by those who know, and took from each and all their *dimensiones*, which we then compared with one another. Omitting the extremes on both sides, we took the mean figures.[9]

Since Vitruvius, writers had insisted that the proportions of the human body embodied the harmony of the universe. Villard d'Honnecourt had laid out rough and ready systems for determining the proportions and contours of human subjects. But Alberti apparently transformed the study of the body into a purely empirical discipline.[10] And the techniques he offered impressed contemporary and later readers like the scholar Angelo Poliziano, a lover of technical terms in his own right, who quoted Alberti's description of the sculptor at work, and sculptors like Leonardo.[11]

Alberti's list of ideal measurements—and the illustration that accompanied it in one manuscript—in fact derived from traditional values for human proportions.[12] And he retained many elements of his own earlier thinking, like his belief that an eclectic, comparative study of many individuals would yield a higher form of beauty, one not embodied in any single one of them. But Alberti's enterprise still had its radical side. He defined the sculptor's task as empirical and verifiable. He devised techniques for carrying it out in a rigorous way. And he summarized them in one short and generally lucid text—one that unlike On Painting, does not seem to be directed at particular sculptural projects but that drew systematically on all the experience he had gained in the 1440s and afterward as surveyor, architect, and writer on technical subjects.[13]

Alberti, in other words, made sculpture a branch of engineering, in the period sense of the term. And he showed his undimmed faith in technology in at least one other highly revealing way. In order to bring On Painting to the attention of a reading public, he dedicated both the Italian and the Latin versions of it to men whose names could give his work authority: the architect Brunelleschi and the great nobleman Giovanni Francesco Sforza. When he published On Sculpture, he dedicated it to a fellow member of the curia, Giovanni Andrea Bussi, bishop of Aleria. Typically, Alberti asked Bussi to "emend, alter, or even delete" whatever he wanted to.[14] What he did not ask—but almost certainly hoped for—was that Bussi, who became editorial adviser to Sweynheym and Pannartz in 1468, might print his work as well.[15] Alberti, late in life, still hoped for help from new technologies as he set out one last time to improve his contemporaries' artistic and technical practices. He also—to judge from a short dedicatory text that accompanies On Sculpture in some manuscripts—retained his faith in the analogy between rhetoric and other arts like painting. "In writing," he commented,

> it is not he who knows the very best writings, who will become a writer, but he who has become so familiar with all of literature that there is not a single text which he cannot appropriately and fittingly use in writing, in its proper place.[17]

Though he was primarily based in Rome and at courts in Urbino and Mantua, Alberti continued to visit Florence as well. Cristoforo Landino, noted for his commentaries on Italian and Latin poetry, recalled that he took a leading place in literary discussions in the circle of the young Lorenzo de' Medici. Alberti set his late work *On Ruling the Household* in the city, at a dramatic date in the later 1460s or early 1470s.[16] As he took care to show, he saw this dialogue as a considered statement of his views about his family's native city. Walking downhill on a sunny day from the Church of San Miniato, Alberti the character finds his friends Niccolò Cerretani and Paolo Niccolini on the bridge over the Arno. Meeting Alberti's nephews, they view the turbulent river with some alarm and then retire to the chimney corner to hold forth on values and how to put them into practice. The movement from public to private, from the sunny city street to the family palace, adumbrates the argument of the work as a whole.

Alberti and his spokesmen in the dialogue make no bones about their disapproval of the new luxury that became fashionable in Florence during the decades of Medici hegemony. Niccolò criticizes the new mania for high living that has ruined country life. Once even the richest men took only a bed and a few vessels with them to their villas. Now madness reigns: each house has more beds than its inhabitants could possibly need, and their dining rooms and tables rival those of great prelates. Battista attacks the "arrogance" that has led to "the creation of new institutions and destruction of the order that has been confirmed by use and experience." The new system of taxation that the Florentine government introduced at the end of the 1460s, which enabled the government to "remove money from private purses with public authority," is only one "intolerable thing" among many.[18] Every social and political innovation—even an apparently harmless change in costume— brings with it many costs and few if any benefits. Alberti clearly retained the stout political conservatism to which he had adhered for decades.

Some conservatives, in Florence, saw the Medici as corrupters of the city's ancient constitution.[19] Alberti, firm believer in order that he was, certainly did not mean to challenge the "veiled Signory" of Medicean rule. Indeed, he admits that cities need a single ruler, "with an authority that enables him to rule his fellow citizens in an honorable life and the ability to punish those who disobey the laws of their fatherland."[20] Writing around 1470, he would have known of Lorenzo's genuine regard for old families, but the innovative practices that would extend and deepen Medicean power still lay in the decades to come.[21]

But he also argued, in contrast to *On the Family*, that a young man could learn to lead a civic life better within a clan than in the city. Cities, after all, owed their founding to chance; families owed theirs to love, and their "primary chain" consisted of "piety and love." After serving as the prudent "rector" of the miniature society that each great family constituted, one would be more than able "to attain, among your own and in the republic, to a lofty rank."[22] The city of Florence has become, by Alberti's own confession, an oligarchy, and only "fortunate young men" like those who took part in the dialogue, born to good families, can hope to participate in public life. The republic has developed a nobility of its own, and the separate public and private worlds of *On the Family* have seemingly collapsed into one another.[23]

Yet Alberti's acknowledgment that times had changed did not imply resignation. He still insisted that activity was always good, inactivity always bad. He still urged young men to pursue virtue. They must study good authors, and—perhaps harder—listen to the wise advice of their elders (as their elders must, in turn, learn to enjoy their company). Once well informed, they would see that in most matters, one must seek a proper balance. Wealth, for example, deserved their interest only to the extent that it made virtuous action possible. By making themselves the objects of constant therapeutic oversight, they would maintain their mental and physical health through establishing balance in all their pursuits.[24]

The young man who followed this advice would become wise and capable of "showing himself to be virtuous" while holding a magistracy or other office. But he would need more than a knowledge of abstract principles. Wisdom—even real wisdom—must be embodied in a suitable form, or it would make no impression. Accordingly, Alberti and his friends give the young men tips on conduct. "When I was your age I liked to ride," says Battista:

> so I used to listen very hard when horses were discussed. A prudent old gentleman said this: "There are some things in which one must commit himself with his whole mind, with all his diligence, and with all his effort, to do them well. And apparently, this involves nothing more than doing it with great modesty, combined with lightness and a lordly air, to please those who watch you. These are riding, dancing, walking in the street and so on. But it is necessary above all to control your gestures and countenance and your motions and your entire appearance with a very precise examination and with a very correct

form of art, so that nothing seems to be done with tricks that required extensive thought, but the onlooker thinks that all of your accomplishment is the innate gift of nature."[25]

Alberti's "old gentleman" was, of course, his own earlier self—the brilliant scholar-courtier who had offered the same counsels about the art of presenting the self in his precocious autobiography, more than thirty years before.

If the Alberti of *On Sculpture* was still an ambitious lover of technology, the Alberti of *On Ruling the Household* was still an ambivalent moralist—at once radical in his critique of the corruption of society and conservative in his abhorrence of attempts at revolution. As in his earlier years, so now, he saw the art of effective performance and persuasion, the building of an attractive facade that expressed the genuine virtues of the man beneath, as the key to the kingdom of political and social power. As in his earlier years, so now, he saw this art as a real one—one with its own exacting discipline and high standards, and one that did not necessarily conflict with the rules of true morality. For only the truly refined performer could rise to be the ruler of the organic "body" of a clan or the artificial "body" of the state.

The Alberti of 1472, like the Alberti of the 1430s, was still a master builder. He built churches, but he also helped create new, carefully defined social and political groups, career structures, and the protocols of a new etiquette that, in the next century, would spread through the courts of Europe. He still hoped for glory. And he still knew that he would find it not outside, in the "public squares" he had once evoked, but inside defined circles, whose members could both approve of and "emend" his efforts. A prophet of individualism and the cult of glory, a tightrope performer of self-creation, Alberti knew, as he always had, that if he lost his audience, the lights would be extinguished, the curtain would fall, and he would find himself alone and lost in the dark, unable to move his audience. In the last years of his wonderfully productive life, he kept busy, as he always had. He thereby avoided the lethargy and depression that had always threatened him. But he did more as well. He made his life, until the end, a conscious performance and a continuous act of reflection on the problems that had gripped him since his troubled, isolated youth. Nothing that he built of stone expressed Alberti's ideals more fully than his lifelong effort to create a rich and responsive social world: to make, out of the rhetoric he prized so deeply, not only an art of composition, but a model for all forms of intellectual and artistic community.

NOTES

INDEX

NOTES

1. This setting—imagined by Alberti for a comedy that was never performed—was the first such fully realized visualization of a comic stage: see E. Battisti, "La visualizzazione della scena comica nella commedia umanistica," *Rinascimento e barocco* (Turin, 1960), 96–111 at 102–104. On the role of the theater in Alberti's thought and language, see the masterly article of L. Cesarini Martinelli, "Metafore teatrali in Leon Battista Alberti," *Rinascimento*, 2d ser., 29 (1989), 3–51.

2. "L. B. Alberti, *Philodoxeos fabula*. Edizione critica a cura di Lucia Cesarini Martinelli," *Rinascimento*, 2d ser., 17 (1977), 111–234, 150.

3. All quotations from Alberti's *Philodoxeos fabula* are from the Martinelli edition cited in n. 2; they appear on pp. 144, 162, 184–85, and 202–204.

4. For Alberti's life, see esp. G. Mancini, *Vita di Leon Battista Alberti*, 2d ed. (Florence, 1911), still the standard full-length work; C. Grayson, in *Dizionario biografico degli italiani*, s.v. L. B. Alberti; C. Grayson, "Leon Battista Alberti: Vita e opere," in *Leon Battista Alberti*, ed. J. Rykwert and A. Engel (Milan, 1994), 28–37, repr. in C. Grayson, *Studi su Leon Battista Alberti*, ed. P. Claut (Florence, 1999),·419–33; R. Tavernor, *On Alberti and the Art of Building* (New Haven and London, 1998). *Alberti*, ed. Rykwert and Engel, the catalog of a massive exhibition on Alberti held in Mantua, offers rich and up-to-date bibliographical information. Good bibliographies of secondary work appear in M. Jarzombek, *Leon Battista Alberti: His Literary and Aesthetic Theories* (Cambridge, Mass., and London, 1989), and in L. B. Alberti, *Apologhi*, ed. M. Ciccuto (Milan, 1983). For the older literature on Alberti's architectural work see G. Mirolli, "Saggio di bibliografia albertiana," *Studi e documenti di architettura* 1 (1972), 11–56.

5. J. Burckhardt, *Die Kultur der Renaissance in Italien: Ein Versuch*, ed. L. Geiger, 11th ed. (Leipzig, 1913), I, 154–56.

6. J. Gadol, *Leon Battista Alberti: Universal Man of the Early Renaissance* (Chicago, 1969).

7. See esp. E. Panofsky, *Renaissance and Renascences in Western Art* (New York and London, 1972).

8. R. Wittkower, *Architectural Principles in the Age of Humanism* (London, 1949; 3d ed., 1962, repr. 1967).

9. J. von Schlosser, "Ein Künstlerproblem der Renaissance: L. B. Alberti," *Akademie der Wissenschaften in Wien*, *Sitzungsberichte* 210, 2 (1929); see R. de Mambro Santos, *Viatico Viennese* (Rome, 1998). Contrast this treatment of Alberti as artist with von

Schlosser's treatment of Alberti the theorist in *Die Kunstliteratur*, ed. O. Kurz (Vienna, 1924), tr. into Italian as *La letteratura artistica*, tr. F. Rossi, 3rd ed. (Florence, 1977; repr. 1979), 121–29.

10. See esp. E. Garin, "Studi su L. B. Alberti," *Rinascite e rivoluzioni* (Bari, 1975), 133–96; M. Tafuri, " 'Cives esse non licere': The Rome of Nicholas V and Leon Battista Alberti. Elements Toward a Historical Revision," *Harvard Architectural Review* 6 (1987), 60–75; M. Tafuri, *Ricerca del Rinascimento* (Turin, 1992), chap. 2; and Jarzombek, *Alberti*.

11. On Burckhardt's method see E. H. Gombrich, *In Search of Cultural History* (Oxford, 1969) and P. Ganz, "Jacob Burckhardts *Kultur der Renaissance in Italien*. Handwerk und Methode," *Deutsche Vierteljahrsschrift für Literaturwissenschaft und Geistesgeschichte* 62 (1988), 24–59.

12. Both Burkhardt quotations in W. Kaegi, *Jacob Burckhardt: Eine Biographie* (Basel/Stuttgart, 1956), III: 666, 658. The historian in question was Ludwig von Pastor, himself the author of a still standard history of the popes.

13. M. P. Gilmore, "Introduction," in *Renaissance Princes, Popes and Prelates: The Vespasiano Memoirs*, tr. W. George and E. Waters (New York, Evanston, and London, 1963).

14. See Alberti, *Opere volgari*, ed. A. Bonucci (Florence, 1843), I, lxxxix n. Bonucci reprinted the Latin text from volume 25 of the eighteenth-century scholar Ludovico Antonio Muratori's *Rerum italicarum scriptores*, and appended a facing translation in Italian (Alberti, *Opere volgari*, xc–cxvii).

15. The first quotation comes from R. Fubini and A. Menci Gallorini, "L'autobiografia di Leon Battista Alberti: Studio e edizione," *Rinascimento*, 2d ser., 12 (1972), 21–78 at 76. For another translation, see R. Neu Watkins, "L. B. Alberti in the Mirror: An Interpretation of the *Vita* with a New Translation," *Italian Quarterly* 30 (1989), 5–30 at 15. These two articles offer deeply informed and incisive commentaries on Alberti's autobiography. The second quotation is from Fubini and Menci Gallorini, "L'autobiografia," 76–77; Watkins, "L. B. Alberti," 16.

16. See M. Baxandall, "Alberti's Self," *Fenway Court* (1990–91), 31–36.

17. These four quotations come from Fubini and Menci Gallorini, "L'autobiografia," 73, 77, and 76, and Watkins, "L. B. Alberti," 12, 15, and 14–15.

18. G. Gorni, "L. B. Alberti e le lettere dell'alfabeto," *Interpres* 9 (1989), 257–66 at 260.

19. These two quotations come from Fubini and Menci Gallorini, "L'autobiografia," 68–70 and 71; Watkins, "L. B. Alberti," 8 and 9.

20. Cf. C. Kallendorf, "From Virgil to Vida: The *Poeta Theologus* in Italian Renaissance Commentary," *Journal of the History of Ideas* 56 (1995), 41–62.

21. Quotations come from the translations of Bruni's lives in D. Thompson and A. F. Nagel, *The Three Crowns of Florence* (New York, Evanston, San Francisco, and London, 1972), 57–83; the original texts are in L. Bruni, *Humanistisch-philosophische Schriften* (Leipzig and Berlin, 1928; repr. Wiesbaden, 1969), 50–69.

22. See C. Quillen, *Rereading the Renaissance* (Ann Arbor, 1998).

23. The three quotations in this paragraph come from Diogenes Laertius, *Lives of the Philosophers*, 1.27; 1.26; 1.23. See Fubini and Menci Gallorini, "L' autobiografia."

24. These two quotations come from Fubini and Menci Gallorini, "L'autobiografia," 74 and 75; Watkins, "L. B. Alberti," 12 and 13.

25. For Alberti's commitment to the traditional art of rhetoric see now the comprehensive essay by B. Vickers, "Humanismus und Kunsttheorie in der Renaissance," *Theorie der Praxis*, ed. K. W. Forster and H. Löcher (Berlin, 1999), 9–74.

26. *Trivia senatoria*, in Alberti, *Opuscula*, ed. G. Massaini (Florence, 1502). For the medieval antecedent of Alberti's wheel, the "wheel of Virgil," see E. Faral, *Les arts poétiques du xiie et du xiiie siècle* (Paris, 1924), 87; M. Carruthers, *The Book of Memory* (Cambridge, 1990; repr. 1992), 251–53. For a more modern conceptual apparatus, see E. F. Goffman, *The Presentation of Self in Everyday Life* (Garden City, 1959).

27. Fubini and Menci Gallorini, "L'autobiografia," 55, pointing out that Lapo's testimony derives from the *Vita*.

CHAPTER II

1. Both quotations from L. B. Alberti, *De commodis litterarum atque incommodis*, ed. L. Goggi Carotti (Florence, 1976), 46–47, 60–61.

2. Ibid., 78–82. Alberti's *De commodis* strikingly departs from the conventions of Italian humanist writing by insisting that scholarship can play little or no role in public life, and preferring the pure realm of philosophical contemplation to the applied one of rhetoric, the art of effective speech. For discussions, see C. Grayson, *"De commodis litterarum atque incommodis," Modern Language Review* 83 (1988), xxxi–xlii, reprinted in C. Grayson, *Studi su Leon Battista Alberti*, ed. P. Claut (Florence, 1999), 389–405; J. Oppel, "Alberti on the Social Position of the Intellectual," *Journal of Medieval and Renaissance Studies* 19 (1989), 123–58; M. Regoliosi, "Gerarchie culturali e sociali nel *De commodis litterarum atque incommodis* di Leon Battista Alberti," *"Sapere e/è potere": Discipline, dispute e professioni nell'Università Medievale e Moderna. Il caso bolognese a confronto*, I: *Forme e oggetti della disputa delle arti*, ed. L. Avellini (Bologna, 1990), 151–70; A. Jori, "L'eden capovolto. Patologia del sociale nel *De commodis* de Leon Battista Alberti," *Civiltà Mantovana*, 3rd ser., 29 (1994), 131–39. For an interesting and plausible effort to redate the work—normally dated, on the basis of the anonymous *Vita* of Alberti, at ca. 1428—to early in the 1430s, see L. Boschetto, "Nuovi documenti su Carlo di Lorenzo degli Alberti e una proposta per la datazione del *De commodis litterarum atque incommodis*," *Albertiana* 1 (1998), 43–60. Though Boschetto does not explore the possibility, it also seems conceivable that Alberti, an inveterate reviser, drafted the work in 1428 and revised it later.

3. See D. Hughes, "Distinguishing Signs: Ear-Rings, Jews and Franciscan Rhetoric in the Italian Renaissance City," *Past and Present* 112 (1986), 3–59; V. Groebner, "Losing Face, Saving Face: Noses and Honour in the Late Medieval Town," tr. P. Selwyn, *History Workshop Journal* 40 (1995), 1–15; and V. Groebner, "Inside Out: Clothes, Dissimulation and the Arts of Accounting in the Autobiography of Matthäus Schwarz, 1496–1574," *Representations* 66 (1999), 100–21.

4. See A. Neri, in *Giornale Ligustico di archeologia, storia e letteratura* 9 (1882), 165;

A. Mancini, "Nuovi documenti e notizie sulla vita e sugli scritti di Leon Battista Alberti," *Archivio storico italiano*, 4th ser., 19 (1887), 190–212 at 191.

5. Alberti, *De commodis*, ed. Goggi Carotti, 105.

6. See Goggi Carotti's commentary and Boschetto, "Nuovi documenti."

7. On the rise of the universities and the social aspirations of students, see in general A. Murray, *Reason and Society in Medieval Europe* (Oxford, 1978; repr. with corrections, 1985), pt. 3. The Italian phenomena described in the text, as Murray and many others have shown, were specific cases of a Europe-wide development.

8. See P. F. Gehl, *A Moral Art: Grammar, Society and Culture in Trecento Florence* (Ithaca, 1993); and P. Grendler, *Schooling in Renaissance Italy: Literacy and Learning, 1300–1600* (Baltimore, 1989).

9. Alberti, *De commodis*, ed. Goggi Carotti, 86.

10. See, e.g., P. Herde, "Politik und Rhetorik in Florenz am Vorabend der Renaissance. Die ideologische Rechtfertigung der Florentinischen Aussenpolitik durch Coluccio Salutati," *Archiv für Kulturgeschichte* 47 (1965); J. E. Seigel, *Rhetoric and Philosophy in Renaissance Humanism: The Union of Wisdom and Eloquence, Petrarch to Valla* (Princeton, 1968); R. Witt, *Coluccio Salutati and His Public Letters* (Geneva, 1976); R. Witt, *Hercules at the Crossroads* (Durham, 1985); L. Martines, *Lawyers and Statecraft in Renaissance Florence* (Princeton, 1968).

11. See in general P. O. Kristeller, *Renaissance Thought and Its Sources*, ed. M. Mooney (New York, 1979); Murray, *Reason and Society*; N. Siraisi, *Medieval and Early Renaissance Medicine* (Chicago and London, 1990).

12. See, e.g., N. Siraisi, *Taddeo Alderotti and His Pupils* (Princeton, 1985); Martines, *Lawyers and Statecraft*.

13. A. Beccadelli, *Hermaphroditus* II.1, ed. F. Wolff-Untereichen (Leipzig, 1908), 68; more recent edition by D. Coppini, I (Rome, 1990); prose translation in M. de Cossart, *Antonio Beccadelli and the Hermaphrodite* (Liverpool, 1984), 45. Beccadelli gave classic form to a sentiment that had originally been expressed in very unclassical Latin jingles; see Murray, *Reason and Society*.

14. Alberti, *De commodis*, ed. Goggi Carotti, 69.

15. Alberti, *De commodis*, ed. Goggi Carotti, 89. For the symbolic value of book stands and the heavy canonical texts they held, see B. Scala, "Dialogus de legibus et iudiciis," ed. L. Borglia, *La Bibliofilia* 42 (1940), 252–82.

16. Alberti, *De iure*, in C. Grayson, "Il *De iure* di Leon Battista Alberti," *Tradizione classica e letteratura umanistica: Per Alessandro Perosa*, ed. R. Cardini, E. Garin, L. Cesarini Martinelli, and G. Pascucci (Rome, 1985), 173–94, repr. in Grayson, *Studi*, 373–88, at 377 (text, lines 9–10).

17. This important thesis was put forward and demonstrated by P. O. Kristeller. See, e.g., "Humanism and Scholasticism in the Italian Renaissance," *Byzantion* 17 (1944–45), 346–74, repr. in *Renaissance Thought and its Sources*, ed. Mooney.

18. On the role of the mendicants in Italy, see Hughes, "Distinguishing Signs"; G. A. Brucker, "Monasteries, Friaries and Nunneries in Quattrocento Florence," *Christianity and the Renaissance*, ed. T. Verdon and J. Henderson (Syracuse, 1990), 41–63; and N. Rubinstein, "Lay Patronage and Observant Reform in Fifteenth-Century Florence," in ibid., 63–82.

19. On this point, see above all the classic studies of P. O. Kristeller, e.g., *Studies in Renaissance Thought and Letters* (Rome, 1986), II, 209–38; C. Vasoli, *Tra "Maestri" umanisti e teologi* (Florence, 1991).

20. See, e.g., D. Lesnick, "Civic Preaching in the Early Renaissance," in *Christianity and the Renaissance*, ed. Verdon and Henderson, 208–25; the great book of I. Origo, *The World of San Bernardino* (New York, 1962); and F. Mormando, *The Preacher's Demons* (Chicago and London, 1999).

21. Petrarch, "Epistula posteritati," *Opere*, ed. G. Ponte (Milan, 1968), 886–900; English translation in *Petrarch: A Humanist Among Princes*, ed. D. Thompson (New York, Evanston, and London, 1971), 1–13, adapting Ovid, *Tristia*, IV, 10.

22. See P. de Nolhac, *Pétrarque et l'humanisme*, 2d ed., 2 vols. (Paris, 1907); C. E. Quillen, *Rereading the Renaissance* (Ann Arbor, 1998); and the excellent summary in L. D. Reynolds and N. G. Wilson, *Scribes and Scholars*, 3rd ed. (Oxford, 1991), 128–34. J. E. Seigel argues in *Rhetoric and Philosophy in Renaissance Humanism*, section II, that Petrarch was the model on which most humanists of the fifteenth century tried to shape their careers as scholars and writers. For Alberti's debt to Petrarch, see esp. D. Marsh, "Introduction," in L. B. Alberti, *Dinner Pieces*, tr. D. Marsh (Binghamton, N.Y., 1987), 1–11, esp. 1: "Petrarch provided an important model for Alberti's literary ambitions, and although Alberti never names him, his influence is pervasive."

23. For general surveys of various aspects of humanist culture, see R. Sabbadini, *Il metodo degli umanisti* (Florence, 1922); E. Garin, *L'Umanesimo italiano* (Bari, 1952); Kristeller, *Renaissance Thought and its Sources*, ed. Mooney; Seigel, *Rhetoric and Philosophy*; A. Grafton and L. Jardine, *From Humanism to the Humanities* (London and Cambridge, Mass., 1986); Reynolds and Wilson, *Scribes and Scholars*; J. Hankins, "The Popes and Humanism," *Rome Reborn*, ed. A. Grafton (Washington, New Haven, London, and Vatican City, 1993), 47–85; and F. Rico, *El sueño del humanismo: De Petrarca a Erasmo* (Madrid, 1993). A. Rabil, ed., *Renaissance Humanism: Foundations, Forms, and Legacy*, 3 vols. (Philadelphia, 1988), offers useful survey articles on most aspects of humanism in Italy and outside.

24. See Gehl, *A Moral Art*; Grendler, *Schooling in Renaissance Italy*.

25. See P. O. Kristeller, "The Modern System of the Arts," *Renaissance Thought* (Princeton, 1980), II; E. Garin, *La disputa delle arti nel Quattrocento* (Rome, 1982); P. Rossi, *Philosophy, Technology and the Arts in Early Modern Europe*, tr. S. Attanasio, ed. B. Nelson (New York, Evanston, and London, 1970).

26. G. Mancini, "Nuovi documenti e notizie sulla vita e sugli scritti di L. B. Alberti," *Archivio storico italiano*, 4th ser., 19 (1887), 201–205; R. Cessi, "Il soggiorno di Lorenzo e Leon Battista Alberti a Padova," in ibid., 5th ser., 43 (1909), 351–59; *Dizionario biografico degli italiani*, s.v. L. B. Alberti, by C. Grayson. On Barzizza's school, see provisionally R.G.G. Mercer, *The Teaching of Gasparino Barzizza* (London, 1979).

27. See Barzizza's letter to Lorenzo Alberti in Mancini, "Nuovi documenti," 203.

28. See Antonio Beccadelli, *Hermaphroditus*, ed. Coppini, I, xci (pointing out that it would have been more classical for Barzizza to direct this poem to an absent friend, and suggesting that he may have directed other poems as well to Alberti).

29. P. Findlen, "Humanism, Politics and Pornography in Renaissance Italy," *The Invention of Pornography*, ed. L. Hunt (New York, 1993), 49–108 at 83–86; B. Talvacchia, *Taking Positions* (Princeton, 1999).

30. Beccadelli, *Hermaphroditus*, II.37, ed. Wolff-Untereichen, 130–34; ed. Coppini, I, 137–38; prose translation in de Cossart, *Antonio Beccadelli*, 62–63.

31. Beccadelli, *Hermaphroditus*, I.19, ed. Wolff-Untereichen, 30; ed. Coppini, I, 38–39; prose translation in de Cossart, *Antonio Beccadelli*, 33.

32. J. Morelli, *Operette* (Venice, 1820), II, 271–72.

33. Alberti, *De commodis*, ed. Goggi Carotti, 37–38.

34. Goggi Carotti (ed. *De commodis*, 38 n. 3) cites as parallels Cicero, *Brutus*, 302: "*nullum enim patiebatur esse diem quin aut in foro diceret aut meditaretur extra forum*" and 305: "*cotidieque et scribens et legens et commentans oratoriis tantum exercitationibus contentus non eram.*"

35. G. W. Pigman, "Barzizza's Treatise on Imitation," *Bibliothèque d'Humanisme et Renaissance* 44 (1982), 341–52; see also M. Baxandall, *Giotto and the Orators* (Oxford, 1971).

36. Mancini, "Nuovi documenti," 203.

37. See in general A. Moss, *Printed Common-Place Books and the Structuring of Renaissance Thought* (Oxford, 1996); A. Blair, "Humanist Methods in Natural Philosophy: The Commonplace Book," *Journal of the History of Ideas* 53 (1992), 541–51; Blair, *The Theater of Nature* (Princeton, 1997); and for the wider context, W. Ong, "Commonplace Rhapsody: Ravisius Textor, Zwinger and Shakespeare," *Classical Influences on European Culture, 1500–1700*, ed. R. R. Bolgar (Cambridge, 1976), 91–126; Z. S. Schiffman, "Montaigne and the Rise of Skepticism in Early Modern Europe: A Reappraisal," *Journal of the History of Ideas* 45 (1984), 499–516; and above all, W. Schmidt-Biggemann, *Topica universalis* (Hamburg, 1983) and F. Goyet, *Le sublime du "lieu commun"* (Paris, 1996).

38. Both quotations from Guarino da Verona, *Epistolario*, ed. R. Sabbadini (Venice 1915–19), II, 270; I, 594–95.

39. For case studies in the humanists' practice of creative literary reuse, see, e.g., J. W. O'Malley, *Praise and Blame in Renaissance Rome* (Durham, 1979); C. Kallendorf, *In Praise of Aeneas* (Hanover and London, 1989); G. McClure, *Sorrow and Consolation in Italian Humanism* (Princeton, 1991); and K. Gouwens, *Remembering Rome* (Leiden, 1998).

40. For Beccadelli's role see R. Sabbadini, "Cronologia della vita del Panormita e del Valla," in L. Barozzi and R. Sabbadini, *Studi sul Panormita e sul Valla* (Florence, 1891), 23; Sabbadini, *Un biennio umanistico (1425–26) illustrato con nuovi documenti, Giornale storico della letteratura italiana*, supplement 6 (1903), 112; G. Ponte, *Leon Battista Alberti: umanista e scrittore* (Genoa, 1981), 148–57, esp. 149.

41. "L. B. Alberti, *Philodoxeos fabula*. Edizione critica a Cura di Lucia Cesarini Martinelli," *Rinascimento* 17 (1977), 111–234, at 146–47.

42. The passage is in Alberti, *Profugiorum ab aerumna libri iii*, in *Opere volgari*, ed. C. Grayson (Bari, 1960–73), II, 160–62. See the full analysis by R. Cardini, *Mosaici* (Rome, 1990), 4–5.

43. These three quotations come from Alberti, *De commodis*, ed. Goggi Carotti, 111–12, 88, 93; cf. 96.

44. Alberti, *"Philodoxeos fabula*, ed. Cesarini Martinelli,"* 146.

45. Quotations in this paragraph come from Alberti, *De commodis*, ed. Goggi Carotti, 72–73.

46. See in general G. Holmes, *The Florentine Enlightenment* (New York, 1968; new ed., Oxford and New York, 1992); and J. Gill, *The Council of Florence* (Cambridge, 1959). C. Celenza provides a full and lucid description of the curia as Alberti knew it in *Renaissance Humanism and the Papal Curia: Lapo da Castiglionchio the Younger's "De curiae commodis"* (Ann Arbor, 1999), chap. 3. On the situation of the church in this period, see more generally R. W. Southern, *Western Society and the Church in the Middle Ages* (Harmondsworth, 1970) and G. Bossy, *Christianity in the West, 1400–1700* (Oxford, 1985). For the Italian scene, see also the important articles collected in *Christianity and the Renaissance*, ed. Verdon and Henderson, and *Women and Religion in Renaissance Italy*, ed. D. Bornstein and R. Rusconi (Chicago and London, 1996).

47. I follow the excellent description in Celenza, *Renaissance Humanism*. For further details, see J. D'Amico, *Renaissance Humanism in Papal Rome* (Baltimore and London, 1983); and P. Partner, *The Pope's Men* (Oxford, 1990).

48. Lapo da Castiglionchio, Jr., *De curiae commodis*, ed. and tr. in Celenza, *Renaissance Humanism*, 173 (slightly altered).

49. R. Trexler, *Public Life in Renaissance Florence* (New York, 1980); and V. Breidecker, *Florenz, oder: "Die Rede, die zum Auge spricht": Kunst, Fest und Macht im Ambiente der Stadt* (Munich, 1990; 2d ed. 1992).

50. See in general Herde, "Politik und Rhetorik"; H. Baron, *In Search of Florentine Civic Humanism*, 2 vols. (Princeton, 1988); Witt, *Salutati* and *Hercules*.

51. E. Walser, *Poggius Florentinus* (Leipzig and Berlin, 1914); Holmes, *Florentine Enlightenment*.

52. A. Ryder, "Antonio Beccadelli: A Humanist in Government," *Cultural Aspects of the Italian Renaissance: Essays in Honour of Paul Oskar Kristeller*, ed. C. H. Clough (Manchester and New York, 1976), 123–40; and J. Bentley, *Politics and Culture in Renaissance Naples* (Princeton, 1987).

53. See V. de Matteis, s.v. Stefano Fieschi in *Dizionario biografico degli italiani* (with bibliography).

54. G. Aliotti, *Epistolae et opuscula*, ed. G. M. Scarmalius, 2 vols. (Arezzo, 1769), e.g. Aliotti to Bartolomeo Zabarella, 1444, I, 96: "I have many reasons for desiring to leave the curia. For if you want peace of mind, and tranquillity, and to live innocently and keep your conscience clear: you cannot seek peace, where there is none, where quarrels continually rage, where the noise of lawsuits is continually heard. If you want leisure for your studies, what leisure can there be amidst all this noise and tumult? If you want to attain honors, and higher things, this is the vice of ambition: and ambition must be restrained by reason. And then, in addition, you know how hard it is these days for a poor and low-born man to arrive at glory. What then do I have to do with the curia, where the intellect slumbers, the senses are dulled, and time is wasted, while one wastes all one's leisure waiting outside the gates?"

55. Lapo to Angelo da Recanate, 24 June 1436; Paris, Bibliothèque Nationale, MS lat. 11388, fol. 27 ro; published by F. P. Luiso. "Studi su l'epistolario e le traduzioni di Lapo da Castiglionchio iuniore," *Studi italiani di filologia classica* 8 (1899), 205–99 at 229.

56. Lapo to Angelo da Recanate, 16 June 1436, in ibid., 24 ro; published by Luiso, 227.

57. Lapo to the duke of Milan, late 1435, in ibid., 37 vo.

58. For for this quotation, see the vivid description by Jacopo Angeli, in his letter to Manuel Chrysoloras, in L. Dati, *Epistolae xxxiii*, ed. L. Mehus (Florence, 1743), 61–95, 67–70.

59. See in general Holmes, *Florentine Enlightenment*, and Walser's still classic biography of Poggio, *Poggius Florentinus*, chaps. 5–8.

60. Poggio Bracciolini, *Facetiae*, ed. and tr. M. Ciccuto (Milan, 1983), 406–408.

61. For details on the famous fight of 4 May 1452 between Poggio Bracciolini and George of Trebizond, see J. Monfasani, *George of Trebizond* (Leiden, 1976), 109–11.

62. See in general F. Rico, *Nebrija frente a los bárbaros* (Salamanca, 1978) and S. Rizzo, "Il latino nell'Umanesimo," *Letteratura italiana*, ed. A. Asor Rosa, V: *Le questioni* (Turin, 1986), 379–408. For a case study, see B. L. Ullman, *The Humanism of Coluccio Salutati* (Padua, 1963), chap. 7. On the later history of Latin in the modern world, see F. Waquet, *Le latin ou l'empire d'un signe, xvie–xxe siècle* (Paris, 1998).

63. R. L. Kaster, *Guardians of Language* (Chicago and London, 1986).

64. L. B. Alberti, *The Family in Renaissance Florence*, tr. R. N. Watkins (Columbia, S.C., 1969), 82; original in *Opere volgari*, ed. Grayson, I, 71. Cf. C. Grayson, " 'Cartule e gregismi' in L. B. Alberti,' *Lingua nostra* 13 (1952), 105–106, repr. in C. Grayson, *Studi su Leon Battista Alberti*, ed. P. Claut (Florence, 1998), 45–46. See also G. Billanovich, "Leon Battista Alberti, il Grecismus e la Chartula," in *Lingua nostra*, 15 (1954), 70–71. The *Chartula* was a poem widely used as a textbook; the *Grecismus*, a grammar by Eberhard of Bethune.

65. R. Pfeiffer, "Küchenlatein," *Philologus* 86 (1931) 455–59, reprinted in Pfeiffer, *Ausgewählte Schriften*, ed. W. Bühler (Munich, 1960), 183–87.

66. J. Perry, "A Fifteenth-Century Dialogue on Literary Taste: Angelo Decembrio's Account of Playwright Ugolino Pisani at the Court of Leonello d'Este," *Renaissance Quarterly* 39 (1986), 613–34.

67. M. Baxandall, "Bartholomaeus Facius on Painting. A Fifteenth-Century Manuscript of the *De viris illustribus*," *Journal of the Warburg and Courtauld Institutes* 27 (1964), 90–107.

68. S. Rizzo, "Il latino del Petrarca nelle *Familiari*," *The Uses of Greek and Latin: Historical Essays*, ed. A. C. Dionisotti et al. (London, 1988), 41–56.

69. Nolhac, *Pétrarque et l'humanisme*, II, 92. Quintilian cautioned in *Institutio oratoria*, X.iii.32–33, against the lack of blank space that could cause "laziness in correction" (*pigritiam emendandi*); "*Verissimum et expertum*," wrote Petrarch in his copy, Paris, Bibliothèque Nationale, MS lat. 7720, fol. 91 verso.

70. Petrarch to Donato degli Albanzani, *The Renaissance Philosophy of Man*, ed. E. Cassirer, P. O. Kristeller, and J. H. Randall (Chicago and London, 1948), 48, quoting Suetonius, *Nero*, 52; for the original, see Petrarch, *Le traité de sui ipsius et multorum*

ignorantia, ed. L. M. Capelli (Paris, 1906), 16. Two autograph copies survive; both include the corrections Petrarch described. See also P. Rajna, "Il codice Hamiltoniano 493 della R. Biblioteca de Berlino," *Rendiconti dell'Accademia dei Lincei*, 5th ser., 18 (1909), 479–508.

71. Ullman, *Salutati*, 22; see also his *Studies in the Italian Renaissance* (Rome, 1955), 241.

72. F. Biondo, *Scritti inediti o rari*, ed. B. Nogara (Vatican City, 1927), 146–47.

73. Pius II, *Memoirs of a Renaissance Pope*, tr. F. A. Gragg, ed. L. C. Gabel (New York, 1959), 323. Pius went on to reflect, "Some one may perhaps say the same of us, and rightly, for though what we write is true, yet we set down the important or unimportant alike, we are without eloquence, and have woven together a rude and unorganized narrative. Perhaps someday another will shed light on what Biondo and we have put together and will reap the fruit of others' toil." Pius's *Memoirs* (*Commentarii*) were in fact submitted to the posthumous editorial judgment of another specialist in the field, Giannantonio Campano, who professed himself satisfied with the pope's eloquence: see his judgment in Campano, *Opera* (Venice, 1502), II, fols. II recto–III verso, reprinted in *Epistolae et poemata*, ed. J. B. Mencke (Leipzig, 1707), 1–13, esp. his conclusion: "I was given the power of deleting what seemed superfluous, correcting what seemed confused, and clarifying what seemed to be obscurely put. But the whole text seemed so elegant, so brilliant, that it not only requires no outside correction to improve its qualities, but will inspire all who hope to imitate it with despair."

74. Lapo to Biondo, 8 April 1437, in M. Regoliosi, " 'Res gestae patriae' e 'res gestae ex universa Italia': La lettera di Lapo da Castiglionchio a Biondo Flavio," *La memoria e la città*, ed. C. Bastia and M. Bolognani (Bologna, 1995), 273–305, at 292–93. This edition of the text supersedes the earlier one in M. Miglio, *Storiografia pontifica del Quattrocento* (Milan, 1975), 189–201, though Miglio's commentary (31–59) remains important.

75. E. H. Gombrich, "From the Revival of Antiquity to the Reform of the Arts: Niccolò Niccoli and Filippo Brunelleschi," *Essays in the History of Art Presented to Rudolf Wittkower*, ed. D. Fraser et al. (London, 1967), 71–82, reprinted in E. H. Gombrich, *The Heritage of Apelles* (Ithaca, 1976), 93–110.

76. L. Valla, *De voluptate*, ed. M. Panistella Lorch (1977), 188–90.

77. Tacitus, *De oratoribus*, 2–3.

78. *Texts and Transmission*, ed. L. D. Reynolds (Oxford, 1983), 410–11; P. Burke, "Tacitism," in *Tacitus*, ed. T. A. Dorey (New York, 1969), 149–71; K. C. Schellhase, *Tacitus in Renaissance Political Thought* (Chicago and London, 1976).

79. P. Stadter, "Niccolò Niccoli: Winning Back the Knowledge of the Ancients," *Vestigia: Studi in onore di Giuseppe Billanovich*, ed. R. Avesani et al. (Rome, 1984), II, 747–64. See further B. L. Ullman and P. A. Stadter, *The Public Library of Renaissance Florence* (Padua, 1972); and E. Garin, *La biblioteca di San Marco* (Florence, 1999).

80. See, e.g., J. Alsop, *The Rare Art Traditions* (New York, 1982), 322–36.

81. Vespasiano, "Vita di Niccolò Niccoli," *Vite di uomini illustri del secolo XV* (Florence, 1938).

82. M. C. Davies, "An Emperor Without Clothes? Niccolò Niccoli Under Attack," *Italia Medioevale e Umanistica* 30 (1987), 95–148.

83. L. Bruni, *Dialogi ad Petrum Paulum Histrum*, ed. S. U. Baldassari (Florence, 1994), 254–55 (translation from *The Humanism of Leonardo Bruni: Selected Texts*, ed. and tr. G. Griffiths, J. Hankins, and D. Thompson [Binghamton, N.Y., 1987], 73). On the interpretation of this much-discussed text, see esp. D. Quint, "Humanism and Modernity: A Reconsideration of Bruni's *Dialogus*," *Renaissance Quarterly* 38 (1985), 423–45.

84. One of the greatest students of Florentine humanism, Hans Baron, based large segments of his interpretative work on the theory that Bruni changed his mind on major questions in politics and culture after writing the preface and first book of the *Dialogues*, and that book two expresses his new views. See, e.g., *The Crisis of the Early Italian Renaissance*, 2 vols. (Princeton, 1955; 2d ed., Princeton, 1966); *From Petrarch to Leonardo Bruni* (Chicago, 1968); and *In Search of Florentine Civic Humanism*, 2 vols. (Princeton, 1988). More recent scholarship has demonstrated that Bruni composed the whole work as a philosophical and literary unit. See Quint, "Humanism and Modernity"; L. B. Mortensen, "Leonardo Bruni's *Dialogus*: A Ciceronian Debate on the Literary Culture of Florence," *Classica et Mediaevalia* 37 (1986), 259–302; Baldassari's introduction to his edition of the *Dialogi*; and, for a review of the literature, the sharp survey by J. Hankins, "The 'Baron Thesis' after Thirty Years and Some Recent Studies of Leonardo Bruni," *Journal of the History of Ideas* 56 (1995), 309–38.

85. Quotation from *Renaissance Princes, Popes and Prelates*, ed. M. P. Gilmore, tr. W. George and E. Waters (New York, Evanston, and London, 1963), 400, slightly altered; original text in Vespasiano, *Vite*, 501.

86. Poggio Bracciolini, *De infelicitate principum*, ed. D. Canfora (Rome, 1999), chap. 17, 13. See H. Harth, "Niccolò Niccoli als literarischer Zensor: Untersuchungen zur Textgeschichte von Poggios *De avaritia*," *Rinascimento* NS 7 (1967), 29–53 at 29–30; and G. Germano, "Nota critica al testo," in Poggio Bracciolini, *Dialogus contra avaritiam*, ed. G. Germano (Livorno, 1994), promising a fuller study.

87. For this dialogue and its context, see, in addition to the English translation and introduction in B. G. Kohl and R. W. Witt, *The Earthly Republic* (Philadelphia, 1978); Walser, *Poggius Florentinus*, 110–34; H. Baron, "Franciscan Poverty and Civic Wealth as Factors in the Rise of Humanistic Thought," *Speculum* 13 (1938), 1–37, revised and expanded in *In Search of Florentine Civic Humanism*, I, chaps. 7–9; D. Marsh, *The Quattrocento Dialogue* (Cambridge, Mass., 1980); J. W. Oppel, "Poggio, San Bernardino of Siena and the Dialogue *On Avarice*," *Renaissance Quarterly* 30 (1977), 564–87; H. M. Goldbrunner, "Poggios Dialog über die Habsucht. Bemerkungen zu einer neuen Übersetzung," *Quellen und Forschungen aus italienischen Archiven und Bibliotheken* 59 (1979), 436–52.

88. Poggio to Niccoli, 10 June 1429, in *Two Renaissance Book Hunters*, ed. and tr. P.W.G. Gordan (New York and London, 1974), 142–46 at 143, 145 (slightly changed); original in Poggio Bracciolini, *Epistole*, ed. H. Harth, 3 vols. (Florence, 1984–87), I, 115–18 at 115, 118. Ambrogio Traversari, another member of the circles in which Alberti moved, also "emended" Latin texts at the request of young

writers; see, e.g., Traversari to Niccoli, 16 March 1432, *Latinae epistolae*, ed. L. Mehus (Florence, 1759; repr. Bologna, 1968), VIII.1, 350–51.

89. Lapo to Flavio Biondo, 8 April 1437, in Regoliosi, " 'Res gestae patriae,' " 292–93; Leonardo Dati to Tommaso Ceffi, 23 May 1443, in Dati, *Epistolae xxxiii*, ed. L. Mehus (Florence, 1743), 22–25 (e.g., the characteristic remark on 25: "Well, you will say, Dati doesn't think anything of anyone; but you're wrong"). Cf. Traversari to Niccoli, 16 March 1432, *Latinae epistolae*, ed. Mehus, VIII.1, 351.

90. The extent of Alberti's knowledge of Greek literature—and his command of the language—remain unclear. He regularly took advantage of new Latin translations from the Greek, as D. Marsh shows in his detailed study of Alberti and other readers and reusers of Lucian in the fifteenth century: *Lucian and the Latins* (Ann Arbor, 1998). For further evidence that Alberti's knowledge of Greek literature, though extensive, rested chiefly on translations, see L. Bertolini, *"Grecus sapor"* (Rome, 1998).

91. L. B. Alberti, *Vita S. Potiti e Musca*, ed. C. Grayson (Florence, 1954). On Lucian in the Renaissance, see C. F. Robinson, *Lucian* (London, 1979); E. Mattioli, *Luciano e l'umanesimo* (Naples, 1980); and above all, Marsh, *Lucian*.

92. Last two quotations in this paragraph come from L. B. Alberti, *Dinner Pieces*, tr. D. Marsh (Binghamton, N.Y., 1987), 116, 119; originally published as *Intercenali inedite*, II, ed. E. Garin (Florence, 1965).

93. See esp. Baron, *In Search of Florentine Civic Humanism*, chaps. 7–9.

94. See Kohl and Witt, *Earthly Republic*.

95. These two quotations come from Alberti, "Wealth," *Dinner Pieces*, tr. Marsh, 52–53, 175–76. For Alberti's political conservatism, see Marsh's notes, 239, 241, 257.

96. These quotations come from Alberti, "Garlands," in ibid., 103, 211–12, 217; cf. p. 232 n. 4. On Alberti's quotation from Plutarch, see also D. Marsh, "Textual Problems in the *Intercenales*," *Albertiana* 2 (1999), 125–35 at 133–35.

97. See Alberti, *De commodis*, ed. Goggi Carotti, 42 and n. 15; Alberti, *Dinner Pieces*, tr. Marsh, 35; Alberti, *Apologhi ed elogi*, ed. R. Contarino (Genoa, 1984), 46. Note also "Leon Battista Alberti, *Philodoxeos fabula*. Edizione critica a cura di Lucia Cesarini Martinelli," *Rinascimento*, 2d ser., 17 (1977), 111–234 at 147. In his "commentarium," Alberti described the process of revision to which he had subjected his own text: *"Cum autem ad hec studia philosophie rediissem, hec fabula elimatior et honestior mea emendatione facta."*

98. These quotations come from Alberti, *Dinner Pieces*, tr. Marsh, 127, 98–125, 67; cf. G. Ponte, "Lepidus e Libripeta," *Rinascimento* 12 (1972), 237–65, 66–69. Cf. also R. Fubini and A. Menci Gallorini, "L'autobiografia di Leon Battista Alberti: Studio e edizione," *Rinascimento*, 2d ser., 12 (1972), 21–78 at 70: "He thanked those who slandered his writing, so long as they gave him their opinion face to face, and expressed his gratitude for their effort to make him more smooth and correct by their instruction."

99. See Alberti to Bartolomeo Dal Pozzo, c. 1433, *Opera inedita et pauca separatim impressa*, ed. G. Mancini (Florence, 1890), 272–77.

100. Poggio, *De varietate fortunae*, in *Visitiamo Roma nel Quattrocento*, ed. C. D'Onofrio (Rome, 1989); and Chapter 7 below.

101. Alberti, *Vita Potiti*, ed. Grayson; cf. R. Weiss, *The Renaissance Discovery of Classical Antiquity* (Oxford, 1988); E. Cochrane, *Historians and Historiography in Renaissance Italy* (Chicago and London, 1981).

102. Alberti, *Vita Potiti*, ed. Grayson, 63–64.

103. See *Dizionario biografico degli Italiani*, s.v. Leonardo Dati, by R. Ristori.

104. See Cochrane, *Historians*.

105. These six quotations come from Alberti, *Vita Potiti*, ed. Grayson, 86, 87, 65, 66, 70.

106. See in general G. Nadel, "Philosophy of History before Historicism," *History and Theory* 3 (1964), 291–315; R. Landfester, *Historia magistra vitae* (Geneva, 1972); M. Miglio, *Storiografia pontificia del Quattrocento* (Bologna, 1975); R. Koselleck, "Historia magistra vitae: Über die Auflösung des Topos im Horizont neuzeitlich bewegter Geschichte," *Vergangene Zukunft* (Frankfurt, 1984), 38–66; E. Kessler, "Das rhetorische Modell der Historiographie," *Formen der Geschichtsschreibung*, ed. R. Koselleck et al. (Munich, 1982), 37–85; and for the larger context, Cochrane, *Historians*.

107. See, e.g., M. Carruthers, *The Book of Memory* (Cambridge, 1990); J. Hamburger, *The Visual and the Visionary* (New York, 1998); P. Tinagli, *Women in Italian Renaissance Art* (Manchester, 1997), chap. 5.

108. Alberti, *Vita Potiti*, ed. Grayson, 83, quotation on 72.

109. See Chapter 5 below.

110. Quotation comes from Alberti, *Vita Potiti*, ed. Grayson, 78–79, 88.

111. See Chapter 5 below.

112. Baxandall, *Giotto and the Orators*; cf. C. Smith, *Architecture in the Culture of Early Humanism* (New York, 1992).

113. These three quotations come from Alberti, *Dinner Pieces*, tr. Marsh, 56, 54, 57.

CHAPTER III

1. Alberti's letter to Brunelleschi is preserved in Florence, Biblioteca Nazionale, Cod. II. IV. 38, fols. 120 recto–136 verso, which is also one of the four manuscripts to contain the Italian version of the work. The Italian text was completed (according to a note by Alberti at the end) on 17 July 1436. (L. B. Alberti, *Opere volgari*, ed. C. Grayson [Bari, 1960–73], III, 299.) Alberti completed the work itself—as he recorded in his copy of Cicero's *Brutus*, now in Venice, Biblioteca Marciana, Cod. Lat. 67, cl. XI—on 26 August 1435: "Die Veneris ora xx 3/4 quae fuit dies 26 Augusti 1435 complevi opus de Pictura Florentiae." We do not know if this refers to the Latin or the Italian text (in ibid., 305). But it is clear that Alberti had written the text, in one language or another, by 1435, and completed the Italian version of it within a year. Most manuscripts of the Latin version derive from a revised version that Alberti completed early in the 1440s.

2. Most scholars accept the view that Alberti completed *De pictura*, the Latin form of his work, in Florence by 1435, and *Della pittura*, the Italian form, before July 1436, when he dedicated it to Filippo Brunelleschi. See C. Grayson, "Studi su Leon Bat-

tista Alberti," *Rinascimento* 4 (1953), 45–62 at 54–62, and "The Text of Alberti's *De pictura*," *Italian Studies* 23 (1968), 71–92, both reprinted in his *Studi su Leon Battista Alberti*, ed. P. Claut (Florence, 1999), 57–66, 245–69. In a provocative counterargument, M. Picchio Simonelli, "On Alberti's Treatises of Art and their Chronological Relationship," *Yearbook of Italian Studies* (1971), 75–102, tried to demonstrate the priority of the Italian version, but it has generally found less acceptance than the close analysis of the text conducted by N. Maraschio, "Aspetti del bilinguismo albertiano nel *De pictura*," *Rinascimento*, 2d ser., 12 (1972), 183–228, who treated the Italian as a translation from the Latin. See most recently J. M. Greenstein, *Mantegna and Painting as Historical Narrative* (Chicago and London, 1992), 235–36 n. 1; J. M. Greenstein, "On Alberti's 'Sign': Vision and Composition in Quattrocento Painting," *Art Bulletin* 79 (1997), 669–98 at 669; and for a different formulation cf. D. Rosand, "*Ekphrasis* and the Renaissance of Painting: Observations on Alberti's Third Book," *Florilegium columbianum*, ed. K.–L. Selig and R. Somerville (New York, 1987), 147–63 at 147 n. 1. But L. Bertolini's pointed summary of the *status quaestionis* emphasizes that some solid internal evidence supports the priority of the Italian text. See *Leon Battista Alberti*, ed. J. Rykwert and A. Engel (Milan, 1994), 423–24.

3. For the Italian text, see L. B. Alberti, *On Painting and On Sculpture*, ed. C. Grayson (London, 1972), 32; it may also be found in Alberti, *Opere volgari*, ed. Grayson, III, 7–8. For the English text, see Alberti's *On Painting and On Sculpture*, ed. Grayson, 33 (slightly altered).

4. Pliny, *Ep.*, 6.21.1–3: "I am one of those who admire the ancients, without—as some do—despising the intellects of our own day. For it is not true that nature, being, so to speak, worn out, produced nothing nowadays that is worthy of praise. Recently, for example, I heard Vergilius of Rome reading a comedy, one modeled on an ancient comedy, aloud to a small audience—one so well executed that it too could someday serve as an exemplar."

5. Lucretius, *De rerum natura*, 2.1150–53.

6. See J. Bialostocki, "The Renaissance Concept of Nature and Antiquity," *The Renaissance and Mannerism: Studies in Western Art. Acts of the Twentieth International Congress of the History of Art* (Princeton, 1963), II, 19–30, esp. 20: Alberti uses the term *nature* in an active sense, meaning not only the creation but "a live power that directs and governs life in men, animals, and plants, as well as the growth of a work of art." See also H. W. Janson, *Apes and Ape Lore in the Middle Ages and the Renaissance* (London, 1952), chap. 10.

7. See esp. E. H. Gombrich, "A Classical Topos in the Introduction to Alberti's *Della Pittura*," *Journal of the Warburg and Courtauld Institutes* 20 (1957), 173, and the very close examination of the passage in C. Smith, *Architecture in the Culture of Early Humanism* (New York, 1992). Smith's argument that Alberti also drew on Manuel Chrysoloras rests on general analogies that do not prove her case, rather than on a solid proof of textual descent. But her meticulous interpretation of the whole text rewards study even when it does not convince.

8. See Smith, *Architecture*, 22–23.

9. See Chapter 2 above.

10. C. W. Westfall, "Painting and the Liberal Arts: Alberti's View," *Journal of the History of Ideas* 30 (1969), 487–506; cf. M. Warnke, *Der Hofkünstler: Zur Vorgeschichte des modernen Künstlers* (Cologne, 1985), 63, on the courtly context in which such claims to freedom from guild restrictions arose.

11. See A. Manetti, *The Life of Filippo Brunelleschi*, ed. H. Saalman, tr. C. Enggass (University Park and London, 1970), 38–39.

12. J. Burckhardt, *Die Baukunst der Renaissance in Italien* (Darmstadt, 1955), 19. The approach Burckhardt adumbrated to Alberti here has been developed in some later works—e.g. L. Olschki, *Geschichte der neusprachlichen wissenschaftlichen Literatur*, I: *Die Literatur der Technik und der angewandten Wissenschaften vom Mittelalter bis zur Gegenwart* (Heidelberg, 1919) 45–88, now a largely forgotten classic, as well as the more recent work of Smith.

13. Paris, Bibliothèque Nationale, MS fr. 19093, fols. 6 recto, 9 verso, 15 verso, 24 recto, 24 verso: reproduced in *Carnet de Villard de Honnecourt*, ed. A. Erlande-Brandenbourg, R. Pernoud, J. Gimpel, and R. Bechmann (Paris, 1986; repr. 1994), plates 11, 18, 30, 47–48.

14. Ibid., fol. 15 verso (plate 29); cf. fol. 5 recto (plate 9). On the importance of Villard's terminology here, see E. Panofsky, *Gothic Architecture and Scholasticism* (New York, 1957), 87.

15. Paris, Bibliothèque Nationale, MS fr. 19093, fol. 1 verso (Villard, *Carnet*, plate 2).

16. J. Gimpel, *La révolution industrielle au Moyen Age* (Paris, 1975).

17. See the classic article by L. White, "Medical Astrologers and Late Medieval Technology," *Viator* 6 (1975), 295–308, and the superb recent synthesis by P. Long, "Power, Patronage and the Authorship of Ars: From Mechanical Know-How to Mechanical Knowledge in the Last Scribal Age," *Isis* 88 (1997), 1–41. For a historical overview, see H. Vérin, *La gloire des ingénieurs* (Paris, 1993). Further studies of the engineers' manuscripts include B. Gilles, "Etudes sur les manuscrits d'ingénieurs du xve siècle: Le manuscrit de la guerre hussite," *Techniques et civilisations* 5 (1956), 77–86; Gilles, *Engineers of the Renaissance* (Cambridge, Mass., 1966); and B. Hall, *The Technological Illustrations of the so-called "Anonymous of the Hussite Wars": Codex Latinus Monacensis 117, part 1* (Wiesbaden, 1979).

18. *Prima di Leonardo: Cultura delle macchine a Siena nel Rinascimento*, ed. P. Galluzzi (Milan, 1991); and J. J. Berns, *Die Herkunft des Automobils aus Himmelstrionfo und Höllenmaschine* (Berlin, 1996).

19. *Two Memoirs of Renaissance Florence*, ed. G. Brucker, tr. J. Martines (New York, Evanston, and London, 1967), 78–79; for the original see the edition by L. Pandimiglio, *Bullettino dell'Istituto Storico Italiano* 92 (1985). Cf. the brilliant case study by N. Adams, "Architecture for Fish: The Sienese Dam on the Bruna River—Structures and Designs, 1468–ca. 1530," *Technology and Culture* 25 (1984), 768–97.

20. See Vérin, *La gloire*, 19–42. For a case study of the way in which one Renaissance engineer combined his technical work with literary pursuits, see L. Makkai, "De Taccola à Vercanzio. L'ingénieur de la Renaissance en Hongrie," *Mélanges en l'honneur de Fernand Braudel* (Toulouse, 1973), I, 337–47.

21. S. P. Lambros, "Ipomnima tou Kardinaliou Vissarionos eis Konstantinon ton Palaiologon," *Neos Hellinomnimon* 3 (1906) 12–50 at 26; for the translation and the larger context, see C. Cipolla, *Clocks and Culture 1300–1700* (New York, 1967), 27; cf. I. Sevcenko, "The Decline of Byzantium seen through the eyes of its Intellectuals," *Dumbarton Oaks Papers* 15 (1961), 167–86.

22. See C. Cipolla, *Guns and Sails in the Early Phase of European Expansion* (London, 1963); B. Hall, *Weapons and Warfare in Renaissance Europe* (Baltimore, 1997).

23. M. Taccola, *De rebus militaribus*, ed. and tr. E. Knobloch (Baden-Baden, 1984), 62–63; C. Kyeser, *Bellifortis*, ed. G. Quarg (Düsseldorf, 1967).

24. For near-contemporary evidence that Alberti's list of his own skills could be seen as connecting him to the world of artists and engineers, cf. the similar list that Ghiberti, following Vitruvius, prescribed, probably around 1450: "It is fitting that the sculptor and painter have a solid knowledge of the following liberal arts: grammar, geometry, philosophy, medicine, astrology [i.e., astronomy and astrology], perspective [i.e., optics and perspective], history, anatomy, theory, design, arithmetic"; *I commentarii*, ed. L. Bartoli (Florence, 1998), 46. Vitruvius' list was slightly different: it included drawing, geometry, history, philosophy, music, medicine, law, astrology, and astronomy (*De architectura* 1.1.3).

25. E. Panofsky, "Artist, Scientist, Genius: Notes on the 'Renaissance-Dämmerung,' " *The Renaissance: A Symposium* (New York, 1953), 77–93.

26. See in general Warnke, *Der Hofkünstler*; but cf. the important qualifications made by E. S. Welch, *Art and Authority in Renaissance Milan* (New Haven and London, 1995), pt. 5.

27. C. Ginzburg, *Jean Fouquet: Ritratto del buffone Gonella* (Modena, 1996).

28. Taccola, *De rebus bellicis*, color plate in *Prima di Leonardo*, ed. Galluzzi, III.b.15.

29. See in general P. Panza, *Leon Battista Alberti: Filosofia e teoria dell'arte* (Milan, 1994), 99–112.

30. R. Fubini and A. Menci Gallorini, "L'autobiografia di Leon Battista Alberti: Studio e edizione," *Rinascimento*, 2d ser., 12 (1972), 72, 77; translations from R. N. Watkins, "L. B. Alberti in the Mirror: An Interpretation of the *Vita* with a New Translation," *Italian Quarterly* 30 (1989), 5–30.

31. See, e.g., W. Newman, "Alchemical and Baconian Views on the Art/Nature Division," *Reading the Book of Nature: The Other Side of the Scientific Revolution*, ed. A. Debus and M. Walton (Kirksville, Missouri, 1998), 81–90.

32. Roger Bacon, *Opus maius*, I.10, ed. J. H. Bridges (Oxford, 1897), I, 23; for a full translation of the passage, see Bacon, *Opus majus*, tr. R. B. Burke (Philadelphia, 1928), I, 25. The passage quoted in the text is also quoted by Vérin, *La gloire*, 47, but she does not note Bacon's further remark: "simple folk and the ignorant so reckoned know frequently great facts which escape the learned, as Aristotle shows in his second book on Sleep and Wakefulness."

33. In the course of the sixteenth century, artists like Jan van der Straet and Giuseppe Arcimboldo and organizers of *Kunst- und Wunderkammern* would devise strategies for the visual representation of technological progress as well. See U. Bernsmeier, *Die Nova Reperta des Jan van der Straet* (Diss. Hamburg, 1986); T. DaC. Kaufmann,

" 'Ancients and Moderns' in Prague: Arcimboldo's Drawings for Silk Manufacture," *Leids Kunsthistorisch Jaarboek* 2 (1983 [1984]), 179–207, repr. in T. DaC. Kaufmann, *The Mastery of Nature* (Princeton, N.J., 1993), 151–73; and H. Bredekamp, *Antikensehnsucht und Maschinenglauben* (Berlin, 1993), tr. with corrections by A. Brown as *The Lure of Antiquity and the Cult of the Machine* (Princeton, 1995).

34. On this tradition, see W. Van Egmond, *Practical Mathematics in the Italian Renaissance: A Catalog of Italian Abbacus Manuscripts and Printed Books to 1600* (Florence, 1980); F. J. Swetz, *Capitalism and Arithmetic* (La Salle, Ill., 1987; repr. 1989); and I. Rowland, "Abacus and Humanism," *Renaissance Quarterly* 48 (1995), 695–727.

35. See the fine analysis by P. Souffrin, "La geometria practica dans les *Ludi rerum mathematicarum*," *Albertiana* 1 (1998), 87–104.

36. See L. B. Alberti, *Ludi rerum mathematicarum,* in *Opere volgari,* ed. Grayson, III, 135 ("*come qui vedete la pittura*") and *passim.*

37. L. B. Alberti, *De commodis litterarum atque incommodis,* ed. L. Goggi Carotti (Florence, 1976), 88.

38. *Prima di Leonardo,* ed. Galluzzi, I.b.1. For Fontana, see esp. E. Battisti and G. Saccaro Battisti, *Le macchine cifrate di Giovanni Fontana* (Milan, 1984).

39. Alberti, *Opere volgari,* ed. Grayson, III, 163–66.

40. See Chapter 7 below.

41. See *Prima di Leonardo,* ed. Galluzzi, II.c.1–2.

42. See Alberti, *De statua,* 5, in *On Painting and On Sculpture,* ed. Grayson, 122–23.

43. Alberti, *De pictura,* 19, in *On Painting and On Sculpture,* ed. Grayson, 56 (translation 55).

44. Fubini and Menci Gallorini, "L'autobiografia," 73; Watkins, "L. B. Alberti," 11.

45. Cf. Welch, *Art and Authority.*

46. See two recent accounts: by H. Rauterberg, *Die Konkurrenzreliefs: Brunelleschi und Ghiberti im Wettbewerb um die Baptisteriumtür in Florenz* (Münster, 1996), and A. Niehaus, *Florentiner Reliefkunst von Brunelleschi bis Michelangelo* (Munich and Berlin, 1998), 46–60.

47. G. Pochat, "Brunelleschi and the 'Ascension' of 1422," *Art Bulletin* 60 (1978), 232–34.

48. G. Dondi dell'Orologio, *Tractatus astrarii,* ed. A. Barzon, E. Morpurgo, A. Petrucci, and G. Francescato (Vatican City, 1960).

49. See, e.g., P. Morel, *Les grottes maniéristes en Italie au xvie siècle* (Paris, 1998).

50. This passage, from Munich, clm 197 II, 107 verso has been published repeatedly: F. Prager, "A Manuscript of Taccola, Quoting Brunelleschi, on Problems of Inventors and Builders," *Proceedings of the American Philosophical Society* 112 (1968), 131–49; M. Taccola, *Liber tertius de ingeneis ac edifitiis non usitatis,* ed. J. H. Beck (Milan, 1969), 15; B. Degenhart and A. Schmitt, with H.–J. Eberhardt, *Corpus der italienischen Zeichnungen 1300–1450,* Teil II: *Venedig, Addenda zu Süd- und Mittelitalien,* 4: *Katalog 717–719, Mariano Taccola* (Berlin, 1982), 121 n. 14; also in the facsimile of the entire manuscript, edited by F. Prager, G. Scaglia, and U. Montag (Wiesbaden, 1984), 134–35.

51. Taccola, *De rebus militaribus,* ed. Knobloch, 121 (on a ship with crow's nest): "*ac*

dicte naves in bello marino sunt preliabiles contra hostes tuos prout facile in designo cerni-tur ab asuetis in guerris marinis expertisque"; 159 (on military wagon with crow's nests): "*Notandum est/quod expertis ac doctis de rebus militaribus/non opportet dicere cum quibus ducuntur currus ac machine/quod quilibet debet scire/trahuntur a bobus/bubalis et ab aliis iumentis . . .*" 197 (on a winch): "*Hoc designum pondera levandi/ad opus faciendi/non potest clarius demonstrari/nisi videatur a bove/sic iumentis girari/dificile est quod oretenus declaretur/et cetera.*"

52. Taccola, *De rebus militaribus,* ed. Knobloch, 368–69. For Alberti's measuring devices and their context see esp. the rich study by G. Scaglia, "Instruments Perfected for Measurements of Man and Statues Illustrated in Leon Battista Alberti's *De statua,*" *Nuncius* 8 (1995), 555–96.

53. Fubini and Menci Gallorini, "L'autobiografia," 73; Watkins, "L. B. Alberti," 12.

54. Alberti, *Opere volgari,* ed. Grayson, III, 146, 148, 166.

55. For the demonstrations, see Alberti, *De pictura,* 1.19, in *On Painting and On Sculpture,* ed. and tr. Grayson, 55–56 (translation altered).

56. See in general N. Pastore and E. Rosen, "Alberti and the Camera Obscura," *Physis* 26 (1984), 259–69.

57. O. Pächt, "Giovanni da Fano's Illustrations for Basinio's Epos *Hesperis,* with Two Appendices by A. Campana," *Studi Romagnoli* 2 (1951), 91–112; cf. J.J.G. Alexander in *The Painted Page: Italian Renaissance Book Illumination,* ed. J.J.G. Alexander (Munich and New York, 1994), no. 30, 91. I use Bodleian library, MS Canon. Class. Lat. 81. True, the illuminations do not all follow a single visual code. The stunning view of Florence creates no coherent system of space or proportion but rather uses a hallucinatory, Caligari-like juxtaposition of white marble planes to evoke the impression made by Italy's most spectacular city. Another scene, representing an army encamped on the shore, also fails to work out the consequences of its high viewpoint consistently. Multiple intersecting outlines of tents, spears, and standards create an impression of military movement and confusion. But even these are dramatized, like the rest, by their highly unusual, illusionistic marble frames.

58. See P. Galluzzi, *Renaissance Engineers: From Brunelleschi to Leonardo da Vinci* (Florence, 1996).

59. Alberti, *Della pittura,* 1.11, in *Opere volgari,* ed. Grayson, III, 26.

60. S. Y. Edgerton, Jr., *The Renaissance Rediscovery of Linear Perspective* (New York, 1976).

61. Alberti, *De pictura,* 1.20, in *On Painting and On Sculpture,* ed. Grayson, 56 (tr. Grayson, 57).

62. Fubini and Menci Gallorini, "L'autobiografia," 73; Watkins, "L. B. Alberti," 11 (slightly altered).

63. Manetti, *Life of Brunelleschi,* ed. Saalman, tr. Enggass, 42–47, quotation on 44–45. Cf. the ingenious reconstruction offered by Edgerton, *Renaissance Rediscovery,* and M. Kemp, "Science, Non-Science and Nonsense: The Interpretation of Brunelleschi's Perspective," *Art History* 1 (1978), 134–61.

64. See now J.V. Field, *The Invention of Infinity* (Oxford, 1996).

65. Manetti, *Life of Brunelleschi,* ed. Saalman, tr. Enggass, 67–69.

66. F. Prager, "Brunelleschi's Patent," *Journal of the Patent Office Society* 27 (1946), 109–35.

67. Cf. Long, "Power, Patronage, and the Authorship of *Ars*."

68. G. Campori, *Artisti degli Estensi: Orologieri, architetti ed ingegneri* (Modena, 1882; repr. Bologna, 1980), 34–35, 55–56.

69. For the further development of humanist reflection on new and old technologies, see esp. B. P. Copenhaver, "The Historiography of Invention in the Renaissance: The Sources and Composition of Polydore Vergil's *De inventoribus rerum I–III*," *Journal of the Warburg and Courtauld Institutes* 41 (1978), 192–214.

70. Dondi based his work not on an ancient source but on the *Theorica planetarum* of the thirteenth-century astronomer Campanus of Novara, the subtlety of which he praised. (Campanus had also designed a model of the planetary motions.) No doubt Dondi felt the friend who praised his work as superior to the sphere of Archimedes was only doing him justice.

71. These two quotations come from N. W. Gilbert, "A Letter of Giovanni Dondi dell'Orologio to Fra' Guglielmo Centueri: A Fourteenth-Century Episode in the Quarrel of the Ancients and the Moderns," *Viator* 8 (1977) 299–346, 336 (Latin text) and 344–45 (English translation).

72. See, e.g., the wise treatments of R. Krautheimer and T. Krautheimer-Hess, *Lorenzo Ghiberti*, 3d ptg. (Princeton, 1982; repr. 1990), 296–97; and R. Weiss, *The Renaissance Discovery of Classical Antiquity*, 2d ed. (Oxford, 1988), 50.

73. See esp. Seneca, *Epistulae morales*, 86 and 90.

74. Manetti, *Life of Brunelleschi*, ed. Saalman, tr. Enggass, 42–43.

75. Alberti, *Della pittura*, 1.11, in *Opere volgari*, ed. Grayson, III, 26.

76. See esp. Long, "Power, Patronage, and the Authorship of *Ars*," which makes this point with a wealth of concrete examples.

77. L. Bek, "Voti frateschi, virtù di umanista e regole di pittore. Cennino Cennini sub specie Albertiana," *Analecta Romana Instituti Danici* 6 (1971), 63–105, compares the two treatises very precisely.

78. C. Cennini, *Il libro dell'arte*, ed. F. Brunello (Vicenza, 1982; repr. 1998), cap. i, 2. On the sources and limits of Cennini's concept of *fantasia*, see L. Magagnato, "Introduzione," in ibid., v–xxvii at xi–xiv; M. Kemp, *Behind the Picture* (New Haven and London, 1997), 84–90 and *passim*.

79. See Degenhart and Schmidt, with Eberhardt, *Corpus der italienischen Zeichnungen*, esp. 29.

80. A manuscript of *Della pittura* (Paris, Bibliothèque Nationale, MS it. 1692, 1 recto) contains a note according to which Alberti wrote the work first in Latin and then translated it into Italian, for the use of—among others—"unlettered practitioners of the art." But this late note, however plausible its content, has no authority as a guide to Alberti's intentions. See R. Watkins, "Note on the Parisian MS of L. B. Alberti's Vernacular *Della Pittura*," *Rinascimento* 6 (1955), 369–72; P. H. Michel, *Un idéal humain au xvie siècle: La pensée de Leon Battista Alberti* (Paris, 1930), 22; P. H. Michel, "Le traité de la peinture de Léon-Baptiste Alberti: Version latine et vulgaire," *Revue des études italiennes* (1962), 80–91; C. Grayson, "The Text of Al-

berti's *De Pictura*," *Italian Studies* 23 (1968), 71–92, repr. in Grayson, *Studi su Leon Battista Alberti*, ed. P. Claut (Florence, 1999), 254–69. For a more modern argument in the same direction, see esp. M. Baxandall, *Giotto and the Orators* (Oxford, 1971), 126, arguing that *De pictura* "is, first, for people able to read neo-classical Latin quite freely: that is, humanists." Baxandall does not express an opinion on the intended readers of *Della pittura*.

81. Paris, Bibliothèque Nationale, MS lat. 12052; see esp. the colophon to *Elementa*, 42 vo: "*Neapoli per Arnaldum de Bruxella. 1476. die 11. februarii. ante ortum solis.*"

82. For Ghiberti's wide reading in the medieval literature on optics and perspective, from which he composed the mosaiclike third book of his *Commentaries*, see esp. K. Bergdolt, *Der dritte Kommentar Lorenzo Ghibertis: Naturwissenschaft und Medizin in der Kunsttheorie der Frührenaissance* (Weinheim, 1988), and L. Bartoli, "Introduzione," in Ghiberti, *I commentarii* (Florence, 1998), 33–37.

83. See M. Kemp, "From Mimesis to *Fantasia*: The Quattrocento Vocabulary of Creation, Inspiration and Genius in the Visual Arts," *Viator* 8 (1977), 347–98.

84. G. Aliotti to Niccolò Corbizo, n.d., in Aliotti, *Epistolae et opuscula*, ed. G. M. Scaramalius (Arezzo, 1769), I, 406.

85. Diagrams appear in some manuscripts, notably the Paris and Florence manuscripts of *Della pittura*, for which see Grayson, "The Text of Alberti's *De Pictura*," 268–69, and a Brescia manuscript of *De pictura*.

86. Fubini and Menci Gallorini, "L'autobiografia," 72–73; Watkins, "L. B. Alberti," 11.

87. Three works of sculpture are associated with Alberti in Kurt Badt, "Drei plastische Arbeiten von Leone Battista Alberti," *Mitteilungen des Kunsthistorischen Institutes in Florenz* 8 (1958), 78–87: the Washington plaquette, a similar one in the Louvre (now regarded as a fake), and a bust of Lodovico Gonzaga in Berlin (*On Painting*, ed. Grayson, plate VIII). D. Lewis, in *The Currency of Fame: Portrait Medals of the Renaissance*, ed. S. K. Scher (New York, 1994), 41–43, suggests that "[t]he closest antique parallel for it is the British Museum's noble cameo portrait of Augustus, appropriated with a 'rebaptism' and the addition of a new diadem by Constantine the Great. That work—or others like it—provided a precedent for the size, shape, relief handling, costume and iconography of Alberti's creation." Lewis also calls it "one of the true milestones in Western art. It is the first major Renaissance revival of a Roman imperial cameo, as well as the first monumental post-classical profile portrait and the first labeled self-portrait of an artist." (G.A.M. Richter, *Engraved Gems of the Romans* [London, 1971], 99–100, no. 474.) See also J. Pope-Hennessy, *Renaissance Bronzes from the Samuel H. Kress Collection, Reliefs, Plaquettes, Statuettes, Utensils and Mortars* (London, 1965), 7–8 and no. 1, fig. 1; C. C. Wilson, *Renaissance Small Bronze Sculptures and Associated Decorative Arts at the National Gallery of Art* (Washington, 1983), 12; and A. F. Radcliffe in *Italian Renaissance Sculpture in the Time of Donatello* (Detroit, 1985), 163–64.

88. A number of scholars have followed Kurt Badt in suggesting that Alberti deliberately fashioned the hair of his self-portrait as "leonine": either in the literal sense, by imitating the hair of Roman images of lions, or in the figurative, by imitating that of Leonello d'Este of Ferrara, who would soon make that city into a humanist

paradise. But comparison with the closest contemporary evidence—the early medals of the Estensi done by Pisanello—does not offer much support for this argument. Alberti represented his hair not as a coherent mass but as a series of overlapping, curving masses, roughly scored to indicate the individual hairs. It matches neither the long, soft waves of a lion's hair, as Pisanello represented it, nor the closely interwoven curls of Leonello's. But the shortcut that Alberti used to represent his own hair is revealing nonetheless. For all its attractiveness, the portrait is in some respects technically unimpressive.

89. See esp. the rich discussion in J. Woods-Marsden, *Renaissance Self-Portraiture* (New Haven and London, 1998), 71–77 (quotation from 73).

90. For some notable examples, see *The Painted Page*, ed. J.J.G. Alexander (New York, 1994). *Immaginare l'autore: il ritratto del letterato nella cultura umanistica. Ritratti riccardiani*, ed. G. Lazzi (Florence, 1998).

91. See in general R. Weiss, *The Renaissance Discovery of Classical Antiquity* (Oxford, 1988), 23. For Petrarch's remark that Gordian *"malum habuit sculptorem,"* see F. Haskell, *History and its Images* (New Haven and London, 1993), 13.

92. L. Mehus, ed., *Ambrogii Traversari . . . latinae epistolae*, (Florence, 1759; repr. Bologna, 1968), VIII, Ep. 45, cited in C. Stinger, "Ambrogio Traversari and the 'Tempio degli Scolari' at S. Maria degli Angeli in Florence," *Essays Presented to Myron P. Gilmore*, ed. S. Bertelli and G. Ramakus (Florence, 1978), 1.271–86 at 277, also describing a gold ring with an onyx stone carved with an image of Hadrian that Stefano Porcari gave Traversari in the fall of the same year. See also A. Traversari, *Hodeporicon*, ed. and tr. V. Tamburini (Florence, 1985), 126. On Cyriac's slightly later passion for identifying images of great ancient thinkers like Aristotle, see P. W. Lehmann and K. Lehmann, *Samothracian Reflections* (Princeton, 1973), 15ff. (from October 1444).

93. Vespasiano da Bisticci, *Vite di uomini illustri del secolo xv* (Florence, 1938), 500; Krautheimer and Krautheimer-Hess, *Ghiberti*, esp. 13: Ghiberti took the image in question, which actually represents the flaying of Marsyas, as depicting the three ages of man.

94. E. Wind, *Pagan Mysteries in the Renaissance*, 2d ed. (London, 1966).

95. For these two quotations, see L. B. Alberti, *Dinner Pieces*, tr. D. Marsh (Binghamton, N.Y., 1987), 156, 154. The fullest and most insightful account of these developments is in B. Curran, "Ancient Egypt and Egyptian Antiquities in Italian Renaissance Art and Culture," Ph.D. diss., Princeton University, 1997, 154.

96. At the end of the work, however, Alberti apparently challenged his own hermeneutics. The philosopher's friends laughingly warn him, "Whether you are right or wrong, others may judge. But you should know that there will be others, some bold and some learned and ingenious, who will take your remarks in a different spirit." And they point out that when a boy spilled oil from a lamp on a splendid book, he could claim that he had done no harm. The philosopher, after all, had said that "evil will ensure if a lamp goes out." But the lamp, in this case, had continued to burn. Taking their point, the philosopher insists not on the age and profundity, but rather on the originality and wittiness of his teachings: "I won't deny that I in-

vented some of these sayings in my leisure, and improvised others as I spoke. No matter how you and other scholars receive them, I shall consider myself fortunate if I do not appear indolent, and if I amuse those who enjoy my works." Here too, in other words, Alberti was also out to prove himself a master of rhetoric—one who could argue all sides of any given question.

97. These three quotations come from Alberti, *Dinner Pieces*, tr. Marsh, 213, 215, 215–16.

98. See in general *The Hieroglyphics of Horapollo*, ed. with an introduction by G. Boas (New York, 1950; repr. with a new foreword by A. Grafton, Princeton, 1993); E. Iversen, *The Myth of Egypt and its Hieroglyphs in European Tradition* (Copenhagen, 1961; repr. Princeton, 1993); E. Iversen, "The Hieroglyphic Tradition," *The Legacy of Egypt*, ed. J. R. Harris, 2d ed. (Oxford, 1971); R. Wittkower, "Hieroglyphics in the Early Renaissance," *Allegory and the Migration of Symbols* (London, 1977), 114–28; C. Dempsey, "Renaissance Hieroglyphic Studies and Gentile Bellini's *Saint Mark Preaching in Alexandria*," *Hermeticism and the Renaissance*, ed. I. Merkel and A. G. Debus (Washington, London, and Toronto, 1988), 342–65; S. Sider, "Horapollo," *Catalogus translationum et commentariorum*, ed. F. E. Cranz, P. O. Kristeller, and V. Brown (Washington, D.C., 1960–), VI, 15–29.

99. Cf. L. Schneider, "Leon Battista Alberti: Some Biographical Implications of the Winged Eye," *Art Bulletin* 72 (1990), 261–70.

100. Badt emphasizes the "leonine" hair of the first medal and the amateur quality shown by its bad finish on cheek and neck. This line of argument is taken further by U. Middeldorf, "On the Dilettante Sculptor," *Apollo* 107 (April 1978), 310–22, who emphasizes the strong draftsmanship, the weak modeling of the underlying bony structure, and the prominent ear, which show the amateur hand at work.

101. Alberti, *De pictura*, 58, in *On Painting and On Sculpture*, ed. Grayson, 100: "*Certior enim ac facilior est sculptura quam pictura . . . Prominentiae vero facilius reperiuntur sculptura quam pictura*" (tr. ibid., 101).

102. Alberti, *De pictura*, 35, in *On Painting and on Sculpture*, ed. Grayson, 72: "*[i]n qua vero facie ita iunctae aderunt superficies ut amena lumina in umbras suaves defluant, nullaeque angulorum asperitates extent*" (tr. ibid., 73)—as opposed to the face with big hollows and bumps. Cf. 2.41 (80, tr. 81) where he talks a bit about physiognomics, and 2.42 (ibid) on the difficulty of representing emotions in faces.

103. Vasari, life of Alberti: "*In Fiorenza medesimamente è in casa di Palla Rucellai un ritratto di se medesimo, fatto alla spera*" ("Also in Florence, in the house of Palla Rucellai, there is a self-portrait, done with the aid of a mirror"); quoted and translated in Alberti, *On Painting and on Sculpture*, ed. Grayson, 144.

104. See the fine analysis in Woods-Marsden, *Renaissance Self-Portraiture*, esp. 76–77.

105. J. Pope-Hennessy, *The Portrait in the Renaissance* (Washington, 1966), 66–69 and fig. 67.

CHAPTER IV

1. On Cyriac, see P. Brown, *Venice and Antiquity* (New Haven and London, 1996); and *Ciriaco d'Ancona e la cultura antiquaria dell'Umanesimo*, ed. G. Paci and S. Sconocchia (Reggio Emilia, 1998).

2. Francesco Scalamonti, *Vita viri clarissimi et famosissimi Kyriaci Anconitani*, ed. and tr. C. Mitchell and E. W. Bodnar, S.J., Transactions of the American Philosophical Society, 86, pt. 4 (Philadelphia, 1996), no. 101–103, 131–32.

3. Scalamonti, *Vita viri clarissimi*, 131–32.

4. See M. Wackernagel, *Der Lebensraum des Künstlers in der florentinischen Renaissance* (Leipzig, 1938); tr. with valuable commentary by A. Luchs as *The World of the Florentine Renaissance Artist* (Princeton, 1981), chaps. 11–14.

5. See D. Rosand, "Ekphrasis and the Renaissance of Painting: Observations on Alberti's Third Book," *Florilegium columbianum*, ed. K.–L. Selig and R. Somerville (New York, 1987), 147–63.

6. C. Nauert, "C. Plinius Secundus (Naturalis Historia)," *Catalogus translationum et commentariorum*, ed. F. E. Cranz et al. (Washington, D.C., 1980), III, 297–422; A. Borst, *Das Buch der Naturgeschichte*, 2d ed. (Heidelberg, 1995).

7. L. B. Alberti, *De pictura*, 2.26, in *On Painting and On Sculpture*, ed. and tr. C. Grayson (London, 1972), 62–63 (translation altered); and in L. B. Alberti, *Opere volgari*, ed. C. Grayson (Bari, 1960–73), III, 46–47.

8. See L. Barkan, *Unearthing the Past* (New Haven and London, 1999).

9. See C. Cennini, *Il libro dell'arte*, ed. F. Brunello (Vicenza, 1982; repr. 1998); and L. Bek, "Voti frateschi, virtù di umanista e regole di pittore: Cennino Cennini sub specie Albertiana," *Analecta Romana Instituti Danici* 6 (1971), 63–105.

10. See Rosand, "Ekphrasis."

11. See Bek, "Voti frateschi."

12. On Alberti and Cennini see, in addition to Bek, "Voti frateschi," the excellent chapter in M. Kemp, *Behind the Painting: Art and Evidence in the Italian Renaissance* (New Haven and London, 1997).

13. Alberti, *De pictura*, 3. 52, in *On Painting and On Sculpture*, ed. and tr. Grayson, 94–95 (translation slightly altered); and in *Opere volgari*, ed. Grayson, III, 90–91.

14. Alberti, *De pictura*, 2.25, in *On Painting and On Sculpture*, ed. and tr. Grayson, 60–61; and in *Opere volgari*, ed. Grayson, III, 44–45.

15. See esp. M. Baxandall, "Alberti's Self," *Fenway Court* (1990–91), 31–36.

16. See esp. H. Mühlmann, *Aesthetische Theorie der Renaissance* (Bonn, 1981), and his "Über den humanistischen Sinn einiger Kerngedanken der Kunsttheorie seit Alberti," *Zeitschrift für Kunstgeschichte* 33 (1970), 135.

17. This approach to Renaissance art theory was first pursued by R. W. Lee, who emphasized the role of poetics in his classic article "Ut pictura poesis," *Art Bulletin* 22 (1940), 197ff., later reprinted in book form, as *Ut pictura poesis* (New York, 1967); for Alberti and rhetoric, see esp. app. 2, "Inventio, Dispositio, Elocutio." The role of ancient literary theory in Alberti's work was clarified by C. Gilbert, "Antique Frameworks for Renaissance Art Theory: Alberti and Pino," *Marsyas* 3 (1943–45),

87–106. More recent studies, while differing on the structure and models for On Painting, have tended to stress rhetoric more than poetics; see esp. J. R. Spencer, "Ut rhetorica pictura: A Study in Quattrocento Theory of Painting," Journal of the Warburg and Courtauld Institutes 20 (1957), 26–44; A. Chastel, "Die humanist-ischen Formeln als Rahmenbegriffe der Kunstgeschichte und Kunsttheorie des Quattrocento," Kunstchronik 5 (1954), 119–22; A. Chastel, Art et humanisme à Flo-rence au temps de Laurent le Magnifique (Paris, 1959); S. L. Alpers, "Ekphrasis and Aesthetic Attitudes in Vasari's Lives," Journal of the Warburg and Courtauld Institutes 23 (1960), 190–215; A. Ellenius, De arte pingendi (Uppsala and Stockholm, 1960); C. W. Westfall, "Painting and the Liberal Arts: Alberti's View," Journal of the History of Ideas 30 (1969), 487–506; M. Baxandall, Giotto and the Orators (Oxford, 1971); M. Baxandall, Painting and Experience in Fifteenth-Century Italy (Oxford, 1972); N. Maraschio, "Aspetti del bilinguismo albertiano nel De pictura," Rinasci-mento, 2d ser., 12 (1972), 183–228, esp. 187–99; D. R. Edward Wright, "Alberti's De pictura: Its Literary Structure and Purpose," Journal of the Warburg and Courtauld Institutes 47 (1984), 52–71; Rosand, "Ekphrasis"; R. Kuhn, "Albertis Lehre über die Komposition als die Kunst in der Malerei," Archiv für Begriffsgeschichte 28 (1984), 123–78; N. Michels, Bewegung zwischen Ethos und Pathos (Münster, 1988), esp. 1–65; P. Panza, Leon Battista Alberti: Filosofia e teorie dell'arte (Milan, 1994), 115–26; G. Wolf, " 'Arte superficiem illam fontis amplecti': Alberti, Narziss, und die Erfindung der Malerei," Diletto e maraviglia, ed. C. Göttler, U. M. Hofstede, K. Patz, and K. Zollikofer (Emsdetten, 1998), 10–39. M. Gosebruch, "Varietas bei L. B. Alberti und der wissenschaftliche Renaissancebegriff," Zeitschrift für Kunstgeschichte 20 (1957), 229–38 [cf. also Kunstchronik 9 (1956), 301–302]; Mühlmann, Aesthe-tische Theorie der Renaissance; and C. Smith, Architecture in the Culture of Early Hu-manism (Oxford, 1992) concentrate on connections between rhetoric and architecture in Alberti's thought but have much to offer students of On Painting as well. K. Patz, "Zum Begriff der Historia in L. B. Albertis De pictura," Zeitschrift für Kunstgeschichte 49 (1986), 269–87; J. Greenstein, "Alberti on Historia: A Renais-sance View of the Structure of Significance in Narrative Painting," Viator 21 (1990), 273–99; J. Greenstein, Mantegna and Painting as Historical Narrative (Chicago and London, 1992); and S. Deswarte-Rosa, "Introduction," in Alberti, De la peinture, tr. J. L. Schefer (Paris, 1992; repr. 1993), 29–44, all rightly stress Al-berti's originality and eclecticism in the use of classical sources. Cf. most recently P. Galand-Hallyn, "La rhétorique en Italie à la fin du Quattrocento (1475–1500)," Histoire de la rhétorique dans l'Europe moderne, 1450–1950, ed. M. Fumaroli (Paris, 1999), 131–90 at 151–54, and H. Locher, "Leon Battista Albertis Erfindung des 'Gemäldes' aus dem Geist der Antike: der Traktat De pictura," in Theorie der Praxis, ed. K. W. Forster and H. Locher (Berlin, 1999), 75–107.

18. See M. Winterbottom, "Quintilian," Texts and Transmission, ed. L. D. Reynolds (Oxford, 1983), 332–34.

19. See esp. Wright, "Alberti's De pictura," and Patz, "Zum Begriff der Historia." For a very different view, see M. Jarzombek, "The Structural Problematic of Leon Battista Alberti's De pictura," Renaissance Studies 4 (1990), 273–85.

20. Lee, *Ut pictura poesis*, remains the classic study. On the fluidity of borders between poetry and rhetoric in the classical tradition, see Patz, "Zum Begriff der *Historia*."

21. Cf. Kemp, *Behind the Picture*.

22. See, e.g., the recent works of A. Vasaly, *Representations* (Berkeley, Los Angeles, and London, 1993) and M. Gleason, *Making Men* (Princeton, 1996). R. Williams is now at work on a comprehensive study of decorum in Renaissance culture.

23. Alberti, *De pictura*, 2.36, in *On Painting and On Sculpture*, ed. and tr. Grayson, 72–73 (translation altered); and in *Opere volgari*, ed. Grayson, III, 62–63. The other quotations come from *De pictura* 2.43, in *On Painting and On Sculpture*, ed. and tr. Grayson, 82–83, following Quintilian's *Institutio oratoria* 11.3.105. See Michels, *Bewegung*, for a full discussion.

24. Alberti, *De pictura* 2.45, in *On Painting and On Sculpture*, ed. and tr. Grayson, 86–87; and in *Opere volgari*, ed. Grayson, III, 78–79.

25. See A. Niehaus, *Florentiner Reliefkunst von Brunelleschi bis Michelangelo* (Cologne, 1998).

26. Alberti, *De pictura*, 2.28, in *On Painting and On Sculpture*, ed. Grayson, 64–67; and in *Opere volgari*, ed. Grayson, III, 50–53. Interestingly, in the Italian text, Alberti remarks on his "amazement" at this; the Latin version speaks only of his pleasure. Much later, Leonardo would cite the leisurely character of painting as an argument for its superiority to the dirtier, sweatier art of sculpture; but Michelangelo would emphasize, in his poems, just how sweaty and dirty painting could also be.

27. The passages in question come from Alberti, *De pictura*, 1.12, 1.23, 2.43, and 3.36 in *On Painting and On Sculpture*, ed. and tr. Grayson, 48–49, 58–59, 82–83 (translation altered); and in *Opere volgari*, ed. Grayson, III, 26–27, 42–43, 74–75.

28. L. Ghiberti, *I commentarii*, ed. L. Bartoli (Florence, 1998), 73–74 at 73; cf. 19 and H. van de Waal, "The *Linea summae tenuitatis* of Apelles: Pliny's Phrase and Its Interpreters," *Zeitschrift für Aesthetik und allgemeine Kunstwissenschaft* 12 (1967), 5–32.

29. Alberti, *De pictura*, 1.1, in *On Painting and On Sculpture*, ed. and tr. Grayson, 36–37; and in *Opere volgari*, ed. Grayson, III, 10–11.

30. L. B. Alberti, *Opera inedita et pauca separatim impressa*, ed. G. Mancini (Florence, 1890), 68. On this text, see L. Bertolini in *Leon Battista Alberti*, ed. J. Rykwert and A. Engel (Milan, 1994), 424–25.

31. Alberti, *De pictura*, 2.47, in *On Painting and On Sculpture*, ed. and tr. Grayson, 88–89; and in *Opere volgari*, ed. Grayson, III, 84–85.

32. P. Hills, *The Light of Early Italian Painting* (New Haven and London, 1987), 44. On Alberti's color theory, see also S. Y. Edgerton, Jr., "Alberti's Colour Theory: A Medieval Bottle Without Renaissance Wine," *Journal of the Warburg and Courtauld Institutes* 32 (1969), 109–34.

33. S. Y. Edgerton, Jr., *The Renaissance Rediscovery of Linear Perspective* (New York, 1975), and for a very different approach see L. Gérard-Marchand, "Les indications chromatiques dans le *De pictura* et le *Della pittura* d'Alberti," *Histoire de l'Art* 11 (1990), 23–36.

34. Alberti, *On Painting and On Sculpture*, ed. and tr. Grayson, 72–75; and in *Opere volgari*, ed. Grayson, III, 62–65.

35. F. Ames-Lewis, *Drawing in Early Renaissance Italy* (New Haven and London, 1981).

36. Alberti, *De pictura*, 3.61, in *On Painting and on Sculpture*, ed. and tr. Grayson, 102–105 (translation altered); and in *Opere volgari*, ed. Grayson, III, 102–105.

37. Alberti had already studied Masaccio's frescoes. But expert opinion is not agreed as to whether Masaccio used the technique Alberti recommended in the sinopia for the face of the Virgin in his *Trinity* fresco in Santa Maria Novella. See E. Borsook, *The Mural Painters of Renaissance Tuscany from Cimabue to Andrea del Sarto*, 2d ed. (Oxford, 1980), 59–60.

38. See, e.g., F. Borsi and P. Borsi, *Paolo Uccello* (Milan, 1992).

39. These quotations come from Alberti, *De pictura*, 2.46, 3.52, and 1.12, in *On Painting and On Sculpture*, ed. and tr. Grayson, 94–95, 88–89, 48–49 (translation altered); and in *Opere volgari*, ed. Grayson, III, 90–91, 82–83, 26–29.

40. See esp. Edgerton, *Rediscovery*, and, for the traditions Alberti knew and his use of them, D. C. Lindberg, *Theories of Vision from Al-Kindi to Kepler* (Chicago and London, 1976), 149–54. Both provide guidance to the ample older literature. See also D. C. Lindberg, *Roger Bacon and the Origins of Perspectiva in the Middle Ages* (Oxford, 1996).

41. Lindberg, *Theories*, 154. See also J. A. Aiken, "Truth in Images: From the Technical Drawings of Ibn-al-Razzaz al-Jazzari, Campanus of Novara and Giovanni de' Dondi to the Perspective Projection of Leon Battista Alberti," *Viator* 25 (1994), 325–59.

42. L. B. Alberti, *Ludi rerum mathematicarum*, in *Opere volgari*, ed. Grayson, III, 136–38.

43. See Kemp, "Science, Non-Science and Nonsense"; J. Kuhn, "Measured Appearances: Documentation and Design in Early Perspective Drawing," *Journal of the Warburg and Courtauld Institutes* 53 (1990), 114–32; and M. Trachtenberg, "What Brunelleschi Saw: Monument and Site at the Palazzo Vecchio in Florence," *Journal of the Society of Architectural Historians* 47 (1988), 14–43.

44. See, e.g., A. Dürer, *The Painter's Manual*, ed. and tr. W. L. Strauss (New York, 1977), 386–93.

45. For further discussion, see esp. E. Panofsky, "Die Perspektive als 'symbolische Form,'" *Vorträge der Bibliothek Warburg* 4 (1924–25), 258–330, tr. with an important introduction by C. S. Wood as *Perspective as Symbolic Form* (New York, 1991); Edgerton, *Rediscovery*; and J. Elkins, *The Poetics of Perspective* (Ithaca and London, 1994).

46. See, e.g., C. Cennini, *Il libro dell'arte*, ed. F. Brunello (Vicenza 1982; repr. 1998), chaps. 27–28, 25–26 (advising selectivity and recourse to nature as well).

47. Alberti, *De pictura*, 2.58, in *On Painting and On Sculpture*, ed. and tr. Grayson, 100–101: and in *Opere volgari*, ed. Grayson, III, 98–101.

48. Alberti, *De pictura*, 2.31, in *On Painting and On Sculpture*, ed. and tr. Grayson, 68–69; and in *Opere volgari*, ed. Grayson, III, 54–57.

49. See M. Pardo, "Veiling the *Venus of Urbino*," in *Titian's Venus of Urbino*, ed. R. Goffen (Cambridge, 1997), 108–28.

50. See esp. J. R. Spencer, "Introduction," in Leon Battista Alberti, *On Painting*, tr. J. R. Spencer (New Haven and London, 1956; new ed., 1966); Patz, "Zum Begriff der *Historia*"; Greenstein, "Alberti on *Historia*"; and Greenstein, *Mantegna*.

51. The quotations in this paragraph come from Alberti, *De pictura*, 3.60, 2.42, in *On Painting and On Sculpture*, ed. and tr. Grayson, 102–103, 82–83; and in *Opere volgari*, ed. Grayson, III, 102–103, 74–75. For Cicero's phrase and Renaissance adaptations of it, see esp. G. Nadel, "Philosophy of History before Historicism," *History and Theory* 3 (1964), 291–315: and R. Landfester, *Historia magistra vitae* (Geneva, 1972).

52. L. B. Alberti, *De commodis litterarum atque incommodis,* ed. L. Goggi Carotti (Florence 1976), 41; L. B. Alberti, *Opuscoli inediti di Leon Battista Alberti. "Musca," "Vita S. Potiti,"* ed. C. Grayson (Florence, 1954), 86–87.

53. On the term *historia* in Greek and Latin, see K. Keuck, *"Historia,"* Diss., Münster (Emsdetten, 1934); and F. Hartog, *L'histoire d'Homère à Augustin* (Paris, 1999).

54. On Cicero's usage, see esp. Keuck, *"Historia,"* 16–19. In *De pictura*, 2.26, Alberti describes the story of Narcissus—which he calls a *fabula* in Latin—as a *storia* in Italian, further evidence of the lability of the term's meaning (*Opere volgari*, ed. Grayson, III, 46–47).

55. See P. Toynbee, "A Note on *Storia, Storiato*, and the Corresponding Terms in French and English, in Illustration of *Purgatorio* X, 52, 71, 73," *Mélanges offerts à Emile Picot par ses amis et ses élèves* (Paris, 1913), I, 195–208; Patz, "Zum Begriff der *Historia*"; and the forthcoming study by L. Barkan, which will shed new light on the Dantesque elements in Alberti and much else.

56. In 1431, for example, the Sienese Ser Mariano described the gates of the Church of the Holy Sepulchre in Jerusalem as *molto belle, e storiate di petre*—"very lovely, and adorned with histories in stone."

57. Niehaus, *Florentiner Reliefkunst,* 24–26.

58. C. Guasti, *Il pergamo di Donatello nel Duomo di Prato* (Florence, 1887), 19.

59. R. Krautheimer and T. Krautheimer-Hess, *Lorenzo Ghiberti,* 5th ed. (Princeton, 1990), 229.

60. D. S. Chambers, *Patrons and Artists in the Italian Renaissance* (Columbia, S.C., 1971), 48; for the original document see Krautheimer and Krautheimer-Hess, *Ghiberti,* 372–73, with discussion at 169–73.

61. Alberti, *De pictura*, 1.21, in *On Painting and On Sculpture,* ed. and tr. Grayson, 57–58; and in *Opere volgari,* ed. Grayson, III, 40–41.

62. See most recently Niehaus, *Florentiner Reliefkunst.*

63. Quotations in this paragraph come from Alberti, *De pictura*, 2.37, 2.45, in *On Painting and On Sculpture*, ed. and tr. Grayson, 76–77, 86–87, 74–75; and in *Opere volgari*, ed. Grayson, III, 64–67, 78–81, 64–65.

64. This point is powerfully made by H. Kaufmann, *Donatello* (Berlin, 1935), 63–66. Alberti's ideal *historia* represented, as Krautheimer brilliantly showed, less a detailed prescription than a recipe for compromise between two opposing aesthetic ideals. The *historia* must be varied, containing "a properly arranged mixture of old men, youths, boys, matrons, children, domestic animals, dogs, birds, horses, sheep, buildings and provinces." But variety had limits: the painter must observe restraint, modesty, and dignity, and should not try, without good artistic reason, "to appear rich or to leave no space empty." A good *historia* should have some nine or ten characters,

posed in different attitudes (2.40). Many of the Florentine relief panels produced in Alberti's time conform to these ideals for painting. No wonder that he argued explicitly that painters and sculptors in fact followed the same set of rules, which his art of painting prescribed (2.26). On Alberti and contemporary art see also F. Balters, "Leon Battista Albertis 'De pictura.' Die kunsttheoretische und literarische Legitimierung von Affektübertragung und Kunstgenuss," *Georges-Bloch-Jahrbuch* 4 (1997), 23–39.

65. Sallust, *Jugurtha*, 4.5–6.

66. One of the most original and influential modern students of the rhetorical tradition and its application to the visual arts, David Summers, has acknowledged this point. Cicero, he points out, urged not in one of his rhetorical works but in his moral treatise *De officiis* that the painter and the writer seek as systematically as possible for criticism, asking ordinary laymen to judge their work: "painters and sculptors and even poets, too, wish to have their works reviewed by the public, in order that, if any point is criticized by many, it may be improved [1.41.147]." (D. Summers, *The Judgment of Sense* [Cambridge, 1987], 132–33.) As this passage suggests, even in antiquity the analogy most widely made was between painting and poetry—two arts designed to produce finished, not improvised, works. The classical tradition in rhetoric in fact provides no single complete model for Alberti's art of painting.

67. Alberti, *On Painting*, 3.53, in *On Painting and On Sculpture*, ed. and tr. Grayson, 94–97; and in *Opere volgari*, ed. Grayson, III, 92–93.

68. See esp. R. Förster, "Die Verleumdung des Apelles in der Renaissance," *Jahrbuch der Königlich-Preussischen Kunstsammlungen* 8 (1887), 29–56, 89–113; 15 (1894), 27–40; R. Förster, "Wiederherstellung antiker Gemälde durch Künstler der Renaissance," ibid., 43 (1933), 126–36; D. Cast, *The Calumny of Apelles* (New Haven and London, 1981); J.–M. Massing, *Du texte à l'image: La Calomnie d'Apelle et son iconographie* (Strasbourg, 1990); and D. Marsh, *Lucian and the Latins* (Ann Arbor, 1998), 22–23.

69. J.A.W. Heffernan, "Alberti on Apelles: Word and Image in *De pictura*," *International Journal of the Classical Tradition* 2 (1996), 345–59.

70. See, e.g., H. Bredekamp, *Sandro Botticelli: La Primavera* (Frankfurt, 1988); and C. Dempsey, *The Portrayal of Love* (Princeton, 1992), with full references to earlier literature.

71. These two quotations come from Alberti, *De pictura*, 3.62, in *On Painting and On Sculpture*, 104–105 (altered; Latin text); and in *Opere volgari*, ed. Grayson, III, 104–107.

72. See esp. Ghiberti, *Commentarii*, ed. Bartoli, 14 (list of passages used), 19, 23–25, 30, and n. 43, 53, 68, 73; and cf. the classic study of E. H. Gombrich, "The Renaissance Conception of Artistic Progress and Its Consequences," *Norm and Form* (London, 1966), 1–10.

73. Pliny, *Natural History*, 35.84, 35.85–86, tr. Jex-Blake.

74. Translation from Chambers, *Patrons and Artists*, 66; original in Guasti, *Il pergamo di Donatello*, 19.

75. Ghiberti, *Commentarii*, ed. Bartoli.

76. See esp. Westfall, "Painting and the Liberal Arts," 487–506; for the larger context and long-term course of these developments, see, e.g., P. Burke, "The Italian Artist and His Roles," *History of Italian Art*, tr. E. Bianchini and C. Dorey (Cambridge, 1994; repr. 1996), I, 1–28; *The Changing Status of the Artist*, ed. E. Barker, N. Webb, and K. Woods (New Haven and London, 1999).

77. L. B. Alberti, *Pontifex*, written 13–17 October 1437; in Alberti, *Opera inedita et pauca separatim impressa*, ed. G. Mancini (Florence, 1890), at 77, using *emendare* in an interesting sense—as a moral term: "*Utrumne igitur* [asks the jurisconsult Alberto Alberti], *vel hanc ipsam ob rem pontificis quam patrisfamilias cura erit familiaris gravior; quod ille suos ex se et in suorum gremio natos et adultos, sui amantissimos fidissimosque alat; idem suos, si petant, multis possit modis percommode emendatiores reddere monendo, castigando, spem dando adimendorum legatorum atque haereditatum . . .*" Cf. also 113–14, and Alberti, *I libri della famiglia*, in *Opere volgari*, ed. Grayson, I, 309–10 ("*Quasi come pochissime ti si avengano in ogni ragionamento attissime vie con parole emendarli*"). In his short treatise *Villa*, Alberti remarks that one can "emend" farmland by draining or fertilizing it (in ibid., 359).

78. B. Facio, *De viris illustribus liber*, ed. L. Mehus (Florence, 1745), 4, on Alberti's friend Beccadelli: "No one else was so quick or so sharp at noting others' faults and virtues in speech and writing—a quality for which the learned Leonardo Bruni gave him special praise."

79. Alberti, *De pictura*, 2.37, in *On Painting and On Sculpture*, ed. and tr. Grayson, 76–77; and in *Opere volgari*, ed. Grayson, III, 66–67.

80. H. Harth, "Niccolò Niccoli als literarischer Zensor. Untersuchungen zur Textgeschichte von Poggios *De avaritia*," *Rinascimento*, 2d ser., 7 (1967), 29–53.

81. These two quotations come from Alberti, *De pictura*, 2.38, 2.39, in *On Painting and On Sculpture*, ed. and tr. Grayson, 76–77 (translation altered); and in *Opere volgari*, ed. Grayson, III, 66–67, 68–69. See also 2.37.

82. J. Bialostocki, "Ars auro potior," *Mélanges de littérature et philologie offertes à Mieczyslaw Brahmer* (Warsaw, 1966), 55–63.

83. See the important article by C. Hope, "Artists, Patrons and Advisers in the Italian Renaissance," *Patronage in the Renaissance*, ed. G. F. Lytle and S. Orgel (Princeton, 1981), 293–343.

84. See A. Warburg, "Sandro Botticelli's *Birth of Venus* and *Spring*," *The Renewal of Pagan Antiquity*, ed. K. W. Forster, tr. D. Britt (Los Angeles, 1999), 95–98.

85. Alberti, *De pictura*, 3.63, in *On Painting and on Sculpture*, ed. and tr. Grayson, 106–107. Grayson points out that Alberti adapted Cicero's *Brutus*, 18.71, in his conclusion (106 n. 79).

86. Alberti, *On Painting*, 2.42, in *On Painting and On Sculpture*, ed. and tr. Grayson, 82–83; *Opere volgari*, ed. Grayson, III, 74–75.

87. Pliny, *Natural History*, 35.73; Valerius Maximus, *Facta et dicta memorabilia*, 8.11, ext. exempl. 6.

88. Cicero, *Orator*, 22.72; Quintilian, *Institutio oratoria*, 2.13.13. Cf. the interesting treatment in Heffernan, "Alberti on Appelles," 350–52.

89. Cf. Baxandall, *Painting and Experience*, pt. 2.

90. M. Barasch, *Gestures of Despair in Medieval and Renaissance Art* (New York, 1976), 106–109.

91. D. de Robertis, "Ut pictura poesis (uno spiraglio sul mondo figurativo albertiano)," *Interpres* 1 (1978), 27–42.

92. Westfall, "Painting and the Liberal Arts," 493.

93. Borsook, *Mural Painters*, 77–78; J. Pope-Hennessy, *Paolo Uccello*, 2d ed. (London, 1969); Borsi and Borsi, *Paolo Uccello*, 304–307.

94. B. Degenhart and A. Schmitt, *Corpus der italienischen Zeichnungen 1300–1450* 1.2 (Berlin, 1968), 383.

95. A. Manetti, *The Life of Brunelleschi*, ed. H. Saalman, tr. C. Enggass (University Park and London, 1970), 54–55: "if certain authors in pagan times gave precepts about that method, such as Battista degli Alberti has done in our period, they were not much more than generalities." The two quotes in this paragraph come from 46–49.

96. M. Baxandall, "A Dialogue on Art from the Court of Leonello d'Este. Angelo Decembrio's *De Politia Litteraria* Pars LXVIII," *Journal of the Warburg and Courtauld Institutes* 26 (1963), 304–26.

97. Alberti, *De pictura*, 3.56, in *On Painting and On Sculpture*, ed. and tr. Grayson, 98–101; and in *Opere volgari*, ed. Grayson, III, 97–99.

98. Cicero, *De inventione*, 2.1; Pliny, *Natural History*, 35.64.

99. Pliny really set the work in the Temple of Hera Lacinia.

100. See Maraschio, "Aspetto del bilinguismo albertiano."

101. Pliny's shorter text was much blunter on the point at issue. Zeuxis, he said, "inspected the Agrigentine virgins, naked, and chose five"—*ut . . . inspexerit virgines eorum nudas et quinque elegerit* (*Natural History*, 35.64).

102. Victorinus, the fourth-century rhetorician who wrote a standard commentary on Cicero's work, saw this point clearly. A typical schoolmaster, he tried to distract his students at this potentially worrying point. Accordingly, he described Zeuxis—against the clear intent of Cicero's text—as a specialist in painting the faces, the *vultus*, of women.

103. Alberti, *De pictura*, 3.53, in *On Painting and On Sculpture*, ed. and tr. Grayson, 96–97; and in *Opere volgari*, ed. Grayson, III, 92–93. For the original passages and the contemporary translations by Guarino and Lapo, see Cast, *Calumny of Apelles*, 198–202.

104. E. Panofsky, *Studies in Iconology* (New York, 1939; repr. New York, 1967), 158–59 at 159.

105. For an excellent account of another apparently deliberate misreading, see Grayson's edition of *De pictura* and *De statua*, 20–21, 24. See also *De statua*, 12, in *On Painting and On Sculpture*, ed. and tr. Grayson, 134–35: "I proceeded accordingly to measure and record in writing, not simply the beauty found in this or that body, but, as far as possible, that perfect beauty distributed by Nature, as it were in fixed proportion, among many bodies." See the classic study of E. Panofsky, *Idea* (Leipzig, 1924; tr. J. S. Peake [Columbia, S.C., 1968]), which follows the adventures of this story with exemplary intelligence and wit. The other quotation comes from ibid., 59–60 at 60.

106. For some possible portraits of Alberti, see R. Tavernor, "La ritrattistica e l'interesse dell'Alberti per il futuro," in *Leon Battista Alberti*, ed. J. Rykwert and A. Engel (Milan, 1994), 64–69, with older bibliography; cf. J. Pieper, "Un ritratto di Leon Battista Alberti architetto: osservazioni su due capitelli emblematici nel duomo di Pienza," in ibid., 54–63.

107. See M. Gosebruch, "Ghiberti und der Begriff von *Copia e Varietà* aus Albertis Malertraktat," *Lorenzo Ghiberti nel suo tempo* (Florence, 1980), II, 269–82; and H. van Veen, "L. B. Alberti and a Passage from Ghiberti's *Commentaries*," in ibid., 343–48.

108. A. Averlino, *Trattato di architettura*, ed. A. M. Finoli and L. Grassi (Milan, 1972), II, 646, 581–86, 662–63, 666, 669–70, and *passim*.

109. A. Dürer, *Schriftlicher Nachlass*, ed. H. Rupprich (Berlin, 1956), I, 327; cited and discussed by B. Hinz, "Cnidia, oder: Des Aktes erster Akt," *Der nackte Mensch*, ed. D. Hoffmann (Marburg, 1989), 51–79 at 75, 79 n. 78.

110. See, e.g., Lee, *Ut pictura poesis*; Panofsky, *Idea*; T. Frangenberg, *Der Betrachter: Studien zur florentinischen Kunstliteratur des 16. Jahrhunderts* (Cologne, 1990); and R. Williams, *Art, Theory and Culture in Sixteenth-Century Italy* (Cambridge, 1997).

CHAPTER V

1. *Two Memoirs of Renaissance Florence: The Diaries of Buonaccorso Pitti and Gregorio Dati*, ed. G. Brucker, tr. J. Martines (New York, Evanston, and London, 1967), 124.

2. See in general L. Jardine, *Worldly Goods* (New York, 1996; repr. New York, 1998).

3. L. B. Alberti, *Opere volgari*, ed. C. Grayson (Bari, 1960–73), I, 367–80.

4. W. Sombart, *The Quintessence of Capitalism*, tr. M. Epstein (New York, 1915), 104.

5. M. Weber, *The Protestant Ethic and the Spirit of Capitalism*, tr. T. Parsons (New York, 1958), 194–95.

6. See the valuable edition of *Della famiglia* by R. Romano and A. Tenenti (Turin, 1969).

7. Brunner, *Adeliges Landleben und europäischer Geist* (Salzburg, 1949), esp. 208. Cf. V. Groebner, "La forza, i concetti ed il classico. Otto Brunner letto da Gadi Algazi," *Rivista storica italiana* 111 (1999), 227–34.

8. M. Danzi, "Fra *oikos* e *polis*: Sul pensiero familiare di Leon Battista Alberti," *La memoria e la città*, ed. C. Bastia and M. Bolognani (Bologna, 1995), 47–62.

9. See the characteristically deft quotations of Alberti in I. Origo, *The Merchant of Prato* (New York, 1957; repr. Boston, 1986), 97, 224, 268.

10. R. Fubini and A. Menci Gallorini, "L'autobiografia di Leon Battista Alberti: Studio e edizione," *Rinascimento*, 2d ser., 12 (1972), 1–78 at 70. See also R. Neu Watkins, "L. B. Alberti in the Mirror: An Interpretation of the *Vita* with a New Translation," *Italian Quarterly* 30 (1989), 5–30 at 8.

11. See C. Grayson's account in Alberti, *Opere volgari*, ed. Grayson, I, 78–410. But see Fubini and Menci Gallorini, "L' autobiografia" 71–72 (cf. Watkins, "L.B. Alberti" 10). For textual evidence that suggests that book four of *On the Family*, in its pres-

ent form, was actually composed around 1441, in direct connection with the *certame coronario*, see L. Bertolini, "Un idiografo del IV libro della Famiglia," *Rivista di letteratura italiana* 6 (1988), 275–97 and Danzi, "Fra *oikus* e *polis*," 53 and n. 22. But given the likely date of the autobiography (1437 or 1438), it seems more likely that Alberti wrote an early nucleus of book four in the 1430s and then revised it into its current form in 1441.

12. T. Kuehn, *Law, Family and Women: Toward a Legal Anthropology of Renaissance Italy* (Chicago, 1991), chap. 6.

13. Virgil, *Eclogues*, 10.38–39.

14. G. Gorni, "Storia del Certame Coronario," *Rinascimento* 12 (1972), 135–81 at 139 n. 2.

15. Leon Battista Alberti, *The Family in Renaissance Florence*, tr. R. N. Watkins (Columbia, S.C., 1969), 153–54; Alberti, *Opere volgari*, ed. Grayson, III, 156.

16. Alberti, *Opere volgari*, ed. Grayson, III, 164; Alberti, *Family*, tr. Watkins, 161.

17. See D. Marsh, *The Quattrocento Dialogue* (Cambridge, Mass., 1980).

18. Quotations here and from previous paragraph come from Alberti, *Opere volgari*, ed. Grayson, I, 116–17, 141; Alberti, *Family*, tr. Watkins, 120–21, 141.

19. See, e.g., C. Bec, *Les marchands écrivains: Affaires et humanisme à Florence, 1375–1434* (Paris and The Hague, 1967); G. Brucker, *Renaissance Florence* (New York, 1968).

20. L. Trilling, "Manners, Morals and the Novel," *The Liberal Imagination* (New York, 1950; repr. Garden City, 1953), 200–15 at 204–205.

21. R. Goldthwaite, *Private Wealth in Renaissance Florence: A Study of Four Families* (Princeton, 1968); F. W. Kent, *Household and Lineage in Renaissance Florence: The Family Life of the Capponi, Ginori and Rucellai* (Princeton, 1971); D. Herlihy and C. Klapisch-Zuber, *Tuscans and Their Families: A Study of the Florentine Catasto of 1427* (Cambridge, Mass., 1986). For recent discussions of the structure and solidity of the Florentine family, see esp. L. Fabbri, *Alleanza matrimoniale e patriziato nella Firenze del '400* (Florence, 1991); and A. Molho, *Marriage Alliance in Late Medieval Florence* (Cambridge, Mass., 1994).

22. Alberti, *Opere volgari*, ed. Grayson, I, 205, 219; Alberti, *Family*, tr. Watkins, 197, 209.

23. See G. Brucker, "Introduction," in *Two Memoirs*; V. Branca, *Mercanti scrittori* (Milan, 1986).

24. Quoted by Bec, *Les marchands écrivains*, 51, who notes the similarity to Giannozzo's statement.

25. Alberti, *Opere volgari*, ed. Grayson, I, 215–16; Alberti, *Family*, tr. Watkins, 206.

26. See Herlihy and Klapisch-Zuber, *Tuscans*. For specimens of the 1427 *catasto* in English translation, see G. Brucker, *The Society of Renaissance Florence* (New York, 1971), 6–13.

27. J. Burckhardt, *Die Kultur der Renaissance in Italien, Ein Versuch* (Darmstadt, 1955), 52–54.

28. G. Ponte, *Leon Battista Alberti: umanista e scrittore* (Genoa, 1981), 69.

29. Cf. M. Becker, *Florence in Transition* (Baltimore, 1967–68), and D. Kent and F. W.

Kent, *Neighbours and Neighbourhood in Renaissance Florence* (Locust Valley, N.Y., 1982). Quotations from Alberti, *Opere Volgari*, ed. Grayson, I, 156; Alberti, *Family*, tr. Watkins, 154.

30. For a very helpful introduction to this tradition, see Xenophon, *Oeconomicus: A Social and Historical Commentary*, ed. S. B. Pomeroy (Oxford, 1994; repr. 1995), with rich bibliography. On the diffusion of Xenophon's work, see 68–90 and D. Marsh, "Xenophon," *Catalogus translationum et commentariorum*, ed. V. Brown et al. (Washington, D.C., 1992), VII, 177–89.

31. J. Soudek, "The Genesis and Tradition of Leonardo Bruni's Annotated Latin Version of the ps.-Aristotelian *Economics*," *Scriptorium* 12 (1958), 260–68, 179–80, 182–84; J. Soudek, "Leonardo Bruni and his Public: A Statistical and Interpretative Study of his Annotated Latin Version of the ps.-Aristotelian *Economics*," *Studies in Medieval and Renaissance History* 5 (1968), 49–136; J. Soudek, "A Fifteenth-Century Humanistic Bestseller: The Manuscript Diffusion of Leonardo Bruni's Annotated Version of the ps.-Aristotelian *Economics*," in *Philosophy and Humanism: Renaissance Essays in Honor of Paul Oskar Kristeller*, ed. E. P. Mahoney (Leiden, 1976), 129–43; H. Goldbrunner, "Leonardo Brunis Kommentar zu seiner Übersetzung der ps.-aristotelischen Oekonomik: Ein humanistischer Kommentar," *Der Kommentar in der Renaissance*, ed. A. Buck and O. Herding (Bonn, 1975); and the translation of Bruni's text in Griffiths, Hankins, and Thompson, *Humanism of Leonardo Bruni*, 300–17.

32. M. King, *Venetian Humanism in an Age of Patrician Dominance* (Princeton, 1986).

33. I follow here the brilliant article by Danzi, "Fra *oikos* e *polis*."

34. L. B. Alberti, *Profugiorum ab aerumna libri*, ed. G. Ponte (Genoa, 1988), 81–83. Cf. R. Cardini, *Mosaici: Il 'nemico' dell'Alberti* (Rome, 1990).

35. See esp. H. Baron, "Leon Battista Alberti as an Heir and Critic of Florentine Civic Humanism," in *In Search of Florentine Civic Humanism* (Princeton, 1988), I, 264–68.

36. Xenophon, *Oeconomicus* 10.2, 10.3–10, in *Oeconomicus*, ed. Pomeroy, 161–63.

37. Brucker, *Society*, 195.

38. Alberti, *Opere volgari*, ed. Grayson, I, 227–28; Alberti, *Family*, tr. Watkins, 216.

39. I. Origo, *The World of San Bernardino* (New York, 1962), chap. 2; D. O. Hughes, "Distinguishing Signs: Ear-Rings, Jews, and Franciscan Rhetoric in the Italian Renaissance City" *Past and Present* 112 (1986), 3–59; records of some prosecutions in Brucker, *Society*, 181–83.

40. For different perspectives on Alberti's attitude toward women see F. Furlan, "L'idea della donna e dell'amore nella cultura tardomedievale e in L.B. Alberti," *Intersezioni* 10 (1990), 211–38; M. Wigley, "Untitled: The Housing of Gender," *Sexuality and Space*, ed. B. Colomina (Princeton, 1992), 327–89; Gisela Ecker, "Leon Battista Alberti: Ordnungen des Hauses, des Sehens und der Geschlechter," *Geschlechterperspektiven: Forschungen zur Frühen Neuzeit*, ed. H. Wunder and G. Engel (Königstein/Taunus, 1998), 348–57; and K. Imesch, "Misogynie im literarischen und architekturtheoretischen Werk Leon Battista Albertis," *Theorie der Praxis*, ed. K. W. Forster and H. Locher (Berlin, 1999), 233–73. For the social background see esp. J. Brown, "A Woman's Place was in the Home: Women's Work in Renaissance

Tuscany," in *Rewriting the Renaissance*, ed. M. Ferguson, M. Quilligan, and N. Vickers (Chicago and London, 1986), 206–24 and S. Cohn, "Donne in piazza e donne in tribunale a Firenze nel Rinascimento," *Studi storici* 22 (1981), 515–33.

41. Giovanni di Pagolo Morelli, *Ricordi*, ed. V. Branca (Florence, 1969), 177–80.

42. See the articles by Strocchia and Pandimiglio in *Palazzo Strozzi: Metà millennio, 1489–1989*, ed. D. Lamberini (Rome, 1991); C. Klapisch-Zuber, *Women, Family and Ritual in Renaissance Italy*, tr. L. Cochrane (Chicago, 1985); H. Gregory, ed. and tr., *Selected Letters of Alessandra Strozzi* (Berkeley and Los Angeles, 1997).

43. For a case in point, see Rucellai, *Zibaldone*, I, 28–29.

44. These three quotations come from Alberti, *Opere volgari*, I, 235, 232, 234; Alberti, *Family*, tr. Watkins, 223, 220, 222.

45. Klapisch-Zuber, *Women, Family, and Ritual*.

46. Griffiths, Hankins, and Thompson, *Humanism of Leonardo Bruni*, 315, 311.

47. Alberti, *Opere volgari*, ed. Grayson, I, 153–54; Alberti, *Family*, tr. Watkins, 151–53.

48. F. Biondo, *De verbis romanae locutionis*; M. Tavoni, *Latino, grammatica, volgare. Storia di una questione umanistica* (Padua, 1974), 197–215.

49. These quotations come from L. Bruni, *Humanistisch-philosophische Schriften*, ed. H. Baron (Leipzig and Berlin, 1928; repr. Wiesbaden, 1969), 216–21; English translation in Griffiths, Hankins, and Thompson, *Humanism of Leonardo Bruni*, 229–34.

50. L. Bruni, "Vita di Dante," *Humanistisch-philosophische Schriften*, ed. H. Baron, 61; translation in *The Three Crowns of Florence*, ed. D. Thompson and A. F. Nagel (New York, Evanston, San Francisco, and London, 1971), 71.

51. On this debate, see R. Fubini's classic article "La coscienza del latino negli umanisti," *Studi medievali*, 3d ser., 2 (1961), 505–50; M. Tavoni, *Latino, grammatica, volgare*; A. Mazzocco, *Linguistic Theories in Dante and the Humanists* (Leiden and New York, 1993); and G. Patota, "Introduzione," in L. B. Alberti, *Grammatichetta e altri scritti sul volgare* (Rome, 1996), xiv–xxiv.

52. Alberti, *Opere volgari*, ed. Grayson, I, 154; Alberti, *Family*, tr. Watkins, 152.

53. G. Cipriani, *Il mito etrusco nel rinascimento fiorentino* (Florence, 1980).

54. This quotation comes from G. Aliotti, *Epistolae et opuscula*, ed. F. M. Scaramalius (Arezzo, 1769), I, 33–34; see also 44, 45, 67. These letters can be found somewhat more readily in A. Traversari, *Latinae epistolae*, ed. L. Mehus (Florence, 1759; repr. Bologna, 1968), cols. 1053–58.

55. See, e.g., C. Grayson, "Alberti and the Vernacular Eclogue in the Quattrocento," *Italian Studies* 11 (1956), 16–29, repr. in Grayson, *Studi su Leon Battista Alberti*, ed. P. Claut (Florence, 1999), 103–18; and A. Cecere, *Leon Battista Alberti, Deifira: Analisi tematica e formale* (Naples, 1999).

56. See, e.g., T. E. Mommsen, *Medieval and Renaissance Studies*, ed. E. F. Rice, Jr. (Ithaca, N.Y., 1959), 101–105.

57. For Cyriac, see G. Arbizzoni, "Ciriaco e il volgare," *Ciriaco d'Ancona e la cultura antiquaria dell'Umanesimo*, ed. G. Paci and S. Sconocchia (Reggio Emilia, 1998), 217–33.

58. These four quotations come from L. Bertolini, ed., *De vera amicitia. I testi del primo Certame coronario* (Ferrara, 1993), 224, 226, 254–260, 355.

59. Alberti, "Protesta," in ibid., 506.

60. "Diceria," in ibid., 516. In formal terms, the judges acknowledged that the poets had reached a high standard at the three forms of composition defined by classical rhetoric: invention (finding the proper subject matter), disposition (laying out the argument), and elocution (style).

61. Alberti, "Protesta," 503–13. See also A. Altamura, *Il Certame Coronario* (Naples, 1952); Gorni, "Storia del Certame Coronario."

62. Gorni, "Storia del Certame Coronario," 150; quotation in this paragraph comes from 149.

63. See esp. S. Niccoli, "Le *Rime* Albertiane nella prospettiva poetica Quattrocentesca," *Interpres* 3 (1980), 7–28.

64. See *Dizionario biografico degli Italiani*, s. v. Leonardo Dati, by R. Ristori.

65. L. Dati, *Epistolae xxxiii*, ed. Lorenzo Mehus (Florence, 1743), Ep. xiv, to Alberti, Florence, 8 June 1443, 21–22; pp. xxvi–xxviii, esp. xxviii; Ep. i, Dati to Niccolò della Luna, undated, 1–2; pp. xlvii–lii and Ep. xxxiii, Dati to Matteo Palmieri, Lateran, 4 April 1466, 59–60; Ep. xv, Dati to Ceffi, Florence, 23 May 1443, 22–25; and Ep. xiii, Dati and Ceffi to Alberti, Florence, 6 June 1443, 18–20. The chronology of Dati's efforts is not quite clear; cf. *Libro del Poema chiamato Citta di Vita composto da Matteo Palmieri Fiorentino*, ed. M. Rooke, Smith College Studies in Modern Languages, VIII, 1–2 (1926–27); IX, 1–4 (1927–28), I, xi–xvi.

66. Quotations in C. Grayson, "Leon Battista Alberti and the Beginnings of Italian Grammar," *Proceedings of the British Academy* 49 (1963), 291–311 at 293. The text of Alberti's grammar appears in *Opere volgari*, ed. Grayson, III, 177–93, and in the newer critical edition of the *Grammatichetta* by Patota [cited in 51 above]; quotations ibid., 15; and see also ibid., lxv. Patota gives a very full and helpful analysis of the content of Alberti's work.

67. *Giovanni Rucellai ed il suo Zibaldone* I: G. Rucellai, *Il Zibaldone Quaresimale*, ed. A. Perosa (London, 1960), 3–19, 139 n. 1.

68. Alberti, *Dinner Pieces*, tr. D. Marsh (Binghamton, N.Y.), 23–27; also in *Prosatori latini del Quattrocento*, ed. E. Garin (Milan and Naples, 1952), 644–57. The importance of this text was recognized by A. Doren, "Fortuna im Mittelater und in der Renaissance," *Vorträge der Bibliothek Warburg*, II: 1922–1923, pt. 1 (1924), 71–144 at 132–33 n. 128.

69. Origo, *Merchant of Prato*, chaps. 3–4. For further discussion, see B. Nelson, *The Idea of Usury* (Princeton, 1949; repr. Chicago, 1969); Nelson, "The Usurer and the Merchant Prince: Italian Businessmen and the Ecclesiastical Law of Restitution, 1100–1500," *Journal of Economic History* 7, supp. 7 (1947), 104–22; J. Kirshner, *Pursuing Honor While Avoiding Sin: The Monte delle Doti of Florence* (Milan, 1978); C. Bresnahan Menning, *Charity and State in Late Renaissance Italy: The Monte di Pietà of Florence* (Ithaca and London, 1993). On the background for Bernardino's preaching see now J. Kaye, *Economy and Nature in the Fourteenth Century* (Cambridge, 1998).

70. Brucker, *Society*, 23–24.

71. Alberti, *Opere volgari*, ed. Grayson, I, 248; Alberti, *Family*, tr. Watkins, 234.

72. A. Warburg, "Francesco Sassetti's letztwillige Verfügung," *Gesammelte Schriften* (Leipzig and Berlin, 1932; repr. Berlin, 1998), I, 127–58 at 141; "Francesco Sassetti's Last Injunctions to his Sons," *The Renewal of Pagan Antiquity*, ed. K. W. Forster, tr. D. Britt (Los Angeles, 1999), 223–62 at 237.

73. See Rucellai, *Zibaldone*, ed. Perosa, I, 114–16.

74. See esp. Danzi, "Fra *oikos* e *polis*," 51–52.

75. These four quotations come from Alberti, *Opere volgari*, ed. Grayson, I, 180, 183–84, 142–43, 202; Alberti, *Family*, tr. Watkins, 175, 178, 143, 194. See the fascinating development of this position by Giovanni Rucellai in *Zibaldone*, ed. Perosa, I, 39–43; Alberti, *Opere volgari*, ed. Grayson, I.

76. See Baron, *In Search*, I, 261–68, 278–80.

77. B. Vickers, "Humanismus und Kunsttheorie in der Renaissance," *Theorie der Praxis*, ed. K. W. Forster and H. Löcher (Berlin, 1999), 9–74.

78. Alberti, *De pictura*, 2.49, in *On Painting and On Sculpture*, ed. C. Grayson (London, 1972), 92–93.

79. Alberti, *Della pittura*, 2.47, in *Opere volgari*, ed. Grayson, III, 84.

80. Alberti, *Opere volgari*, ed. Grayson, I, 141, 210. See A. D. Fraser Jenkins, "Cosimo de' Medici's Patronage of Architecture and the Theory of Magnificence," *Journal of the Warburg and Courtauld Institutes* 33 (1970), 162–70 at 163–64. Quotation comes from *Opere volgare* I, 202; Alberti, *Family*, tr. Watkins, 194.

81. M. Phillips, *Marco Parenti: A Life in Medici Florence* (Princeton, 1987); R. Goldthwaite, *The Building of Renaissance Florence: An Economic and Social History* (Baltimore, 1980); and *Wealth and the Demand for Art in Italy, 1300–1600* (Baltimore, 1993).

82. M. Baxandall, *Painting and Experience in Fifteenth-Century Italy* (Oxford, 1972), pt. 1. Quotation from Alberti, *Opere volgari*, ed. Grayson, I, 225; Alberti, *Family*, tr. Watkins, 214.

83. See F. W. Kent, "The Making of a Renaissance Patron of the Arts," *Giovanni Rucellai ed il suo Zibaldone* II: *A Florentine Patrician and his Palace* (London, 1981), 9–95 at 42–44.

84. Alberti, *Opere volgari*, ed. Grayson, I, 177; Alberti, *Family*, tr. Watkins, 172.

85. See J. Le Goff, "Labor Time in the 'Crisis' of the Fourteenth Century: From Medieval Time to Modern Time," *Time, Work and Culture in the Middle Ages*, tr. A. Goldhammer (Chicago and London, 1980), 43–52 at 51–52; Baron, *In Search*, II, 52–53; R. Glasser, *Time in French Life and Thought*, tr. C. G. Pearson (Manchester, 1972), chaps. 4–5.

86. Rucellai, *Zibaldone*, ed. Perosa, I, 18.

87. Warburg, "Francesco Sassetti".

88. Alberti, *Dinner Pieces*, tr. Marsh, 215; R. Watkins, "Leon Battista Alberti's Emblem, the Winged Eye and his Name," *Mitteilungen des Kunsthistorischen Institutes in Florenz* 9 (1959–60), 256–58.

89. K. Reichert, *Fortuna, oder die Beständigkeit des Wechsels* (Frankfurt, 1985); cf. Doren, "Fortuna in Mittelalter."

90. These two quotations come from Alberti, *Opere volgari*, ed. Grayson, I, 194–201, at 198 and 197; Alberti, *Family*, tr. Watkins, 187–93, at 191 and 190.

91. Alberti, *Villa*, in *Opere volgari*, ed. Grayson, I, 359–63 at 363; for the date and Alberti's use of Hesiod, see 456–57.
92. See D. Coffin, *The Villa in the Life of Renaissance Rome* (Princeton, 1979), esp. 11; and J. Ackerman, *The Villa* (Princeton, 1990), chap. 3.
93. Cf. M. Baxandall, "Alberti's Self," *Fenway Court* (1990–91), 31–36.

CHAPTER VI

1. See L. B. Alberti, *De equo animante*, ed. C. Grayson, J.-Y. Boriaud, and F. Furlan, *Albertiana* 2 (1999), 191–235 at 204–207, 232–33. (This edition supersedes the older one by A. Videtta [Naples, 1991].) On the sources Alberti used, see S. Salomone, "Fonti greche nel *De equo animante* di Leon Battista Alberti," *Rinascimento*, 2d ser., 26 (1986), 241–50, arguing that he drew on Xenophon's *Peri hippikes*, then untranslated; cf. 197.
2. Alberti, *De equo animante*, ed. Grayson et al., 206–207.
3. See Chapter 4 above.
4. Alberti, *De equo animante*, ed. Grayson et al., 209–13, 212–15, 216–23, 225. Quotation from first paragraph comes from 208–209.
5. Ibid., 146, 150. First quotation comes from 230–31; note that Alberti goes on to raise and answer two more questions, in a form that resembles that of the *Vita anonyma*; second quotation comes from 214–15.
6. E. H. Kantorowicz, "The Este Portrait by Roger van der Weyden," *Journal of the Warburg and Courtauld Institutes* 3 (1939–40), 165–80, repr. in Kantorowicz, *Selected Studies* (Locust Valley, N.Y., 1965), 366–80; admittedly, on one "luckless day" in 1468, "Francesco's charger refused to gallop along the lists" (373).
7. See K. Weil-Garris Brandt, "The Relation of Sculpture and Architecture in the Renaissance," *The Renaissance from Brunelleschi to Michelangelo: The Representation of Architecture*, ed. H. Millon and V. M. Lampugnani (New York, 1997), 75–98 at 90.
8. L. Dati, *Epistolae xxxiii*, ed. Lorenzo Mehus (Florence, 1743), Ep. xix, Dati to Aliotti, Florence, 14 November 1443, 31–33 at 32.
9. On the connections among Dati, Alberti, and Palmieri, see esp. G. Gorni, "Tre schede per l'Alberti volgare," *Interpres* 1 (1978), 43–58 at 45–53.
10. On Alberti's changes of direction in the late 1430s and early 1440s, see the important studies of G. Gorni, "Dalla famiglia alla corte: Itinerari e allegorie nell'opera di L. B. Alberti," *Bibliothèque d'Humanisme et Renaissance* 43 (1981), 241–56; G. Ponte, "La crisi della 'compagnia di Corte': L'intercenale *Erumna* e il prologo alla *Famiglia* di L. B. Alberti," *Tradizione classica e letteratura umanistica: Per Alessandro Perosa*, ed. R. Cardini et al. (Rome, 1985), I, 159–71; M. Danzi, "Fra *oikos* e *polis*: Sul pensiero familiare di Leon Battista Alberti," *La memoria e la città*, ed. C. Bastia and M. Bolognani (Bologna, 1995), 47–62.
11. J. Gill, *The Council of Florence* (Cambridge, 1959; repr. with corrections, New York, 1982).
12. Lapo da Castiglionchio, *Dialogus de curiae commodis*, in *Prosatori latini del Quattro-*

cento, ed. E. Garin (Milan and Naples, 1952), 190. For a critical text and translation of the whole work, see C. Celenza, *Renaissance Humanism and the Papal Curia:
Lapo da Castiglionchio the Younger's "De curiae commodis"* (Ann Arbor, 1999), here,
130–32.

13. See Celenza's introduction in ibid., esp. chap. 2, for a sensitive and erudite interpretation of Lapo's work and his ambivalence.

14. Quotations from previous paragraph and this paragraph come from L. B. Alberti,
Opuscula inedita et pauca separatim impressa, ed. G. Mancini (Florence, 1890),
67–121 at 68, 97, 100–101.

15. Ibid., 80, 78, 80–81, 77.

16. Ibid., 119–20; these four quotations come from 121, 103–104, 108–109, 107.

17. These six quotations come from L. B. Alberti, *Opere volgari*, ed. C. Grayson (Bari,
1960–73), I, 269, 270, 283–91, 281, 279, 274; L. B. Alberti, *The Family in Renaissance Florence*, tr. R. N. Watkins (Columbia, S.C., 1969), 252, 264–72, 262,
260–61, 256.

18. R. Fubini and A. Menci Gallorini, "L'autobiografia di Leon Battista Alberti: Studio
e edizione," *Rinascimento*, 2d ser., 12 (1972), 71.

19. Alberti, *Opere volgari*, ed. Grayson, I, 267–68; Alberti, *Family*, tr. Watkins, 250–51.

20. See T. Dean, *Land and Power in Late Medieval Ferrara* (Cambridge, 1988).

21. G. Mattingly, *Renaissance Diplomacy* (New York, 1955).

22. See E. G. Gardner, *Dukes and Poets at Ferrara* (London, 1904); W. Gundersheimer,
Ferrara: The Style of a Renaissance Despotism (Princeton, 1973); *La corte e lo spazio:
Ferrara estense*, ed. G. Papagno and A. Quondam, 3 vols. (Rome, 1982); *Le muse e il
principe* (Modena, 1991); T. Tuohy, *Herculean Ferrara* (Cambridge, 1996);
A. Grafton, *Commerce with the Classics* (Ann Arbor, 1997), chap. 1.

23. *Peregrinatio metropolitae Isidori ad concilium Florentinum*, in *Acta Slavica Concilii
Florentini. Narrationes et documenta*, ed. J. Krajcar, S.J. (Rome, 1976), 24. See
P. Castelli, " 'Veni creator spiritus.' Da San Giorgio a Santa Maria Novella: Immagini conciliari," *Firenze e il Concilio del 1439*, ed. P. Viti (Florence, 1994), I,
289–316, at 297 and n. 20.

24. A. T. Grafton and L. Jardine, *From Humanism to the Humanities* (London, 1986),
chap. 1.

25. Lapo, *Dialogus de curiae commodis*, in *Prosatori latini*, ed. Garin, 174 (cf. Celenza, *Renaissance Humanism*, 108–109).

26. A. Decembrio, *De politia literaria*, 2.21, Biblioteca Apostolica Vaticana MS Vat. lat.
1794, fol. 47 recto.

27. Aeneas Silvius Piccolomini, *De Europa*, chap. 52, in *Opera quae extant omnia*
(Basel, 1551; repr. Frankfurt a.M., 1967), 450–51.

28. Poggio Bracciolini, *Lettere*, II: *Epistolarum familiarium libri*, ed. H. Harth (Florence,
1984), 251–52.

29. Decembrio, *De politia*, MS Vat. lat. 1794, fol. 183 recto.

30. Poggio, *Lettere*, II, 170, 198–99, 253.

31. J. W. Oppelt, "Peace vs. liberty in the Quattrocento: Poggio, Guarino and the
Scipio-Caesar Controversy," *Journal of Medieval and Renaissance Studies* 4 (1974),

221–65; M. Pade, "Guarino and Caesar at the Court of the Este," *La corte di Ferrara ed il suo mecenatismo, 1441–1598: The Court of Ferrara and its Patronage*, ed. M. Pade, L. W. Petersen, and D. Quarta (Copenhagen and Ferrara, 1990), 71–91.

32. E. Walser, *Poggius Florentinus, Leben und Werke* (Leipzig and Berlin, 1914), 172 n. 2, 170–71.

33. Alberti, *Opere volgari*, ed. Grayson, I, 271; Alberti, *Family*, tr. Watkins, 252–54.

34. See, e.g., M. Biagioli, *Galileo Courtier* (Chicago and London, 1993).

35. Vespasiano da Bisticci, *Vite di uomini illustri del secolo xv* (Florence, 1938), 71.

36. Alberti, *Opere volgari*, ed. Grayson, I, 291–92; Alberti, *Family*, tr. Watkins, 272.

37. L. B. Alberti, *Philodoxeos fabula*. Edizione critica a cura di Lucia Cesarini Martinelli," *Rinascimento*, 2d ser., 17 (1977), 111–234 at 144.

38. J. P. Perry, "A Fifteenth-Century Dialogue on Literary Taste: Angelo Decembrio's Account of Playwright Ugolino Pisani at the Court of Leonello d'Este," *Renaissance Quarterly* 39 (1986), 613–43.

39. Poggio, *Lettere*, ed. Harth, II, 260.

40. Alberti, *Canis*, in *Apologhi ed elogi*, ed. R. Contarino (Genoa, 1984), 166; quotation from 156–58.

41. M. Baxandall, *Giotto and the Orators: Humanist Observers of Painting in Italy and the Discovery of Pictorial Composition, 1350–1450* (Oxford, 1971), 78–96; D. Marsh, *Lucian and the Latins: Humor and Humanism in the Early Renaissance* (Ann Arbor, 1998), esp. chap. 5.

42. For Poggio's letters to Niccoli and Marescalco, see Poggio, *Lettere*, ed. Harth, II, 223; for book acquisition, see ibid., 224, and Walser, *Poggius Florentinus*, 528.

43. Walser, *Poggius Florentinus*, 307–308 n. 2; cf. 540–41.

44. Poggio, *Lettere*, ed. Harth, II, 171.

45. Walser, *Poggius Florentinus*, 224.

46. On patronage in Renaissance society see D. W. Kent's classic case study, *The Rise of the Medici* (Oxford, 1978); the pioneering methodological essay by W. Gundersheimer, "Patronage in the Renaissance: An Exploratory Approach," *Patronage in the Renaissance*, ed. G. F. Lytle and S. Orgel (Princeton, 1981), 3–23; the more recent collection of essays on *Patronage, Art, and Society in Renaissance Italy*, ed. F. W. Kent and P. Simons with J. C. Eade (Canberra and Oxford, 1987); and Biagioli, *Galileo Courtier*. Cf. also A. Field, *The Origins of the Platonic Academy of Florence* (Princeton, 1988).

47. L. B. Alberti, *Apologhi ed elogi*, ed. R. Contarino (Genoa, 1984), 46; the previous six quotations come from 44; XXV, 54; LIII, 60; LXXXVIII, 72; LIV, 60; XXXIX, 56.

48. Ibid., XXI, 52; the quotation in this paragraph comes from XXIII, 52.

49. See C. Baskins, "Echoing Narcissus in Alberti's *Della pittura*," *Oxford Art Journal* 16 (1993), 25–33; M. Wolf, " 'Arte superficiem illam fontis amplecti': Alberti, Narziss und die Erfindung der Malerei," *Diletto e Maraviglia*, ed. C. Göttler, U. M. Hofstede, K. Patz, and K. Zollikofer (Emsdetten, 1998), 10–39. The three quotes in this paragraph come from LXXXIII, 70; LXVIII, 66; LV, 62; LVIII, ibid.

50. Kantorowicz, "The Este Portrait," 168, repr. in *Selected Studies*, 370; Alberti,

Apologhi, ed. Contarino, XCVII, 74–76. The quotations in this paragraph come from XCIII, 74; XCIX, 76.

51. These four quotations come from M. Baxandall. "A Dialogue on Art from the Court of Leonello d'Este," *Journal of the Warburg and Courtauld Institutes* 26 (1963), 304–26 at 314, 318, 316.

52. N. Forti Grazzini, "Leonello d'Este nell'autunno del Medioevo. Gli arazzi delle 'Storie di Ercole,' " *Le muse e il principe,* 53–62.

53. See C. Rosenberg, *The Este Monuments and Urban Development in Renaissance Ferrara* (Cambridge, 1997), 53–54.

54. Rosenberg, *Este Monuments;* cf. J. Reiss, "The Civic View of Sculpture in Alberti's *De re aedificatoria,*" *Renaissance Quarterly* 32 (1979), 1–17.

55. Rosenberg, *Este Monuments,* 56 and figs. 17–18.

56. The document is in Rosenberg, *Este Monuments,* 209 n. 31, but read *"Pro utraque"* for *"Quod utraque,"* as in A. Franceschini, *Artisti a Ferrara in età umanistica e rinascimentale. Testimonianze archivistiche. Parte I, dal 1341 al 1471* (Ferrara and Rome, 1993), no. 511, 240.

57. Alberti, *De equo animante,* ed. Grayson et al., 202–203.

58. See the fine account in Rosenberg, *Este Monuments,* chap. 4.

59. Baxandall, "Dialogue," 324.

60. S. K. Scher, ed., *The Currency of Fame: Portrait Medals of the Renaissance* (New York, 1994), pl. 4 rev.

61. K. Badt, "Drei plastische Arbeiten von Leone Battista Alberti," *Mitteilungen des Kunsthistorischen Institutes in Florenz* 8 (1958), 78–87.

62. U. D. Asmus, *Corpus quasi vas. Beiträge zur Ikonographie der italienischen Renaissance* (Berlin, 1977), chap. 1.

63. Scher, *Currency,* pl. 11 obv. and rev.

64. The four quotes found in this paragraph are found in L. B. Alberti, *Ludi rerum mathematicarum,* in *Opere volgari,* ed. Grayson, III, 133, 173, 151, 161.

65. See M. Taccola, *De rebus militaribus,* ed. and tr. E. Knobloch (Baden-Baden, 1984), at 159, 133, 140.

66. So, at least, it is represented in the Riccardiana MS; Alberti, *Opere volgari,* ed. Grayson, III, 139.

67. These four previous quotations come from ibid., 142, 156, 163, 171, 148; cf. J. Shearman, *Mannerism* (Harmondsworth, 1967).

68. Cf. Dean, *Land and Power.*

69. On the sources and limitations of the *Ludi* see J. K. Gadol, *Leon Battista Alberti: Universal Man of the Italian Renaissance* (Chicago, 1969), chap. 4; L. Vagnetti, "Considerazioni sui *Ludi matematici,*" *Studi e documenti di architettura* 1 (1972), 175–79; and esp. P. Souffrin, "La *Geometria practica* dans les *Ludi rerum mathematicarum,*" *Albertiana,* 1 (1998), 87–104.

70. Alberti, *Opere volgari,* ed. Grayson, III, 156.

CHAPTER VII

1. F. De Marchi, *Della architettura militare* (Rome, 1810), chaps. 82–84, I, 90–94; cf. E. Concina, *Navis. L'umanesimo sul mare 1470–1740* (Turin, 1990), 105–107.

2. G. Ucelli, *Le navi di Nemi* (Rome, 1950; repr. 1983).

3. J. Adhémar, *Influences antiques dans l'art du Moyen Age français* (London, 1939; repr. Paris, 1996); M. Greenhalgh, *The Survival of Roman Antiquities in the Middle Ages* (London, 1989); P. Brown, *Venice and Antiquity* (New Haven and London, 1996), pt. 1. The classic survey of the history of antiquarianism is A. D. Momigliano, "Ancient History and the Antiquarian," *Journal of the Warburg and Courtauld Institutes* 13 (1950), 285–315, repr. in Momigliano, *Contributo alla storia degli studi classici* (Rome, 1955), 67–106; see also his later treatment of the subject in *Classical Foundations of Modern Historiography*, ed. R. Di Donato (Berkeley, Los Angeles, and London, 1990), chap. 3.

4. G. Seibt, *Anonimo romano* (Stuttgart, 1992). See also the rich material collected by R. Weiss, *The Renaissance Discovery of Classical Antiquity* (Oxford, 1969; 2d ed., 1988); and C. Nardella, *Il fascino di Roma nel Medioevo: Le "Meraviglie di Roma" di Maestro Gregorio* (Rome, 1997).

5. Poggio Bracciolini, *De varietate fortunae*, in C. D'Onofrio, *Visitiamo Roma nel Quattrocento* (Rome, 1989), 69.

6. G. Fabricius, *Roma* (Helmstedt, 1670), 105; cf. 3.

7. F. Haskell, *History and Its Images* (New Haven and London, 1992).

8. L. B. Alberti, *De re aedificatoria* (hereafter *DRA*), VI.1, translated as *On the Art of Building in Ten Books*, tr. J. Rykwert, N. Leach, and R. Tavernor (Cambridge, Mass., and London, 1988; repr. 1989), 154 (altered); *L'Architettura*, ed. G. Orlandi, tr. P. Portoghesi (Milan, 1966), II, 441–43.

9. Alberti, *DRA*, VI.1, tr. Rykwert et al., 154–55; ed. Orlandi and Portoghesi, II, 443.

10. Alberti, *DRA*, III.16, ed. Orlandi and Portoghesi, I, 257; II.8, ed. Orlandi and Portoghesi, I, 137, on stones; VI.13 *ad fin*, ed. Orlandi and Portoghesi, II, 527, on laying out and making templates for columns: "*Haec a veteribus tradita non invenimus, sed diligentia studioque ex optimorum operibus annotavimus.*" Cf. II.8 *ad fin*, ed. Orlandi and Portoghesi, I, 139: "*Neque hic praetermittenda censeo digna memoratu quaedam, quae de nonnullis lapidibus veteres meminere*" (these follow in II.9, ed. I, 139ff.).

11. A. Manetti, *The Life of Brunelleschi*, ed. H. Saalmann, tr. C. Enggass (University Park and London, 1970), 54 (original text, 55). Next quote comes from 52 (slightly altered; original, 53).

12. H. Burns, "A Drawing by L. B. Alberti," *Architectural Design* 49, nos. 5–6 (1979), 45–56; R. Tavernor, *On Alberti and the Art of Building* (New Haven and London, 1998), chap. 9.

13. P. Jacks, *The Antiquarian and the Myth of Antiquity* (Cambridge, 1993), 160, 328.

14. H. Burns, "Quattrocento Architecture and the Antique: Some Problems," *Classical Influences on European Culture, A.D. 500–1500*, ed. R. R. Bolgar (Cambridge, 1971), 269–87; A. Nesselrath, "I libri di disegni di antichità. Tentativo di una tipologia," *Memoria dell'antico nell'arte italiana* (Turin, 1984–86), III, 89–147.

15. Alberti, *De pictura*, 2.37, in *On Painting and On Sculpture*, ed. and tr. C. Grayson (London, 1972), 75 (slightly altered; original 74–76).

16. L. Barkan, unpublished lecture, Gauss Seminars, Princeton University, spring 1997.

17. M. Baxandall, *Giotto and the Orators* (Oxford, 1971), 81. For a full English translation of Chrysoloras's work, see C. Smith, *Architecture in the Culture of Early Humanism* (Oxford, 1992).

18. F. Biondo, *Roma instaurata*, I.58, in D'Onofrio, *Visitiamo Roma*, 129.

19. Baxandall, *Giotto*, 81. On the diffusion of Chrysoloras's brilliant reading of the city, see Smith, *Architecture*, and G. Lombardi, "La città, libro di pietra. Immagini umanistiche di Roma prima e dopo Costanza," *Alle origini della nuova Roma. Martino V (1417–1431)*, ed. M. Chiabò et al. (Rome, 1992), 17–45.

20. Cf. Lombardi, "La città," esp. 33–34.

21. Nesselrath, "I libri di disegni," 99–100. See also P. Pray Bober, *Drawings after the Antique by Amico Aspertini* (London, 1957), pt. 1; B. Degenhart and A. Schmitt, "Gentile da Fabriano in Rom und die Anfänge des Antikenstudiums," *Münchener Jahrbuch der bildenden Kunst* 11 (1960), 59–151; G. Schweikhart, *Der Codex Wolfegg* (London, 1986), chap. 1; A. Cavallaro, "I primi studi dall'antico nel cantiere del Laterano," *Alle origini della nuova Roma*, ed. Chiabò et al., 401–12.

22. See Brown, *Venice and Antiquity*, 81–91, with full references to the older literature. Especially rich are B. Ashmole, "Cyriacus of Ancona," *Proceedings of the British Academy* 45 (1959), 25–41; C. Mitchell, "Archaeology and Romance in Renaissance Italy," *Italian Renaissance Studies. A Tribute to the Late Cecilia M. Ady*, ed. E. F. Jacob (London, 1960), 468–83; E. Mandowsky and C. Mitchell, *Pirro Ligorio's Roman Antiquities* (London, 1963); Weiss, *Renaissance Discovery*; K. Lehmann and P. W. Lehmann, *Samothracian Reflections* (Princeton, 1973); and F. Scalamonti, *Vita viri clarissimi et famosissimi Kyriaci Anconitani*, ed. and tr. C. Mitchell and E. W. Bodnar, S.J., *Transactions of the American Philosophical Society* 86, 4 (1996).

23. Alberti, *DRA*, VIII.4, ed. Orlandi and Portoghesi, II, 697: "*Earum notae imitantur Graecas, imitantur etiam Latinas, sed quid moneant, intelligit nemo.*"

24. L. Dati, *Epistolae xxxiii*, ed. Lorenzo Mehus (Florence, 1743), lxii–lxvi, esp. lxiii–lxiv.

25. See in general G. Cipriani, *Il mito etrusco nel rinascimento fiorentino* (Florence, 1980).

26. See C. Sperling, "Leon Battista Alberti's Inscription on the Holy Sepulchre in the Capella Rucellai, San Pancrazio," *Journal of the Warburg and Courtauld Institutes* 52 (1989), 221–28; for the wider context, see E. H. Gombrich, "From the Revival of Letters to the Reform of the Arts," *The Heritage of Apelles* (Ithaca, N.Y., 1976), 93–110.

27. G. Mardersteig, "Leon Battista Alberti e la rinascita del carattere lapidario romano nel '400," *Italia Medioevale e Umanistica* 2 (1959).

28. A. Petrucci, "L'Alberti e le scritture," in *Leon Battista Alberti*, ed. J. Rykwert and A. Engel (Milan, 1994), 276–81 at 280–81.

29. Cf. also the classic studies of G. Mardersteig, *Felice Feliciano Veronese, Alphabetum Romanum* (Verona, 1960); M. Meiss, "Toward a More Comprehensive Renaissance

Palaeography," *The Painter's Choice* (New York, Hagerstown, San Francisco, and London, 1976), 151–75; "Alphabetical Treatises in the Renaissance," in ibid., 176–86.

30. Cyriac to the bishop of Ragusa, 1441, in K. A. Neuhausen, "Die vergessene 'göttliche Kunst der Totenerweckung': Cyriacus von Ancona als Begründer der Erforschung der Antike in der Frührenaissance," *Antiquarische Gelehrsamkeit und bildende Kunst*, Atlas, Bonner Beiträge zur Renaissanceforschung, 1 (1996), 51–68 at 68.

31. A. Campana, "Ciriaco d'Ancona e Lorenzo Valla sull'inscrizione greca del tempio dei Dioscuri," *Archeologia classica* 25–26 (1973–74 [1975]), 84–102; and M. A. Lavin, "The Antique Source for the Tempio Malatestiano's Greek Inscriptions," *Art Bulletin* 59 (1977) 421–22.

32. G. Olmi, *L'inventario del mondo* (Bologna, 1992); and P. Findlen, *Possessing Nature* (Berkeley, Los Angeles, and London, 1994).

33. J. M. Huskinson, "The Crucifixion of St. Peter: A Fifteenth-Century Topographical Problem," *Jounal of the Warburg and Courtauld Institutes* 32 (1969) 135–61.

34. Biondo, *Roma instaurata*, I.100, in D'Onofrio, *Visitiamo Roma*, 160–61.

35. Biondo to Leonello d'Este, 1 February 1446, in Biondo, *Scritti inediti o rari*, ed. B. Nogara (Vatican City, 1927), 159–60.

36. Biblioteca Apostolica Vaticana, MS Chigi VII 149, fol. 3 verso: *"eaque excogitavi quo pacto, quivis vel mediocri ingenio praeditus, bellissime et commodissime pingere quantacunque voluerit in superficie possit."* Critical text and translation by G. Orlandi in L. Vagnetti, "Lo studio di Roma negli scritti albertiani," *Convegno internazionale indetto nel v centenario di Leon Battista Alberti* (Rome, 1974), 73–137 at 112–27, here 112. See now L. B. Alberti, *Descriptio urbis Romae*, ed. M. Furno and M. Carpo (Geneva, 2000), 27.

37. L. B. Alberti, *Elementa picturae*, in *Opere volgari*, ed. C. Grayson III, (Bari, 1960–73), III, 112.

38. Alberti, *Ludi rerum mathematicarum*, in *Opere volgari*, ed. Grayson, III, 163, 164.

39. See in general the fine analysis by T. Campbell, "Portolan Charts from the Late Thirteenth Century to 1500," *The History of Cartography* I: *Cartography in Prehistoric, Ancient and Medieval Europe and the Mediterranean*, ed. J. B. Harley and D. Woodward (Chicago and London, 1987), 371–463.

40. Alberti, *Ludi*, in *Opere volgari*, ed. Grayson, III, 164.

41. See esp. Vagnetti, "Lo studio di Roma"; S. Y. Edgerton, Jr., "Florentine Interest in Ptolemaic Cartography as Background for Renaissance Painting, Architecture and the Discovery of America," *Journal of the Society of Architectural Historians* 33 (1974), 275–92; Jacks, *Antiquarian*, 99–110; M. Carpi, "*Descriptio urbis Romae*: Ekfrasis geografica e cultura visuale all'alba della rivoluzione tipografica," *Albertiana* 1 (1998), 121–42. For the larger context, see esp. J. Pinto's classic article, "The Renaissance City Image," *The Rational Arts of Living*, ed. A. C. Crombie and N. Siraisi (Northampton, 1987), 205–54 (a revised form of "Origins and Development of the Iconographic City Plan," *Journal of the Society of Architectural Historians* 35 [1976], 35–50), and the important works of C. W. Westfall, *In This Most Perfect Paradise*

(University Park and London, 1974); J. Schulz, "Jacopo de' Barbari's View of Venice: Map Making, City Views and Moralized Geography before the Year 1500," *Art Bulletin* 60 (1978), 425–74; P.D.A. Harvey, "Local and Regional Cartography in Medieval Europe," in *History of Cartography* I, ed. Harley and Woodward, 464–501; S. Maddalo, *In figura Romae* (Rome, 1990); L. Nuti, "The Perspective Plan in the Sixteenth Century: The Invention of a Representational Language," *Art Bulletin* 76 (1994), 105–28; L. Nuti, *Ritratti di città* (Venice, 1996); and the catalogue A *volo d'uccello* (Venice, 1999).

42. See esp. Jacks, *Antiquarian*, and Carpi, *"Descriptio urbis Romae."*

43. Poggio Bracciolini, *De infelicitate principum*, ed. D. Canfora (Rome, 1998), 7–8.

44. Alberti, *Opuscoli*, ed. Grayson, 57. Alberti later canceled the description of Ptolemy's maps in the Riccardiana MS.

45. For Alberti's use of astronomical terminology see *Descriptio*, ed. Furno and Carpo, 102–104. Regiomontanus's letter to Bianchini, 1464, in M. Curtze, "Der Briefwechsel Regiomontan's mit Giovanni Bianchini, Jacob von Speier und Christian Roder," *Urkunden zur Geschichte der Mathematik um Mittelalter und in der Renaissance*, ed. Curtze, 1 (Leipzig, 1902), 264.

46. See esp. N. Swerdlow, "The Recovery of the Exact Sciences of Antiquity: Mathematics, Astronomy, Geography," *Rome Reborn: The Vatican Library and Renaissance Culture*, ed. A. Grafton (Washington, D.C., Vatican City, New Haven, and London, 1993), 125–67, 149–50.

47. L. B. Alberti, *Dinner Pieces*, tr. D. Marsh (Binghamton, N.Y., 1987), 15, ending: "My dear Paolo, continue to love your friend Leon Battista. When you find time from your more important pursuits to read this book, please emend it, mindful of our long friendship."

48. R. Fubini and A. Menci Gallorini, "L'autobiografia di Leon Battista Alberti: Studio e edizione," *Rinascimento*, 2d ser., 12 (1972), 21–78 at 76; L. B. Alberti, *Dinner Pieces*, tr. Marsh, 252 n. 3.

49. Alberti, *De statua*, 5, in *On Painting and On Sculpture*, ed. and tr. Grayson, 123 (Latin 122).

50. P. Whitfield, *The Mapping of the Heavens* (San Francisco, 1995), 68–69, 75. It has even been suggested that Alberti helped to create the painted circular painted sky map that adorns the cupola of the old sacristy of San Lorenzo. See J. Beck, "Leon Battista Alberti and the 'Night Sky' at San Lorenzo," *Artibus et historiae* 19 (1989), 9–35.

51. See Vagnetti, "Lo studio di Roma"; Alberti, *Descriptio*, ed. Furno and Carpo, 98–99, 128.

52. The manuscript is Vat. lat. 2224; see Maddalo, *In figura Romae*, 191–99.

53. B. Rucellai, *De urbe Roma*, in *Codice topografico della città di Roma*, ed. R. Valentini and G. Zucchetti (Rome, 1940–53), IV, 455.

54. See Weiss, *Renaissance Discovery*, 113–14; *Dizionario biografico degli italiani*, s.v. Flavio Biondo, by A. Campana; N. Thomson de Grummond, ed., *An Encyclopedia of the History of Classical Archaeology* (Westport Conn.: 1996), II, 800–801 (s.v. Nemi); O. Clavuot, *Biondos "Italia Illustrata"—Summa oder Neuschöpfung?* (Tübin-

gen, 1990), 53; Concina, *Navis*, 4–21. A. M. Brizzolara, "La Roma instaurata di Flavio Biondo: Alle origini del metodo archeologico," *Atti dell'Accademia delle Scienze dell'Istituto di Bologna*, Cl. di scienze morali, Memorie 76 (1979/80), 29–74.

55. Biondo to Leonello d'Este, 13 November 1444, in *Scritti*, ed. Nogara, 156, quoting Suetonius, *Divus Iulius*, 46.

56. F. Biondo, *De Roma triumphante libri decem* (Basel, 1531), I, 325–26.

57. See Alberti, *DRA*, Prologus, ed. Orlandi and Portoghesi I, 16, for his promise to add a treatise called "navis" to the work. For reactions, see for example the wishful thinking of L. G. Giraldi, *De re nautica libellus*, ded. to Ercole II of Ferrara, in his *Opera omnia* (Leiden, 1696), I, cols. 599–676, at cols. 599–600.

58. Alberti, *DRA*, V.12, IV.6; V.12, IV.6, X.12.

59. See Ucelli, *Le navi di Nemi*; L. Mariani, *Le navi di Nemi nella bibliografia* (Rome, 1941).

60. See Alberti, *DRA*, V.12, ed. Orlandi and Portoghesi, I, 389; Biondo, *De Roma triumphante*, 326.

61. Alberti, *DRA*, VI.9, ed. Orlandi and Portoghesi, II, 505.

62. Biondo, *De Roma triumphante*, 326: "*Pulchrum autem et pene mirum est videre clavos maiores aeneos, quibus cubitalibus navis constructa erat, ita integros, ita politos, ut nuper a fabri ferrarii incudibus exisse videantur*"; cf. Alberti, *DRA*, III.11, ed. Orlandi and Portoghesi, I, 221, on the superior durability of bronze cramps to iron ones, which rust and damage stone: "*aes vero durare et prope aeternum esse.*"

63. See Alberti, *DRA*, X.7, ed. Orlandi and Portoghesi, II, 931, on how lead water pipes should mate: "*Pixidatis commissuris tubuli alter in alterum inibit,*" and II, 933, on how to lay pipe across a lake bottom. For Giraldi's summary of Alberti's and Biondo's findings, see *De re nautica*, cap. vii, at col. 612.

64. C. Grayson, "Un codice del *De re aedificatoria* posseduto da Bernardo Bembo," in *Studi letterari. Miscellanea in onore di Emilio Santini* (Palermo, 1956), 181–88; repr. in C. Grayson, *Studi su Leon Battista Alberti*, ed. P. Claut (Florence, 1999), 119–27.

65. *Memoirs of a Renaissance Pope: The Commentaries of Pius II. An Abridgement*, tr. F. A. Gragg, ed. L. C. Gabel (New York, 1959), 319; Pius II, *I Commentarii*, ed. L. Totaro (Milan, 1984), II, 2242.

66. The erudite encyclopedist Raffaele Maffei thought that Alberti later changed his mind about the purpose of the ships, deciding that they had served not as pleasure barges but as pumping stations that sent water from the lake to neighboring areas. See R. Maffei, *Commentariorum urbanorum . . . octo et triginta libri* (Basel, 1559), 125; F. Biondo, *Roma ristaurata, et Italia illustrata*, tr. L. Fauno (Venice, 1542), "Annotationi," sig. [HH viii recto].

67. See E. Iversen, *Obelisks in Exile I: The Obelisks of Rome* (Copenhagen, 1968), 19–46.

68. Biondo, *De Roma triumphante*, 145.

69. Alberti, *DRA*, II.1; ed. Orlandi and Portoghesi, I, 97.

70. See esp. R. W. Gaston, "Introduction," *Pirro Ligorio: Artist and Antiquarian*, ed. R. W. Gaston (Florence, 1988), 11–18.

71. See Concina, *Navis*; N. G. Wilson, "Vettor Fausto, Professor of Greek and Naval Architect," in *The Uses of Greek and Latin*, ed. A. C. Dionisotti et al. (London, 1988), 89–95.

72. B. Curran and A. Grafton, "A Fifteenth-Century Site Report on the Vatican Obelisk," *Journal of the Warburg and Courtauld Institutes* 58 (1995 [1996]), 234–48. For detailed studies of Alberti's investigations and interpretations of Roman ruins see the fascinating case studies by L. Pellecchia, "Architects Read Vitruvius: Renaissance Interpretations of the Atrium of the Ancient House," *Journal of the Society of Architectural Historians* 51 (1992), 377–416, and H. Günther, "Albertis Vorstellung von antiken Häusern." *Theorie der Praxis*, ed. K. W. Forster and H. Locher (Berlin, 1999), 157–202.

73. Alberti, *DRA*, VIII.8, tr. Rykwert et al., 279; ed. Orlandi and Portoghesi, II, 753. Cf. P. Ligorio, *Della antichità di Roma*, ed. D. Negri (Rome, 1989), 37: "*Le misure del Circo sono tanto confuse dalle ruine; che non se puo fare un vero, & certo giudicio.*"

74. B. Rucellai, *Commentarius in Publ. Victorem de regionibus urbis*, RIS, *Supplementum II* (Florence, 1770), 1077: "*Nos autem vidimus duce Baptista Alberto in ea parte ubi fuit fragmenta praegrandia Numidici lapidis pene obruta quae adhuc videre facile est funditus fundentibus.*" See Iversen, *Obelisks in Exile*, 67–69.

75. Alberti *DRA*, VII.11, ed. Orlandi and Portoghesi, II, 615. The two quotations in this paragraph come from VI.11, VII.10, tr. Rykwert et al., 179, 219; ed. Orlandi and Portoghesi, II, 511, 605.

76. Alberti to Matteo de' Pasti, in C. Grayson, with M. Paolo and A. G. Cassani, "Alberti and the Tempio Malatestiano," *Albertiana* 2 (1999), 238–74 at 255 (slightly altered); original 253.

77. F. Biondo, *Roma instaurata*, 3.65–66, in D'Onofrio, *Visitiamo Roma nel Quattrocento*, 249.

78. See esp. T. Buddensieg, "Criticism and Praise of the Pantheon in the Middle Ages and the Renaissance," in *Classical Influences*, ed. Bolgar, 259–67.

79. See G. Cugnoni, "Diritti del Capitolo di S. Maria della Rotonda nel età di mezzo," *Archivio della R. Società Romana di Storia patria* 8 (1885), 577–89, esp. 582–83; see O. Verdi, *Maestri di edifici e di strade a Roma nel secolo XV* (Rome, 1997), 36; A. Modigliani, *Mercati, botteghe e spazi di commercio a Roma tra Medioevo ed Età Moderna* (Rome, 1998), 95–106, esp. 100–103.

80. See esp. P. Williams Lehmann, "Alberti and Antiquity: Additional Observations," *Art Bulletin* 70 (1988), 388–400; and C. Syndikus, "Zu Leon Battista Albertis Studium des Basilica Aemilia auf dem Forum Romanum," *Zeitschrift für Kunstgeschichte* 57 (1994), 319–29. Only in Alberti's practice as an architect, similarly, does it become clear that he took as deep an interest as Traversari showed in his magnificent description of Ravenna (*Latinae epistolae*, ed. L. Mehus [Florence, 1759; repr. Bologna, 1968], VIII.52, 420–22) in the colors and surfaces of different types of stone.

81. See, e.g., Weiss, *Renaissance Discovery*, 135–38.

82. Alberti, *DRA*, VII.2; Staatsbibliothek zu Berlin Preussischer Kulturbesitz, MS Hamilton 254, fol. 84 verso.

83. Alberti, *DRA*, VI.4, tr. Rykwert et al., 160; ed. Orlandi and Portoghesi, II, 461–63. Previous quotation found in ibid., VII.2, ed. Orlandi and Portoghesi, II, 541: "*Quale autem apud quosque per eam posteritatem fuerit templum, non satis constat; mihi quidem facile persuadebitur fuisse, quale apud Athenas in arce, qualeve apud Romam in Capito-*"

lio." Cf. MS Hamilton 254, fols. 85 recto-verso and E. W. Bodnar, S. J., *Cyriacus of Ancona and Athens* (Brussels, 1960), and "Athens in 1436," *Archaeology* 23 (1970), 96–105, 188–99.

84. Poggio Bracciolini, *Facezie*, ed. M. Ciccuto (Milan, 1983), 200–203.

85. Alberti, *DRA*, VIII.5, tr. Rykwert et al., 257; ed. Orlandi and Portoghesi, II, 699.

86. L. A. Smoller, *History, Prophecy and the Stars* (Princeton, 1994).

87. Rucellai, *De urbe Roma*, 445.

88. Pius II, *I Commentarii*, ed. Totaro, II, 2232.

89. See the great study of R. Krautheimer, "Alberti and Vitruvius," *The Renaissance and Mannerism. Studies in Western Art: Acts of the Twentieth International Congress of the History of Art* (Princeton, 1963), II, 42–52. See also the valuable study of the antiquarian as "service professional" by T. A. Griggs, "Promoting the Past: The *Hypnerotomachia Poliphili* as Antiquarian Enterprise," *Word and Image* 14 (1998), 17–39.

90. G. Budé, subscription in his composite copy of Pliny's letters, Bodleian Library Auct.L.4.3: "*Hae Plinii iunioris epistolae ex vetustissimo exemplari Parisiensi et restitutae et emendatae sunt opera et industria Ioannis Iucundi praestantissimi architecti hominis imprimis antiquarii.*" Giocondo also read Vitruvius with Budé, commenting on both ancient and modern buildings and machines; see V. Juren, "Fra Giovanni Giocondo et le début des études vitruviennes en France," *Rinascimento*, 2d ser., 14 (1974), 101–15.

91. On the further development of antiquarian scholarship, in addition to the works already cited, see M. Di Macco, *Il Colosseo* (Rome, 1971); V. Farinella, *Archeologia e pittura a Roma tra Quattrocento e Cinquecento* (Turin, 1992); I. Rowland, *The Culture of the High Renaissance* (Cambridge, 1998); N. Dacos, *Roma quanta fuit* (Rome, 1995); *Fiamminghi a Roma, 1508–1608* (Milan, 1995); A. Grafton, *The Footnote: A Curious History* (Cambridge, Mass., 1997), chap. 6; and J. Cunnally, *Images of the Illustrious* (Princeton, 1999).

CHAPTER VIII

1. Biondo to Leonello, 13 November 1444, *Scritti inediti e rari*, ed. B. Nogara (Rome, 1927), 154–59 at 155–56.

2. On Biondo's vision of Rome, see M. G. Blasio, "Memoria filologica e memoria politica in Biondo Flavio. Il significato della 'instauratio urbis,'" *La memoria e la città*, ed. C. Bastia and M. Bolognani (Bologna, 1995), 307–17.

3. Biondo to Gregorio Lolli Piccolomini, 18 September and 30 September 1461, *Scritti*, ed. Nogara, 202–207 at 206. Cf. R. Olitsky Rubinstein, "Pius II's Piazza S. Pietro and St. Andrew's Head," *Essays in the History of Architecture Presented to Rudolf Wittkower*, ed. D. Fraser, H. Hibbard, and M. J. Lewine (London 1967), 22–33; and C. Frommel, "Francesco del Borgo: Architekt Pius' II und Pauls I: Pt. I," *Römisches Jahrbuch für Kunstgeschichte* 20 (1983), 107–54.

4. C. Smith, *Architecture in the Culture of Early Humanism* (Oxford, 1992).

5. See, e.g., M. Kemp, "Ideal Cities," in *Circa 1492*, ed. J. A. Levenson (New Haven

and London, 1991); and K. Weil-Garris Brandt, "The Relation of Sculpture and Architecture in the Renaissance," *The Renaissance from Brunelleschi to Michelangelo: The Representation of Architecture*, ed. H. Millon and V. Lampugnani (New York, 1997), 75–98.

6. R. Krautheimer, "The Panels in Urbino, Baltimore and Berlin Reconsidered," in ibid., 233–57.

7. See Smith, *Architecture*, chap. 2; and A. Tönnesmann, *Pienza* (Munich, 1990).

8. For strong interpretations stressing Alberti's own elaborate sense of constraint, see M. Jarzombek, *Leon Battista Alberti: His Literary and Aesthetic Theories* (Cambridge, Mass., and London, 1989) and M. Tafuri, *Ricerca del Rinascimento* (Turin, 1992), chap. 2.

9. See N. Adams, "The Construction of Pienza (1459–1464) and the Consequences of *Renovatio*," in *Urban Life in the Renaissance*, ed. S. Zimmerman and R.F.E. Weissman (Newark, Del., London, and Toronto, 1989), 50–79.

10. L. B. Alberti, *Ludi rerum mathematicarum*, in *Opere volgari*, ed. C. Grayson (Bari, 1960–73), III, 156.

11. For a full discussion, see C. W. Westfall, *In This Most Perfect Paradise* (University Park, 1974).

12. See C. Grayson, "The Composition of L. B. Alberti's *Decem libri de re aedificatoria*," *Münchener Jahrbuch der bildenden Kunst* 11 (196), 152–61, repr. in C. Grayson, *Studi su Leon Battista Alberti*, ed. P. Claut (Florence, 1999), 173–92.

13. L. B. Alberti, *De commodis litterarum atque incommodis*, ed. L. Goggi Carotti (Florence, 1976), 50–51.

14. Alberti, *Ludi*, in *Opere volgari*, ed. Grayson, III, 135.

15. L. B. Alberti, *De re aedificatoria* (hereafter *DRA*), V.12, *On the Art of Building in Ten Books*, tr. J. Rykwert, N. Leach and R. Tavernor (Cambridge, Mass., and London, 1988; repr. 1989); *L'Architettura*, ed. G. Orlandi, tr. P. Portoghesi (Milan, 1966), I, 391–93. For Alberti's comment, see *DRA*, II.6; ed. Orlandi and Portoghesi, 2, 123.

16. See J. Ackerman, " 'Ars sine scientia nihil est': Gothic Theory of Architecture at the Cathedral of Milan," *Distance Points* (Cambridge, Mass., and London, 1991), 211–68; E. Welch, *Art and Authority in Renaissance Milan* (New Haven and London, 1995), chap. 3.

17. See in general N. Adams and L. Nussdorfer, "The Italian City, 1400–1600," *The Renaissance*, ed. Millon and Lampugnani, 205–30.

18. Westfall, *Most Perfect Paradise*, 88–89.

19. H. Burns, "Quattrocento Architecture and the Antique: Some Problems," *Classical Influences on European Culture, A.D. 500–1500*, ed. R. R. Bolgar (Cambridge, 1971), 269–87 at 273.

20. See *Giovanni Rucellai ed il suo Zibaldone*, I, *Il Zibaldone Quaresimale*, ed. A. Perosa (London, 1960), 76.

21. A. D. Fraser Jenkins, "Cosimo de' Medici's Patronage of Architecture and the Theory of Magnificence," *Journal of the Warburg and Courtauld Institutes* 33 (1970), 162–70.

22. L. A. Ciapponi, "Il *De architectura* di Vitruvio nel primo umanesimo," *Italia Medioe-*

vale e Umanistica 3 (1960), 59–99. For the transmission of the text in the Middle Ages and after, see C. H. Krinsky, "Seventy-eight Vitruvius Manuscripts," *Journal of the Warburg and Courtauld Institutes* 30 (1967), 36–70; and S. F. Weiskittel and L. D. Reynolds, "Vitruvius," in *Texts and Transmission*, ed. L. D. Reynolds (Oxford, 1983), 440–45.

23. M. Moressi, "Humanistic Interpretations of Vitruvius in the Fifteenth Century," *The Princeton Journal: Thematic Studies in Architecture* 3: *Canon* (1988), 81–100.

24. The two quotations in this paragraph come from Vitruvius, *Ten Books on Architecture*, 1.2.6, 5.1.1, ed. T. N. Howe with I. D. Rowland and M. J. Dewar; tr. I. D. Rowland (Cambridge, 1999), 25, 64. See also "Introduction," esp. 15–17, and A. A. Payne, *The Architectural Treatise in the Italian Renaissance* (Cambridge, 1999), chap. 2.

25. P. de la Ruffinière du Prey, *The Villas of Pliny: From Antiquity to Posterity* (Chicago and London, 1994).

26. John of Olmüz, *Vita* of Cardinal Branda Castiglione, in "Notiziario," *Aevum* 9 (1935), 474–79 at 477.

27. De la Ruffinière du Prey, *Villas*, 26.

28. On Pizolpasso, see A. Paredi, *La biblioteca del Pizolpasso* (Milan, 1961); R. Fubini, "Tra umanesimo e concilio," *Studi medievali*, 3d ser., 7 (1966), 322–70; J. Hankins, *Plato in the Italian Renaissance* (Leiden, 1990), I, 125–26.

29. See Paredi, *La biblioteca*, 124–25; Moressi, "Humanistic Interpretation."

30. The text appears in Paredi, *La biblioteca*, 181–92, and in T. Foffano, "La construzione di Castiglione in un opuscolo inedito di Francesco Pizolpasso," *Italia Medioevale e Umanistica* 3 (1960); a fine analysis in Moressi, "Humanistic Interpretations."

31. Paredi, *La biblioteca*, 180.

32. Alberti, *DRA*; tr. J. Rykwert et al., 4; ed. Orlandi and Portoghesi, I, 11–13.

33. M. Baxandall, *Painting and Experience in Fifteenth-Century Italy* (Oxford, 1972).

34. L. B. Alberti, *De pictura*, in *On Painting and On Sculpture*, ed. and tr. C. Grayson (London, 1972), 36, 48; cf. Weil-Garris Brandt, "Sculpture and Architecture."

35. R. Krautheimer, "Alberti and Vitruvius," *The Renaissance and Mannerism. Studies in Western Art: Acts of the Twentieth International Congress of the History of Art* (Princeton, 1963), II, 42–52; see further F. Choay, *La règle et le modèle* (Paris, 1980), tr. as *The Rule and the Model*, ed. D. Bratton (Cambridge, Mass., and London, 1997); V. Biermann, *Ornamentum* (Hildesheim, Zürich, and New York, 1997); and Payne, *Architectural Treatise*, esp. chap. 4.

36. O. Neugebauer and N. Swerdlow, *Mathematical Astronomy in Copernicus's "De revolutionibus"* (New York, Berlin, Heidelberg, and Tokyo, 1984), 48–54.

37. See A. Grafton, *Commerce with the Classics* (Ann Arbor, 1997), chap. 2.

38. See esp. Krautheimer, "Alberti and Vitruvius." For the strains that this structure exerted on Alberti's work, see Choay, *La règle*, chap. 2.

39. See esp. V. Biermann, *Ornamentum* (Hildesheim, Zürich, and New York, 1997); C. Van Eck, "The Structure of *De Re Aedificatoria* Reconsidered," *Journal of the Society of Architectural Historians* 57 (1998), 280–97.

40. Alberti, *DRA*, tr. Rykwert et al., 4; ed. Orlandi and Portoghesi, I, 11–13.

41. Alberti, *DRA*, IX.10, tr. Rykwert et al., 315–16; ed. Orlandi and Portoghesi, II, 855–57.

42. Vitruvius, *On Architecture*, 8.3.27, tr. Rowland, 103.

43. Alberti, *DRA*, II.4, tr. Rykwert et al., 38–39; ed. Orlandi and Portoghesi, I, 111.

44. Alberti, *DRA*, I.4, tr. Rykwert et al., 14.; ed. Orlandi and Portoghesi, I, 39. Cf. VI.6, ed. Orlandi and Portoghesi II, 475: *"Haec brevissime collecta ab ipsis auctoribus prolixius discenda linquimus"*; I.6, ed. Orlandi and Portoghesi, I.51 (examples of cities with bad fortune): *"Sed ista sinamus, quorum refertissimae sunt historiae"*; and, for sharper statements, II.8, ed. Orlandi and Portoghesi, I, 137: *"Verum hi, quales pro locorum varietate et natura sint, usu et experientia pulcherrime innotescunt, ut iam ex veterum aedificiis cuiusque lapidis vim et virtutem didicisse plenius possis quam ex philosophantium scriptis et monimentis"*; III.16, ed. Orlandi and Portoghesi, I, 257: *"Haec, quae hactenus recensuimus, ex Plinio atque in primis Vitruvio interpretati sumus. Nunc, quae de pavimentis ex veterum operibus summa et cura et diligentia collegerim, referam; a quibus plura me longe quam a scriptoribus profiteor didicisse."*

45. Alberti, *DRA*, 4.3, tr. Rykwert et al., 102.

46. See the detailed account in L. Kanerva, *Defining the Architect in Fifteenth-Century Italy* (Helsinki, 1998), esp. chaps. 3–4.

47. See A. Blair, "Humanist Methods in Natural Philosophy: The Commonplace Book," *Journal of the History of Ideas* 53 (1992), 541–51; A. Blair, *The Theatre of Nature* (Princeton, 1997); A. Moss, *Printed Commonplace-Books and the Structuring of Renaissance Thought* (Oxford, 1996).

48. Further sources used by Alberti include Diodorus Siculus' *Historical Library*, a massive compilation of materials on geography, ethnography, and mythology, assembled by its erudite author in the late first century B.C.E.; Eusebius' *Preparation for the Gospel*, a massive work of Christian apologetics, written in the fourth century C.E. to show that pagan philosophy and the Roman Empire had prepared the way for the coming of Jesus.

49. See in general Hankins, *Plato*.

50. L. Valla, *Epistole*, ed. O. Besomi and M. Regoliosi (Padua, 1984), 345.

51. L. Bertolini, *Grecus sapor* (Rome, 1998).

52. See D. Marsh, *Lucian and the Latins* (Ann Arbor, 1998).

53. See *Rome Reborn*, ed. A. Grafton (Washington, D.C., New Haven, London, and Vatican City, 1993).

54. This argument was first made, on the basis of much more limited evidence, by O. Hoffman, *Studien zu Albertis zehn Büchern "De re aedificatoria"* (Frankenberg i.S., 1883); cf. also E. Garin, *Rinascite e rivoluzioni* (Bari, 1975), 184; Westfall, *Most Perfect Paradise*; Grafton, *Commerce*, 70–73. It is possible, and even likely, that Alberti read some or all of these texts in Greek, perhaps with the help of a more skillful Hellenist. Machiavelli, though he had no Greek, managed to gain access to the theories about Roman society presented by the Greek historian Polybius in book six of his *Histories*, before it was translated into Latin. Similarly, Alberti cited passages from Aeschylus, Plutarch, and other Greek writers that had not yet been translated

into Latin when he used them. Friends could always be kind enough to provide a reference or summarize a passage; Alberti himself could presumably have analyzed some of the Greek sources. But the massive work of excerpting that Alberti carried out seems to presuppose the existence of Latin versions to be excerpted, sorted, and recycled. And only the curia of the 1450s could have provided Alberti, at this date, with all these tools—and with the learned assistance he would have needed to work through so many demanding and difficult Greek texts. See Bertolini, *Grecus sapor*.

55. See three remarkable books: W. Braunfels, *Mittelalterliche Stadtbaukunst in der Toskana* (Berlin, 1953; 6th ed., 1988); V. Breidecker, *Florenz, oder: die Rede die zum Auge spricht. Kunst, Fest und Macht im Ambiente der Macht* (Munich, 1990; 2d ed., 1992); and M. Trachtenberg, *Dominion of the Eye: Urbanism, Art, and Power in Early Modern Florence* (Cambridge, 1997).

56. Braunfels, *Mittelalterliche Stadtbaukunst*, 102 and n. 342; 104 and n. 355. See the fine analysis of the creation of this space in Trachtenberg, *Dominion of the Eye*, pt. 3.

57. Braunfels, *Mittelalterliche*, 128, 252; Trachtenberg, *Dominion of the Eye*, 32.

58. Trachtenberg, *Dominion of the Eye*, esp. pt. 4.

59. This text is known in recent research as G. Manetti, "Oratio," ed. E. Battisti, *Umanesimo e esoterismo* (Padua, 1960), 310–20, from Vat. lat. 2919; note that the same text is ascribed to Lapo da Castiglionchio in Paris, Bibliothèque Nationale, 1616, from which F. P. Luiso edited it in *Firenze in festa per la consecrazione di Santa Maria del Fiore, 1436* (privately printed). Though Battisti describes the work as a formal oration (208–209), it in fact takes the form of a letter addressed to one Angelo; and Angelo da Recanate was one of Lapo's closest friends and correspondents. The ascription should perhaps be reconsidered.

60. See C. Warren, "Brunelleschi's Dome and Dufay's Motet," *Musical Quarterly* 59 (1973), 92–105; Smith, *Architecture*, 94. S. Zak, "Der Quellenwert von Giannozzo Manettis Oratio über die Domweihe von Florenz 1436 für die Musikgeschichte," *Die Musikforschung* 40 (1987), 2–32 offers the fullest analysis of this text.

61. Manetti [Lapo], "Oratio," ed. Battisti, 315 (Lapo, in Luiso, *Firenze*, 30–31).

62. Alberti, *DRA*, VI. 1, tr. Rykwert et al., 154; ed. Orlandi and Portoghesi, II, 441.

63. Alberti, *DRA*, VI.13, tr. Rykwert et al. 186; ed. Portoghesi and Orlandi, II, 525. Cf. Alberti, *DRA*, VI.1, ed. Orlandi and Portoghesi, II, 441–45, where he cites the difficulty "*et rerum explicandarum et nominum inveniendorum et materiae pertractandae.*"

64. Alberti, *DRA*, V.1, tr. Rykwert et al., 155; ed. Orlandi and Portoghesi, II, 443–45.

65. See Ciapponi, "Il *De architectura* di Vitruvio."

66. O. Besomi, "Dai *Gesta Ferdinandi regis Aragonum* del Valla al *De orthographia* del Tortelli," *Italia Medioevale e Umanistica* 9 (1966), 75–121.

67. Alberti, *DRA*, VI.7, ed. Orlandi and Portoghesi, II, 481–83.

68. Alberti, *DRA*, IX.10, tr. Rykwert et al., 317; ed. Orlandi and Portoghesi, II, 861–63.

69. The text is in Alberti, *Opere volgari*, III, ed. Grayson, 109–29. He dates the Latin text and ep. ded. to Gaza to their time together in Rome, 1450–55. In the ep. ded. to the Italian text, Alberti promised that "*chi forse per sé non sa designare, e' mostrerà vera e certa ragione e modo a diventare perfetto disegnatore*" (111); in the Latin, that

even if readers "*alioquin rudes atque imperiti sint, habeant tamen quo pacto picturae cupidos et studiosos instruant levi labore, talesque brevi reddant quales eruditissimi probare soliti sint . . .*" (112). Unlike *De pictura* itself, *Elementa* had a notably wide and enthusiastic reception: see Lucia Bertolini in *Leon Battista Alberti*, ed. J. Rykwert and A. Engel (Milan, 1994), 425–26, accepting Grayson's dating. She rightly points out that "*il pubblico elettivo di questi 'Elementa picturae' è, al sentimento stesso dell'Alberti, quello dei dotti umanisti suoi 'familiares'* " (426). Filarete cites the work; Alberti himself, in *Opera inedita et pauca separatim impressa*, ed. G. Mancini (Florence, 1890), mentioned that an unidentified friend had begun to read the *Elementa* "*summo studio et multa cum voluptate*" (426); Bussi approved of the work.

70. Cusanusstift, Bernkastel-Kues, cod. 112.
71. Alberti, *DRA*, II.11, tr. Rykwert et al., 56; ed. Orlandi and Portoghesi, I, 157–59.
72. On the diffusion of *On the Art of Building*, see Orlandi's "Nota sul testo" and "Appendice," II, 1005–28; L. Bertolini in *Alberti*, ed. Rykwert and Engel, *Alberti*, 414–16.
73. See, e.g., Alberti, *DRA*, IX.5, ed. Orlandi and Portoghesi, II, 813; VI.2 (II, 447).
74. See M. Wigley, "Untitled: The Housing of Gender," *Sexuality and Space*, ed. B. Colomina (Princeton, 1992), 327–89; K. Imesch, "Misogynie im literarischen und architekturtheoretischen Werk Leon Battista Albertis," *Theorie der Praxis*, ed. K. W. Forster and H. Locher (Berlin, 1999), 233–73; and, above all, the wonderful study by K. Weil-Garris and J. D'Amico, *The Renaissance Cardinal's Ideal Palace* (Rome, 1980).
75. Alberti, *DRA*, V.3, V.7, V.8, V.15–16, V.17, IX.4.
76. Alberti, *DRA*, III.2, ed. Orlandi and Portoghesi, I, 179–81.
77. Alberti, *DRA*, IV.6, X.4, V.14, X.17, V.2, V.17, IX.2.
78. Alberti, *DRA*, IX.2, tr. Rykwert et al., 295; ed. Orlandi and Portoghesi, II, 793; V.17, ed. Orlandi and Portoghesi, I, 415.
79. Alberti, *DRA*, II.5, VIII.1.
80. Alberti, *DRA*, II.5, VIII.1, and esp. X.17, ed. Orlandi and Portoghesi, II, 1001.
81. These quotations come from Alberti, *DRA*, IX.9, IX.10, tr. Rykwert et al., 315, 314; ed. Orlandi and Portoghesi, II, 855: "*De re enim aedificatoria laus omnium prima est iudicare bene quid deceat.*"
82. Alberti, *DRA*, I.7, V.1, V.2, VIII.17, I.9, II.2; cf. Kanerva, *Defining the Architect*, esp. 114–17.
83. Alberti, *DRA*, IX.7, tr. Rykwert et al., 310; ed. Orlandi and Portoghesi, II, 837–39; *DRA*, IX.10, tr. Rykwert et al., 315; ed. Orlandi and Portoghesi, II, 859–61.
84. See esp. Payne, *Architectural Treatise*, 76–70, and Biermann, *Ornamentum*, chap. iv.
85. See esp. Braunfels, *Stadtbaukunst*, 101, and cf. Smith, *Architecture*, and Trachtenberg, *Dominion of the Eye*.
86. See Chapter 5 above.
87. See J. Rykwert, "Theory as Rhetoric: Leon Battista Alberti in Theory and in Practice," in *Paper Palaces: The Rise of the Renaissance Architectural Treatise*, ed. V. Hart with P. Hicks (New Haven and London, 1998), 33–50.
88. See esp. Payne, *Architectural Treatise*; *Paper Palaces*, ed. Hart with Hicks.

CHAPTER IX

1. L. B. Alberti, *Opere volgari*, ed. C. Grayson (Bari, 1960–73), III, 295; and R. Tavernor, *On Alberti and the Art of Building* (New Haven and London, 1998), 159. Tavernor's survey of Alberti's architectural career lays out the history of each project and the problems connected with it in detail and with great clarity. It also presents stunning three-dimensional reconstructions of Alberti's original projects, which, though necessarily conjectural, shed much light on his work.

2. Cf. A. Tönnesmann, *Pienza* (Munich, 1990); C. Smith, *Architecture in the Culture of Early Humanism* (Oxford and New York, 1992), both of whom see Alberti's involvement as probable and use his work to support their rich interpretations of the city.

3. M. Jarzombek, *On Leon Battista Alberti: His Literary and Aesthetic Theories* (Cambridge, Mass., and London, 1989).

4. See, in addition to Tavernor, *On Alberti*, the following recent accounts, which are especially well informed: *Leon Battista Alberti*, ed. J. Rykwert and A. Engel (Milan, 1994), containing detailed essays on each of Alberti's major projects; H. Burns, "Leon Battista Alberti," in *Storia dell'architettura italiana: Il Quattrocento*, ed. F. P. Fiore (Milan, 1998), 114–65; C. L. Frommel, "Roma," in ibid., 374–433 (cf. the review of this volume by A. G. Cassani in *Albertiana* 2 [1998], 339–51); and J. Rykwert, "Theory as Rhetoric: Leon Battista Alberti in Theory and in Practice," in *Paper Palaces*, ed. V. Hart with P. Hicks (New Haven and London, 1998), 33–50. Of the older literature, see esp. R. Wittkower, *Architectural Principles in the Age of Humanism* (London, 1949; rev. ed., London, 1973).

5. G. Dehio, "Die Bauprojekte Nikolaus des Fünften und L. B. Alberti," *Repertorium für Kunstwissenschaft* 3 (1880), 241–75; for the development of the scholarly discussion since Dehio, see M. Tafuri, " 'Cives esse non licere.' Niccolò V e Leon Battista Alberti," *Ricerca del Rinascimento* (Turin, 1992), 33–88 at 68 n. 1. In addition to the works cited below, see esp. V. Fontana, *Artisti e committenti nella Roma del Quattrocento* (Rome, 1973).

6. Giannozzo Manetti described Nicholas's plans at length in his life of the pope, written after Nicholas's death in 1455. It was published, minus an excurses on dreams, by L. A. Muratori, *Rerum italicarum scriptores* (Milan, 1734), III, 2, cols. 907–60; for the excised passage, see L. Onofri, "Sacralità, immaginazione e proposte politiche: La vita di Niccolò V di Giannozzo Manetti," *Humanistica lovaniensia* 28 (1979), 27–77 at 73–77. The entire Latin text has now been translated into Italian, with illuminating notes, by A. Modigliani: G. Manetti, *Vita di Niccolò V*, ed. A. Modigliani with a "Premessa" by M. Miglio (Rome, 1999). Modigliani is also preparing a critical edition of the original Latin.

7. T. Magnusson edited and translated the section on Nicholas's urbanistic project into English with a detailed commentary in "The Project of Nicholas V for Rebuilding the Borgo Leonino in Rome," *Art Bulletin* 36 (1954), 89–115 at 92–94; C. D'Onofrio reproduces Magnusson's Latin text with an Italian translation in *Visitiamo Roma nel Quattrocento* (Rome, 1989), 50–53. For detailed analysis of

Nicholas's plans—leaving aside for the moment the question of how much was ever realized—see esp. Magnusson, "Project of Nicholas V," and C. W. Westfall, *In This Most Perfect Paradise* (University Park, 1974).

8. See D'Onofrio, *Visitiamo Roma*, 56–59; Manetti, *Vita*, tr. Modigliani, 179–88.

9. P. P. Vergerio, *Epistolario*, ed. L. Smith (Rome, 1934), 216–17; quoted with commentary by M. Miglio, "Materiali e ipotesi per una ricerca," *Scritture, scrittori e storia* II: *Città e Corte a Roma nel Quattrocento* (Rome, 1993), 26. See also M. Miglio, "L'immagine dell'onore antico. Individualità e tradizione della Roma municipale," in ibid., 149–61.

10. See esp. M. Miglio, *Storiografia pontifica nel Quattrocento* (Bologna, 1975); Onofri, "Sacralità" and " 'Sicut fremitus leonis ita et regis ira': Temi neoplatonici e culto solare nell'orazione funebre per Niccolò V di Jean Jouffroy," *Humanistica lovaniensia* 32 (1982), 1–28; H. Goldbrunner, " 'Quemcumque elegerit Dominus, ipse sanctus erit': Zur Leichenrede des Jean Jouffroy auf Nikolaus V," *Quellen und Forschungen aus italienischen Bibliotheken und Archiven* 64 (1984), 385–96; S. Simoncini, "Roma come Gerusalemme celeste nel Giubileo del 1450: La Renovatio di Niccolò V e il *Momus* di Leon Battista Alberti," in *Le due Rome del Quattrocento*, ed. S. Rossi and S. Valeri (Rome, 1997), 322–45; Miglio, "Premessa," in Manetti, *Vita*, ed. and tr. Modigliani.

11. For an excellent survey, see C. L. Stinger, *The Renaissance in Rome* (Bloomington, 1985; repr. with a new preface, 1998). On urban planning see esp. Frommel, "Roma."

12. For the history of ideas about Rome, see esp. C. W. Westfall, *Most Perfect Paradise*; S. Maddalo, *In figura Romae* (Rome, 1990); P. Jacks, *The Antiquarian and the Myth of Antiquity* (Cambridge, 1993); I. Rowland, *The Culture of the High Renaissance* (Cambridge, 1998).

13. See O. Verdi, *Maestri di edifici e di strade a Roma nel secolo xv* (Rome, 1997).

14. For the text of the statute, see D'Onofrio, *Visitiamo Roma*, 17–18.

15. See esp. C. Burroughs, *From Signs to Design* (Cambridge, Mass., and London, 1990), who gives a vivid sense of the urban physiognomy of Rome in the mid-fifteenth century, with rich photographic material.

16. M. Miglio, "La rinascita politica dell'antico," *Scritture, scrittori e storia* II, 188–89.

17. See esp. Verdi, *Maestri*, and A. Modigliani's wonderfully rich *Mercati, botteghe e spazi di commercio a Roma tra Medioevo ed età moderna* (Rome, 1998).

18. Westfall, *Most Perfect Paradise*, 92–101.

19. Previous quotation comes from D'Onofrio, *Visitiamo Roma*, 26; cf. C. Burroughs, "Below the Angel: An Urbanistic Project in the Rome of Pope Nicholas V," *Journal of the Warburg and Courtauld Institutes* 45 (1982), 197–207.

20. Burroughs, *From Signs to Design*, 78.

21. Frommel, "Roma."

22. Miglio, "Rinascita politica," 203.

23. Miglio, "Premessa," and Manetti, *Vita*, ed. Modigliani.

24. J. Pinto, *The Trevi Fountain* (New Haven and London, 1986).

25. See the brilliant treatment in Burroughs, *From Signs to Design*, 72–76.

26. Burroughs, *From Signs to Design*, 93–98.

27. Modigliani, *Mercati*, 276–84.

28. L. B. Alberti, *Ludi rerum mathematicarum*, in *Opere volgari*, ed. C. Grayson (Bari, 1960–73), III, esp. 139–42; *DRA*, X.2–13.

29. G. Vasari, *The Lives of the Artists*, tr. J. Conaway Bondanella and P. Bondanella (Oxford and New York, 1991; repr. 1998), 179–80: "Leon Battista happened to arrive in Rome during the reign of Pope Nicholas V, who had turned Rome upsidedown with his methods of building, and through the intercession of Flavio Biondo from Forlì, his close friend, he came to be on close terms with the pope, who had earlier taken advice on architectural matters from Bernardo Rossellino. . . . As a result, by depending upon the judgment of the one and the ability of the other to execute a project, the pope constructed many things which were useful and worthy of praise; among them were the refitting of the water pipes to the Acqua Vergine fountain, which had fallen into disrepair, and the construction of the fountain in the Piazza de' Trevi with the marble decorations that can be seen there today, upon which are found the coat of arms of that pontiff and of the Roman people." Obviously, much of this is not to be taken literally. For a very different account, using new archival evidence to emphasize the role of Nello da Bologna, see Tafuri, " 'Cives esse non licere,' " 39–41.

30. See the account in Manetti, *Vita*, ed. Modigliani, 116–17.

31. L. B. Alberti, *Opera inedita et pauca separatim impressa*, ed. G. Mancini (Florence, 1890), 308.

32. Alberti, *DRA*, X.9, VIII.6.

33. Vasari, *Lives*, tr. Conaway Bondanella and Bondanella, 183; see also Alberti, *On Painting and On Sculpture*, ed. and tr. C. Grayson (London, 1972), 144, for discussion of the drawings attributed to Alberti.

34. See Burroughs, *From Signs to Design*, esp. 42.

35. M. Palmieri, "De temporibus suis," ed. G. M. Tartini, *Rerum italicarum scriptores* I (Florence, 1748), 241; tr. in Westfall, *Most Perfect Paradise*, 169 (altered).

36. Westfall, *Most Perfect Paradise*, esp. 167–84.

37. Tafuri, " 'Cives esse non licere,' " esp. 62–67. For the interpretation of Alberti that Tafuri followed, see esp. E. Garin, *Rinascite e rivoluzioni* (Bari, 1976).

38. Vespasiano da Bisticci, *Vite di uomini illustri del secolo xv* (Florence, 1938), 35, 48–49.

39. Tafuri, " 'Cives esse non licere,' " *passim*.

40. D. Marsh, *Lucian and the Latins* (Ann Arbor, 1998), 114. Marsh's account of the work is excellent (114–29).

41. L. B. Alberti, *Momo o del principe*, ed. R. Consolo (Genoa, 1986), 231–34.

42. The standard edition is *Momo*, ed. Consolo; see also *Momus oder von Fürsten*, ed. and tr. M. Boenker (Munich, 1993), and *Momus ou le prince*, tr. C. Laurens (Paris, 1993).

43. Alberti, *Momo*, ed. Consolo, 303–304. Quotation comes from 288–89; cf. A Perosa, "Considerazioni su testo e lingua del *Momus* dell'Alberti," *The Languages of Literature in Renaissance Italy*, ed. P. Hainsworth et al. (Oxford, 1988), 45–62.

44. Marsh, *Lucian*, 127–28.

45. See Alberti, *Momo*, ed. Consolo, 288–90, nn. 58, 60; cf. P. Laurens, "Préface," in *Momus*, tr. Laurens, 30–33 and *passim*.

46. Cf. Marsh, *Lucian*, as well as the literature cited below.

47. A. Modigliani, *I Porcari* (Rome, 1994), esp. 454–55.

48. Miglio, "Premessa," in Manetti, *Vita*, ed. Modigliani.

49. In addition to Modigliani, see the detailed narrative in F. Gregorovius, *Geschichte der Stadt Rom im Mittelalter*, 4th ed. (Stuttgart, 1894), VII, 99–102, 127–37.

50. Alberti, "De Porcariana coniuratione," in *Opera inedita*, ed. Mancini.

51. R. Fubini and A. Menci Gallorini, "L'autobiografia di Leon Battista Alberti. Studio e edizione," *Rinascimento* 12 (1972), 3–78 at 57; A. G. Cassani, "*Libertas, frugalitas, aedificandi libido*: Paradigmi indiziari per Leon Battista Alberti a Roma," in *Le due Rome del Quattrocento*, ed. Rossi and Valeri, 296–321 at 310–11.

52. Alberti, "De porcariana conjuratione," *Opera inedita*, ed. Mancini, 260.

53. In fact, Alberti's version of the speech is probably the most faithful, ideologically, to Porcari; see Modigliani, *I Porcari*, 495.

54. See esp. Cassani, "*Libertas*," and Simoncini, "Roma come Gerusalemme," both in *Le due Rome*, ed. Rossi and Valeri.

55. Alberti, *DRA*, VII.13, tr. Rykwert et al., 229; ed. Orlandi and Portoghesi, II, 628–20.

56. Alberti, *Momo*, ed. Consolo, 36. Quotation comes from 222.

57. See A. P. Frutaz, *Il torrione di Niccolò V in Vaticano* (Vatican City, 1956), 11–22, esp. 18, 20; Manetti, *Vita*, tr. Modigliani, 135–37.

58. Alberti, *Momo*, ed. Consolo, 34, 64.

59. For a subtle analysis of the figure of the beggar, see M. Martelli, "Minima in Momo libello Adnotanda," *Albertiana* 2 (1998), 21–36 at 22–31, showing that he combines traits of the mendicant friar and the Stoic philosopher.

60. Alberti, *Momo*, ed. Consolo, 122.

61. L. Boschetto, "Ricerche sul *Theogenius* e sul *Momus* di Leon Battista Alberti," *Rinascimento* 2d ser., 33 (1993), 3–52 at 38–50.

62. See esp. Fubini and Menci Gallorini, "L'autobiografia," 57.

63. Quoted in Marsh, *Lucian*, 127 n. 67.

64. See J. Monfasani, "Pseudo-Dionysius the Areopagite in Mid-Quattrocento Rome," in *Supplementum Festivum: Studies in Honor of Paul Oskar Kristeller*, ed. J. Hankins, J. Monfasani, and F. Purnell, Jr. (Binghamton, 1987), repr. in his *Language and Learning in Renaissance Italy* (Aldershot, 1994), chap. 9—an article that has the compulsive interest of a detective story.

65. J. Monfasani, *George of Trebizond* (Leiden, 1976), 104–13.

66. Alberti, *DRA*, I.7, I.10, X.17.

67. B. Curran and A. Grafton, "A Fifteenth-Century Site Report on the Vatican Obelisk," *Journal of the Warburg and Courtauld Institutes* 58 (1995 [1996]).

68. Onofri, "Sacralità."

69. L. Kanerva, *Defining the Architect in Fifteenth-Century Italy* (Helsinki, 1998).

70. Manetti, *Vita*, ed. Modigliani, 136, 151.

71. Alberti, *DRA*, V.8, tr. Rykwert et al., 129; ed. Orlandi and Portoghesi, I, 369–71.

72. See, e.g., J. H. Hexter, *The Vision of Politics on the Eve of the Reformation* (New York, 1973).

73. D'Onofrio, *Visitiamo Roma*, 48.

74. Cf. Modigliani, *Mercati*, 276.

75. L. Rainey, *Ezra Pound and the Monument of Culture* (Chicago and London, 1991).

76. Vasari, *Lives*, tr. Conaway Bondanella and Bondanella, 180.

77. C. Hope, "The Early History of the Tempio Malatestiano," *Journal of the Warburg and Courtauld Institutes* 55 (1992), 51–154.

78. Literature on the Tempio is profuse and contentious. The classic older study by C. Ricci, *Il Tempio Malatestiano* (Milan and Rome, 1924), was reprinted in Rimini in 1974, with an appendix by P. G. Pasini reviewing "Cinquant'anni di studi sul Tempio Malatestiano." Hope, "Early History," discusses the entire history of the building in great detail, making rich use of the older secondary literature and of the archaeological evidence and revising many accepted views. Tavernor, *On Alberti*, goes over the whole ground in detail as well, in chapter 6, offering reconstructions of Alberti's original plans by the Alberti Group that often differ from Hope's. For a very recent review of the discussion, see A. G. Cassani, "Il disegno scomparso," *Albertiana* 2 (1998), 259–74. The documents are now most fully accessible in O. Delucca, *Artisti a Rimini fra Gotico e Rinascimento* (Rimini, 1997).

79. See Tavernor, *On Alberti*, chap. 7. On the Rucellai family palace and loggia, see further B. Preyer, "The Rucellai Loggia," *Mitteilungen des Kunsthistorischen Institutes in Florenz* 21 (1977), 183–97, and "The Rucellai Palace," *Giovanni Rucellai ed il suo Zibaldone* II: *A Florentine Patrician and his Palace*, ed. A. Perosa (London, 1981), 156–225.

80. R. A. Goldthwaite, *The Building of Renaissance Florence* (Baltimore and London, 1980).

81. A. Averlino detto il Filarete, *Trattato di Architettura*, ed. A. M. Finoli and L. Grassi (Milan, 1972), I, 227–28. Vasari credits Alberti with the design, which he criticizes: *Lives*, tr. Conaway Bondanella and Bondanella, 180–81. For the controversy over Alberti's connection with the palace, see Tavernor, *On Alberti*.

82. Vasari, *Lives*, tr. Conaway Bondanella and Bondanella, 180–81.

83. Once again, the history of the buildings Alberti designed for the Gonzaga is highly controversial; once again, their construction took place largely in his absence and lasted until long after his death. Sant'Andrea, in particular, differs radically from Alberti's original plan. For a full account, see Tavernor, *On Alberti*, chap. 8. Also important are E. S. Johnson, *S. Andrea in Mantua: The Building History* (University Park and London, 1975); R. Lamoureux, *Alberti's Church of San Sebastiano in Mantua* (New York and London, 1979); and A. Calzona and L. Volpi Ghirardini, *Il San Sebastiano di Leon Battista Alberti* (Florence, 1994).

84. See Johnson, *S. Andrea*, 64, and Tavernor, *On Alberti*, 159.

85. Alberti, *DRA*, II.1, tr. Rykwert et al., 33–34; ed. Orlandi and Portoghesi, I, 97.

86. Alberti, *DRA*, tr. Rykwert et al., 34; ed. Orlandi and Portoghesi, I, 99.

87. Alberti, *DRA*, IX.8, tr. Rykwert, et al., 313; ed. Orlandi and Portoghesi, II, 847.

88. C. Grayson, with M. Paoli and A. G. Cassani, "Alberti and the Tempio Malatestiano," *Albertiana* 2 (1998), 237–74 at 255 (original at 253).

89. "Manetto" has been identified as both Antonio and Giannozzo Manetti: either interpretation is possible.

90. Grayson, "Alberti and the Tempio." The round windows in question were probably considered for the nave (see Hope, "Early History"), though they have also been seen as applying to the drum supporting the dome.

91. See W. Forster, "Templum, Laubia, Figura: L'architettura di Alberti per una nuova Mantua," in *Alberti*, ed. Rykwert and Engel, 162–77.

92. The quotations in these two paragraphs come from Filarete, *Trattato*, I, 229–31.

93. These two quotations quoted by Tavernor, *On Alberti*, 159, 143.

94. Delucca, *Artisti*, 357, 338.

95. Alberti, *DRA*, VII.11, tr. Rykwert et al., 222; ed. Orlandi and Portoghesi, II, 614–15 n. 4.

96. See esp. Tavernor, *On Alberti*.

97. For a serious effort to resolve some of the tensions discussed here, see V. Biermann, *Ornamentum* (Hildesheim, Zurich, and New York, 1997).

98. Wittkower made this point central to his classic study of Alberti's architecture, *Architectural Principles*.

99. See esp. Goldthwaite, *Building of Renaissance Florence*.

100. Alberti, *DRA*, VIII. 6, tr. Rykwert et al., 268; ed. Orlandi and Portoghesi, II, 723.

101. Alberti, *DRA*, VI.10, tr. Rykwert et al., 177–78; ed. Orlandi and Portoghesi, II, 505–507.

102. Alberti, *DRA*, VIII.6; tr. Rykwert et al., 265, ed. Orlandi and Portoghesi, II, 717–19.

103. Pius II, *Memoirs of a Renaissance Pope*, ed. L. C. Gabel, tr. F. A. Gragg (New York, 1959), 110.

104. R. Krautheimer, *Rome: Profile of a City, 312–1308* (Princeton, 1980), 26–31, 114.

105. See esp. Burroughs, *From Signs to Design*, and A. Calzona, "Leon Battista Alberti e l'immagine di Roma fuori di Roma: Il Tempio Malatestiano," in *Le due Roma*, ed. Valeri and Rossi, 346–63.

106. Alberti, *DRA*, VII.13, tr. Rykwert et al., 229; ed. Orlandi and Portoghesi, II, 627–29.

EPILOGUE

1. Alberti, *De cifra*, in *Opera inedita et pauca separatim impressa*, ed. G. Mancini (Florence, 1890), 310.

2. Alberti, *De iciarchia*, in *Opere volgari*, ed. C. Grayson (Bari, 1960–73), II, 265. Quotation comes from 242.

3. On the datings proposed for this work, see J. Andrews Aiken, "Leon Battista Alberti's System of Human Proportions," *Journal of the Warburg and Courtauld Institutes* 43 (1980), 68–96; Alberti, *De statua*, ed. and tr. M. Spinetti (Naples, 1999),

9–13; M. Collareta, "Considerazioni in margine al *De statua* ed alla sua fortuna," *Annali della Scuola Normale Superiore di Pisa*, 3d ser., 12 (1982), 171–87; L. Bertolini in *Leon Battista Alberti*, ed. J. Rykwert and A. Engel (Milan, 1994), 414–15, 421–23; Alberti, *De statua*, ed. M. Collareta (Livorno, 1998), 48–49; O. Bätschmann, "Leon Battista Alberti: *De statua*," in *Theorie der Praxis*, ed. K. W. Forster and H. Locher (Berlin, 1999), 109–28.

4. Alberti, *De statua*, in *On Painting and On Sculpture*, ed. and tr. C. Grayson (London, 1972), 120–21 (translation altered).

5. See the classic article by H. W. Janson, "The Image Made by Chance in Renaissance Thought," *Essays in Honor of Erwin Panofsky*, ed. M. Meiss (New York, 1961), 254–66. Cf. A.W.G. Poséq, "Alberti's Theory of Primitive Sculpture," *Mitteilungen des Kunsthistorischen Institutes in Florenz* 33 (1989), 380–84.

6. See Grayson's introduction, *On Painting and On Sculpture*, 21–22.

7. See Collareta, "Considerazioni," 174, and his edition, 36.

8. See also F. Balters and P. Gerlach, "Zur Natur von Albertis *De Statua*," *Kunsthistorisches Jahrbuch Graz* 23 (1987), 38–54.

9. Alberti, *De statua*, 4–12, in *On Painting and On Sculpture*, ed. and tr. Grayson, 132–33, 122–23, 124–29, 128–33, 132–35.

10. Cf. E. Panofsky, "Die Entwicklung der Proportionslehre als Abbild der Stilentwicklung," *Monatshefte für Kunstwissenschaft* 14 (1921), 199–219; and F. Saxl, "Science and Art in the Italian Renaissance," *Lectures* (London, 1957), I, 111–24 at 115–17.

11. See Collareta, "Considerazioni," and Bertolini, as in n. 3 above.

12. Cf. P. Morselli, "The Proportions of Ghiberti's Saint Stephen: Vitruvius's *De Architectura* and Alberti's *De statua*," *Art Bulletin* 60 (1978), 235–41; Aiken, "Alberti's System"; G. Scaglia, "Instruments Perfected for Measurements of Man and Statues Illustrated in Leon Battista Alberti's *De statua*," *Nuncius* 8 (1995), 555–96.

13. Cf. Collareta, "Considerazioni," and Bertolini, as in n. 3 above.

14. Alberti to Bussi, n.d., in *On Painting and On Sculpture*, ed. Grayson, 118–19.

15. Cf. *De statua*, ed. Collareta, p. 49.

16. M.P. Simonelli, "On Alberti's Treatises of Art and their Chronological Relationship," *Yearbook of Italian Studies* (1971), 75–101 at 97–98; the date of this text is quite uncertain. Similarly, Alberti argued, the student had to master his entire textbook, the *Elements of Painting*, before he could hope to paint himself. The old Alberti was as much a humanist as the young author of *On the Advantages and Disadvantages of Letters* had been.

17. Alberti describes a flood (*Opere volgari*, ed. Grayson, III, 187–88) and a change in taxation (262); the former, according to Grayson, would suggest a date after 1465, the latter after 1469 (442). But it also seems possible that the latter passage refers to the 1470 reforms of the *Monte Comune*, or public debt, and *Monte delle doti*, or dowry bank, which greatly favored a small group of Lorenzo's followers at the expense of the larger Florentine public and that were introduced only against fierce opposition. See L. F. Marks, "The Financial Oligarchy in Florence under Lorenzo," *Italian Renaissance Studies*, ed. E. F. Jacob (London, 1960), 123–47. The title of the work is one of Alberti's coinages, from the Greek *oikos* (household) and *archeia* (rule or government).

18. L. B. Alberti, *De iciarchia*, in *Opere volgari*, ed. Grayson, II, 203. Quotation comes from 262. Cf. Marks, "Financial Oligarchy," for the reforms to which Alberti may well be referring.

19. Cf. A. Brown, "Lorenzo and Public Opinion in Florence: The Problem of Opposition," in *Lorenzo il Magnifico ed il suo mondo*, ed. G. C. Garfagnini (Florence, 1994), 61–85.

20. Alberti, *De iciarchia*, in *Opere volgari*, ed. Grayson, II, 195. See A. Brown, *The Medici in Florence* (Florence and Perth, 1992), 230.

21. See F. W. Kent, "Lorenzo, . . . amico agli uomini da bene. Lorenzo de' Medici and Oligarchy," in *Lorenzo*, ed. Garfagnini, 43–60; W. J. Connell, "Changing Patterns of Medicean Patronage. The Florentine Dominion During the Fifteenth Century," in ibid., 87–107. On the ways in which humanists gradually decided to live with and serve the Medici, see the fine study by A. Field, *The Origins of the Platonic Academy of Florence* (Princeton, 1988).

22. Alberti, *De iciarchia*, in *Opere volgari*, ed. Grayson, II, 265–66.

23. See the moving analysis of H. Baron, *In Search of Florentine Civic Humanism*, (Princeton, 1988), I, 281–85.

24. Cf. M. Baxandall, "Alberti's Self," *Fenway Court* (1990–91), 31–36 at 31.

25. Alberti, *De iciarchia*, in *Opere volgari*, ed. Grayson, II, 229–30.

INDEX

Note: Page numbers in italics indicate illustrations.

READ MORE IN PENGUIN

In every corner of the world, on every subject under the sun, Penguin represents quality and variety – the very best in publishing today.

For complete information about books available from Penguin – including Puffins, Penguin Classics and Arkana – and how to order them, write to us at the appropriate address below. Please note that for copyright reasons the selection of books varies from country to country.

In the United Kingdom: Please write to *Dept. EP, Penguin Books Ltd, Bath Road, Harmondsworth, West Drayton, Middlesex UB7 0DA*

In the United States: Please write to *Consumer Services, Penguin Putnam Inc., 405 Murray Hill Parkway, East Rutherford, New Jersey 07073-2136.* VISA and MasterCard holders call 1-800-631-8571 to order Penguin titles

In Canada: Please write to *Penguin Books Canada Ltd, 10 Alcorn Avenue, Suite 300, Toronto, Ontario M4V 3B2*

In Australia: Please write to *Penguin Books Australia Ltd, 487 Maroondah Highway, Ringwood, Victoria 3134*

In New Zealand: Please write to *Penguin Books (NZ) Ltd, Private Bag 102902, North Shore Mail Centre, Auckland 10*

In India: Please write to *Penguin Books India Pvt Ltd, 11 Community Centre, Panchsheel Park, New Delhi 110017*

In the Netherlands: Please write to *Penguin Books Netherlands bv, Postbus 3507, NL-1001 AH Amsterdam*

In Germany: Please write to *Penguin Books Deutschland GmbH, Metzlerstrasse 26, 60594 Frankfurt am Main*

In Spain: Please write to *Penguin Books S. A., Bravo Murillo 19, 1°B, 28015 Madrid*

In Italy: Please write to *Penguin Italia s.r.l., Via Vittorio Emanuele 45la, 20094 Corsico, Milano*

In France: Please write to *Penguin France, 12, Rue Prosper Ferradou, 31700 Blagnac*

In Japan: Please write to *Penguin Books Japan Ltd, Iidabashi KM-Bldg, 2-23-9 Koraku, Bunkyo-Ku, Tokyo 112-0004*

In South Africa: Please write to *Penguin Books South Africa (Pty) Ltd, P.O. Box 751093, Gardenview, 2047 Johannesburg*

READ MORE IN PENGUIN

On Painting   Leon Battista Alberti

Translated by Cecil Grayson with an Introduction and Notes by Martin Kemp

Alberti wrote *De Pictura* in Latin in 1435 and in true Renaissance spirit made an Italian translation the following year. He unfolds his theories step by step. In Book One he explains the process of vision, in Book Two he sets out 'to instruct the painter how he can present with his hand what he has understood with his mind'. Book Three stipulates the moral and artistic prerequisites of the painter.

The genius of *De Pictura* surfaced almost immediately – signs are there in Ghiberti's Baptistery Doors in Florence, in the paintings of Fra Angelico and Domenico Veneziano – and it remains a living classic of art theory.

This edition at last makes widely available Cecil Grayson's translation from the Latin, the best English version of Alberti's text. It contains diagrams integrated into the text and an introduction by Martin Kemp which discusses *De Pictura* in the light of Alberti's life and philosophy.